*POPULATION AGING, HUMAN
CAPITAL ACCUMULATION,
AND PRODUCTIVITY GROWTH*

POPULATION AGING, HUMAN CAPITAL ACCUMULATION, AND PRODUCTIVITY GROWTH

Alexia Prskawetz
David E. Bloom
Wolfgang Lutz
Editors

POPULATION AND DEVELOPMENT REVIEW
A Supplement to Volume 34, 2008

POPULATION COUNCIL
New York

©2008 by The Population Council, Inc. All rights reserved.

Library of Congress Cataloging-in-Publication Data

Population aging, human capital accumulation, and productivity growth / Alexia Prskawetz, David E. Bloom, Wolfgang Lutz, editors.
   p. cm.
  Based on a symposium co-sponsored by the European Union and the Vienna Institute of Demography.
  "Population and development review, a supplement to volume 34, 2008."
  ISBN 978-0-87834-116-0 (pbk)
  1. Population aging--Case studies. 2. Saving and investment--Case studies. 3. Industrial productivity--Case studies. I. Prskawetz, Alexia. II. Bloom, David E. (David Elliot), 1955- III. Lutz, Wolfgang. IV. Population Council. V. Population and development review ; vol. 34, 2008 (Supplement)
  HQ1061.P663 2008
  338.4'5--dc22

                                   2008061101

ISSN 0098-7921
ISBN 978-0-87834-116-0

Printed in the United States of America.

CONTENTS

Acknowledgments   vii

Introduction   3

    DAVID E. BLOOM
    WOLFGANG LUTZ
    ALEXIA PRSKAWETZ

PART I. THE ECONOMIC SIGNIFICANCE OF GLOBAL AGING

Global Demographic Change: Dimensions and Economic Significance   17

    DAVID E. BLOOM
    DAVID CANNING

The Impact of Global Aging on Labor, Product, and Capital Markets   52

    AXEL H. BÖRSCH-SUPAN

Aggregate Evidence on the Link Between Age Structure and Productivity   78

    JAMES FEYRER

PART II. THE ROLE OF HUMAN CAPITAL ACCUMULATION IN ECONOMIC GROWTH

Declining Mortality Among British Scientists During the Age of Enlightenment   103

    RYAN D. EDWARDS

Demographic, Economic, and Institutional Factors in the Transition to Modern Growth in England: 1530–1860   126

    RAOUF BOUCEKKINE
    DAVID DE LA CROIX
    DOMINIQUE PEETERS

The Population Dynamics of Human Capital Accumulation   149

    WOLFGANG LUTZ
    ANNE GOUJON
    ANNABABETTE WILS

PART III. PRODUCTIVITY STUDIES AT VARIOUS LEVELS OF ANALYSIS

Age and Productivity Potential: A New Approach Based on
Ability Levels and Industry-Wide Task Demand   191

    VEGARD SKIRBEKK

Charting the Economic Life Cycle   208

    RONALD LEE
    SANG-HYOP LEE
    ANDREW MASON

Productivity Consequences of Workforce Aging:
Stagnation or Horndal Effect?   238

    BO MALMBERG
    THOMAS LINDH
    MAX HALVARSSON

Older Workers and National Productivity in Japan   257

    ROBERT L. CLARK
    NAOHIRO OGAWA
    SANG-HYOP LEE
    RIKIYA MATSUKURA

Growth Effects of Age-Related Productivity Differentials
in an Aging Society: A Simulation Study for Austria   275

    HELMUT HOFER
    THOMAS URL

Workforce Aging and Labor Productivity: The Role of
Supply and Demand for Labor in the G7 Countries   298

    ALEXIA PRSKAWETZ
    THOMAS FENT
    ROSS GUEST

AUTHORS   325

ACKNOWLEDGMENTS

This volume grows out of a symposium on "Population Aging and Economic Productivity" held within the framework of the Macro-Demographic Working Group, which comprises the following five institutes: The Institute for Futures Studies (Stockholm), The East-West Center (Honolulu), the Vienna Institute of Demography (Vienna), the Program on the Global Demography of Aging (PGDA), Harvard University (Cambridge), and Nihon University (Tokyo). The conference was co-sponsored by the European Union, via the Research Training Network on "Demographic Sustainability and European Integration," and the Vienna Institute of Demography.

Publication of this volume was made possible by support from The East-West Center (US National Institute on Aging Grant #3 R01 AG025488-02S1 from the National Institutes of Health (NIH)), the PGDA, Harvard University (Grant #5 P30 AG024409 from NIA, NIH), the John D. and Catherine T. MacArthur Foundation, the Vienna Institute of Demography, and the International Institute for Applied Systems Analysis (IIASA). The contents of the volume are solely the responsibility of the authors and do not necessarily represent the official views of the NIH or any other donor.

We extend our thanks to Guenther Fink, Jocelyn Finlay, Larry Rosenberg, and the staff of *Population and Development Review* for their assistance in producing this volume.

A.P.
D.E.B.
W.L.

INTRODUCTION

Introduction

DAVID E. BLOOM
WOLFGANG LUTZ
ALEXIA PRSKAWETZ

The twentieth century was an era of sustained population growth, and the twenty-first century will be an era of population aging. Demographers and economists concerned with population growth in the past must now turn to understanding the implications of population aging and the options for adapting to it. Although the extent of population aging, current and anticipated, constitutes a new phenomenon in human history, research may draw on previous studies of the mechanisms that link demographic change and economic outcomes.

Two broad population trends have been observed over the past decades. On the one hand, the "population explosion" about which so much has been written seems to be continuing in some parts of the world—particularly in Africa, the Arab world, and parts of South Asia. On the other hand, in a number of countries the birth rate has fallen so much that the population is rapidly aging, and in some cases beginning to shrink. Hence the world includes countries where rapid population growth is considered a major development obstacle, but also ones where policymakers believe that their fertility level is already too low and that the associated rapid population aging will negatively affect old-age security, international competitiveness, and hence economic growth.

Today's world is demographically divided because the universal process of demographic transition—a movement from high fertility and mortality rates to first lower mortality rates and subsequently lower fertility rates—is at different stages in different parts of the world. This demographic divide does not always follow the traditional line between industrialized and developing countries. Some developing countries have recently seen very rapid fertility declines, and the number of "poor" countries with sub-replacement fertility is increasing. China is the most prominent example, where the period total fertility rate has recently fallen to a level estimated at between 1.3 and 1.7.

During the coming two decades China will experience both further population growth (the result of its population momentum) and rapid population aging. Between 2005 and 2030 China is expected to grow by more than 100 million people; at the same time, the proportion of the population above age 60 will more than double from 11 percent to around 25 percent. Surprising to some, the United States will also simultaneously experience population growth and population aging. Unlike Europe, the United States is expected to grow significantly because of relatively high immigration and birth rates.

Over the last few years awareness of a direct influence of population age structure on the macro economy, and in particular on economic growth, has increased. The "neutralist" viewpoint first articulated by Bloom and Freeman asserted that "developing economies can, but need not, grow rapidly in the presence of rapid population growth" (Bloom and Freeman 1986: 382). This view was adopted in a series of widely cited reports that stressed the lack of significant correlation between population growth and economic growth (see, for example, National Research Council 1986; Blanchet 1991; and Kelley and Schmidt 1995). By contrast, several authors have recently concluded that demography indeed matters if one abandons the assumption of symmetry in the effects of population growth that arise from changes in mortality and changes in fertility (Bloom and Freeman 1988). If one incorporates the age structure of the population into empirical growth regressions, a significant and robust correlation between demographic change and economic growth emerges (Bloom and Williamson 1998). As argued in Kelley and Schmidt (2005: 277), "What has changed with the evolution of modeling in the 1990s is a clearer interpretation of the channels and sizes of demographic changes on the economy."

The variation of age structure generated by the demographic transition helps to identify the effects of demographic change on economic outcomes. The heterogeneity in the extent and speed of the demographic transition across and within countries produces variation that makes identification of the demographic–economic interrelationships feasible.

When fertility falls the resulting demographic shifts may create a window of opportunity for the realization of a demographic dividend. This window appears because the growth rate of the total population is slower than the growth rate of the working-age population, so the share of persons in their working age relative to the total population increases. The demographic dividend has been found to account for roughly one-third of the East Asian growth "miracle" (Bloom and Williamson 1998; Bloom, Canning, and Malaney 2000). Similarly, in most industrialized countries, demographic change in the period after World War II led to a demographic dividend that began in the 1970s when the baby boom generation entered the labor market. This aspect of the demographic dividend is called the accounting effect. The dividend also operates through a behavioral effect, as discussed below.

The theoretical foundation of the reduced-form models applied in econometric studies is the variation in the economic needs and contributions of individuals over their life cycles: young people require investment in health and education, prime-age adults supply labor and savings, and the elderly require health care and retirement income (cf. Modigliani 1986 and the more recent Bloom, Canning, and Graham 2003; Zhang et al. 2003). The age-specific needs and contributions themselves are country-specific and depend on institutional settings, cultural norms, and economic environment.

The same demographic shifts that create the demographic dividend may subsequently lead to a demographic burden, as fertility continues to decline and life expectancy, now benefiting the elderly in particular, improves. The growth rate of the working-age population will fall short of the growth rate of the total population. Most of the industrialized countries will experience the demographic burden, as will many developing countries (albeit with some time lag).

The results of the various studies of demographic structure and economic growth are generally compatible, despite differences in the setup of the models (with respect to the choice of explanatory variables and time periods) and the methods of estimation (cross-country vs. panel regressions). One of the most robust demographic variables that are positively and significantly linked to output-per-worker growth is the growth rate of the working-age population. This variable not only determines the accounting effect (the difference between the growth rate of the working-age and the total population) but also influences the behavioral component (the productivity term as represented by the growth rate of output per worker). The accounting and behavioral effects add up to the growth rate of output per capita. Kelley and Schmidt (2005) find that for Europe the accounting effect was exhausted in the 1970s, while the decline in the youth dependency ratio had a strong positive effect on the growth rate of output per worker during the 1970s and 1980s. Other authors obtain findings similar to those of Kelley and Schmidt. Bloom and Williamson (1998) find a positive effect of the growth rate of the economically active population on growth in output per capita. Moreover, they find a significant interaction between demographic variables and policies: good policies lead to higher economic growth, and the impact of demographic change is greater when institutions are of higher quality. They further argue that the interaction of a faster demographic transition and better economic policies in East Asia can account for 40 percent of the difference in the growth rate of per capita income between East Asia and Latin America. The RAND study by Bloom, Canning, and Sevilla (2003), which includes case studies on the role of the demographic transition for economic growth within aggregate world regions, stresses that open economies, a flexible labor force, and modern institutions are necessary for a country to reap the demographic dividend. More recent work (Agosín et al. 2007; Rodrik 2001, 2006) has raised questions about the value of these measures and has pointed to the need for more country-specific analysis.

In summary, recent empirical evidence supports the argument that demographic factors matter for economic growth just as much as, or sometimes even more than, the factors commonly stressed in the growth literature (i.e., technological change, innovation, and political/institutional settings). Because the age structure of the population reflects these demographic factors in a comprehensive form, it is most informative to relate changes in the age structure to the economic processes under consideration. Nevertheless it should be kept in mind that macro-level econometric studies are not adequate to identify the underlying mechanisms and causalities that link economic and demographic factors. Demographic changes interact with several other determinants of economic growth. For example, in many developing countries rapid population growth has made it more difficult to improve school enrollment rates. In addition, rapid aging of the population in many countries requires longer and more intense use of existing human capital.

Economic implications of population aging: The role of human capital accumulation and productivity growth

According to many economists, an aging population leads to negative consequences in terms of growth of output per capita for two reasons. The first is an accounting effect. A decreasing ratio of the working-age population to the total population increases the ratio of dependents to workers. This contributes negatively to growth of output per capita. The second is a behavioral effect on growth of output per worker, namely, the negative effect of an aging population on economic productivity as measured by output per worker. The latter effect is the focus of much of the current supplement volume to *Population and Development Review*.

Labor productivity is the heart of economic growth. Trends in the demographic composition of the workforce play a crucial role in shaping productivity and income growth at the aggregate level. Overall, productivity and pay tend to rise at a decreasing rate over the working life. The factors that lie beneath these simple patterns are less obvious than the patterns themselves. Productivity and wages are not solely attributes of an individual; they are also the outcome of the economic system. Thus the impact of an aging workforce needs to be understood at both the micro and macro levels. Firm dynamics and practices are also influential, and these constitute an additional meso-level at which these phenomena should be studied.

We know with considerable accuracy how much population aging will take place in the next half-century. We can also project future improvements in human capital by age, although perhaps not with the same accuracy as population aging. What remains to be gauged is the extent to which improving education, accelerating technological change, and increasing labor force participation rates can compensate for and mitigate potential problems caused by population aging. Changing proportions of different age groups in the workforce will put pressure on labor market institutions and policies to adapt, so as to take full advantage of the different opportunities for growth.

As important as the change in the composition of the workforce is the change in the quantity and composition of human capital. Human capital is one of the key driving factors of productivity growth (Lindh 2004). Therefore, it is necessary to understand its change over time and along cohort lines in order to assess its importance in the context of population aging. Although human capital is often defined as people with a given level of education and health status, here we focus mostly on the education dimension. We emphasize human capital accumulation because it is the stock of knowledge and skills that matter for economic growth, as opposed to the process (flow) of acquiring education that is the focus of most education-related research. Most countries have seen impressive growth in their stocks of human capital over the past decades, with the younger cohorts generally having more education than the older ones (Lutz et al. 2007). Because of the momentum of educational improvements along cohort lines, this growth is the basis for expecting further improvements in the average educational attainment of the labor force.

The theory of optimal life-cycle human capital investment through education and training has been developed by Ben-Porath (1967), Mincer (1974), and Becker (1964) (see Weiss 1986 for an extensive review of the theoretical literature). Because this theory predicts that human capital accumulation will be concentrated at the early phases of life, human capital in an economy characterized by population aging will be of an "older vintage." From a country-level perspective, and in a context of rapid technological change, the fact that education continues to be almost exclusively concentrated at younger ages poses challenges for rapidly aging populations. From a firm-level perspective (meso-level), human capital investment or upgrading is less common for the older workforce because they face less time remaining until retirement. Hence, the relationship between age and human capital investment and consequently productivity growth cannot be seen in isolation from organizational and institutional factors at the macro, firm, and individual levels.

In December 2004 the Vienna Institute of Demography organized a workshop on "Population Aging and Economic Productivity" at which the papers included in this volume were presented. A debate session during which several arguments were advanced for and against a possible negative effect of population aging on economic productivity concluded the workshop. It seems useful to briefly recall the main arguments on both sides.

The positive view suggested that population aging would not have negative impacts on productivity. This view was based on the reasoning that although there would be relatively fewer people in the workforce, the productivity of workers would increase and compensate for this decline. Its proponents argued that companies would react to population aging if they were given time to adjust to the compositional change in the labor force. It was noted that Europe will also see an increase in the number of highly experienced workers in the coming years (i.e., before the baby boom generation starts retiring in large numbers), which could constitute an opportunity for productivity growth. Increasing efforts across European countries to facilitate the compatibility of motherhood and labor force participation also have the potential to bring more well-educated and productive young women into the labor force and hence increase average productivity. Finally, one particularly interesting conjecture raised at the workshop was that although productivity growth in Europe may be lower now and in the coming years, this may not be a consequence of population aging but rather the natural end of a productivity boost that accompanied the past rapid gains in educational attainment and is now simply flattening out. Exploring the validity of this conjecture would be an interesting and potentially important new line of inquiry.

Other workshop participants countered these assessments with several arguments for negative effects of population aging on productivity. First, labor markets in Europe may not be flexible enough to adapt to the changing age structure of the workforce; therefore, they will not be able to bring the specific skills of the older workers to productive use. It was also suggested that as long as investment in older people does not pay off, owing to the short period of its yield, productivity may decline when the workforce ages. Finally, declining productivity in Europe as compared to other parts of the world may promote outmigration of some of the most talented and mobile young Europeans to regions with more economic promise. This would reduce the innovative capacity of their home countries.

Although this list of arguments is not exhaustive, the initial discussion at the workshop made evident the need for clearly distinguishing whether the discussion is about labor productivity or total factor productivity and whether it is aimed at the individual level, firm level, or macro level. As illustrated in several chapters in this volume, both the assumptions we make in our models (e.g., closed versus open economies) and the measures of productivity we apply will critically influence our evaluation of the effects of population aging on economic productivity. The answers we propose will also be influenced by our judgments about the flexibility of institutional settings in adjusting to an aging workforce. Although several workshop participants were skeptical about the possibility of European labor markets making adjustments, a look at countries such as Japan that are even further advanced in the aging process shows that labor policies have indeed adjusted to the changing composition of the workforce. We clearly need more studies that investigate individual retirement decisions in the context of different prevailing institutional settings. As a bottom line this debate made it clear that the question whether population aging implies lower productivity in the future has no simple and unique answer. We need more in-depth studies at different levels of analysis and in different settings to understand empirically the relationship between age and productivity.

Economic theory provides no clear view as to how aging affects productivity. Because productivity growth will in the end determine economic growth and therefore many dimensions of our individual and societal well-being, gaining a better scientific understanding of the relationship between aging and productivity is indispensable. To this end the chapters in this volume range from simulation studies of population aging and economic productivity at the global and country level to models of human capital accumulation and empirical studies at the macro, firm, and individual level. These studies are grouped into three sections.

Structure of the volume

The first section, on the economic significance of global population aging, reviews recent demographic changes and links these changes to the past as well as the likely future development of economic productivity. The chapters by Bloom and Canning and by Börsch-Supan deal with global demographic change, its dimensions, and its economic significance. Drawing on the cases of Ireland and Taiwan, Bloom and Canning discuss the beneficial economic consequences of a change from high mortality and fertility to low mortality and fertility. These benefits arise through increased incentives to invest in education and to save for retirement. Bloom and Canning stress that the potential benefits associated with the demographic transition are dependent on the institutions and policies that prevail. The contribution by Börsch-Supan assesses the impact of global population aging on labor, product, and capital markets. Although population aging is global, the speed and extent of aging vary across countries and these differences lead to trade and factor movements.

The final chapter in this section, by Feyrer, aims to test empirically the correlation between age structure and economic productivity. Feyrer presents evidence based on cross-country regressions which show that having an older, more experienced workforce is significantly and positively correlated with changes in aggregate productivity. He concludes that almost one-quarter of the OECD's persistent productivity advantage over low-income countries may be related to their different demographic structures. The fact that these results are much larger than microeconomic estimates of age–productivity profiles suggests that there are significant externalities to the age distribution.

The second group of chapters is devoted to the role of human capital accumulation in economic growth. Population aging will change the composition of human capital and consequently also affect economic growth. By studying historical developments, as in the first two chapters in this section, we may learn more about the mechanisms in place. Edwards argues that lengthening life may facilitate more rapid scientific discovery. Put differently, the mortality decline may be more of an input into than a product of technological change. To verify this hypothesis Edwards studies the mortality of the fellows of the Royal Society of London. He finds that their life spans were increasing long before widespread mortality declines were achieved and argues that this has enhanced scientific progress and hence general productivity. Edwards concludes by gauging the likelihood that future extension of the length of life will continue to enhance the development of ideas.

The chapter by Boucekkine, de la Croix, and Peeters discusses the determinants of the English transition to modern economic growth. The authors set up a model and present a calibrated version to measure the impact of mortality, fertility, and technological progress on school density, literacy, and economic growth. The findings indicate that one-third of the rise in literacy over the period 1530–1850 can be directly related to the effect of cohort size, while one-sixth is linked to higher longevity and one half to exogenous total factor productivity growth. Identifying the mechanisms and factors that led to growth in past centuries might offer greater insight into today's economic effects of demographic change. Ultimately we are interested in the future composition of human capital and in how to link it to potential economic growth. While the micro evidence is rather clear cut (identifying positive returns to human capital investment), findings concerning the macro-level link between human capital accumulation and economic growth so far have been inconsistent, presumably as a consequence of measurement problems.

The final chapter of this section, by Lutz, Goujon, and Wils, presents a consistent and comprehensive framework for capturing the dynamics of human capital accumulation by age, sex, and levels of educational attainment. The framework also considers the fact that people with different levels of education have different fertility and mortality rates. Based on demographic multi-state methods, this approach helps to overcome some of the relevant measurement problems. The chapter demonstrates that this approach is feasible for reconstructing and projecting the dynamics of human capital accumulation even for countries with limited empirical data.

The third section of the volume is devoted to specific productivity studies at various levels of analysis. In his presentation on age and productivity, Skirbekk focuses on the level of the individual and discusses age variation in work performance, related in particular to age variation of cognitive abilities and the role of experience. The shape and peak of the age–productivity profile varies over time according to the changing labor market demand for abilities. If experience has a reasonably strong effect on productivity, peak productivity potential is found to occur at ages 35–44.

Lee, Lee, and Mason focus on age profiles of consumption and production in order to disentangle the relationship between changes in population structure and the macroeconomy. They challenge conventional assumptions about these age profiles and stress the importance of distinguishing between compositional and behavioral effects. The former effect measures the change in overall consumption and production that results from keeping age profiles constant but accounting for shifts in the population structure. The behavioral effect captures the change in the age profile itself when the population age structure changes. As indicated by Lee, Lee, and Mason, measuring age-structured profiles of consumption and production is a challenging task in itself, but it is essential for judging the broader influence of population aging on economic productivity.

In their study on Sweden, Malmberg, Lindh, and Halvarsson investigate the productivity consequences of workforce aging at the meso-level, that is, the firm or plant level, as opposed to the macro level discussed by Feyrer. They use a panel of employer–employee matched data from Sweden covering the period 1985–96 and focus on the manufacturing and mining industries. Their results indicate that when plant-level effects are controlled for, high shares of older adults are associated with higher productivity, whereas high shares of young adults have a negative effect on productivity. Malmberg, Lindh, and Halvarsson argue that their findings may have great relevance for the current practice of early retirement because this practice may risk depressing productivity.

The retirement decisions of the elderly are discussed in the chapter by Clark, Ogawa, Lee, and Matsukura, which considers the case of Japan. In contrast to the European pattern—that of declining labor force participation rates among older people—the labor force participation of the elderly in Japan (the country most advanced in the process of population aging) has been and remains high. The Japanese experience suggests that eliminating the employment restrictions that confront older workers and modifying the social security benefit system may also help to raise employment rates among the elderly in other countries.

The last two chapters consider workforce aging and economic productivity in Austria. Hofer and Url present a simulation study for Austria that incorporates the age-related productivity differentials suggested by Skirbekk and allows for a highly disaggregated labor supply. A long-run neoclassical growth model constitutes the framework of the simulation. Hofer and Url show that under perfect substitutability of labor, the consequences of population aging for long-run growth potential are negligible. Introducing imperfect substitutability of workers of different ages creates relatively small long-run effects on average productivity, real output, and per-worker wages, although the influence on growth rates over the first years of the simulation is pronounced. Similarly, varying the age-specific productivity profiles does not impair long-run economic performance.

Prskawetz, Fent, and Guest scrutinize the demand for labor. In a series of simulations they study the sensitivity of projected economic productivity, measured by output per worker, with respect to alternative projections of the quantity and quality of labor supply as measured by individual productivity. They also consider productivity with respect to alternative assumptions about the substitutability of workers at different ages. The authors show that in a pure labor economy, the assumption of imperfect substitution of workers at different ages implies an increase in relative economic productivity during the next two decades, compared to constant or declining economic productivity in the case of the commonly applied additive labor demand function. Although the assumption of a pure labor economy is restrictive—as Hofer and Url's results indicate—these simulations nevertheless demonstrate that assumptions about the substitutability of workers at different ages are at least as important as the age pattern of productivity. The authors further demonstrate that a decline in economic productivity can be attenuated if labor force participation rates can be adjusted to levels similar to those currently observed in northern European countries.

Possible directions for research

Although the contributions to this volume help define the state of the field for this difficult yet highly important area of economic demography, our understanding of the effects of population aging and human capital development on economic productivity is still in an early stage. At this point we see several broad areas that call for further research.

First, it would be useful to understand at a much more detailed level how the age structure of the workforce affects a wide range of socioeconomic outcomes under conditions of population aging. Economic growth, perhaps the most intensely studied of these outcomes, depends on many underlying factors, but the manner in which it is affected by the age structure of the workforce is far from fully understood. Savings and unemployment rates are likely affected by the age structure, and scholarly consideration of these and related relationships at different levels of analysis may yield important policy insights.

Second, the importance of education for productivity is widely acknowledged. New internationally comparable data on educational attainment distributions by age and sex have become available in time-series form for a large number of countries. Because age, health, and skill level (approximated by formal education) jointly characterize a person's human capital and influence his or her individual productivity, empirical studies should consider these dimensions jointly rather than treat them as independent forces. The changing proportions of healthy people across age and skill groups under diverse institutional settings result in different paths of productivity growth. To jointly consider these various dimensions in empirical studies remains a major research challenge.

Population health has also been considered as a factor influencing productivity growth in advanced industrial societies. More attention should be paid to health in the study of future productivity for two reasons. As life expectancies increase, age at retirement may also rise, fostering productive aging, particularly for those who are not affected by disabilities. However, even in modern welfare states a certain proportion of the population is not able to participate in the labor force because of mental health problems and socio-psychological disorders. Although it is not clear whether this proportion has been increasing as is claimed by some, these individuals face greater problems in a more competitive globalized economy. Helping to improve mental health conditions is not only an ethical issue but also directly relevant for average productivity.

Finally, almost all of the contributions to this volume stress the importance of institutional settings for translating the effects of changing age structure and human capital into productivity. The elucidation of these relationships may benefit from case studies of countries where the age structure of the workforce has changed in specific institutional contexts. Such studies could be designed to target the specific pathways from evolving workforce age structure to changes in economic indicators and to the relative value of investments in education and health.

Population aging is likely to accelerate in most countries of the world over the coming decades, reaching levels unprecedented in human history. Because we are unable to look to historical examples in order to understand how such massive population aging affects productivity, our anticipation of the future must be built largely on assumptions and hypotheses. With much at stake, major efforts to understand these issues and to derive policy conclusions and recommendations may help us avoid leaving to future historians the empirical analysis of how economic stagnation or decline could result from the two unquestioned human success stories—individual control over reproduction and longer lives—that in combination lead to population aging.

References

Agosín, M. R., D. E. Bloom, G. Chapelier, and J. Saigal. 2007. "Introduction," in M. R. Agosín, D. E. Bloom, G. Chapelier, and J. Saigal (eds.), *Solving the Riddle of Globalization and Development*. Routledge, pp. 1–16.

Becker, G. 1964. *Human Capital*. Chicago: University of Chicago Press.

Ben-Porath, Y. 1967. "The production of human capital and the life cycle of earnings," *Journal of Political Economy*, 75(4) (Part 1): 352–365.

Blanchet, D. 1991. "Estimating the relationship between population growth and aggregate economic growth," in *Consequences of Rapid Population Growth in Developing Countries*. New York: Taylor & Francis.

Bloom, D. E, D. Canning, and B. Graham. 2003. "Longevity and life-cycle saving," *Scandinavian Journal of Economics* 105(3): 319–338.

Bloom, D. E., D. Canning, and P. N. Malaney. 2000. "Population dynamics and economic growth in Asia," *Population and Development Review* 26(Suppl.): 257–290.

Bloom, D. E., D. Canning, and J. Sevilla. 2003. *The Demographic Dividend: A New Perspective on the Economic Consequences of Population Change*. Rand.

Bloom, D. E. and R. B. Freeman. 1986. "The effects of rapid population growth on labor supply and employment in developing countries," *Population and Development Review* 12(3): 381–414.

———. 1988. "Economic development and the timing and components of population growth," *Journal of Policy Modeling* 10: 57–81.

Bloom, D. E. and J. G. Williamson. 1998. "Demographic transitions and economic miracles in emerging Asia," *World Bank Economic Review* 12(3): 419–455.

Kelley, A. C. and R. M. Schmidt. 1995. "Aggregate population and economic growth correlations: The role of the components of demographic change," *Demography* 32(4): 543–555.

———. 2005. "Evolution of recent economic-demographic modeling: A synthesis," *Journal of Population Economics* 18(2): 275–300.

Lindh, T. 2004. "Medium-term forecasts of potential GDP and inflation using age structure information," *Journal of Forecasting* 23: 19–49.

Lutz, W., A. Goujon, K. C. Samir, and W. Sanderson. 2007. "Reconstruction of populations by age, sex and level of educational attainment for 120 countries for 1970–2000," IIASA Interim Report IR-07-02, in *Vienna Yearbook of Population Research 2007*, pp. 193–235.

Mincer, J. 1974. *Schooling, Experience, and Earnings*. New York: Columbia University Press.

Modigliani, F. 1986. "Life cycle, individual thrift, and the wealth of nations," *American Economic Review* 76: 297–313.

National Research Council. 1986. *Population Growth and Economic Development: Policy Questions*. Washington, DC: National Academy Press.

Rodrik, D. 2001. "Trading in illusions," *Foreign Policy* (March–April): 55–62.

———. 2006. "Goodbye Washington consensus, hello Washington confusion?: A review of the World Bank's *Economic Growth in the 1990s: Learning from a Decade of Reform*," *Journal of Economic Literature* 44(December): 973–987.

Weiss, Y., 1986. "The determination of life cycle earnings: a survey," in O. Ashenfelter and R. Layard (eds.), *Handbook of Labour Economics*, Vol. I. Amsterdam: Elsevier, pp. 603–640.

Zhang, J., J. Zhang, and R. Lee. 2003. "Rising longevity, education, savings, and growth," *Journal of Development Economics* 70(1): 83–101.

PART I.
THE ECONOMIC SIGNIFICANCE OF GLOBAL AGING

Global Demographic Change: Dimensions and Economic Significance

DAVID E. BLOOM
DAVID CANNING

Until the early eighteenth century, global population size was relatively static and the lives of the vast majority of people were "nasty, brutish, and short."[1] Since then, the size and structure of the global population have undergone extraordinary change. More than three decades have been added to life expectancy, with a further gain of one or two more decades commonly projected for this century. World population has increased by an order of magnitude to over 6 billion and is projected to reach 9 billion by mid-century. Past and projected additions to world population have been, and will increasingly be, distributed unevenly across the world. The disparities reflect the existence of considerable heterogeneity in birth, death, and migration rates, both over time and across national populations, races, and ethnic groups. Coupled with the projected increase in global population is a complicated set of age structure dynamics, including a near tripling of the population aged 60 and older by the year 2050.

Demographic realities are substantially determined by economic and social circumstances and institutions. But they also influence those circumstances and institutions through a variety of channels. The microeconomic links between various economic outcomes and demographic indicators have been extensively studied. By contrast, the links that run from demography to economics and that operate at the level of national economies are far less certain. Some of these links arise partly as accounting identities, such as the effect of population size on gross domestic product, or the effects of population age structure on aggregate labor supply and savings. Other links, such as the effect of fertility decline on female labor supply and the effect of longevity on the incentives to save and to retire, are fundamentally behavioral in nature.

The objective of this chapter is to explore the implications of demographic change for macroeconomic performance. The first section reviews major features of the global demographic scene and its evolution. The second section sets out a simple model of economic growth that allows for possible demographic effects. The parameters of this model are estimated using cross-country panel data relating to 1960–95. Insofar as the estimates suggest plausible and powerful links that run from population age structure and health to economic growth, we turn in the third section to examining the labor supply, savings, and education channels through which these demographic factors may affect economic growth, because of either accounting effects or behavioral change. Special attention is paid to population health and age structure as missing factors in a unified explanation of such disparate phenomena as East Asia's "economic miracle" and sub-Saharan Africa's economic failures. We also examine the contribution of demographic change to Ireland's emergence as the "Celtic Tiger" and to the savings boom in Taiwan. The final section looks to the future and stresses the role that market and non-market institutions can play, at both the national and global levels, in allowing economies to cushion adverse macroeconomic impacts of demographic changes and to magnify and capture beneficial impacts.

Global demographic change

Improvements in health and the related rise in life expectancy are among the most remarkable demographic changes of the past century. For the world as a whole, life expectancy more than doubled from around 30 years in 1900 to 66 years by 2005 (and is projected to rise to 81 by the end of this century; Lee 2003). Most of the historical rise reflects declines in infant and child mortality due to public health interventions related to improved nutrition, water, and sanitation, and to medical interventions such as vaccine coverage and the use of antibiotics (Cutler, Deaton, and Lleras-Muney 2006). By contrast, the life expectancy gains observed over the past few decades (especially in high-income countries) and projected into the future are predominantly associated with reductions in age-specific death rates at the middle and older ages. These reductions are typically associated with improvements in medical technology, life-style changes, and income growth.

Figure 1 shows the historical demographic transition for Sweden, one of the few countries for which we have long time-series of demographic data. Concentrating first on the death rate, we see that before 1800 death rates in Sweden were consistently high, with periodic spikes caused by epidemics and famines. Life expectancy in this period was between 20 and 30 years. However, starting around 1820 we see a long-term decline in death rates, and while some spikes in death rates after 1820 remain (the last spike being the 1918–19 influenza epidemic), they are considerably attenuated. The beginning of the historical decline in mortality in Europe after 1820 preceded the germ theory of disease and widespread provision of clean water and sanitation

FIGURE 1 The demographic transition in Sweden

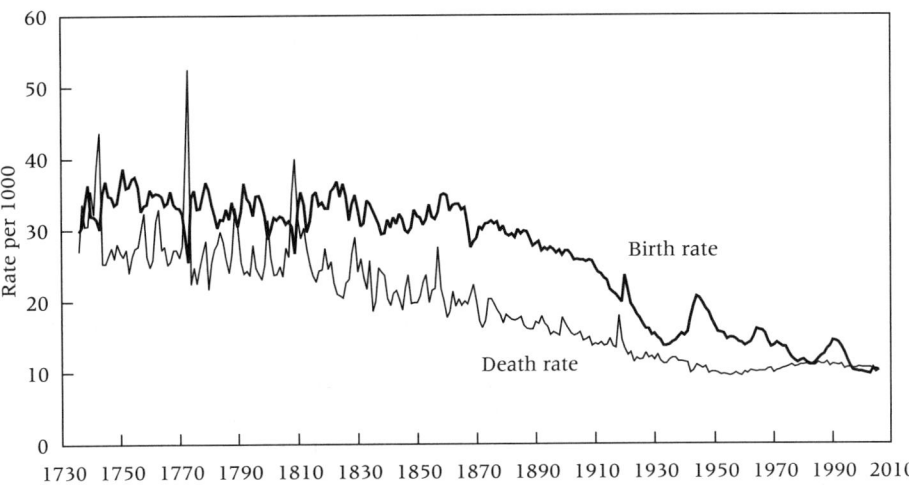

SOURCES: 1736–1987: Chesnais (1992); 1988–99: Statistics Sweden «http://www.scb.se/»; 2000–06: CIA *World Factbook* «https://www.cia.gov/cia/publications/factbook/geos/sw.html».

systems in cities in the second half of the nineteenth century, and may be due to rising living standards and improvements in nutrition. The slight upturn in the crude death rate after 1960 is due to population aging and high death rates among the elderly. More detailed data show that age-specific mortality rates have continued to decline and life expectancy continues to rise.

This pattern of declining death rates is common throughout Europe.[2] In a worldwide perspective, Bloom and Canning (2001) show that mortality rates were high across the world in the nineteenth century, with little difference between poor and rich countries. In the first half of the twentieth century a wide differential opened up, with rich countries enjoying low infant mortality while rates remained very high in developing countries. The second half of the twentieth century saw large improvements in infant mortality, even in very poor countries. While there is undoubtedly a relation between income and health, with higher incomes leading to better health and lower mortality (Preston 1975; Pritchett and Summers 1996), the most important effect has been the downward movement of the whole relationship over time, with improvements in health at every income level.

Along with gains in nutrition, relatively inexpensive public health measures aimed at disease prevention initially, and medical interventions for the prevention and treatment of infectious disease later, were the basis for early improvements in health. More recently, improvements in health have relied on the treatment of non-infectious disease, such as cardiovascular disease and cancer, requiring medical interventions that are more costly.

Turning to the birth rate, we see a fairly high level historically in Sweden. While fertility rates within marriage were high, Europe before 1870 was exceptional in the world in having late marriage for women, with ages at marriage in the late 20s being common. After 1870 (there is some evidence of an effect from around 1800 in France) a large decline occurred in fertility rates within marriage throughout Western Europe, with Sweden exemplifying this pattern. The European Fertility project (Coale and Watkins 1986) found that this decline was widespread and seems to have been fairly independent of economic factors.

In developing countries, the pattern has been for fertility to remain high for a considerable time, but when fertility rates start falling they tend to fall at a rapid pace. Fertility remains high initially because of high desired family size. The causes of the fertility decline in low-income countries can be ascribed to falling infant mortality rates, and to high levels of female education and labor market opportunities that reduce desired fertility, together with the provision of family planning services (Schultz 1997).

The historic pattern of the fertility transition seen in Figure 1 has been repeated in many countries, with the declines in the death rate occurring first followed at a later stage by declines in the birth rate. But the pace of these declines is occurring more rapidly in today's developing countries than it did historically. Insofar as the gap between the birth rate and the death rate in Figure 1 is the rate of population growth (assuming no net migration), one immediate consequence of the demographic transition, since death rates tend to decline prior to the birth rate, is a period of rapid population growth.

On the strength of an average annual growth rate of 1.7 percent, world population more than doubled from 1950 to 2005, increasing from 2.5 to 6.5 billion. The growth rate is projected by the United Nations Population Division to drop sharply during the next half century (to under 0.8 percent) as birth rates decline, but an additional 3 billion people will nevertheless be added to the planet.[3]

But population growth is not the only result of the demographic transition. Changes also occur in the age structure of the population. The initial fall in mortality rates creates a "boom generation," in which there are more people at the young ages than in earlier generations because survival rates—mainly infant and child survival—are higher. After a period of time, fertility rates fall as people realize they do not need as many births to reach their desired family size, or as desired fertility abates as a result of some combination of educational development, income growth, and the expansion of women's opportunities to work outside the home. Improved access to family planning supplies and services may also be an important underlying causal factor (Bongaarts 1994, 1997; although Pritchett 1994 argues otherwise). At that point, the baby boom stops. But the age structure of the population then shows a "bulge" that is created by the nonsynchronous falls in mortality and fertility. The bulge is particularly pronounced if the drops in mortality and fertility are large and if the period between the onset of mortality and fertility decline is short.[4] The bulge works its way through the age structure and, for a period of time, the share of the population that is of working age (generally taken to be 15–64 years) can be significantly higher than it was previously and than it will be in the future. Eventually the bulge will reach the older ages (as reflected in the UN population projections noted above).

In Europe and the United States the demographic transition was relatively slow and produced mild age structure effects. The major reason for the demographic imbalances in these countries is the baby boom that followed World War II. This boom has several explanations, including an echo effect of the baby boom that followed the high mortality rates of the influenza epidemic of 1918–19 (probably to replace children lost during the epidemic, or reflecting childbearing that was postponed during World War I), the postponement in childbearing in the face of the economic hardships and uncertainties of the Great Depression, and spousal separation associated with World War II. The post–World War II baby boom and its echo (a subsequent baby boom after 25 years, as the boomers themselves had children) profoundly destabilized the age structures, for variable periods of time, in many developed countries.

Figures 2–5 illustrate this process in detail for Japan. Figure 2 shows that the crude birth rate (i.e., the number of births per thousand population) following Japan's post–World War II baby boom fell by more than half between 1950 and 2005. The bump in 1970 reflects the echo effect of Japan's baby boom, which occurred during 1946 to 1951. Figure 2 also shows that the birth rate is projected to remain low and that it is already lower than the death rate. The crude death rate is projected to rise. This rise, which seems at first sight to be at odds with the projected rise in life expectancy (Figure 3), reflects the dominance of the increasingly elderly age distribution projected for Japan as the relatively large cohorts born from 1946 to the early 1970s reach the older ages. This baby boom can be seen in Figure 4, which represents a succession of cross-sectional population age distributions (e.g., the first slice—at the far end of the figure—represents the age distribution in 1950, the second slice represents the age distribution in 1955, and so on). In the absence of mortality and migration, the population aged a at time t will become the population aged $a+5$ at time $t+5$. Thus, the diagonal ridges shown in Figure 4 represent two separate 5-year birth cohorts that are part of Japan's baby boom. These ridges begin to reach the older ages in 2010, corresponding to the rise in the rate of elderly dependency in Japan.

Figure 5 offers a two-dimensional view of this secular "age wave" process by plotting the ratio of the working-age population to the non-working-age population (i.e., the ratio of 15–64 years olds to the sum of those below age 15 years and those ages 65 and over). Declining fertility and improving survival rates in Japan are associated with a sizable rise in the working-age ratio (from 1.5 in 1950 to about 2.3 in the 1990s). But going forward, population aging will dominate and the working-age ratio will recede steadily from

FIGURE 2 Japan: Birth and death rates, 1950–55 to 2045–50

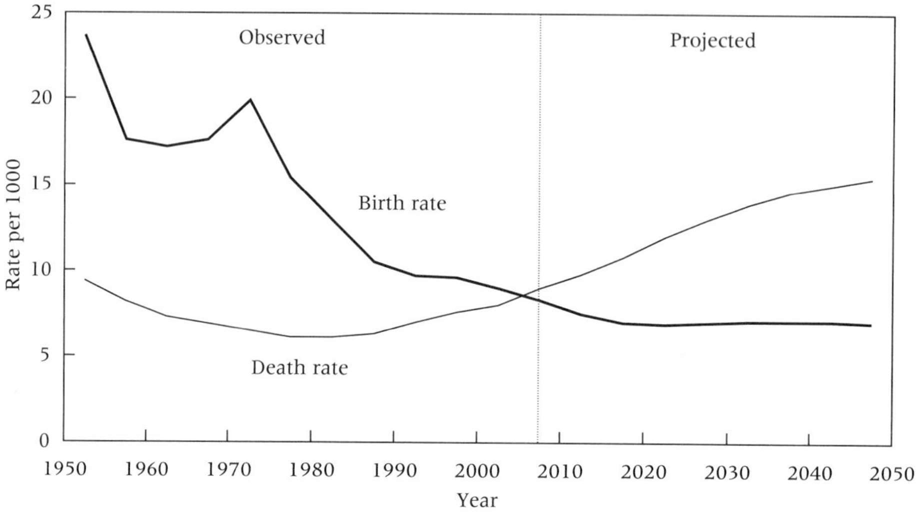

[Figure 2: Line graph showing Japan's birth rate declining from about 24 per 1000 in 1950 to around 7 per 1000 by 2050, and death rate declining from about 9 to about 6 in the 1980s then rising to about 15 by 2050. Vertical dashed line around 2007 separates Observed from Projected.]

SOURCE: UN, *World Population Prospects: The 2006 Revision.*

its recent peak (falling to roughly 1.0 at mid-century, which is slightly below the current level in sub-Saharan Africa).[5]

In fact, population aging in Japan may be more extreme than this. The United Nations projections assume that fertility will gradually rise to 1.85 children per woman, but there is no certainty that this will happen, and indeed, continued low fertility or even further fertility declines seem more likely.

FIGURE 3 Japan: Life expectancy at birth, 1950–55 to 2045–50

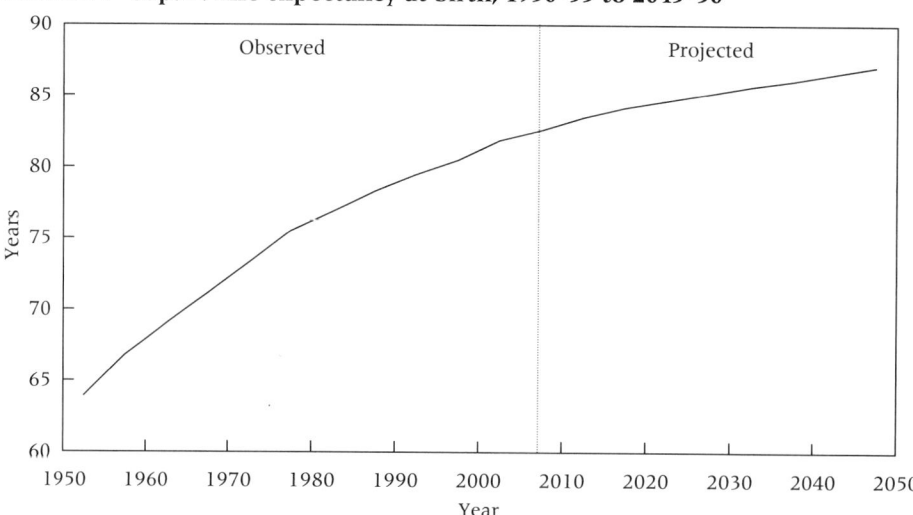

SOURCE: UN, *World Population Prospects: The 2006 Revision.*

FIGURE 4 Japan: Population by age, year, and birth cohort: observed and projected figures 1950–2050

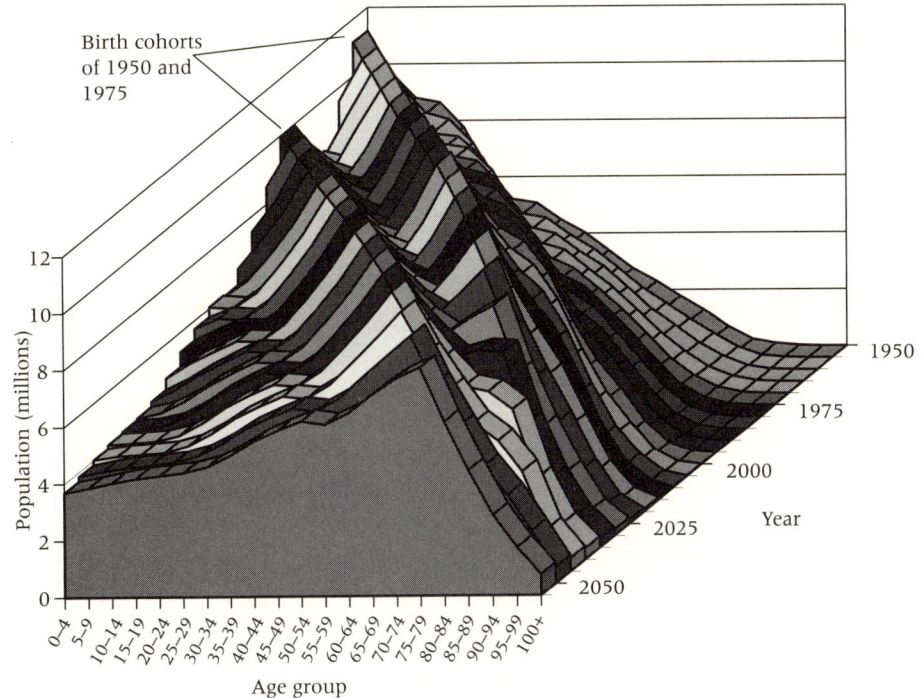

SOURCE: UN, *World Population Prospects: The 2006 Revision*.

The world as a whole is also in the midst of a period of change in its age structure. The world's population aged 60 and older, currently about three-fifths the number of 15–24-year-olds (nearly 1.2 billion people), is rising sharply and projected to surpass 1 billion by 2020 (and to overtake the 15–24 age group by 2030). The population aged 80 and older is projected to increase at an annual rate of 3.4 percent from 2005 to 2050, corresponding to an increase from 1 percent to 4 percent in the global population share of the "oldest old." Moreover, the process of population aging is accelerating. Between 1950 and 2005, the number of people aged 60 or older in the world rose by 468 million (to 673 million); from 2005 to 2050, a 1.3 billion additional increase is projected. Figure 6 shows, for the world as a whole, three different ratios: working-age (15 to 64 year olds) to dependent-age (0–14 years old and those aged 65 or older), working-age to the young, and working age to the elderly. As considered in some region-specific detail below, the world ratio of working-age people to dependents has risen since around 1970 and will reach a peak around 2015. The most dramatic change stems from the rapidly rising number of elderly individuals.

Cross-country heterogeneity is among the most salient features of the global demographic profile. For example, virtually all of the increase

FIGURE 5 Japan: Ratio of working-age (15–64) to dependent (0–14 plus 65 and older) population, 1950–2050

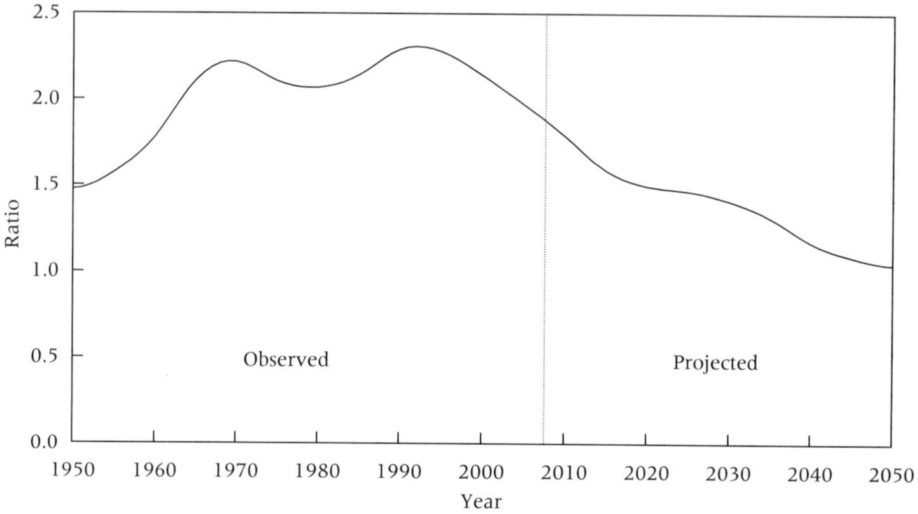

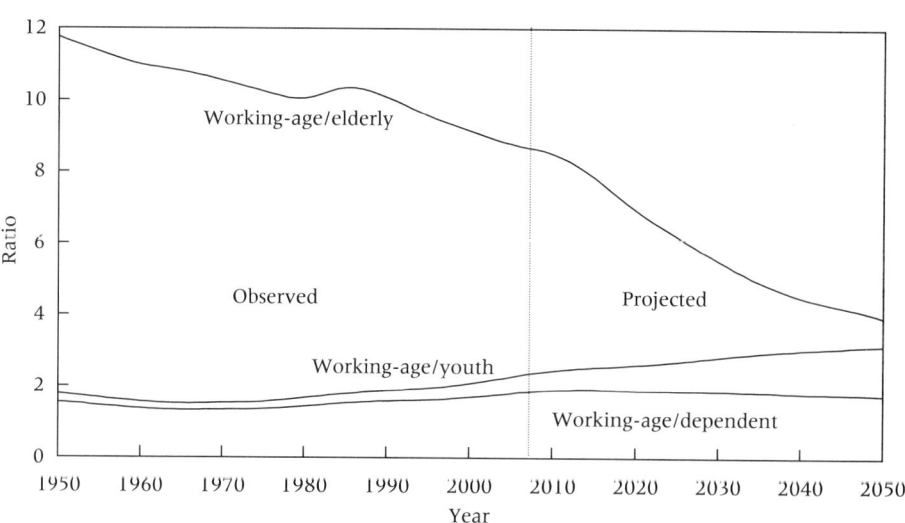

SOURCE: UN, *World Population Prospects: The 2006 Revision.*

projected in world population to 2050 will occur among today's low- and middle-income countries. By contrast, population aging will be most rapid in Western Europe, the United States, and, in particular, Japan, where 44 percent of the population is projected to be aged 60 and older by 2050, with

FIGURE 6 Ratios of working-age population to dependent, youth, and elderly population, 1950–2050

SOURCE: UN, *World Population Prospects: The 2006 Revision.*

15 percent aged 80+. Japan has recently become the first country in history with an average age of over 40. Japan is projected to have nearly 750,000 centenarians (nearly 0.75 percent of the population) by 2050.

Demographic heterogeneity is considerable not just between broad regional groups but also within country groups with similar income levels. For example, fertility rates are well below replacement in Europe, whereas they have been hovering at replacement levels in the United States since 1990. Net migration to Europe (compared with the United States) has been relatively low since 1950, although it has increased somewhat since 2000. The relatively higher migration to the United States has, of course, resulted in a more substantial boost to its population (in part due to the echo effect of above-average fertility among migrants and their children). According to current projections, which reflect the implications of recent fertility and net migration differences, the population of the United States will approach that of Western, Northern, and Southern Europe combined by 2050.

Figure 7 shows the ratio of working-age to non-working-age population in East Asia, South Central Asia, Southeast Asia, Europe, sub-Saharan Africa, Latin America and the Caribbean, and the United States. (The corresponding estimates and projections for Japan alone are shown in Figure 5.) The working-age to non-working-age population ratio rose fastest in East Asia, a consequence of its rapid and pronounced demographic transition. But East Asia, which experienced the most rapid declines in fertility, will exhibit the most sizable drop in this ratio given its projected age structure dynamics in the decades ahead. Europe will follow a path similar to that of East Asia as

FIGURE 7 Ratio of working-age (15–64) to dependent (0–14 plus 65 and older) population, 1950–2050

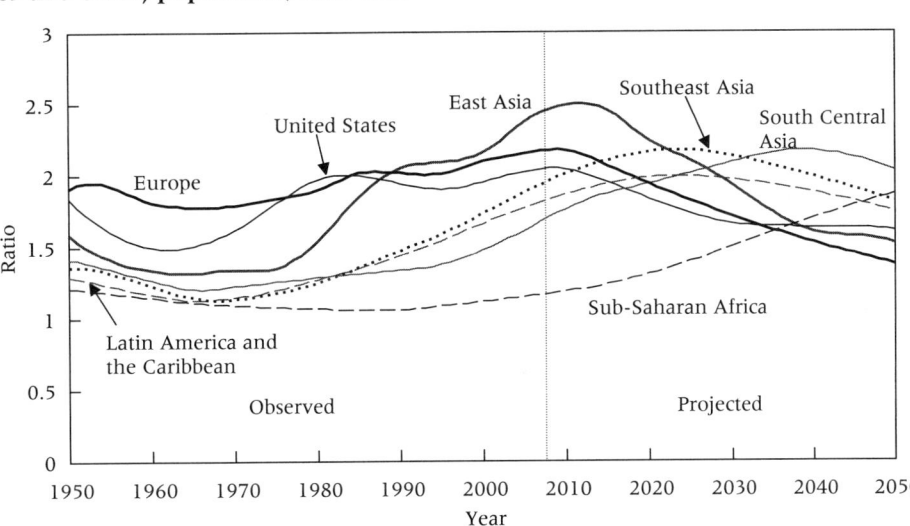

SOURCE: UN, *World Population Prospects: The 2006 Revision.*

a consequence of rapid population aging, while the trajectory of the United States will be qualitatively similar but far less dramatic, with the ratio being supported by somewhat higher fertility and by a somewhat higher level of projected net immigration. Fertility decline is well under way in South Central Asia, most notably in India and Bangladesh, and its working-age ratio already shows signs of increase. Similarly, North Africa and West Asia are now well into the fertility reduction phase of the demographic transition.

At the other end of the demographic spectrum, sub-Saharan Africa continues to experience an extremely sluggish demographic transition. In most countries of the region, children continue to be viewed as a valuable source of labor and insurance for old age. As a result, traditionally high fertility rates and large family sizes have persisted in the face of improvements in infant and child mortality, and now the ravages of HIV/AIDS in some parts of the region are depleting the working-age population.[6] As a result, the average age of the population has remained low, as has the proportion of working-age people.[7] The projection of a rise in the working-age ratio in Figure 7 for sub-Saharan Africa is contingent on the projections of fertility decline in the region actually taking place.

While population aging is occurring in developed countries, it is also likely to come about in developing countries over the next 50 years. Indeed, given the pace of advances in health and lower mortality, and declines in fertility (particularly in China with its stringent birth control policy), large-scale population aging is likely in developing countries before they reach high levels of income. The window of opportunity created by the potential demographic dividend that occurs when birth rates and youth dependency rates fall is temporary, and is replaced by old-age dependency as the baby boom cohort ages.

Effects of demographic change on economic growth

Background and concepts

Although it is often argued that rapid population growth has a negative effect on the growth rate of income per capita, compelling evidence on this point has been elusive and counterarguments abound. Most studies find little cross-country evidence of a significant effect, holding constant myriad other influences on the rate of economic growth. It remains uncertain whether this result reflects the true unimportance of population growth, offsetting negative and positive influences of population growth on economic growth, inadequate control variables or other model specification errors, poor data, or reverse causality. Nonetheless, this body of empirical research has tended to support what has come to be known as the population neutralist view (notably discussed in Kuznets 1960 and 1967): population growth neither systematically impedes nor promotes economic growth. This view has been the dominant academic belief on this topic since the early 1980s and has contributed to the marginalization of policies and programs aimed at affecting population and reproductive health as instruments of economic development among key development agencies like the World Bank (see Ahlburg 2002; Birdsall, Kelley, and Sinding 2001; Bloom, Canning, and Sevilla 2002; Kelley 1988, 2001; and Kelley and Schmidt 2001).

New evidence and thinking have emerged in the past few years that challenge and are beginning to unseat this longstanding view.[8] The new evidence relates to the importance of population age distribution in the determination of macroeconomic performance. There are two main ideas here. The first, as detailed in the preceding section, is that population growth and changes in the age structure of the population are both consequences of the demographic transition. The second is that people's economic needs and contributions vary over the life cycle. For example, young people tend to be net consumers, while working-age people tend to be net producers and savers, with the elderly falling somewhere in between. This implies that the age structure of a population may be very consequential for its economic performance—as measured by income per capita. Large youth and elderly cohorts might slow the pace of economic growth, while large working-age cohorts might speed it. The concentration of labor income in the middle, working years of life requires either saving or borrowing, or governmental or family-based transfer mechanisms, to support consumption of the young and old. Different countries use different mechanisms to accomplish this (Mason, Lee, Tung, Lai, and Miller 2006). The consequences of population aging will depend on the mechanisms in place.

Contrary to the population neutralist view, the emerging evidence indicates that population does matter to economic growth, with age structure playing a central role. As the dependency ratio falls, opportunities for economic growth tend to rise, creating what is now referred to as a "demographic dividend."

East Asia's macroeconomic performance is tracked very closely by its demographic transition and resulting changes in age structure. Estimates indicate that as much as one-third of its "economic miracle" can be accounted for by a "demographic dividend" (Bloom and Williamson 1998; Bloom, Canning, and Malaney 2000; Mason 2001). By contrast, the absence of demographic change also accounts for a large portion of Africa's economic failures (Bloom, Canning, and Sevilla 2002; Bloom and Sachs 1998). In addition, the introduction of demographics has reduced the cogency of the argument that there was something exceptional about East Asia or idiosyncratic to Africa. Most models of economic growth have significant regional dummy variables, usually negative for sub-Saharan Africa and positive for East Asia, indicating that the poor performance of Africa and the exceptionally good growth performance of East Asia cannot be explained within the models. Once age structure dynamics are introduced into an economic growth model, these regions are much closer to obeying common principles of economic growth (Bloom and Canning 2001; Bloom, Canning, and Malaney 2000), and the statistical significance of the regional dummy variables diminishes or even disappears. Bloom, Canning, Fink, and Finlay (2007a) find that the relationship between demographic change and economic growth in Africa is much the same as in other regions, and that sub-Saharan African countries with good institutions and increasing shares of working-age individuals are the ones most likely to reap a demographic dividend. Bloom, Canning, Fink, and Finlay (2007b) find that age structure makes economic growth forecasting more accurate.

It is also clear, both theoretically and empirically, that there is nothing automatic about the link from demographic change to economic growth (Bloom and Canning 2001; Bloom, Canning, and Sevilla 2002; Bloom and Canning 2003a). Age distribution changes merely create potential for economic growth. Whether or not this potential is captured depends on the policy environment, as reflected, for example, by the quality of governmental institutions, labor legislation, macroeconomic management, openness to trade, and education policy. This realm is where Latin America seems to have stumbled. During 1965 to 1990, its demographics resembled those of East and Southeast Asia, but its economic performance lagged well behind. Episodes of high inflation and political instability, and aspects of trade policy and labor relations, appear to have prevented many Latin American countries from exploiting their demographic window of opportunity, at least in its early phases.[9] Numerous other factors also no doubt led to a different pace of economic development in Latin America as compared with East and Southeast Asia.

Model, data, and empirical results

Theoretical model. Income per capita is the major focus of most empirical models of economic growth. It is a convenient summary of the standard of living and a useful measure of the level of economic development. However, in theoretical terms, models of income growth usually rely on a production function that links factor inputs and total factor productivity to output. Dividing the production function through by labor gives us a relationship in which output per worker is due to the level of inputs per worker and the productivity with which inputs are used. Letting z_0 be the initial level of income per worker, we can write the growth rate of income per worker g_z as

$$g_z = \lambda(z^* - z_0)$$

where z^* is the steady-state level of income per worker and λ is the speed of convergence. The steady-state level of income per worker depends on any factors (such as capital stock and education levels per worker, and total factor productivity levels) that may affect labor productivity. We write the vector of variables that can affect steady-state labor productivity as X, which gives us $z^* = X\beta$ and so

$$g_z = \lambda(X\beta - z_0)$$

This type of growth model is discussed extensively in Barro and Sala-i-Martin (1995).

We now wish to develop a theory of the growth of income per capita. We start with an accounting identity that links income per capita (Y/N) to income per member of the working-age population (Y/WA)

$$\frac{Y}{N} = \frac{Y}{L} \frac{L}{WA} \frac{WA}{N}$$

In this identity WA represents the population of working age, L is the labor force, and N the total population. The identity merely states that the level of income per capita equals the level of income per worker, times the participation rate, times the ratio of working-age to total population. If we assume that the participation rate is constant,[10] in growth rate terms this implies that

$$g_{Y/N} = g_{Y/WA} + g_{WA/N}$$

and making the following substitutions,

$$y = \log\frac{Y}{N}, z = \log\frac{Y}{L}, w = \log\frac{WA}{N}, p = \log\frac{L}{WA}$$

we can derive (remembering that p, the participation rate, is assumed constant)

$$g_y = g_z + g_w$$

Hence we have (since $y_0 = z_0 + p\ w_0$)

$$g_y = \lambda(X\beta + p + w_0 - y_0) + g_w$$

This final equation is similar in form to the standard regressions run in economic growth analyses. It relates growth in income per capita to a range of variables, X, and the initial level of income per capita, y_0. We assume that the participation rate p is captured in the constant term of the regression. However, several other terms appear. The ratio of workers to total population appears both as a level term and as a growth term. Because of the identity used to derive this regression, the coefficients on these terms are fixed (equal to

λ, or minus the coefficient on initial income per capita for the level term and equal to one for the growth term).

Data. We construct a panel of 75 countries, including low-, medium-, and high-income countries, observed every five years from 1960 to 1995. Data on GDP per capita are obtained from the Penn World Tables version 6.0 (this data set is an update of Heston and Summers 1991). Data on the working-age (those 15 to 64 years old) and total population come from United Nations (1998).

In addition to these variables, we include in our regressions a number of indicators that potentially explain labor productivity differences across countries (the variables in our vector X in the theory section above). Schooling is measured by the average total years of schooling of the population aged 15 years and older from Barro and Lee (2000). Life expectancy data are from the United Nations (1998). We use these as a proxy for the health of the workforce, even though they measure mortality rates rather than morbidity. Higher life expectancy is generally associated with better health status and lower morbidity (Murray and Chen 1992; Murray and Lopez 1997). Schooling and health can be thought of as indicators of the quality of labor.

We also include a range of geographic and institutional variables that may affect factor productivity. Our governance variable is based on the index created by Knack and Keefer (1995), which gives an average indicator of the quality of public institutions. The index is based on data for 1982 and does not vary within a country over the period we analyze. Data on the percentage of land area in the tropics and a dummy variable for being landlocked come from Gallup, Sachs, and Mellinger (1999). We include some country-specific variables that may affect the long-run level of total factor productivity. We also use a measure of ethno-linguistic fractionalization from Easterly and Levine (1997), and the Sachs and Warner (1995) measure of openness to trade (which also depends to some extent on a country's market institutions).

Empirical results. We explain growth in per capita output in each five-year period by a fairly standard set of explanatory variables but adding our demographic variables, for a panel of countries over the period 1965–95. The results are reported in Table 1. In column 1 we report the results of estimating the relationship by ordinary least squares. We find that open economies, with good institutions and fairly homogeneous populations (i.e., low ethno-linguistic fractionalization), have higher rates of economic growth. In this regression, being landlocked is not statistically significant; neither is being located in the tropics. The average years of schooling of the workforce does not appear to be significant either, although better health in the form of higher life expectancy does have a significant positive effect on growth. The coefficient on the initial level of income per capita is negative, indicating catch-up to a steady state defined by the other variables as set out in the theory section above.

TABLE 1 Estimates of the determinants of the growth rate of income per capita

	1 OLS	2 2SLS	3 2SLS
Constant	0.607*** (3.58)	0.650*** (3.73)	0.531*** (2.84)
Openness of the economy	0.070*** (3.96)	0.067*** (3.86)	0.029 (1.19)
Institutional quality	0.008* (1.73)	0.008* (1.69)	0.009* (1.90)
Ethno-linguistic fractionalization	−0.049* (1.71)	−0.048* (1.73)	−0.046 (1.60)
Landlockedness	−0.013 (0.72)	−0.011 (0.58)	−0.005 (0.27)
Tropical location	−0.032 (1.57)	−0.035* (1.71)	−0.029 (1.44)
Initial average years of schooling	−0.002 (0.48)	−0.002 (0.45)	−0.002 (0.37)
Initial life expectancy	0.005*** (3.41)	0.005*** (2.93)	0.007*** (3.33)
Log initial income per capita	−0.096*** (5.48)	−0.095*** (5.50)	−0.101*** (5.58)
Log initial working-age over total pop.	0.205* (1.71)	0.241* (1.89)	0.165 (1.17)
Growth rate of working age share of total pop.	0.996*** (3.06)	1.394** (2.49)	−0.310 (0.27)
(Growth rate of working-age share of total pop.) times openness			2.524** (2.08)
R squared	0.321	0.318	0.313

* (**, ***) indicates different from zero at the 10% (5%, 1%) significance level.
Based on 507 observations, from 5-year panel of 75 countries, over the period 1965–95. Time dummy variables were included but are not reported. Heteroskedasticity-consistent standard errors are reported in parentheses below the coefficient estimates.

We find that the coefficient on the log of the working-age proportion in the total population has a positive and significant sign as expected. In terms of growth rates, the growth of that proportion has a positive sign and is very close to the expected value of one.

Most of the explanatory variables in this specification are measured at the start of each five-year period and are therefore prior to the economic growth being explained. However, the growth in the ratio of working-age to total population is contemporaneous with the economic growth being explained and may therefore be endogenously determined. It seems quite reasonable to expect periods of strong economic growth to induce a higher ratio of working-age to total population, partly through migration effects but also through an effect on fertility and therefore on the youth dependency rate. To try to control for this potential endogeneity we repeat the analysis reported in column 1 but instrument the growth rate of working-age to total population with its lagged value (from the previous five-year period). The results, shown in column 2, do not change much except that now the negative effect on growth of being located in the tropics appears to be statistically significant.

The estimated coefficients on the demographic variables in Table 1 are, at first sight, difficult to interpret. Since their inclusion comes from an identity (see the theory section above), we could exclude them from the estimation by imposing the parameter restrictions directly from the identity. However, the theoretical accounting model assumes that behavior remains unchanged while the working-age ratio changes, and that all potential workers are productively employed. Increases in the ratio of working-age to total population increase the potential labor force. Provided the measures of human capital (such as health and education) in our model capture any changes in the quality of the labor force during this inflow of workers, and the participation rate of the working-age group remains the same, the coefficients from the identity are correct. However, it seems likely that large expansions of the labor force will lead to changes in average quality in ways our variables do not measure, and in addition there may be a participation rate effect. In particular we might expect that as youth and old-age dependency rates decline (and the working-age to non-working-age ratio rises) the need for care of dependents at home will fall, allowing labor force participation to rise. We estimate, rather than impose, the coefficients on our demographic variables, allowing these labor quality and participation rate effects to potentially be included in our estimates.

The effect of increases in the working-age population on labor supply is to give a supply-side boost to potential output. The availability of extra workers will have little effect, however, if they are not employed. In column 3 of Table 1 we report estimates of the parameters of a regression model that is specified to include an interaction effect between the ratio of working-age to total population and the degree of openness of the economy. This allows us to test whether the effect of increasing the working-age ratio depends on the flexibility of the economy as measured by its openness.

We find a large positive coefficient on this interaction term, indicating that a completely open economy (openness equal to one in our measure) will enjoy nearly twice the growth impact of demographic change as does an average country. In addition, the results in column 3 indicate that a country with a closed economy (openness equal to zero) will have no gain from demographic change (the coefficient on the growth in the working-age ratio in column 3 is negative but not statistically different from zero). This indicates that the impact of demographic change may be to increase labor supply, but how well this extra supply of workers is put to productive employment depends on the economic system and policies being pursued.

Effects of demographic change on labor supply, savings, and education

Table 1 suggests two demographic effects on macroeconomic performance. The first is the effect of age structure, particularly the ratio of the working-age to the total population. The second is the effect of longevity, as measured by life expectancy. We find demographic variables to have positive and large effects on economic growth. In this section we discuss the mechanisms through which these demographic factors appear to operate.

The two mechanisms on which we focus relate to the effects of demography on labor supply per capita and on savings. Given well-established life-cycle variations in behavior, it is reasonable to suppose that changes in age structure will have effects on aggregate outcomes. For example, since labor supply tends to follow an inverted U-shaped pattern with respect to age, changes in the age composition of the population are likely to have effects on aggregate labor supply. Savings rates also vary with age, with the highest rates occurring for 40 to 70 year olds, implying that changes in the age structure will affect aggregate savings rates.

However, in addition to these "accounting" effects (assuming age-specific behavior remains unchanged, we can simply calculate the consequences of age structure change mechanically), there are also behavioral effects. Generational crowding (i.e., being born into a large cohort) may have effects on relative wages and individual labor supply (Easterlin 1980; Bloom, Freeman, and Korenman 1987; Korenman and Neumark 2000). In addition, the decision to reduce fertility and the resulting decline in youth dependency rates may be linked to labor market participation, particularly among women.

The effect of life expectancy that we find can be due to a number of mechanisms. One is that higher life expectancy goes hand in hand with better health, and better health may improve worker productivity (Bloom, Canning, and Sevilla 2004). However, there may also be a demographic effect as a longer prospective life span can change life-cycle behavior, leading to a longer working life or higher savings for retirement (Bloom, Canning, and Graham 2003; Bloom, Canning, and Moore 2004).

We examine these issues more closely by focusing on two cases. The first case relates to the role of demographic factors in the emergence of the "Celtic Tiger": Ireland's remarkable economic boom during the 1990s. In particular, we focus on the effect of age structure changes in Ireland on its labor market and macroeconomic performance. The second case involves the contribution of demographic factors to the savings boom in Taiwan over the period 1960 to 2000.

Labor supply and the Celtic Tiger

Ireland has been slow to complete the demographic transition. The death rate in Ireland, which drifted down only slightly during the period 1950–2005, has been relatively low by international standards (in the neighborhood of 10 per thousand) and comparable to the rest of Europe. By contrast, the birth rate was much higher through the early 1980s (over 20 per thousand). Indeed, Ireland has long been seen as a demographic outlier within Europe, since its fertility rate was still moderately high when the rate in other European countries had fallen to near, or below, replacement level. Figure 8 compares the total fertility rate in Ireland and the United Kingdom; comparisons with other European countries would look similar. The difference between a high birth rate and a low death rate would have led to rapid population growth were it not for Ireland's historically high rate of out-migration.

One reason for Ireland's high fertility rate was undoubtedly the legal ban on the use of contraception. From the founding of the Irish State in 1922 until 1979, Ireland placed severe restrictions on access to contraception, importation of contraceptives, and the circulation of literature about contraception. Irish women and some medical institutions resisted these restrictions, and by the late 1960s women were increasingly obtaining oral contraceptives under the legally acceptable guise of regulating their menstrual cycles. The Irish women's movement took up this issue, and in 1973 the Irish Supreme Court ended the ban on contraception by legalizing the importation of contracep-

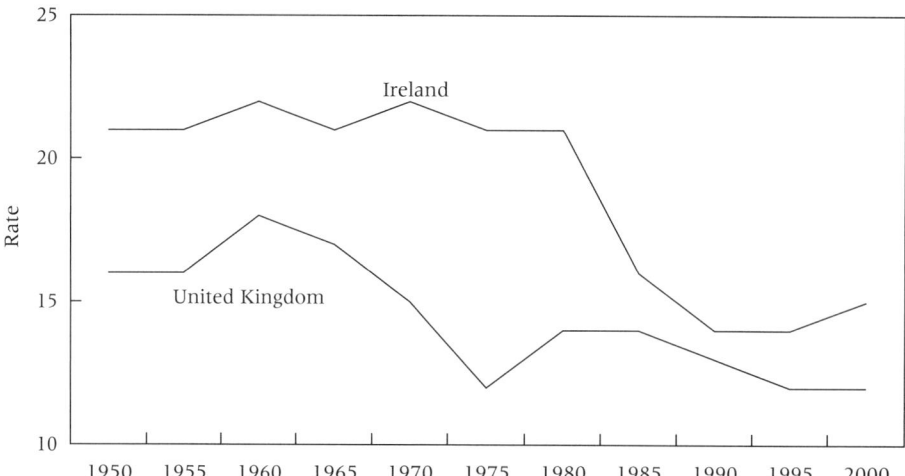

FIGURE 8 Crude birth rate, Ireland and United Kingdom, 1950–54 to 2000–04

SOURCE: UN, *World Population Prospects: The 2006 Revision.*

tives for personal use; this change was not, however, legally implemented until 1979 (see Murphy-Lawless and McCarthy 1999). In that year, the sale of contraceptives for use in family planning was made legal upon presentation of a doctor's prescription. From 1985, contraceptives could be sold to all those aged 18 and older without a prescription.

In the aftermath of societal and legal changes regarding contraception, the decline in fertility rates in Ireland accelerated after 1979, and the crude birth rate fell sharply from 21.0 per thousand in the early 1980s to 14.2 per thousand in the early 1990s. To some extent Ireland represents a "natural experiment" in which the legalization of contraception catalyzed a large demographic change, independent of economic activity.[11]

Ireland's rapidly falling birth rate led to falling youth dependency rates and a higher share of working-age people. Figure 9 shows the ratio of the working-age (15–64) to the non-working-age (<15 or >64) population in Ireland from 1950 to 2005 (and projected to 2050 using UN population projections). Comparative data for the United Kingdom are also shown. It is clear from this figure that the ratio of working-age to dependent individuals in Ireland mirrored that in East Asia through the mid-1970s (see Figure 7). At that point, East Asia's fertility transition, which had begun in the mid-1960s, was well underway and its dependency burden was falling sharply. By contrast, Ireland's dependency burden shows signs of sharp decline by the latter portion of the 1980s, as a consequence of a declining birth rate during the

FIGURE 9 Ratio of working-age (15–64) to dependent (0–14 plus 65 and older) population, Ireland and UK, 1950–2050

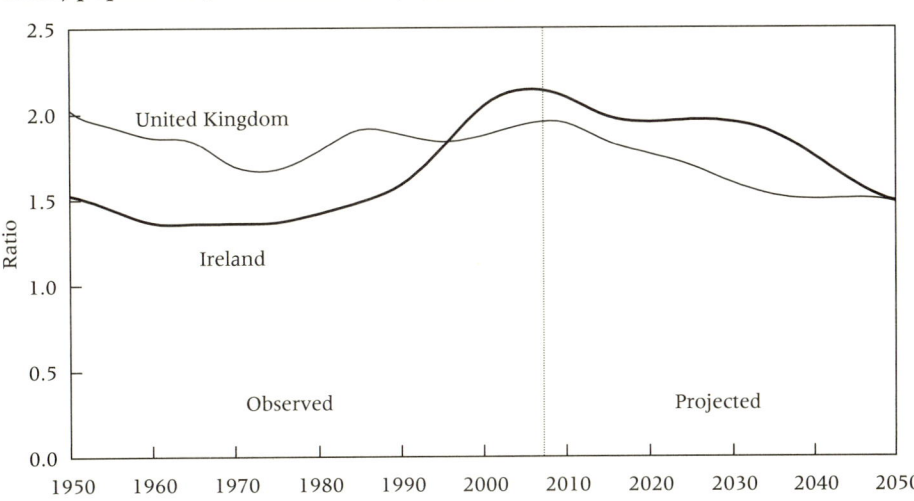

SOURCE: UN, *World Population Prospects: The 2006 Revision.*

1980s. By 2000 the ratio of working-age to dependent individuals in Ireland had risen to a level above that in the United Kingdom.

From 1960 to 1990, the growth rate of income per capita in Ireland was approximately 3.5 percent per annum. In the 1990s, the growth rate jumped to 5.8 percent, which is well in excess of any other European economy, thereby giving rise to the notion of the "Celtic Tiger." This boost in the growth rate coincided closely with the falling dependency rate in Ireland. Thus, the raw data are consistent with the view that demographic change contributed to Ireland's economic surge in the 1990s. Bloom and Canning (2003b) examine this argument more closely and argue that the economic boom that occurred in Ireland in the 1990s is well predicted by estimates of a model similar to that shown in Table 1. As part of their analysis, they also show that the growth in the working-age to total population ratio was matched by an increase in labor supply per capita.

Economic growth in Ireland was also fueled by two additional demography-based factors that increased labor supply per capita. While male labor force participation rates remained fairly static, the period 1980–2000 saw a substantial increase in female labor force participation rates, particularly in the 25–40-year age group (see Figure 10). While one would expect rapid economic growth to encourage female labor market participation, it seems likely that at least some of the increase was due to the availability of contraception and women's increased freedom to choose between working and rearing children. In addition, Ireland has historically had high levels of out-migration of young adults (around 1 percent of the population per year) due to the in-

FIGURE 10 Ireland: Female labor market participation rates, ages 20–24 to 60–64, 1950–2000

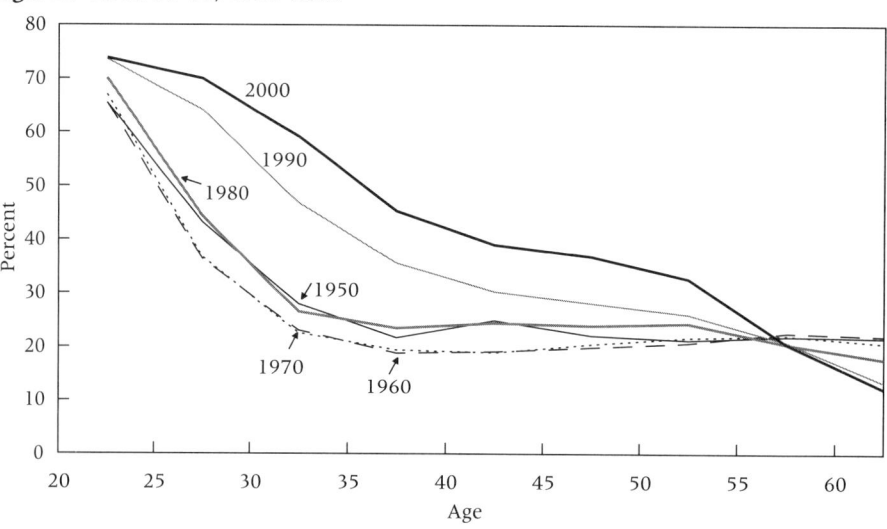

SOURCE: International Labour Organization (1996).

ability of its economy to absorb the large inflows of young workers created by its high fertility rate. The loss of these young workers of course exacerbated the problem of the high youth dependency rate. The decline in youth cohort sizes and rapid economic growth of the 1990s led to a reversal of this flow, resulting in net in-migration of workers, made up partly of return migrants but also for the first time of substantial numbers of foreign migrants.

It is important to note that Ireland, like the "miracle" economies of East Asia, had in place economic and social policies that favored its taking advantage of the demographic shifts it experienced. Two key policies appear to have been at work. First, in the late 1950s, there was recognition that the "closed economy" model of development had failed in Ireland. This led to new policies with an emphasis on encouraging direct foreign investment in Ireland and promoting exports. Second, from the mid–1960s, free secondary education was introduced, leading to a large increase in school enrollments and subsequent expansions in higher education. The resultant high levels of education, combined with export-oriented economic policies, seem to be powerful factors in ensuring that the benefits of the demographic transition are realized.[12]

The savings boom in Taiwan

Central to our understanding of the East Asian "miracle" has been Alwyn Young's work (Young 1994, 1995) showing that rapid economic growth in the region was mainly due to increases in factor inputs—notably labor, capital, and education—and not to improvements in total factor productivity. In order to understand the rise in income levels in East Asia we must therefore understand the driving forces behind the growth in these inputs.

All of the Asian "Tiger" economies enjoyed a surge in savings and investment during their period of rapid economic growth. We focus here on Taiwan, for which there are fairly good data on household savings. The private savings rate in Taiwan rose from around 5 percent in the 1950s to well over 20 percent in the 1980s and 1990s. Savings rates vary by age, being highest in Taiwan for households with heads aged 50–60 years. We would therefore expect changing age structure to be a possible explanation of this increase in aggregate saving. Studies that examine the link between demographic structure and national savings rates do find a strong connection (Fry and Mason 1982; Higgins 1998; Higgins and Williamson 1997; Kelley and Schmidt 1996; Leff 1969; Mason 1987, 1988) and suggest that a large part of the savings boom in East Asia can be explained by the age structure of the population.

However, Deaton and Paxson (2000) show that based on household savings data for Taiwan, changes in age structure account for only a modest increase in the overall savings rate, perhaps 4 percentage points. They show that the rise in the aggregate savings rate has not been mainly due to changes in the age composition of the population but, rather, to a secular rise in the savings rates of all age groups.

The question then arises as to why savings rates rose at each age. One possible explanation, proposed by Lee, Mason, and Miller (2000), is that increased savings rates were due to rising life expectancy and an increasing need to fund retirement income. Tsai, Chu, and Chung (2000) show that the timing of the rise in household savings rates matched the increases in life expectancy of the population.

With a fixed retirement age we would expect such a savings effect. However, Deaton and Paxson (2000) argue that in a flexible economy, without mandatory retirement, the main effect of a rise in longevity will be on the span of the working life, with no obvious prediction for the rate of saving. Bloom, Canning, and Moore (2004) formalize this argument to show that under reasonable assumptions the optimal response to an improvement in health and a rise in life expectancy is to increase the length of working life, although less than proportionately, with no need to raise saving rates at all (because of the gains from enjoying compound interest over a longer life span).

While in theory a longer life span should be associated with a longer working life, in practice this may not be the case. Bloom, Canning, and Graham (2003) find that, even allowing for age structure effects, longer life expectancy is strongly associated with higher national savings rates across countries, which suggests that there is a savings effect.[13] Bloom, Canning, Moore, and Song (2007) find that when people's estimates of their own longevity increase, they save more but do not work for more years, in part because of market failures and institutional constraints.[14] In other words, this savings effect could be due to retirement incentives such as mandatory retirement, which impedes workers from lengthening their working lives. Even in the absence of mandatory retirement, Gruber and Wise (1998) argue that many national social security systems produce strong financial incentives to retire at particular ages and that workers respond to these incentives. For example, the social security system in Taiwan takes 5.85 percent of earnings (jointly from employers and workers), pays a lump sum at retirement of at most 50 months' salary, and takes contributions, but provides no additional benefits, for workers after 35 years of work who are over 65 years old.

While the optimal response with perfect markets may be for workers to have a longer working life as their health improves and they have longer life expectancies, mandatory or conventional retirement ages, coupled with the strong financial incentives to retire that are inherent in many social security systems, seem to result in early retirement and increased need for saving for old age.

Education

Demography can affect educational investments through several mechanisms. Perhaps the most important is the quantity–quality tradeoff whereby fertility choices and human capital investment decisions are jointly made. This framework points to lower fertility being both a cause and a consequence of increased educational investments, with both fertility and schooling determined as well by a common set of factors that affect families' incentives.

Notwithstanding families' desired fertility, actual fertility in the absence of contraception may be much higher. The provision of family planning services to populations in which desired fertility is low can both lower fertility outcomes and increase schooling levels. This effect may be particularly pronounced for girls' schooling because with high fertility girls are frequently kept out of school to help care for their younger siblings. Foster and Roy (1997) show how a randomized trial providing family planning services in Bangladesh affected both fertility outcomes and children's schooling levels.

The quantity–quality tradeoff can also appear to some extent at the national level if schooling is publicly funded. Smaller youth cohorts can increase the availability of educational funding per child and can lead to an expansion of public education (Kelley 1996).

One reason for an increased incentive to invest in education may be the rise in life expectancy. A longer life increases the time over which education investments can be recouped. Kalemli-Ozcan, Ryder, and Weil (2000) argue that the effect of improved health and longevity on educational investments has played a large role in economic growth over the last 150 years.[15] This incentive effect, however, is clearly linked to the prospective working life rather than total life span, suggesting that education levels may be linked to planned retirement ages and social security incentives.

Discussion

For most of the twentieth century the dominant issue in population was the explosion in population numbers caused by the lowering of mortality rates coupled with continuing high fertility rates. The predicted negative consequences of high population densities and a high population growth rate seem not to have been borne out or were overshadowed by the positive effects of other factors. Thus, many of the predictions made about the immiserizing effects of population growth seem in retrospect to have been unduly alarmist.

Following the 1986 National Academy of Sciences report on population growth (National Research Council 1986), the revisionist position came to dominate economists' thinking on population (Kelley 2001). While rapid population growth posed problems, the report argued that market mechanisms and nonmarket institutions were usually sufficiently flexible to overcome or to ameliorate those problems. In particular, projections of the effects of population growth based on unchanged behavior elsewhere in the economy might give a very bleak picture but in general would be very misleading. Changing incentives through price changes, and changing nonmarket institutional arrangements to promote new behaviors, could have large effects and produce responses that would alleviate the problems associated with rapid population growth.

The population debate focused on population numbers and missed to a large extent the issue of age structure changes. Population growth caused by rising fertility and population growth caused by falling mortality are likely to have quite different economic consequences because they have different age structure effects. We have examined some of these consequences above. However, it is important to remember the lessons of the earlier debate. Analysis based on "accounting effects," in particular on the assumption that age-specific behavior remains unchanged as the age structure evolves, may be misleading. When this type of analysis predicts large reductions in welfare, we should be particularly suspicious since these are exactly the conditions that will produce incentives for behavioral change.

The historical experience with which we are familiar is of reductions in infant and child mortality that produce a "baby boom" and that lead to a large working-age cohort. Subsequent reductions in fertility reduce the dependency ratio. This change in the age structure appears to produce a demographic dividend that is overwhelmingly positive in terms of potential economic outcomes. Labor supply per capita rises when the large baby boom cohort enters the working ages and with the increase in female labor force participation that is typically associated with fertility decline. The large working-age cohort saves for retirement, perhaps at a higher rate than before due to its longer life expectancy, producing potential resources for investment. The longer life span and reduced mortality rate may also encourage investments in education.

The potential of this "demographic dividend" is not always realized; economic growth is not an automatic outcome of changes in the population age structure. A large working-age population requires a matching demand for labor if the demographic dividend is to be enjoyed. Without appropriate policies the extra labor supply can result in unemployment or underemployment, with political instability, elevated rates of crime, and the deterioration of social capital as possible further consequences.

In our empirical modeling the benefits of the demographic dividend depend on good policies. We use openness of the economy as a proxy for good policies, but emphasize it is good policies in general that appear to be beneficial, not just openness to trade. We get similar results if we replace openness with a measure of the quality of governmental institutions. Macroeconomic data are not sufficiently rich to distinguish exactly which policies matter most during the transition.

Intuitively, the key determinants of whether a country will capitalize on its demographic opportunity are how flexible the economy is and its ability to absorb a rapidly increasing labor force. A comparison between Latin America and East and Southeast Asia is instructive here. Latin America has a demographic history that is similar to that of East and Southeast Asia (although its

fertility reduction was less rapid), but the Asian regions experienced rapid economic growth, while Latin America stagnated for long periods of time.

Demographic opportunity alone has been insufficient for Latin America. We put forward three possible hypotheses to account for this. First, East and Southeast Asian countries have found ways to engage in international trade that have helped to keep their large cohorts of workers productively employed. The enabling changes involved a phased, careful, and partial opening of economies to international markets, with governments striving to ensure that integration would have coherent, and quickly visible, effects on the local economy and people. In Latin America, too, governments have tried to integrate with the world economy, but they have often done so inconsistently and many countries have suffered long periods of poor macroeconomic management. The results, in terms of economic growth and poverty reduction, have been disappointing. Meanwhile, internal markets have not been sufficiently dynamic to provide employment to the large working-age cohort.

Second, in comparison with Latin America, East and Southeast Asia have had, in general, less restrictive labor laws. Laws providing protection to workers—for example, minimum wages, the right to organize, and restrictions on firing—have been very important in many countries in steering clear of some of the worst abuses of workers. At the same time, less restrictive labor regimes in East and Southeast Asia—although perhaps initially harmful to workers—may have assisted the absorption of the baby boom cohort of workers.

Finally, the financial markets of East and Southeast Asia may have done a better job of mobilizing the potential savings of the baby boom generation toward productive investments. In Latin America, weaker private sector financial institutions, large public sector deficits, and the recurrent risk of loss of savings through hyper-inflation may all have contributed to a wasted economic opportunity.

Well-chosen and effectively implemented policies in these areas—engagement with the global economy, labor practices, and capital markets (and education[16])—are all potential complements to the demographic dividend.

Many developing regions, particularly South Asia and North Africa, and in the more distant future sub-Saharan Africa, can look forward to this demographic dividend. But the future for developed countries is somewhat different. The continuation of improvements in health and reductions in mortality into old age, and continuing reductions in fertility, coupled with the aging of the baby boom generation, are set to produce a new age structure with high levels of old-age dependency. How well these countries cope with the challenge of population aging will likely depend to a large extent on the flexibility of their markets and the appropriateness of their institutions and policies.

It is important to grasp the fact that the projected changes in age structure and falling population numbers expected in the developed countries are unparalleled in history. While we have extensive experience of high rates of youth dependency, and of high ratios of working-age to total population, developed countries are set to experience high rates of old-age dependency and rapidly declining population numbers for the first time. While we can make projections for this, it should be borne in mind that there is little previous evidence to serve as a guide for appropriate policies.

One view is that population aging in the developed countries is likely to have a large effect, reducing income per capita mainly through the fall in labor supply per capita that will accompany the reduction in the share of the working-age population.

However, even if this occurs, it may not be as harmful as it at appears, for three reasons. First, income per capita is not a welfare measure. Nordhaus (2003) estimates that over the twentieth century, improvements in longevity made a contribution to increasing welfare in the United States of roughly the same magnitude as the rise in consumption levels. The longer life expectancies that lead to aging can be thought of as improving welfare directly. Even if rising life expectancy were to lead to reduced consumption levels per period, it is difficult to argue that the net effect of increased longevity on welfare will be negative.

Second, welfare depends on consumption, not income. Typically household income falls at retirement, but consumption may remain relatively high. It follows that we could have two populations, each enjoying the same consumption stream over the same life span, but the population with a larger elderly age cohort will have lower per capita income. For example, the accounting identity given on p. 29 is compatible with income per worker remaining constant while movements in income per capita are driven by the contemporaneous age structure. However, this means that the wage rate and life cycle income and consumption of each person may remain unchanged while the income per capita at each point in time moves with changes in the age structure. It follows that while we predict a reduction in income per capita as a result of population aging, to the extent that this is an accounting effect based on age structure at each point in time it may not affect the welfare of each cohort.

Third, old-age "dependency" is something of a misnomer. Lee (2000) shows that, in all preindustrial societies for which he was able to assemble evidence, the flow of transfers is from the middle-aged and old to the young. In developed countries, on the other hand, both the young and the old benefit from government transfers, and the net pattern of transfers is toward the elderly. However, at the household level in the United States, elderly households make significant transfers to middle-aged households, undoing to some extent the effects of government policy. The dependency burden of the elderly is a function of the institutional welfare systems that are in place rather than an immutable state of affairs.

While the consequences of a fall in per capita income may not be all that bad for welfare, it is not even clear that population aging will lead to a fall in per capita income. Increases in life expectancy in the United States over the last two centuries have been associated with reductions in the age-specific incidence of disease, disability, and morbidity (Costa 1998; Fogel 1994, 1997). Mathers et al. (2001) show that health-adjusted life expectancy (each life year weighted by a measure of health status) rises approximately one for one with life expectancy across countries. This implies that the length of the period of ill health at the end of life appears to be fairly constant and as life expectancy rises health status improves proportionately.

Given longer life spans, people can either work longer or consume less. If they work longer they can keep their consumption levels high and need only save at the same rate as before for old age. If they decide to take extra leisure and retire at the same age as before, they will have lower consumption levels throughout their life and will need higher savings rates while working. Bloom, Canning, and Moore (2004) examine this issue theoretically and argue that when health improves and longevity rises the optimal response is likely to be a longer working life, without the need for higher savings. The tendency toward early retirement is explained by an income effect with people wanting more leisure time as incomes rise.

To the extent that working lives lengthen in response to longer life spans, there is no reduction in income levels. Indeed average income and consumption per capita can remain high. The fixed definition of the working-age population (15–64 years of age) we used in our analysis in the third section (like our assumption of a fixed participation ratio for this group) assumes no behavioral change when in fact such changes may occur.

While projections based on fixed labor supply may suggest a labor shortage, this is exactly the situation in which market responses may be expected to ameliorate the situation. Rising wages will tend to increase labor market participation, particularly of women and the younger elderly and may also to some extent induce inward migration. If these supply responses are sufficiently elastic, the required rise in wages may be small, implying that the ability of the elderly to pay for services out of their retirement income is not diminished significantly.

A greater challenge is to ensure that nonmarket institutions are capable of responding to the problems that arise with an aging population. The two major issues are labor supply and saving. In terms of labor supply, any institutional factors that prevent a supply response to rising wages need to be addressed.

Of particular concern are social security systems that encourage early retirement and financially penalize a longer working life. Gruber and Wise (1998) show that labor market participation of the elderly is quite responsive to social security incentives. Belgium, Italy, France, Germany, and the Netherlands have large incentives to retire early, with implicit tax rates (taking account of taxes and lost benefits) on earnings around age 65 in excess of 60 percent, and corresponding low participation rates of the 55 to 65 age group.

On the other hand, the United States, Canada, Sweden, and in particular Japan have much lower effective tax rates on older workers and correspondingly higher labor force participation. Ideally, tax revenues should be raised in the least distortionary manner possible. In light of the evidence of a large labor supply response to high effective tax rates on older workers, the policy environment seems to afford much scope for improvement (for example, by making social security systems in Europe actuarially neutral, so that workers who work longer receive higher benefits when they do retire, based on their contributions and life expectancy at that point).

Labor shortages and rising wages due to population aging can also be alleviated by allowing greater immigration from less developed countries. The large wage gaps that exist between countries, and the fact that the demographic transitions in different regions are out of phase, create an incentive for such migration.

Figure 11 shows the number and age structure of migrants to the United States between 2000 and 2004. The migrants are overwhelmingly of working age. Figure 12 shows the age structure of the United States population in 2004 and separates out the native and foreign-born populations. The foreign-born population is concentrated in the working-age group, although this is less pronounced than the age structure of recent migrants, reflecting the aging of earlier migrants to the United States. In-migration has made a significant contribution to improving the ratio of workers to nonworkers in the United States. For example, in 2004 the US ratio of working-age to non-working-age

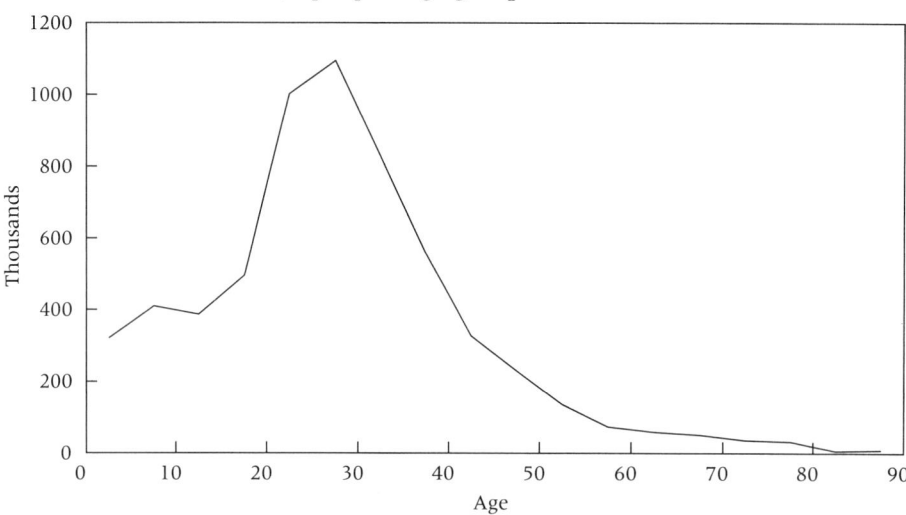

FIGURE 11 Size of the foreign-born population who entered the United States in 2000–04, by 5-year age groups

SOURCE: US Census Bureau (2004).

FIGURE 12 Size of the US population by five-year age groups, by place of birth, 2004

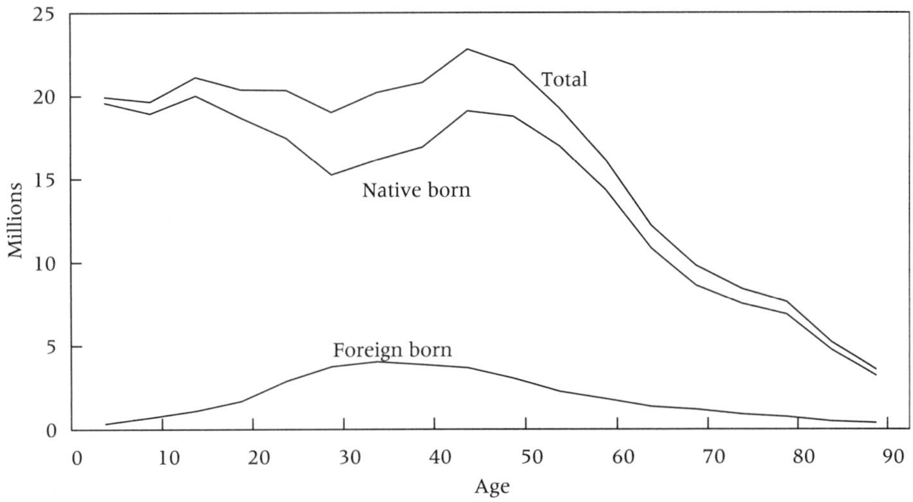

SOURCE: US Census Bureau (2004).

population was 2.02; in the absence of inward migration (that is, counting only the native born) this figure would have been 1.84.

Over the next 45 years, population aging in Western Europe will be more rapid than in the United States, because of a lower birth rate and somewhat lower projected rates of immigration. It seems clear that the incentives to increase labor supply will become large in Western Europe—to provide workers to supply labor-intensive services to the elderly and to shore up the tax base for social security transfer systems. While there may be resistance to longer working lives or to large-scale immigration, the economic incentives for one or both of these responses may grow very strong. In turn, there will be increasing pressures for migration from developing to developed countries that are likely to occur as a result of demographic change, as discussed by Hatton and Williamson (2001, 2002).

For both saving and labor supply, however, markets are not the main mechanisms that need to be addressed. Rather, policy responses are required. In the case of a longer working life, we have already discussed the negative incentives currently in place and argued for a more encouraging tax regime for older workers. In the case of migration the policy issues are more complex. It is clear that the large wage gaps between rich and poor countries mean that there are large potential gains to migration. These gains largely accrue to the migrants themselves. There are, however, negative externalities to the receiving country and possibly to the sending country. Competition for jobs may depress wages, harming workers in the receiving country, while the loss of working-age people and the human capital they embody (the "brain drain" effect) may depress income levels in the sending country. A second issue with migration is its effect on national culture and public goods provision. Alessina and Spolare (2004) make the point that societies that are heterogeneous in ethnic, linguistic, and religious composition appear to be disadvantaged in providing efficient levels of public goods. Levitt (2001) explores the concept of social remittances that coincide with international migration.

The challenge with migration is to devise institutions that turn a large potential efficiency gain into a Pareto improvement by compensating those who lose from the process. Such a scheme would not only help improve welfare but might also remove much of the political opposition to migration by ensuring that it is a win-win proposition. Similar issues occur with trade in commodities, and lessons from that arena may well be applicable to migration. But none of these ideas addresses the perhaps-greater issue of social and political resistance to immigration. As Max Frisch, one of the great Swiss writers of the twentieth century, stated in commenting on immigration in the 1960s, "We wanted workers, but we got people instead."

A second central issue in population aging involves the provision of income to the elderly. The disequilibrium dynamics of the age structure mean that providing for the elderly through a transfer system based on rigid tax rates on workers and benefit rates to retirees is not sustainable. The support of large numbers of elderly will require real resources to be accumulated today to supply their needs in the future.

Social security transfer systems actually undermine this accumulation of resources by reducing the incentives for workers to save. However, social security systems in some form appear to be essential. There is a widespread lack of foresight about the incentives to save for retirement, perhaps owing to time inconsistency in preferences (Feldstein 1985; Laibson 1998; Laibson et al. 1998). There may also be in some countries capital market imperfections (Hubbard and Judd 1987) that may make saving for retirement unappealing.

There is general agreement among academics about the need for institutional changes in developing countries to move away from pay-as-you-go pension systems to at least partially funded systems. There are, however, two difficulties with such policies. The first is that large-scale savings may lower the return on savings to the point where it becomes difficult for a large cohort to generate sufficient resources for retirement. This is partly a case of a low return on investment. As savings surge, investment opportunities become scarce, and there is a worsening in the inter-temporal terms of trade as the low wages of the large baby boom generation are replaced by the high wages of the succeeding small cohort. However, Poterba (2004) argues that demographic factors appear to have had only a small effect on real rates of return historically.

A more worrying prospect than a fall in the long-run rate of return may be a large and long-lasting financial crisis that reduces the returns to a particular cohort. The prospect of such a crisis creates aggregate uncertainty regarding the value of capital, against which neither markets nor governments can provide insurance.

Notes

This is an updated version of a paper presented at the Federal Reserve Bank of Kansas City's 2004 economic symposium on "Global Demographic Change: Economic Impacts and Policy Challenges" at Jackson Hole, Wyoming, 26–28 August, and published in the proceedings of that symposium. The authors thank their discussant, Joel Mokyr, and other Symposium participants for their comments, and Fifi Gosali and Yolanda Kodrzycki for their useful written comments. Larry Rosenberg and Patrick Salyer provided assistance in updating the paper. Financial support was provided by the MacArthur Foundation.

1 This phrase comes from Thomas Hobbes (1588–1679), the English moral and political philosopher, writing about life in an unregulated state of nature in *Leviathan* (1651).

2 One exception is the precipitous fall in male life expectancy in Russia in the 1990s (see Bennett, Bloom, and Ivanov 1998).

3 It has been asserted in recent years that the world no longer faces a "population problem." This assertion has a variety of sources, including a series of downward revisions of global population projections by the United Nations over the past ten years (from 10 billion to slightly over 9 billion by 2050). The assertion also reflects the toll of AIDS mortality and evidence that fertility decline has proceeded faster than previously assumed. While there is some truth to the view that world population has lost its "explosive" character, an increase of 3 billion in this half century is still exceedingly large by historical standards. It is equivalent, for example, to total world population as recently as 1960. It also corresponds to adding nearly three populations the current size of India, or almost five populations the current size of sub-Saharan Africa.

4 The experience of different regions of the developing world in the latter half of the twentieth century shows that the time lag between the onset of the fall in mortality rates and the corresponding decline in fertility rates can occur within widely different time frames, from 15 years upward.

5 The low ratio in sub-Saharan Africa stems from the high share of its population that is under age 15.

6 Nearly one-fourth of all deaths in sub-Saharan Africa are now due to HIV/AIDS, a rate that is overwhelmingly in excess of the corresponding rate in all other developing regions (UNAIDS 2004). This has a potentially large effect on these economies, given that deaths from AIDS are concentrated among prime-age workers, and insofar as the rise in orphans, and decline in prospective longevity, may reduce investments in human capital.

7 Some African nations—notably those in southern Africa, including Namibia, Botswana, South Africa, and Zimbabwe—are beginning to show reductions in fertility.

8 The "new" thinking described here actually stems from the seminal ideas presented in Coale and Hoover (1958).

9 As discussed below, Ireland is, like much of East Asia, an example of a country whose policy environment enabled it to take advantage of its demographic dividend.

10 Bloom and Canning (2003b) attempt to use the participation rate in such a regression but are rather unsuccessful, perhaps due to problems in measuring labor force participation across countries.

11 As suggested to us by Yale biologist Robert Wyman, the legalization of abortion in Japan in 1951 appears to account for the end of its relatively short baby boom, representing another "natural experiment" of sorts.

12 Although we use "openness of the economy" in Table 1 as a factor that may magnify the impact of the demographic dividend, we interpret this variable as a proxy for liberal economic policies in general, not as a specific measure of export orientation.

13 The earlier studies of national savings referenced above omit the life expectancy effect, suggesting that their age structure effects may be biased since longer life expectancy is highly correlated with an older population.

14 Bloom, Canning, Mansfield, and Moore (2007) find that longer life spans lead to higher savings rates in countries where social security systems have incentives that deter lengthening the working life.

15 Alsan, Bloom, and Canning (2006) find related evidence at the international

level: better population health leads to increased foreign direct investment in low- and middle-income countries.

16 Many countries in East Asia have successfully sought to educate the majority of young people and to do so in a fashion that has prepared them for an economy in which workers need to be able to learn new tasks. In an era when production methods change quickly in response to international demands and trends, better-educated workers are more able to adapt to new circumstances and contribute to the success of a wide range of industries and firms. The focus in numerous Asian countries on building a cadre of young people with good general education and technical skills has been invaluable. Although not as remarkable as in East Asia, educational development in Latin America has also been impressive.

References

Ahlburg, D. A. 2002. "Does population matter?," *Population and Development Review* 28(2): 329–350.

Alessina, A. and E. Spolare. 2004. *The Size of Nations*. Cambridge, MIT Press.

Alsan, M., D. Bloom, and D. Canning. 2006. "The effect of population health on foreign direct investment inflows to low- and middle-income countries," *World Development* 34(4): 613–630.

Barro, R. and J. Lee. 2000. "International data on educational attainment: Updates and implications," Working Paper no. 42. Harvard University, Center for International Development, Cambridge, MA.

Barro, R. and X. Sala-i-Martin. 1995. *Economic Growth*. New York: McGraw-Hill.

Bennett, N. G., D. E. Bloom, and S. F. Ivanov. 1998. "Demographic implications of the Russian mortality crisis," *World Development* 26: 1921–1937.

Birdsall, N., A. C. Kelley, and S. W. Sinding (eds.). 2001. *Population Matters: Demography, Growth, and Poverty in the Developing World*. New York: Oxford University Press.

Bloom, D. and D. Canning. 2001. "Demographic change and economic growth: The role of cumulative causality," in N. Birdsall, A. C. Kelley, and S. W. Sinding (eds.), *Population Matters: Demography, Growth, and Poverty in the Developing World*. New York: Oxford University Press, pp. 165–197.

———. 2003a. "From demographic lift to economic liftoff: The case of Egypt," *Applied Population and Policy* 1(1): 15–24.

———. 2003b. "Contraception and the Celtic Tiger," *Economic and Social Review* 34(3): 229–247.

Bloom, D., D. Canning, G. Fink, and J. Finlay. 2007a. "Realizing the demographic dividend: Is Africa any different?," manuscript prepared for the African Economic Research Consortium.

———. 2007b. "Does age structure forecast economic growth?," *International Journal of Forecasting* 23(4): 569–585.

Bloom, D., D. Canning, and B. Graham. 2003. "Longevity and life-cycle savings," *Scandinavian Journal of Economics* 105: 319–338.

Bloom, D., D. Canning, and P. Malaney. 2000. "Demographic change and economic growth in Asia," *Population and Development Review* 26(Supp.): 257–290.

Bloom, D., D. Canning, R. Mansfield, and M. Moore. 2007. "Demographic change, social security systems, and savings," *Journal of Monetary Economics* 54: 92–114.

Bloom, D., D. Canning, and M. Moore. 2004. "Health, longevity, and optimal retirement," NBER Working Paper, August.

Bloom, D., D. Canning, M. Moore, and Y. Song. 2007. "The effect of subjective survival probabilities on retirement and wealth in the US," in Robert Clark, Andrew Mason, and Naohiro Ogawa (eds.), *Population Aging, Intergenerational Transfers and the Macroeconomy*.

Elgar Press. Available as NBER Working Paper 12688 «http://www.nber.org/papers/w12688».

Bloom, D., D. Canning, and J. Sevilla. 2002. *The Demographic Dividend: A New Perspective on the Economic Consequences of Population Change.* Santa Monica, CA: RAND, MR-1274.

———. 2004. "The effect of health on economic growth: A production function approach," *World Development,* 32(1): 1–13.

Bloom, D., R. Freeman, and S. Korenman. 1987. "The labor market consequences of generational crowding," *European Journal of Population* 1987: 131–176.

Bloom, D. and J. D. Sachs. 1998. "Geography, demography and economic growth in Africa," *Brookings Papers on Economic Activity* 2: 207–295.

Bloom, D. and J. G. Williamson. 1998. "Demographic transitions and economic miracles in emerging Asia," *World Bank Economic Review* 12: 419–456.

Bongaarts, J. 1994. "The impact of population policies: Comment," *Population and Development Review* 20: 616–620.

———. 1997. "The role of family planning programmes in contemporary fertility transitions," in Gavin W. Jones, Robert M. Douglas, John C. Caldwell, and Rennie M. D'Souza (eds.), *The Continuing Demographic Transition.* Oxford: Clarendon Press, pp. 422–444.

Chesnais, Jean-Claude. 1992. *The Demographic Transition.* Oxford: Clarendon Press.

Coale, A. J. and E. M. Hoover. 1958. *Population Growth and Economic Development in Low-Income Countries.* Princeton: Princeton University Press.

Coale, A. J. and S. C. Watkins. 1986. *The Decline of Fertility in Europe: The Revised Proceedings of a Conference on the Princeton European Fertility Project.* Princeton: Princeton University Press.

Costa, D. L. 1998. *The Evolution of Retirement: An American Economic History, 1880–1990.* National Bureau of Economic Research Series on Long-Term Factors in Economic Development. Chicago: University of Chicago Press.

Cutler, D., A. Deaton, and A. Lleras-Muney. 2006. "The determinants of mortality," *Journal of Economic Perspectives* 20(3): 97–120.

Deaton A. and C. Paxson. 2000. "Growth, demographic structure, and national saving in Taiwan," *Population and Development Review* 26(Supp.): 141–173.

Easterlin, R. 1980. *Birth and Fortune: The Impact of Numbers on Personal Welfare.* New York: Basic Books.

Easterly, W. and R. Levine. 1997. "Africa's growth tragedy: Policies and ethnic divisions," *Quarterly Journal of Economics* 112(4): 1203–1250.

Feldstein, M. S. 1985. "The optimal level of social security benefits," *Quarterly Journal of Economics* 10: 303–320.

Fogel, R. W. 1994. "Economic growth, population theory, and physiology: The bearing of long-term processes on the making of economic policy." *American Economic Review* 84: 369–395.

———. 1997. "New findings on secular trends in nutrition and mortality: Some implications for population theory," in M. Rosenzweig and O. Stark (eds.), *Handbook of Population and Family Economics,* Vol. 1A. Amsterdam: Elsevier.

Foster, A., and N. Roy. 1997. "The dynamics of education and fertility: Evidence from a family planning experiment." Unpublished manuscript.

Fry, M. and A. Mason. 1982. "The variable rate of growth effect in the life-cycle model," *Economic Inquiry* 20: 426–442.

Gallup, J. L., J. D. Sachs, and A. Mellinger. 1999. "Geography and economic development," *International Regional Science Review* 22: 179–232.

Gruber, J., and D. Wise. 1998. "Social security and retirement: An international comparison," *American Economic Review* 88: 158–163.

Hatton, T. J. and J. G. Williamson. 2001. "Demographic and economic pressure on emigration out of Africa," NBER Working Paper 8124, National Bureau of Economic Research, Cambridge, MA.

———. 2002. "What fundamentals drive world migration?," NBER Working Paper 8124, National Bureau of Economic Research, Cambridge, MA.

Heston, A. and R. Summers. 1991. "The Penn World Table (Mark 5): An expanded set of international comparisons. 1950–1988," *Quarterly Journal of Economics* 106: 327–368.

Higgins, M. 1998. "Demography, national savings, and international capital flows," *International Economic Review* 39: 343–369.

Higgins, M. and J. G. Williamson. 1997. "Age structure dynamics in Asia and dependence on foreign capital," *Population and Development Review* 23: 261–293.

Hubbard, R. G. and K. L. Judd. 1987. "Social security and individual welfare: Precautionary saving, borrowing constraints, and the payroll tax," *American Economic Review* 77: 630–646.

International Labour Organization. 1996. *Estimates and Projections of the Economically Active Population 1950–2050.* Geneva.

Kalemli-Ozcan, S., H. Ryder, and D. N. Weil. 2000. "Mortality decline, human capital investment, and economic growth," *Journal of Development Economics* 62: 1–23.

Kelley, A. C. 1988. "Economic consequences of population change in the third world," *Journal of Economic Literature* 27: 1685–1728.

———. 1996. "The consequences of population growth for human resource development: The case of education," in D. A. Ahlburg, A. C. Kelley, and K. Oppenheim Mason (eds.), *The Impact of Population Growth on Well-being in Developing Countries*, Berlin: Springer-Verlag, pp. 67–137.

———. 2001. "The population debate in historical perspective: Revisionism revised," in Nancy Birdsall, Allen C. Kelley, and Steven Sinding (eds.), *Population Matters: Demographic Change, Economic Growth, and Poverty in the Developing World.* New York: Oxford University Press, pp. 24–54.

Kelley, A. C. and R. M. Schmidt. 1996. "Saving, dependency, and development," *Journal of Population Economics* 9: 365–386.

———. 2001. "Economic and demographic change: A synthesis of models, findings, and perspectives," in N. Birdsall, A. C. Kelley, and S. W. Sinding (eds.), *Population Matters: Demographic Change, Economic Growth, and Poverty in the Developing World.* Oxford: Oxford University Press.

Knack, S. and P. Kiefer. 1995. "Institutions and economic performance: Cross-country tests using alternative institutional measures," *Economics and Politics* 7: 207–227.

Korenman, S. and D. Neumark. 2000. "Cohort crowding and youth labor markets: A cross-national analysis," in D. G. Blanchflower and R. B. Freeman (eds.), *Youth Employment and Joblessness in Advanced Countries.* University of Chicago/NBER, pp. 57–105.

Kuznets, S. 1960. "Population change and aggregate output," in Universities–National Bureau Committee for Economic Research, *Demographic and Economic Change in Developed Countries.* Princeton: Princeton University Press.

———. 1967. "Population and economic growth," *Proceedings of the American Philosophical Society* 111: 170–193.

Laibson, D. 1998. "Life-cycle consumption and hyperbolic discount functions," *European Economic Review* 42: 861–871.

Laibson, D. I., A. Repetto, J. Tobacman, R. E. Hall, W. G. Gale, and G. A. Akerlof. 1998. "Self-control and saving for retirement," *Brookings Papers on Economic Activity 1998*: 91–196.

Lee, R. D. 2000. "Intergenerational transfers and the economic life cycle: A cross cultural perspective," in A. Mason and G. Tapinos (eds.), *Sharing the Wealth: Demographic Change and Economic Transfers Between Generations.* Oxford: Oxford University Press.

———. 2003. "The demographic transition: Three centuries of fundamental change," *Journal of Economic Perspectives* 17: 167–190.

Lee, R. D., A. Mason, and T. Miller. 2000. "Life cycle saving and the demographic transition: The case of Taiwan," *Population and Development Review* 26(Supp.): 194–219.

Leff, N. H. 1969. "Dependency rates and savings rates," *American Economic Review* 59: 886–896.

Levitt, P. 2001. *The Transnational Villager.* Berkeley: University of California Press.
Mason, A. 1987. "National saving rates and population growth: a new model and new evidence," in D. G. Johnson and R. D. Lee (eds.), *Population Growth and Economic Development: Issues and Evidence.* Madison: University of Wisconsin Press.
———. 1988. "Saving, economic growth, and demographic change," *Population and Development Review* 14: 113–144.
——— (ed.). 2001. *Population Change and Economic Development in East Asia: Challenges Met, Opportunities Seized.* Stanford: Stanford University Press.
Mason A., R. Lee, A-C. Tung, M-S. Lai, and T. Miller. 2006. "Population aging and intergenerational transfers: Introducing age into national accounts," NBER Working Papers 12770, National Bureau of Economic Research.
Murphy-Lawless, J. and J. McCarthy. 1999. "Recent fertility change in Ireland and the future of Irish fertility," in *Below Replacement Fertility,* Population Bulletin of the United Nations, Special Issue Nos. 40/41. New York: United Nations, pp. 235–246.
Murray, C. J. L. and L. C. Chen. 1992. "Understanding morbidity change," *Population and Development Review* 18: 481–503.
Murray, C. J. L. and A. D. Lopez. 1997. "Regional patterns of disability-free life expectancy and disability adjusted life expectancy: Global burden of disease study," *Lancet* 349: 1347–1352.
Mathers, C. D., R. Sadana, J. A. Salomon, C. J. L. Murray, and A. D. Lopez. 2001. "Healthy life expectancy in 191 countries, 1999," *Lancet* 357(9269):1685–1691.
National Research Council. 1986. *Population Growth and Economic Development: Policy Questions.* Washington, DC: National Academy Press.
Nordhaus, W. 2003. "The health of nations: The contribution of improved health to living standards," in K. H. Murphy and R. H. Topel (eds.), *Measuring the Gains from Medical Research: An Economic Approach.* Chicago: University of Chicago Press.
Poterba, J. M. 2004. "Impact of population aging on financial markets in developed countries," paper presented to the Symposium on Global Demographic Change, Federal Reserve Bank of Kansas.
Preston, S. H. 1975. "The changing relation between mortality and level of economic development," *Population Studies* 29: 231–248.
Pritchett, L. H. 1994. "Desired fertility and the impact of population policies," *Population and Development Review* 20(1): 1–55.
Pritchett, L. H. and L. H. Summers. 1996. "Wealthier is healthier," *Journal of Human Resources* 31(4): 841–868.
Sachs, J. D. and A. Warner. 1995. "Economic reform and the process of global integration," *Brookings Papers on Economic Activity* 1: 1–118.
Schultz, T. P. 1997. "The demand for children in low-income countries," in M. R. Rosenzweig and O. Stark (eds.), *Handbook of Population and Family Economics,* Vol. 1A, Chapter 8. Amsterdam: North-Holland Publishing.
Tsai I-J, C. Y. C. Chu, and C-F Chung. 2000. "Demographic transition and household saving in Taiwan," *Population and Development Review* 26(Supp.): 174–193.
UNAIDS. 2004. *AIDS Update 2004.* Geneva.
United Nations. 1998. *Demographic Indicators 1950–2050.* New York.
———. 2007. *World Population Prospects: The 2006 Revision.* New York.
US Census Bureau, Immigration Statistics Staff, Population Division. 2004. *Current Population Survey, Annual Social and Economic Supplement.* Washington, DC.
Young, A. 1994. "Lessons from the East Asian NIC's: A contrarian view," *European Economic Review* 38: 964–973.
———. 1995. "The tyranny of numbers: Confronting the statistical realities of the East Asian growth experience," *Quarterly Journal of Economics* 110: 641–680.

The Impact of Global Aging on Labor, Product, and Capital Markets

Axel H. Börsch-Supan

The expected change in population age structure in virtually all industrialized countries—as well as in many developing countries—will lead to a substantially higher proportion of older people in the world. The aging process deeply affects future labor, financial, and commodity markets. On a macroeconomic level, labor is becoming relatively scarce in the aging countries while capital becomes relatively more abundant. This precipitates changes in the relative price of labor, will lead to higher capital intensity, and might generate large international flows of capital from the faster to the slower aging countries. On a microeconomic level, the changing age composition of the labor force might affect labor productivity. Consumption and savings patterns are likely to alter when the elderly become a larger proportion of consumers and savers, with widespread implications for capital and goods markets.

While aging is global, there are marked international differences in the speed and extent of the aging processes. Even within the industrialized countries, differences are large. Europe and Japan already have much older populations than North America; Italy and Germany are aging faster than France and Great Britain. In Asia, some countries start from a relatively young population, but aging is very rapid. A particularly dramatic example is China. Given the globalization of economies, no study of aging can disregard these differential changes. International flows of capital, goods and services, and labor—in descending order of mobility—will be important mechanisms moderating the effects of population aging in each individual country.

A central question for economists and politicians alike is how demographic change will affect the wealth of nations. Which countries will gain, which countries will lose in the international pecking order? Equally important is the question how these gains and losses can be influenced by public policy. With these two core questions in mind, this chapter reviews the most important economic challenges and opportunities posed by global aging.

One way to think about the effects of aging on the wealth of nations is to start from the fundamental components that determine a nation's output and income. Let national output Y (GDP) of a country with N inhabitants be

$$Y = A \cdot F(L, K).$$

From a macroeconomic point of view, the main effect of aging is a reduction of the relative size of the labor force L as a share of total population N. In some countries, L will even decline in absolute size. Unless this decline is compensated by an increase in total factor productivity A and/or an increase in the capital stock K, their national output will decline. Since L is changing quite differently across countries, the growth of Y will reflect these differences. Hence, the list of G8 countries might look very different one or two generations from now from what it is today.

Absolute size may not be the most relevant yardstick. Smaller countries do not need to be unhappier or poorer countries. From a more individualistic point of view, per capita output is

$$Y/N = A \cdot G(L/N, K/L).$$

Per capita output Y/N may stay constant or even increase, in spite of a shrinking population N (and a decreasing total output Y along with it) if labor force participation L/N and capital intensity K/L increase. This is one way of countering the effects of the aging process.

Finally, not all income needs to come from domestic production. In addition to wages and capital income from domestic production, equivalent to Y, foreign direct investment may create capital income from foreign production. Gross national product may become substantially larger than gross domestic product if foreign direct investment creates large returns. Here lie major opportunities during the global aging process.

This chapter is structured according to these sources of output and income changes precipitated by the aging process. It takes predominantly a macroeconomic view. It does not deal in any narrow sense with the central issue of reforming the pension, health, and long-term-care insurance systems. Pension and health care reforms may have important macroeconomic implications, however, and I will discuss them where appropriate. In addition, some central macroeconomic issues, such as the productivity of an aging work force, require my taking a microeconomic view.

The next section briefly depicts the central demographic facts and discusses research issues relevant for the economic analysis. The third section looks at labor markets in terms of what is known about labor supply, labor productivity, and labor mobility, and where more research is needed on labor market effects of population aging. The fourth section discusses the interactions between labor, product, and capital markets. Consumer demand will be deeply affected by aging since an elderly population has very different consumption patterns from a young population. This induces sectoral labor demand shifts, possibly accompanied by higher frictional unemployment. With the increasing importance of private pensions, capital markets and product markets may become more closely linked than they are currently. The fifth section is devoted to capital market issues. Will world capital markets face a shortage of loanable funds when baby boomers retire and withdraw their savings? How much new savings will pension reforms generate? Which capital market issues, such as corporate governance and capital productivity, require more research?

The issues are discussed at a general level; concrete examples are derived from the experience of one aging country, Germany. There are several reasons to study Germany as a particularly interesting example of a country in the midst of global aging. Together with Italy and Japan, Germany is ahead of the United States in terms of aging. Germany's old-age dependency ratio in 2003 corresponded to what is projected for the United States for about 2023, two decades later. Germany has a very globalized economy, with a high trade volume, large foreign direct investments, and the highest immigration rate of the EU. Finally, Germany not only has an old population, it also has an old economic system, with labor, capital market, and social policy institutions created in the 1950s and now under substantial pressure. Germany is an ideal showcase for the challenges—and opportunities—global aging poses for a highly developed economy.

Demographic dimensions

At mid-2000, world population stood at 6.1 billion. While world population has constantly grown, its annual growth rate has decreased from 2.04 percent during the period from 1965 to 1970 to 1.2 percent annually now. This decrease in world population growth is expected to continue. In the medium variant of the United Nations current world population projections, the growth rate is projected to decrease to 0.5 percent by 2050. By then, world population will have increased to 9.3 billion. Most of this increase in the size of the world population will take place in less developed regions (United Nations 2001).

The demographic transition is characterized by falling mortality rates followed by a decline in birth rates. This process results in population aging and thereby reduces the rate of population growth and even turns it to negative. This process is taking place throughout the world. While the patterns of population aging are similar in most countries, the timing differs substantially. There are marked differences in the extent and timing of the aging process even within the industrialized countries, as shown in Figure 1. Japan and Germany have the highest old-age dependency ratios, followed by the EU14, an average of all EU countries (as of the year 2000) except Germany. The United States is considerably younger than the EU, and the remaining industrial countries (OECD 13) are even younger.

FIGURE 1 Old-age dependency ratio (65+/15–64) in selected OECD countries as projected from 2000 to 2050

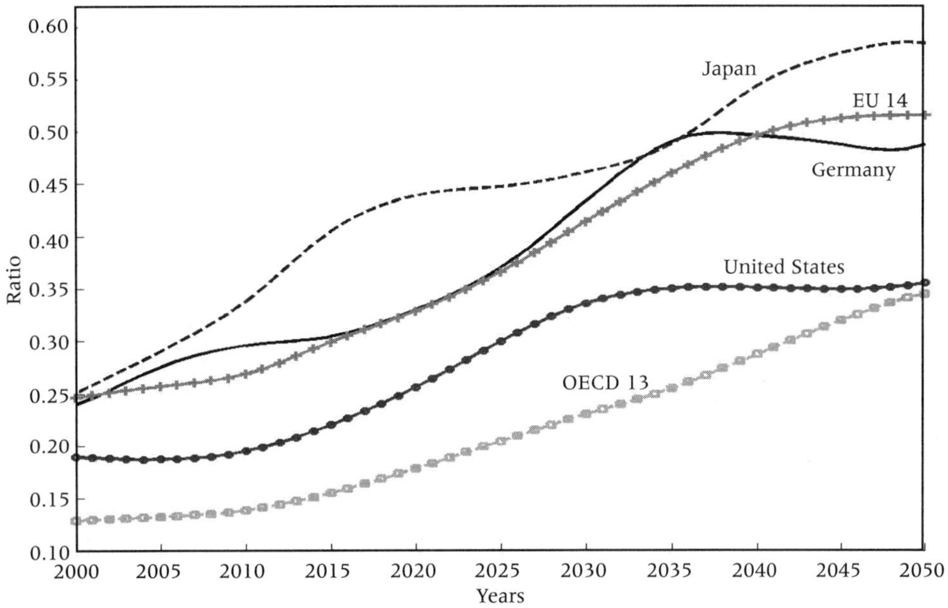

NOTE: EU 14 and OECD 13 show unweighted averages of the country dependency ratios. EU 14 is defined as the EU 15 less Germany. The OECD 13 consists of OECD without EU15, United States, and Japan.
SOURCE: United Nations (2001).

Labor markets

Understanding the development of the labor force during the next decades is crucial for any analysis of global aging because long-run macroeconomic development is dominated by such fundamentals as the relative scarcity of labor and the relative abundance of capital. The macroeconomic effects of population aging are a changing balance between capital and labor, and between labor supply and demand for consumption. An aging society has relatively few workers for the existing capital stock that produces consumption goods for a still relatively large number of consumers. Some countries have been projected to shrink in absolute size, Germany among them. Under most assumptions concerning the size of future international migration, however, this shrinkage will be relatively small until most members of the baby boom generation have died. These changing fundamentals not only affect each country in isolation but also the relation among countries.

This section focuses primarily on the isolated impact of population aging on labor markets and asks to what extent public policy may be able to mitigate potential problems. It sheds light on the structural changes occurring in the labor market—the age structure of workers, their labor productivity, and the wage structure. I also look at interactions between labor and product, and between labor and capital markets. Because the fifth section examines the implications of population aging for capital markets, I postpone a general equilibrium analysis of growth until then. This section may therefore be regarded as a partial analysis dealing with human capital, while the complementary fifth section deals with real capital and the general equilibrium of an aging economy in a globalized world.

Labor supply

Predictions of labor supply have two components: a demographic projection (working-age population) plus assumptions about labor force participation rates specific to age, sex, and other characteristics. Labor force participation rates are policy related; for example, they depend heavily on the rules determining labor market entry (through the education system, see Skirbekk 2004) and retirement (through statutory retirement age and actuarial adjustments, see Gruber and Wise 1999).

Actual employment of course also depends on labor demand. While most economists believe that in the long run employment is determined by supply, the long-lasting unemployment in Europe with its potential structural reasons may also affect employment in the future. Labor market rigidities affect the implications of global aging in several ways. As will be shown below, aging changes the structure of consumption demand, therefore also the sectoral demand for labor. If the Continental European economies keep failing to permit quicker adjustments to changed circumstances, employment will fall more rapidly than the labor supply because of unemployment in those sectors that are shrinking and a lack of available new jobs in the potentially growing sectors. International migration is also heavily influenced by labor market regulations. Unemployment policies that fail to create jobs for less-qualified persons may exacerbate the duality of labor markets in Europe: on the one hand, a rising excess demand for qualified labor is likely to emerge when cohorts become smaller during the aging process; on the other hand, unemployment among less-qualified persons may remain constant because the root cause for such unemployment (the large wedge between marginal productivity and total labor compensation) has not been removed. Since the economic essence of population aging is a scarcity of labor relative to existing capital and population, under-use of labor even at low qualification levels amplifies the negative effects of population aging.

The upper part of Figure 2 depicts projected aggregate employment rates based on OECD (2002) and Börsch-Supan, Ludwig, and Winter (2002). Levels and shapes differ markedly. They lead to "economic dependency ratios" (the number of retired persons as related to the number of workers), shown in the lower part of Figure 2, that are much higher in Europe than in the United States. This economic dependency ratio is the core statistic to judge the economic effects of global population aging. According to these projections, the

FIGURE 2 Aggregate employment rates (employment related to total population) and economic dependency ratios (number of retired persons related to the number employed) in selected OECD countries as projected from 2000 to 2050

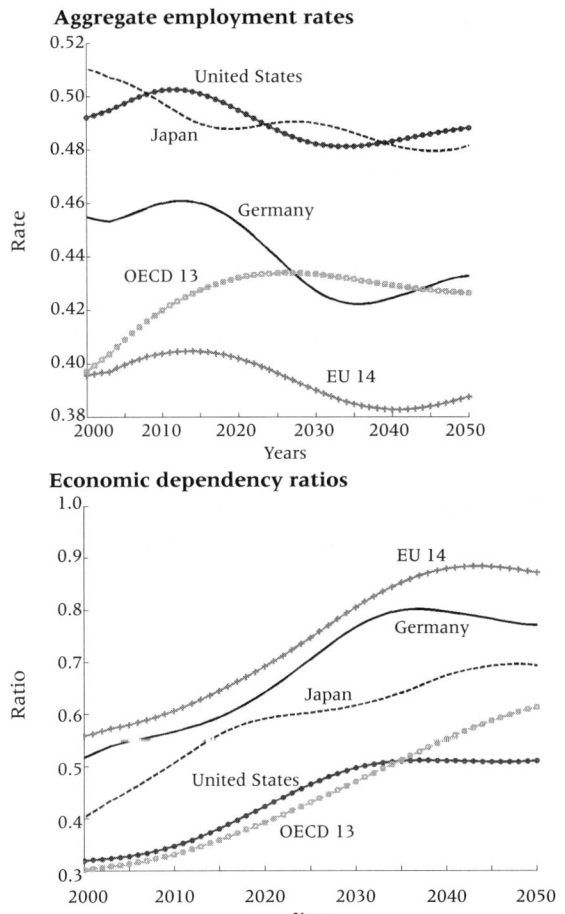

SOURCE: OECD 2002; Börsch-Supan, Ludwig, and Winter 2002.
NOTE: See Note to Figure 1.

United States will never reach the level of economic dependency Germany is already experiencing.

The projections shown in the upper part of Figure 2 show the leverage of employment on the economic implications of aging. Comparing this figure with the purely demographic Figure 1 shows that the higher labor force participation in Japan makes this country less vulnerable to population aging than Europe. By the same token, policies affecting employment, such as earlier labor market entry ages brought about by education reform and later labor market exit ages brought about by pension reform, are crucial ingredients to minimize the economic effects of population aging. Any differential success in implementing such policies will have straightforward implications on global population aging and the relative position of countries in the international pecking order.

The sharply falling employment rates projected for Germany during the 25 years between 2010 and 2035 (Figure 2) translate into a dramatically shrinking labor force. Figure 3 shows the magnitude of this decline under three scenarios.

Details are given in Börsch-Supan (2003); in essence, the very optimistic scenario E3 assumes large increases in the average retirement age and in female labor force participation rates plus an almost complete reduction of unemployment, while the pessimistic scenario E1 assumes no change in age- and sex-specific employment rates at all. Scenario E2 represents the—in my view—most realistic set of assumptions. Despite the increase in participation rates predicted by scenario E2, the size of the labor force as measured in the year 2000 is nonetheless set to fall by around 8 million by mid-century.

It is very unlikely that this decline can be compensated by an equiproportional increase in productivity and/or capital accumulation, as I will show below. Total German GDP will therefore almost surely decline, and Germany is likely to have a declining weight among the G8 countries.

From a domestic consumer's point of view, total GDP is less relevant than GDP per capita. Since the German total population is also likely to decline, labor force as a share of the adult population—the so-called support ratio—will decline more slowly than total labor force. Nevertheless, in the middle scenario E2 shown in Figure 4, the support ratio drops from 56 percent in the year 2000 to 49 percent in the year 2035.

FIGURE 3 Labor force in Germany as projected from 2000 to 2050 under three scenarios concerning the average age of retirement, female labor force participation rates, and the proportion unemployed (in millions)

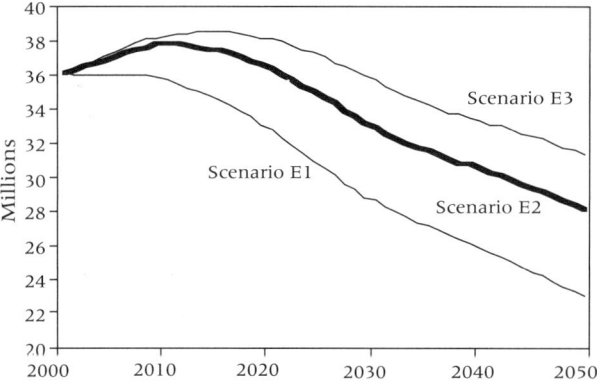

SOURCE: Börsch-Supan 2003.

FIGURE 4 Support ratio (labor force as share of total adult population) in Germany as projected from 2000 to 2050 under three scenarios (percent)

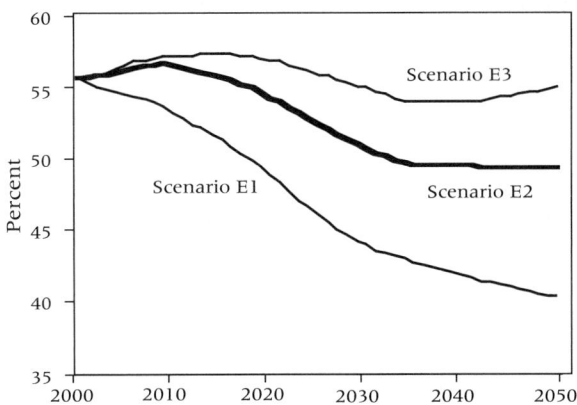

SOURCE: Börsch-Supan 2003.

Figure 4 demonstrates the force of population aging in an understandable metric. A decline of 15 percent in the 25-year period between 2010 and 2035 translates into a negative growth rate of around 0.6 percentage points per annum from 2010 to 2035. The long-term real annual productivity growth of the German economy (1871–1995) has been estimated to be approximately 1.6 percent (Buchheim 1998). In other words, the negative economic force of population aging, simply by reducing the number of workers available to produce goods and services, corresponds to between one-quarter and one-third of the average annual productivity growth. To compensate for the lack of workers by higher productivity of the existing workers, total factor productivity would need to increase by 40 percent, probably an unrealistic figure.

Figure 4 also shows the variability range for this forecast. In the pessimistic scenario E1, the impact of the declining support ratio is huge. On the other hand, in the optimistic scenario E3 the shift in the age structure is compensated for almost entirely by the increase in participation rates.

This example bears several lessons for policy in times of global population aging. First, the huge variability of the projections and the leverage of employment on GDP make clear the imperative to better understand how public policy can influence labor force participation rates. Structural reforms such as education reform and pension reform have potentially large side effects on GDP growth through their impact on employment, over and above the often more prominently discussed impacts on social budgets. Second, the above example shows how strongly the differential force of global population aging depends on the extent to which an increasing quality of labor will compensate for the decreasing quantity of labor. Side effects of structural reforms on productivity may in the long run dominate any direct but static effects, because they change the growth path of the economy.

Labor productivity

Not only the size but also the age structure of the working-age population (age 15–64) will change radically in the coming decades. I again use Germany as an example of how dramatic the change can be. Figure 5 shows the age composition of this population between the years 2000 and 2030. The peak of the age distribution very clearly moves from left to right. The modal age in the year 2000 is 36; ten years later the peak age increases to 46 years; and a further 10 years on it has risen to 54 years. The baby boomers then retire and the age distribution curve flattens out. Projections beyond 2030 (not shown) suggest little change in the following decades.

Correspondingly, the average age of the population aged 15–64 will increase from 29 to 42.5 years in the next 20 years, will then stagnate for 15 years, and will subsequently increase by one further year. The dramatic change in the age structure is exemplified by the projected share of those aged 55–64 within the working-age population (Figure 6). An interesting phenomenon is the temporary "rejuvenation" of the population aged 15–64 after the large baby boom cohorts have retired. The figure, however, also reveals that

FIGURE 5 Age structure of the working-age population of Germany in 2000 and as projected to 2010, 2020, and 2030

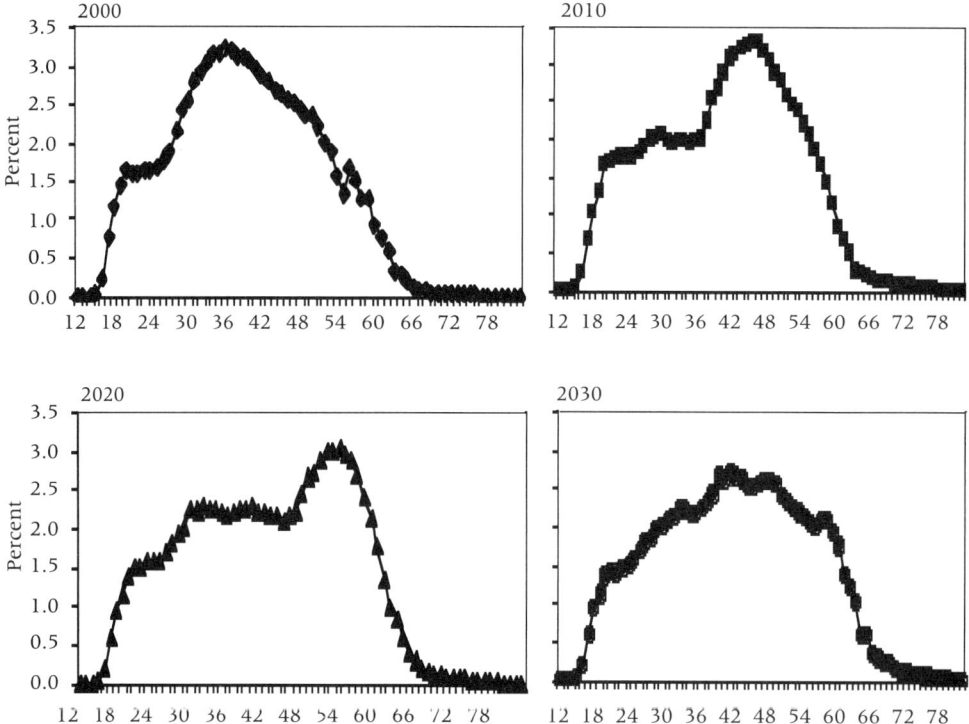

SOURCE: Börsch-Supan 2003.

FIGURE 6 Projected share of the population of Germany aged 55–64 within the working-age population, 2000–50

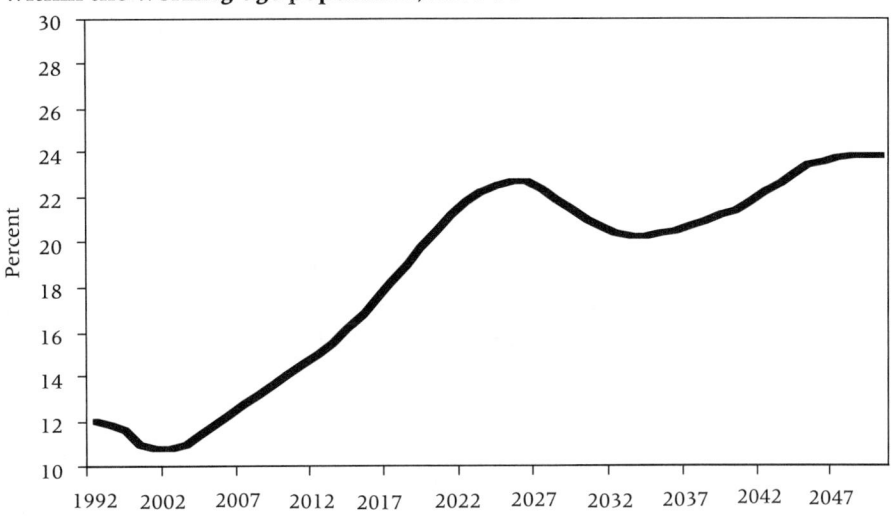

SOURCE: Börsch-Supan 2003.

the shift in the age structure is not a transitory phenomenon that subsides after the decease of the baby boom generation.

This fundamental change in the age structure of the population aged 15–64 will have profound effects on the microeconomics and the sociology of the labor market. The most important—and most controversial—aspect is the potential effect on labor productivity. If labor productivity is age dependent, a shift in the age structure will also bring about a change in aggregate productivity, even if age-specific productivity remains constant. This section provides a rough estimate of the approximate magnitude of this shift in labor productivity.

This is not a simple task because there are no reliable data available on age-specific labor productivity. We apply two extreme estimates of age-specific productivity derived from Kotlikoff and Wise (1989) to the German data, which should roughly capture the range of possible effects. Kotlikoff and Wise evaluated confidential data originating from a major US service enterprise. They provide two estimates. The first estimate uses age- and seniority-specific earnings of sales staff, which are proportionally linked to the value of the sales contracts negotiated by such staff, and interprets them as age- and seniority-specific productivity. Because sales staff, whose pay is wholly performance related, are by no means representative of a modern service economy, we use Kotlikoff and Wise's (1989) salary measures of office workers for our second estimate of age-specific labor productivity. The difficulty here is that salaried workers' pay generally includes a major seniority element that severs the tie between pay and productivity across the life cycle. We therefore take the age–salary pattern of newly recruited staff as our second estimate for age-specific labor productivity. This turns out to be considerably "curvier" than the profile of sales staff. Figure 7 shows the normalized age-productivity estimates. Both feature a distinct bell-shaped curve that peaks for office workers at age 44 years and subsequently falls rapidly while sales employees' productivity maximum is reached four years later followed by a decline that is much less pronounced. In both cases, labor productivity is about 20 percent of its lifecycle maximum at around 16 years and sinks back to this level again at 75 years.

The point of this exercise becomes clear in Figure 8. We now multiply age-dependent productivity (Figure 7) by the gradually changing distribution of the age structure of the population aged 15–64 (Figure 5) in order to estimate the time path of the aggregated productivity of the labor force.

The main lesson from this exercise is that it makes a considerable difference what is assumed to be the true age-productivity profile. If the age-productivity profile is relatively flat, as among sales staff, there is no severe impact of aging on aggregate labor productivity. If the age-productivity profile, however, is better described by the steep profile of office workers, aggregate labor productivity will drop significantly, amplify the negative effects on economic growth, and exacerbate the divergences through global aging.

More research on age-specific productivity is clearly needed to better understand whether aging economies will suffer from a productivity decline, amplifying the effects of a shrinking quantity of labor. At the very least, the difference between the profiles indicates the value of policies fostering further education. Similar arguments apply to the innovative capacity of aging societies.

FIGURE 7 Estimated relative labor productivity by age of sales staff and office workers (age 45 = 1.0)

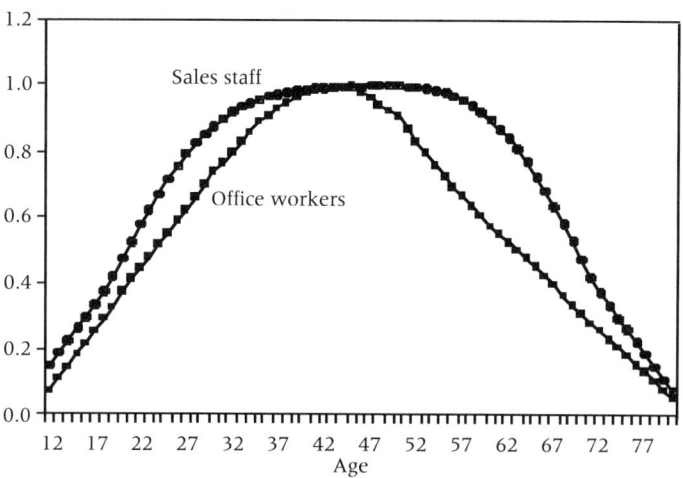

SOURCE: Derived from Kotlikoff and Wise (1989).

FIGURE 8 Potential effect of age-specific labor productivity on aggregate labor productivity under two assumptions concerning the age profile of productivity, Germany 2000–50

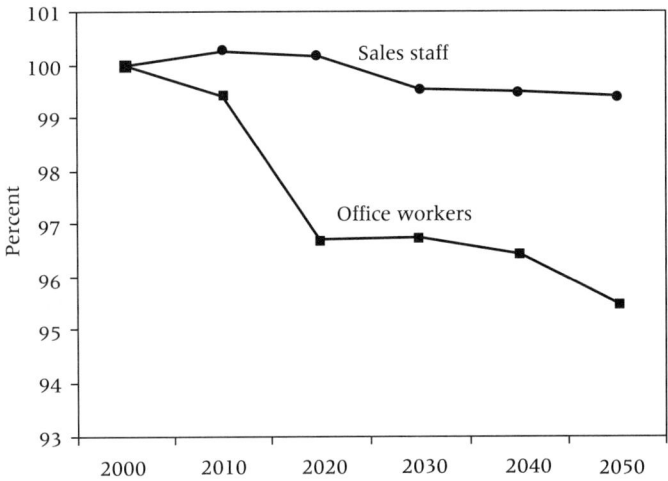

SOURCE: Own calculations based on Figures 5 and 7.

Interactions between labor, product, and capital markets

The labor market is not insulated from other markets. It is not only directly affected by population aging but also indirectly affected by aging-induced changes in product and capital markets. In this brief interim section, we first focus on interactions between labor and product markets, then on interactions between labor and capital markets.

Interactions between labor and product markets

Product demand will change with population aging, since an older population of consumers has different preferences and needs than a younger population. Consumption demand may also decline for at least two reasons. First, GDP per capita will decline in the face of a shrinking labor force unless this is offset by higher capital input and productivity. Second and more subtly, it is likely that more retirement income comes from asset income, which fluctuates more than annuitized pension and labor income. This will increase precautionary savings and depress consumption, given a fixed level of income. We have little evidence to quantify these effects so far.

Somewhat easier to predict are shifts within consumption demand. Consumption behavior changes with increasing age. For example, spending on goods in the group "transport and communication" falls over the life cycle, while goods in the "health and hygiene" group, as well as costs of shelter, account for a growing share of older households' budgets. Hence, if the age distribution of an economy is changing, the composition of consumption will change accordingly. Most notably the aggregated expenditure on health will increase during the aging process while the corresponding spending on transport will decline.

Changing product demand will then precipitate shifts in sectoral labor demand. Using again a simplistic shift-share methodology to obtain a rough idea of the potential order of magnitude, Börsch-Supan (2003) estimates that employment in the health sector will increase by around 7 percent, and fall in the transport sector by around 5 percent. Overall, increases and decreases in employment amount to a total of 18 percent, suggesting that more than one-sixth of all workers will need to change their jobs as the result of population aging.

Interactions between labor and capital markets

Labor supply is also affected by capital market fluctuations. As more retirement income is provided through funded pension income (e.g., 401k plans or other individual accounts invested in the stock market), stock market performance will, at the margin, affect the retirement decision of workers as well as their consumption demand. While there is some evidence that the recent increase in retirement age in the United States is concurrent with the decline in stock market values (Eschtruth and Gemus 2002), these data are too recent and cover too short a period to permit causal analysis.

Understanding this mechanism is important for analyses of global aging since it may substantially amplify capital market disturbances. Stock markets have exhibited huge swings, and we do not fully understand how bubbles emerge and even less how to predict and prevent them. This topic has a clear political dimension since the flexibility of individuals in choosing the retirement age is a core transmission mechanism for these interactions between the capital market on one side and labor and product markets on the other side.

Capital markets

Capital markets play a crucial role in global aging since capital is the factor that moves with the least friction across countries, and it permits the shifting of resources from one time period to another. The first mechanism permits international diversification of demographic risks, the second mechanism permits intertemporal (even intergenerational) substitution of resources.

Both issues are complicated in a system of many countries, some of them aging faster than others, some of them not aging at all. There will be competition across the aging regions for profitable foreign direct investment in regions that age more slowly or not at all. An important area of research is therefore to gauge the relevant orders of magnitude in a system of regions that is tied together by flows of capital combined with reverse flows of goods and services.

Capital market issues cannot be studied in isolation from public policy. Most importantly, the share of private pensions in total retirement income is a major determinant of the supply of loanable funds. Fundamental pension reform therefore has a large impact on capital markets. In turn, the future performance of capital markets will have a huge impact on the success of the current generation of pension reforms. If rates of return stay low, or if an "asset meltdown" will occur owing to falling asset values when the baby boomers retire, funded pensions will not provide the much-searched-for escape from the demographic problems that plague the public pay-as-you-go pension systems.

In this section, we focus on five important capital market issues related to global aging which would benefit from more research but for which we have already some interesting qualitative (and sometimes even quantitative) results.

The supply of savings

Does global aging decrease the supply of global capital? Theoretical arguments that establish this link build on the well-known life-cycle theory of consumption and savings (Modigliani and Brumberg 1954). The aggregation of individual, cohort-specific life-cycle savings leads to a decrease of national saving rates in an aging economy. In a general equilibrium model of forward-looking individuals, it is not only the current demographic structure that alters the time path of aggregate savings, but also future demographic developments. There are two main channels for effects of demographic change on domestic capital formation. First, decreasing labor supply reduces demand for investment goods since less capital is needed. Second, in a closed economy, a decline in national savings leads to a decline in investment by definition. In an open economy, the link between these two aggregates is broken to the extent that capital is internationally mobile.

While the theory is straightforward, it is less clear to what extent the stylized microeconomic savings theory by Modigliani applies to reality. Figure 9 shows German saving rates by age (corrected for cohort effects). While we recognize the hump-shape predicted by Modigliani, we do not observe any dissaving in old age.

This sheds considerable doubt on the realism of predictions based on the simple life-cycle hypothesis. Such predictions are likely to overestimate the decline of saving rates if the true saving behavior looks more like Figure 9. We do not know much, however, about how the current saving behavior might change in the face of global aging. In particular, pension reform away from pay-as-you-go-financed pensions toward funded pensions might change saving behavior because it revives the retirement saving motive. Only international comparisons provide the policy variation needed for such analysis. The potential power of such studies can be seen in Figure 10, which shows median saving rates by age group in France, Germany, Italy, and the Netherlands. They are based on a comparable longitudinal framework, represent life-cycle saving corrected for cohort effects, and employ comparable variable definitions and data sources as part of the International Saving Comparisons Project (Börsch-Supan 2001).

The saving profiles in France, Germany, and Italy are rather flat and show no dissaving in old age. One possible explanation is that the high replacement rates of the public pension systems in these countries have made private retirement income largely unnecessary.[1] If other saving motives, such as precaution and intergenerational transfers, are more important than retirement saving, age-saving profiles are likely to be much flatter than under the textbook life-cycle hypothesis, which predicts saving in young and dissaving in old age. This explanation is in line with work by Jappelli and Modigliani (1998), who argue that the main mechanism for "retirement saving" in Italy is the PAYG system. While we lack the most appropriate counterfactual—French, German, and Italian data from times when these countries had no PAYG systems—Figure 10 depicts the case of the Netherlands, which has, unlike the other three countries, only a small base pension provided

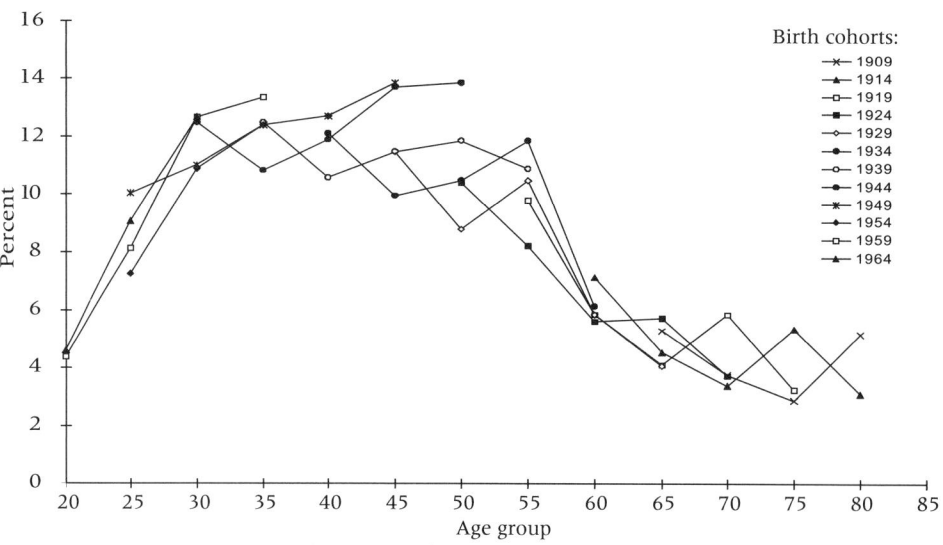

FIGURE 9 Age-specific saving rates in Germany (cohort corrected)

SOURCE: Börsch-Supan, Reil-Held, and Schnabel (2003). The cohort correction is based on the assumption that time effects are absent.

FIGURE 10 Age-specific saving rates (cohort corrected) in four countries

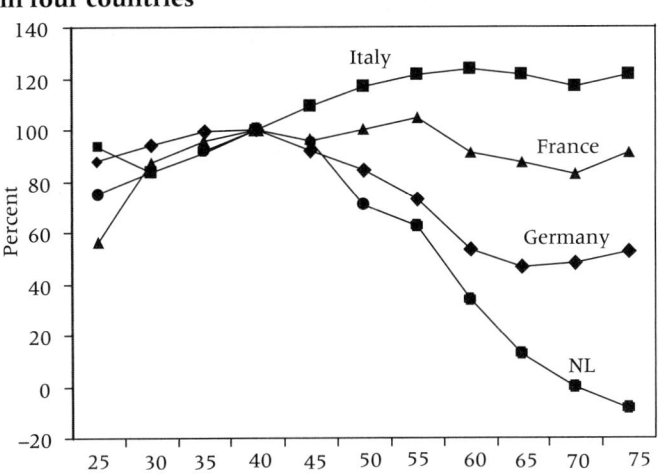

SOURCE: France: Fall, Loisy, and Talon (2001); Germany: Börsch-Supan, Reil-Held, Rodepeter, Schnabel, and Winter (2001); Italy: Brugiavini and Padula (2001); Netherlands: Alessie and Kapteyn (2001).

by its PAYG public pension system. All additional retirement income in the Netherlands has to be provided by (mandatory) savings plans, commonly provided through occupational pension plans. Figure 10 shows that the median Dutch household has a much more pronounced hump-shaped life-cycle savings profile than the median French, German, and Italian households, and it exhibits dissaving among the elderly as they draw down their mandatory saving accounts.

Sophisticated overlapping-generations (OLG) models are in principle able to predict many of the future capital market effects, although they are—so far—not correctly taking into account the risks and uncertainties that generate precautionary savings. The models mainly capture savings accumulated for long-run consumption smoothing, especially for retirement. Figure 11 shows the output of such a model for Germany (Börsch-Supan, Ludwig, and Winter 2004) as part of an EU and an OECD-wide open capital market. We display six variants. In order to show the effect of global capital markets, the three lines in each figure represent the case of Germany as a closed economy, a two-region world consisting of Germany and the other 14 EU countries with free capital mobility between the two regions, and a two-region world extended to all OECD countries. In order to separate the direct effect of population aging and the additional effects of pension reform, we present all projections under the traditional PAYG system and then show the additional (differential) effect of a pension reform that induces a substantial extent of prefunding by freezing the contribution rate to the PAYG value. In an OLG model, prefunding will occur automatically through the consumption-smoothing mechanism. The

FIGURE 11 Projections of the German aggregate saving rate under alternative pension systems and capital mobility scenarios, Germany 2000–50

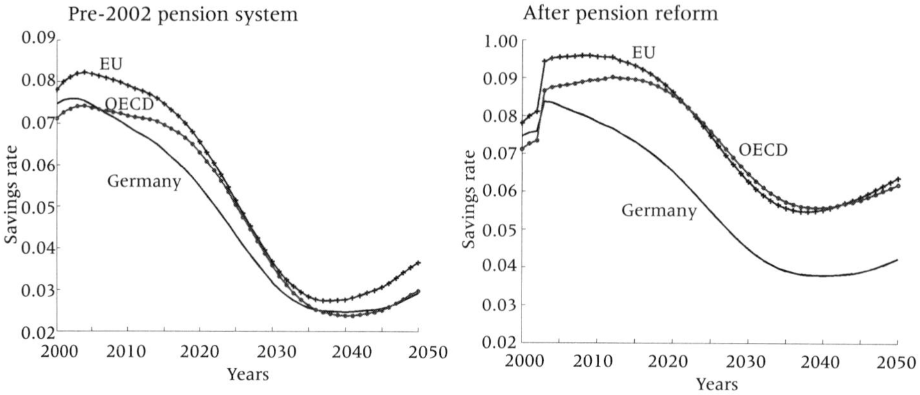

NOTES: This figure shows projections of the aggregate savings of German households as a percentage of GNP. Pension reform only in Germany. Germany: Germany as a closed economy, EU: perfect capital mobility in the EU area, OECD: perfect capital mobility in the OECD area.
SOURCE: Own calculations, based on demographic projections of the United Nations (2001) and age- and sex-specific labor force participation rates by the OECD (2002).

transition process eventually leads to a state in which about one-third of retirement income will come from the funded standard.

Because the baby boom generation decumulates assets, the aggregate saving rate decreases throughout the entire observation period in all capital mobility scenarios. When the aging problem peaks in Germany around 2035–40, the saving rate reaches its trough. The decrease of the savings rate caused by population aging—the difference between the value in 2000 and the minimum reached in 2035–40—is about 5 percentage points in the closed-economy and EU 14 scenarios and 4.7 percentage points if we allow for capital mobility within the OECD. The projected aggregate saving rates under a fundamental pension reform are substantially higher and the effect of a pension reform is stronger in the two open-economy scenarios. An increase in national savings leads to an increase in the capital stock and thereby to a decrease in the rate of return to capital which then crowds out further savings. In the open-economy scenarios, substantially more savings is generated since—as we show below—the rate of return decreases by much less.

Asset meltdown?

Several articles in the popular press have attributed recent rises in stock market prices to population aging and have raised the fear that an asset market meltdown might occur when the baby boom generation decumulates its assets. In the academic literature, there is no consensus on the asset market meltdown hypothesis (see e.g., Poterba 2001; Abel 2001; and Brooks 2002).

According to our view, closed-economy models conventionally used in the academic literature miss the important fact of international capital flows under global aging. Because of international diversification, the meltdown of the asset market is lower than predicted by closed-economy versions of conventional OLG models. Börsch-Supan, Ludwig, and Winter (2004) show that the decrease in the rate of return that results from both population aging and moving toward prefunded pensions is modest, approximately 1.4 percentage points if we assume a closed economy. The return on capital can be improved by international diversification, that is, by investing pension savings in countries with a more favorable demographic transition path than Germany, as shown in Figure 12.

The left panel shows that a decrease in the rate of return on capital is evident for both the closed-economy and the two open-economy scenarios. However, the decrease is much less than often claimed in the public debate. Even in the closed-economy case, a decrease of the rate of return of about 1.4 percentage points—as measured by the difference between the rate of return in 2000 and the minimum for the period 2030–40—is much less than often claimed. Moreover, it is apparent that closed-economy models overestimate this reduction of the rate of return: its projected decrease is only about 1 percentage point for both capital mobility scenarios. In absolute terms, this is not a very large difference (even though the compound effect, over two or three decades, of even such a small difference matters when it comes to analyzing funded pension systems).

The beneficial effects of openness to international capital markets become much more evident when we analyze the effects of a fundamental pen-

FIGURE 12 Projections of the rate of return to capital under alternative pension systems and capital mobility scenarios, Germany 2000–50

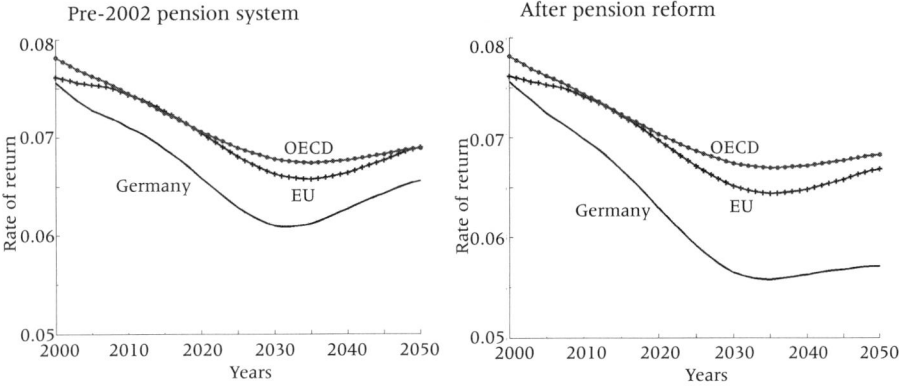

NOTES: This figure shows projections of the rate of return to capital. Pension reform only in Germany. Germany: Germany as a closed economy, EU: perfect capital mobility in the EU area, OECD: perfect capital mobility in the OECD area.
SOURCE: Own calculations, based on demographic projections of the United Nations (2001) and age- and sex-specific labor force participation rates by the OECD (2002).

sion reform. If a fundamental pension reform was implemented in Germany and if Germany was a closed economy, then the additional decrease of the rate of return to capital would be about 0.8 percentage points. But as the right panel shows, there is virtually no difference in the rate of return between the two pension system scenarios if capital is freely mobile within the OECD. In the intermediate case, when capital mobility is restricted to the EU area, the decrease would only be around 0.2 percentage points.

This interaction between global aging and pension reform is an important finding. It suggests that household savings induced by a fundamental pension reform should be invested internationally, not only for reasons of risk diversification (which of course are not present in our deterministic model), but also for the sake of higher returns that are available in other countries with different aging processes and more favorable capital/labor ratios. Our results also confirm our earlier claim that the most important beneficial effects of capital mobility already show up under very modest capital mobility scenarios. Indeed, there is almost no difference between the OECD scenario and a scenario where we allow for perfect capital mobility in the entire world (results not shown).

Portfolio choice and differential rates of return

It is unlikely that all assets are equally affected by global aging. In addition to the international differences in domestic returns, to be equalized by international capital flows as discussed in next section, it is likely that the demand for safe assets will increase relative to the demand for risky assets, simply because an older population tends to prefer safe assets because they have less time left to compensate for economic shocks.

The development of models that are able to generate robust predictions of portfolio choice and differential rates of return is still in its infancy. A major obstacle is the less than perfect understanding of the equity premium puzzle, and the difficulties in modeling dynamic portfolio choice over the life cycle. Following the approach by Constantinides, Donaldson, and Mehra (2002), Börsch-Supan, Ludwig, and Sommer (2003) embed a calibrated dynamic portfolio choice model into an overlapping generations model in order to differentiate the results discussed in the preceding subsection (see Figure 12) by safe and risky assets.

Figure 13 summarizes the main results. The risk-free rate is predicted to decrease relatively sharply during the next 25 years from 3.3 percent to a little above 1.8 percent in the year 2027. This decline is much stronger than the decrease in the rate of return of stocks (7.6 to 6.8 percent). After 2027, the rate for safe assets increases again, while the rate for stocks remains essentially stable. The equity premium increases until 2025 to about 70 basis points. This effect, however, is only temporary. The equity premium goes back

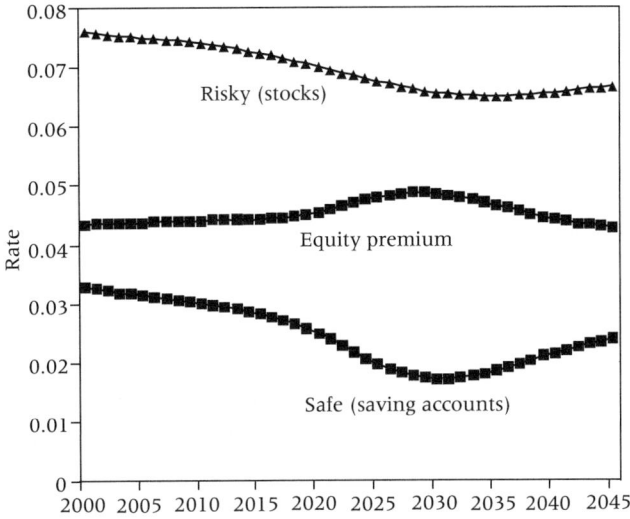

FIGURE 13 Projections of the rate of return to capital assets in three classes of riskiness, Germany 2000–45

SOURCE: Börsch-Supan, Ludwig, and Sommer (2003).

to the pre-aging figures to the extent to which the baby boomers convert their safe assets into consumption.

International capital flows

It is well known that within each country, demographic change alters the time path of aggregate savings, even more so in countries where fundamental pension reforms—that is, a shift toward more prefunding—are implemented (Börsch-Supan 1996; Reisen 2000). To the extent that capital is internationally mobile, population aging will induce capital flows between countries. Figure 14 shows net capital exports of different regions within the OECD as a percentage of GDP. As the left panel indicates, an international OLG model is able to generate capital flows of the correct sign not only for Germany, but also for the other world regions, especially the United States and Japan. As mentioned before, however, levels are overestimated. Given that the United States will continue to have a younger population than other regions, it will also continue to be a capital-import country. For Japan the opposite holds.

Figure 14 also shows how closely related the swings of capital exports are to the differential demographic processes. For example, the swings of Japanese capital exports are exactly opposite to the swings of German exports—just as the aggregate employment ratios are opposites. Also, while the OECD 13 is the youngest area in relative terms as of 2000, it is severely affected by aging.

FIGURE 14 Projections of net capital exports (proportion of GDP) of the OECD area under the assumption of perfect capital mobility within the OECD, 2000–50

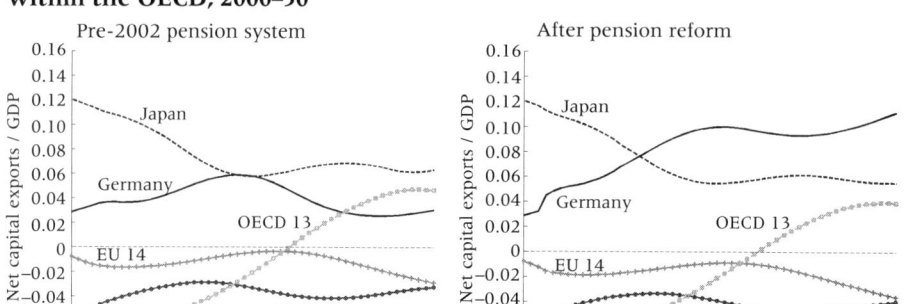

NOTES: This figure shows projections of net capital exports as a percentage of GDP under the assumption of perfect capital mobility within the OECD. Pension reform only in Germany. EU 14: all countries of the European Union except Germany. OECD 13: all OECD countries except for the countries of the European Union, Japan, and the United States.
SOURCE: Own calculations, based on demographic projections of the United Nations (2001) and age- and sex-specific labor force participation rates by the OECD (2002).

Accordingly, capital imports of this region decrease until the current account becomes positive. Under a fundamental pension reform, German capital exports increase substantially and crowd out capital exports of all other world regions by about 8 percentage points in each country until 2050.

For quantitative projections of international capital flows induced by population aging, the degree of capital mobility is crucial. OLG models like those that produced Figures 11–14 assume perfect capital mobility. This is a reasonable assumption within the euro zone. However, capital flows elsewhere are probably overestimated because many important factors that drive international capital flows, such as capital market frictions, capital market risk, home bias, and differential capital income taxation, are ignored.

Feedback effects through corporate governance

There are potentially important feedback effects of global aging on growth through capital market performance. Population aging is precipitating pension reform and with it changes in the nature of capital markets in continental Europe. It is forcing the younger generation to provide more retirement income through private saving. The markets for retirement savings are therefore growing in size, and active institutional investors are becoming more important as intermediaries. A still very controversial research question is to what extent population aging and pension reform, via a change in the savings behavior and portfolio composition of households, and via strengthening capital allocation and corporate governance through active institutional investors, are likely to have beneficial side effects on productivity and growth.

This topic is controversial, not least because it is still uncertain which form of corporate governance works best in the long run. It is an important topic because improved corporate governance might offset some of the negative macroeconomic implications of aging.

To see the strategic importance of this topic, it is helpful to start with three observations. First, France, Germany, and Italy, the three largest economies in continental Europe, have large pay-as-you-go public pension systems that face severe problems due to population aging. At the same time, these countries have thin capital markets in the sense that only a small fraction of households own and control productive capital (either directly or via investment and pension funds). French, German, and Italian savers hold a considerably smaller share of stocks than households in the Netherlands, Britain, and the United States. As a result, stock market capitalization is low in these three countries, and institutional investors such as pension funds play only a minor role in household saving (see Table 1).

Second, France, Germany, and Italy have, in comparison to the United States, poor capital performance as measured by aggregate capital productivity and various aggregate rates of return. While international comparisons of these statistics are not straightforward, the existing evidence summarized in Table 2 yields a clear picture backed up by microeconomic evidence. Third, firms in France, Germany, and Italy have substantially lower capital produc-

TABLE 1 Characteristics of capital markets in countries with pay-as-you-go and funded pensions systems

	Year	Pay-as-you-go systems			Partially funded systems		
		France	Germany	Italy	Netherlands	Britain	United States
Stock market capitalization (% of GDP)[a]	1995	32.6	23.9	19.3	72.1	121.6	95.2
	1998	68.1	50.9	47.5	153.5	168.2	144.9
	2000	111.8	67.6	72.3	174.3	183.8	153.3
Assets held by institutional investors (% of GDP)[b]	1995	77.7	45.3	32.0	154.5	164.0	151.9
	1998	107.3	66.1	79.6	193.2	203.6	192
Assets held by pension funds (% of total assets of institutional investors)[c]	1998	.	5	5	58	38	37
Assets held by pension funds (billion USD)[a]	1995	.	65.3	39.0	352.1	759.7	4,259.5
	1998	.	69.5	37.4	323.0	1,136.5	7,161.6
Pension fund investment (% of household wealth)[d]	1995	1.8	5.6	0.8	35.5	22.3	23.4
	2000	1.5	5.2	1.2	37.7	22.1	23.8

SOURCES: [a]Deutsches Aktieninstitut (2002); [b]OECD (2001); [c]OECD (2000); [d]Babeau and Sbano (2003).

TABLE 2 Capital performance relative to the United States, long-run averages

	France	Germany	Italy
Aggregate return on investment[a]	77	61	50
Mean return on investment (firm sample)[b]	73	72	57
Market sector capital productivity[c]	72	67	—
Total factor productivity[d]	82	81	84

NOTE: All figures are expressed as a percentage of the corresponding US value.
SOURCES: [a]Mueller and Yurtoglu (2000), Table 2. [b]ibid., Table 4. [c]Börsch-Supan (1998), Table 3. [d]Hall and Jones (1996), Table 9.

tivity and return on investment than US companies achieve. Relative to the United States, financial underperformance is also correlated with lower levels of total factor productivity. Many authors claim that an important cause for this underperformance is weak corporate governance (see, e.g., Wenger and Kaserer 1998; Börsch-Supan 1998; Mueller and Yurtoglu 2000).

The relationships between these three observations (large PAYG systems, thin capital markets, and low capital productivity) are not well understood. A clear line of argument can be developed along the following two stages. First, population aging will change households' saving behavior because the internal rate of return generated by the pay-as-you-go pension systems will decrease, making own savings as a vehicle for retirement income both more necessary and more attractive. In many countries, such as France, Italy, and Germany, population aging makes fundamental reform of public pension systems a top priority, strengthening own savings for retirement. Even if no additional savings were created in the aggregate, a larger share of savings would be devoted to retirement and flow through traded shares and bonds, intermediated by institutional investors.

Second, the resulting larger share of intermediated capital will create thick-market externalities and therefore increase productivity and growth. We are not the first to argue that the development of financial markets is an important factor in explaining the sources of productivity and economic growth, but the link to pension systems and pension reform is much less developed.[2] In addition, preliminary microeconomic evidence based on newly assembled firm data in Germany and Great Britain shows that actively managed investment by institutional investors enhances corporate governance and through this channel increases productivity and growth (Köke and Renneboog 2005; Börsch-Supan, Köke, and Winter 2004).

Research on these complex issues has not yet come far, and enthusiasm for capital-market-related research has declined. The stock market crisis after the bubble burst and the ENRON scandal have cast grave doubts on capital market performance everywhere, including the United States. Moreover, evidence on firm performance in fundamentally different institutional settings is scarce, and establishing causality to explain observed differences is difficult. Nonetheless, capital markets will become ever more important as our populations age since capital has to substitute for increasingly scarce labor. Moreover, differential capital performance has important implications for global capital movements and the ability to cope with global aging.

Summary and conclusions

Global population aging will affect labor, product, and capital markets in fundamental ways that will change the growth path of GDP and the wealth of the G20 countries. The discussion above outlines the basic mechanisms behind these changes, traces some of the complex feedback effects in general equilibrium, and suggests the rough magnitudes involved.

Public policy can influence these labor, product, and capital market changes essentially only on a microeconomic level—most directly by adapting the labor market to a situation in which labor is becoming increasingly scarce, which slows down the economy. The main policy tools in order to utilize labor reserves are retirement policies and education policies.

Capital markets can diversify the risks generated by labor scarcity. They are therefore strategic markets in a globally aging world. The supply of capital is directly influenced by pension policies that foster savings. While we do not fully understand the interactions between pension policy and economic growth, we know that policies such as prefunding and privatization have side effects on the growth rate that are particularly welcome in times of global population aging.

The international transmission mechanisms that generate the helpful effects of diversification do not work smoothly. Understanding the frictions affecting the free flow of capital, the sources of instability in global financial markets, and the kind of policies that are appropriate to reduce frictions and instability is a highly policy-relevant research area for global population aging.

Notes

1 See Boeri, Börsch-Supan, and Tabellini (2001) for a comparison of replacement rates.

2 See Levine (1997) for an extensive review of this literature. Köke (2002) reviews the peculiarities of a bank-based system such as in Germany. Börsch-Supan, Köke, and Winter (2004) provide a literature survey tailored to the link between pension reform and capital market performance.

References

Abel, Andrew B. 2001. "Will bequests attenuate the predicted meltdown in stock prices when baby boomers retire?" *Review of Economics and Statistics* 83(4): 589–595.

Alessie, R. and A. Kapteyn. 2001. "Household savings in the Netherlands," *Research in Economics* 55: 61–82.

Babeau, A. and T. Sbano. 2003. "Household wealth in the national accounts of Europe, the United States and Japan," Working Paper 2003/2, Statistics Directorate, OECD, Paris.

Boeri, T., A. Börsch-Supan, and G. Tabellini. 2001. "Would you like to shrink the welfare state? The opinion of European citizens," *Economic Policy* 32: 7–50.

Börsch-Supan, A. 1996. "The impact of population aging on savings, investment and growth in the OECD area," in *Future Global Capital Shortages: Real Threat or Pure Fiction?* Paris: OECD, pp. 103–141.

———. 1998. "Capital productivity and the nature of competition," *Brookings Papers on Economic Activity – Microeconomics* 1998:205–248.

———. 2001. "International comparison of household savings behavior: A study of life-cycle savings in seven countries," *Research in Economics* 55: 1–14.

———. 2003. "Labor market effects of population aging," *Review of Labour Economics and Industrial Relations* 17: 5–44.

Börsch-Supan, A., J. Köke, and J. Winter. 2004. *Pension Reform, Savings Behavior and Capital Market Performance*. Mannheim Research Institute for the Economics of Aging, Mannheim, Germany.

Börsch-Supan, A., A. Ludwig, and M. Sommer. 2003. *Demographie und Kapitalmärkte*. Köln: Deutsches Institut für Altersvorsorge.

Börsch-Supan, A., A. Ludwig, and J. Winter. 2002. "Aging and international capital flows," in A. Auerbach and H. Hermann (eds.), *Aging, Financial Markets and Monetary Policy*. Heidelberg: Springer, pp. 55–83.

Börsch-Supan, A., A. Ludwig, and J. Winter. 2004. "Aging, pension reform, and capital flows." MEA-Discussion Paper, University of Mannheim.

Börsch-Supan, A., A. Reil-Held, R. Rodepeter, R. Schnabel, and J. Winter. 2001. "The German saving puzzle," *Research in Economics* 55: 15–38.

Börsch-Supan, A., A. Reil-Held, and R. Schnabel. 2003. "Household saving in Germany," in A. Börsch-Supan (ed.), *Life Cycle Savings and Public Policy*, Elsevier Science, pp. 57–99.

Brooks, Robin. 2002. "Asset-market effects of the baby-boom and social-security reform," *American Economic Review* 92(2): 402–406.

Brugiavini, A. and M. Padula 2001. "Too much for retirement? Saving in Italy," *Research in Economics* 55: 39–60.

Buchheim, C. 1998. *Industrielle Revolutionen*. Munich: Deutscher Taschenbuch Verlap.

Constantinides, G. M., J. B. Donaldson, and R. Mehra. 2002. "Junior can't borrow: A new perspective on the equity premium puzzle," *Quarterly Journal of Economics* 117: 269–296.

Deutsches Aktieninstitut. 2002. *DIA Factbook*. Frankfurt am Main: Deutsches Aktieninstitut.

Eschtruth, A. D. and J. Gemus. 2002. "Are older workers responding to the bear market? Just the facts," Issue September 2002, Nr. 5, Center for Research on Retirement at Boston College.

Fall, M., C. Loisy, and G. Talon. 2001. "An empirical analysis of household savings in France 1984–1998," *Research in Economics* 55: 155–172.

Gruber, J., and D. Wise. 1999. *Social Security and Retirement Around the World*. Chicago and London: University of Chicago Press.

Hall, R. E. and C. I. Jones. 1996. "The productivity of nations." Working Paper No. 5812, National Bureau of Economic Research, Cambridge, MA.

Jappelli, T. and F. Modigliani. 1998. "The age-saving profile and the life-cycle hypothesis," CSEF Working Paper No. 4, University of Salerno.

Köke, J. 2002. *Corporate Governance in Germany: An Empirical Investigation*. Heidelberg: Physica.

Köke, J. and L. Renneboog. 2005. "Do corporate control and product market competition lead to stronger productivity growth? Evidence from market-oriented and blockholder-based governance regimes," *Journal of Law and Economics* 48: 475–516.

Kotlikoff, L. and D. Wise. 1989. "Employee retirement and a firm's pension plan," in D. A. Wise (ed.), *The Economics of Aging*. Chicago: University of Chicago Press, pp. 279–334.

Levine, R. 1997. "Financial development and economic growth: Views and agenda," *Journal of Economic Literature* 35: 688–726.

Modigliani, F. and R. Brumberg. 1954. "Utility analysis and the consumption function: An interpretation of cross-section data," in K. K. Kurihara (ed.), *Post-Keynesian Economics*. New Brunswick: Rutgers University Press, pp. 388–436.

Mueller, D. C. and B. B. Yurtoglu. 2000. "Country legal environments and corporate investment performance," *German Economic Review* 1: 187–220.

Organisation for Economic Co-operation and Development. 2000. *Institutional Investors – Statistical Yearbook*. Paris: OECD.

———. 2001. *Financial Market Trends*, No. 80. Paris: OECD.

———. 2002. *Labor Force Statistics*. Paris: OECD.

Poterba, J. M. 2001. "Demographic structure and assets returns," *Review of Economics and Statistics* 83(4): 565–584.

Reisen, H. 2000. *Pensions, Savings and Capital Flows: From Aging to Emerging Markets*. Cheltenham, UK: Edward Elgar.

Skirbekk, V. 2004. "Completing education and the timing of births and marriage: Findings from a birth-month experiment in Sweden," Working Paper of the Max Planck Institute for Demographic Research, Rostock, Germany.

United Nations Population Division. 2001. *World Population Prospects: The 2000 Revision*. New York: United Nations.

Wenger, E. and C. Kaserer. 1998. "The German system of corporate governance—A model which should not be imitated," in S. Black and M. Moersch (eds.), *Competition and Convergence in Financial Markets: The German and Anglo-American Models*. Amsterdam: Elsevier, pp. 41–78.

Aggregate Evidence on the Link Between Age Structure and Productivity

JAMES FEYRER

This chapter examines the relationship between the age structure of the workforce and aggregate productivity. It is well known from the labor literature that there is a robust relationship between years of experience and income. If workers are paid their marginal product then this suggests a relationship between worker productivity and age. In the aggregate, therefore, we should expect changes in the age structure of a population to be correlated with changes in productivity.

Feyrer (2007) finds a strong and robust correlation between workforce age structure and total factor productivity. The impact of age structure on productivity is much larger than is estimated by microeconomic evidence on the relationship between wages and experience. The magnitude of the result does not appear to be driven by reverse causality from productivity to workforce age structure through immigration or participation rates. This suggests that the social return to a workforce with a particular experience profile is higher than the private return to experience. This chapter examines the nature of this externality in several ways.

To begin, I explore changes in the age distributions of the US workforce for several subcategories of worker. One mechanism through which the age distribution could produce large externalities is through innovative activity. I examine the evolution of the age distribution of patent holders in the United States over time. Another mechanism through which the age distribution of the workforce may be important is through changes in management. Lucas (1978) suggests that the quality distribution of managers may play a large role in determining output. Using census data, I explore how the entry of the baby boom cohorts into the workforce changed the composition of the managerial workforce over time.

For this reason, it may be useful to identify the scope of the externality. Does it extend to smaller geographic units like US states and localities? This is an important question because different scopes may suggest different mechanisms at work. Does a large proportion of prime-age workers in a city raise productivity in that city alone or do effects spill over to the state and national level?

First, I examine the relationship between age structure and productivity at the country level. Next I discuss the implications of the cross-country results for cross-country economic performance and look at the relative performance of the United States and Japan in light of the results. I suggest channels through which age structure may be affecting output and review evidence from the US census. I then examine US state and metropolitan area data to see if the cross-country effects are evident at lower levels of aggregation.

Cross-country evidence

For use in a cross-country regression, demographic measures have several characteristics that make identification more straightforward than with many variables typically used in the literature on cross-country growth. First, demographic measures are strongly predetermined. The current age structure of the workforce was determined roughly 20 years ago and should be predetermined with respect to current output movements. Second, demographic structure has significant time series variation. This time series variation allows for exploiting the panel nature of the data.

The following results largely follow Feyrer (2007) and focus on total factor productivity. Feyrer (2007) shows that the impact of demographic shifts on physical and human capital accumulation is relatively small and uncorrelated with the productivity effects. For purposes of examining output, productivity is the key variable, and the results would not be substantively different if the dependent variable were to be changed to per worker output. Total factor productivity in country i at time t, $y_{i,t}$, is assumed to be a function of a time-invariant country fixed effect, f_i, a time trend common to all countries, μ_t, and a vector of explanatory variables $x_{i,t}$

$$y_{i,t} = f_i + \mu_t + \beta_{x_{i,t}} + \mu_{i,t}. \tag{1}$$

The regressors are the proportion of the workforce by age group, with W10 indicating workers between ages 10 and 19, W20 workers between 20 and 29, and so on. W60 indicates workers age 60 years and older. Since these variables are proportions, the sum of all the age groups is 1.0 for each country year pair. For this reason, one group is excluded.[1] For most of the reported regressions in this section, first differencing was used to eliminate the country-specific effect.

Productivity is calculated as a residual. I assume a Cobb-Douglas production function taking physical capital, human capital from schooling, and productivity as inputs.

$$y_{i,t} = k_{i,t}^{\alpha}(A_{i,t}h_{i,t})^{1-\alpha}, \quad (2)$$

where $y_{i,t}$ is output, $k_{i,t}$ is capital per worker, $h_{i,t}$ is human capital per worker, and $A_{i,t}$ represents productivity. Capital's share of output, α, is assumed to be 1/3.[2] The human capital production function is assumed to have a Mincer form

$$h_{i,t} = e^{\phi(s_{i,t})}, \quad (3)$$

where $s_{i,t}$ is the average years of schooling in country i at time t and $\phi(s)$ is an increasing function that is assumed to be piecewise linear with decreasing returns to scale.[3] The production function can be solved for log total factor productivity.

$$\log(A_{i,t}) = \log(y_{i,t}) - \frac{\alpha}{1-\alpha}\log\left(\frac{K}{Y}\right)_{i,t} - \log(h_{i,t}). \quad (4)$$

Data for output are from the Penn World Tables version 6.0. Following Hall and Jones (1999), output data are adjusted to exclude income from mining and oil.[4] Data for capital per worker are from Easterly and Levine (2001).[5] The schooling data used to calculate human capital stocks are from Barro and Lee (2001). All variables used in calculating total factor productivity (TFP) are levels from the individual year in question.

The data on workforce composition are from two sources. The International Labor Organization (ILO) has compiled cross-country data on the number of workers by five-year age groups spanning age 10 to age 65. These are available at ten-year intervals starting in 1960. Population by five-year age groups is available from the United Nations. The population data are used to impute the intermediate values for the workforce data.[6]

The availability of both workforce and demographic data allows for the use of instrumental variables (IV) to address several issues. First, if participation rates are systematically related to productivity, results may reflect causality from productivity to participation rates. Instrumenting workforce values on population proportions eliminates this channel. Second, we may worry that immigration is leading people to migrate to high-productivity areas. Instrumenting on lagged population eliminates this channel. Another potential area of concern is that dependency ratios are correlated with workforce age structure. The dependency ratio is added as an additional control and does not change the basic results.

The basic sample contains 87 countries at five-year intervals between 1960 and 1990. The years are limited by the workforce proportion data. The base regressions are also run on an OECD subsample of 21 countries. For the five-year frequency regressions, the workforce data are imputed from the ten-year data and population data. Since the IV strategy uses population data to instrument for the workforce, these imputations cannot be used for

IV. The IV results therefore are at ten-year intervals. The dependent variable is log TFP in all regressions.

Tables 1 and 2 present the results of a series of cross-country regressions. The two tables differ only in their estimation method. Table 1 is estimated in differences and Table 2 is in levels with unreported country-level dummies. The coefficients are directly comparable. In both cases, standard errors are clustered to account for serial correlation. Since the differenced estimator is robust to a unit root in TFP, these estimates are generally preferred. The results are nearly identical, although the differenced estimates are more precisely estimated.

Column (1) is the basic result of total factor productivity versus the age structure of the workforce. All point estimates are negative, indicating that an increase in the size of the excluded group, aged 40–50 years, is associated with higher productivity. The coefficients on W10, W20, and W30 are significant at the 1 percent level. The coefficients on W50 and W60 are significant in all the regressions.

The differences between the age groups are very large. According to the column (1) estimates, a 5 percentage point shift from the 30-year age group to the 40-year age group is associated with over a 16 percent increase in per worker output.[7] Supposing this shift occurred over a 10-year period, this would add approximately 1.6 percentage points to output growth in each year. Column (2) adds in the dependency ratio as an additional control. It does not affect the results. Columns (3) and (4) replicate columns (1) and (2) for the OECD sample with similar results.

Columns (5), (6), and (7) are three robustness checks, which focus on the potential endogeneity problems identified above. Column (5) uses only unimputed values of the demographic measures as regressors. This column tests whether the imputation procedure used to allow five-year data is biasing the results. Columns (6) and (7) report the results of IV estimations where workforce measures are instrumented on population measures. For column (6) contemporaneous population measures are used and are limited to the working-age population. This column tests whether endogeneity of participation rates is biasing the base results. For column (7) lagged values of the population are used as instruments.[8] This column tests whether cross-country migration is significantly biasing the results.

The results for the robustness tests are similar to the base result for each estimation although less precisely estimated because of reductions in the sample size. The 95 percent confidence intervals overlap with the base case for all regressors in all three regressions. For all but the W60 group, all point estimates are negative, indicating that movements into the 40-year-old group from these groups is associated with higher productivity. For the younger groups, the coefficients are significant in all but one case. For the IV results, W60 has positive point estimates, although the standard errors are sufficiently large that the error bands overlap with the base case.

TABLE 1 Effect of changes in workforce composition on changes in total factor productivity: Cross-country regressions

Sample: Imputed W:	(1) OLS nonoil yes	(2) OLS nonoil yes	(3) OLS OECD yes	(4) OLS OECD yes	(5) OLS nonoil no	(6) IVL0 nonoil no	(7) IVL10 nonoil no
ΔW10	−3.774 (1.085)**	−3.797 (1.109)**	−3.996 (0.739)**	−4.063 (0.778)**	−4.42 (1.342)**	−5.753 (1.470)**	−6.254 (1.594)**
ΔW20	−3.152 (1.044)**	−3.704 (1.028)**	−3.095 (0.723)**	−3.233 (0.844)**	−2.766 (1.148)*	−3.022 (1.004)**	−3.02 (1.068)**
ΔW30	−3.312 (1.059)**	−3.661 (1.029)**	−2.323 (0.580)**	−2.395 (0.610)**	−3.296 (1.110)**	−3.468 (1.046)**	−3.317 (1.157)**
ΔW50	−2.661 (0.972)**	−2.731 (0.985)**	−2.04 (0.800)*	−2.122 (0.801)*	−1.877 (1.265)	−1.392 (1.627)	−0.927 (1.784)
ΔW60	−3.046 (1.079)**	−3.309 (1.052)**	−2.709 (0.899)**	−2.81 (0.919)**	−4.305 (1.666)*	1.038 (2.689)	1.444 (3.114)
ΔDependency ratio		−1.812 (0.723)*		−0.4 (0.868)			
Year							
1965	0.183 (0.024)**	0.185 (0.024)**	0.231 (0.020)**	0.229 (0.019)**			
1970	0.044 (0.030)	0.049 (0.031)	0.051 (0.043)	0.052 (0.044)	0.223 (0.035)**	0.243 (0.037)**	0.247 (0.040)**
1975	0.088 (0.038)*	0.071 (0.041)+	0.126 (0.029)**	0.125 (0.029)**			
1980	−0.048 (0.051)	−0.048 (0.051)	−0.127 (0.053)*	−0.132 (0.056)*	0.007 (0.043)	0.05 (0.052)	0.044 (0.058)
1985	0.009 (0.045)	−0.016 (0.049)	0.139 (0.040)**	0.134 (0.037)**			
1990	−0.107 (0.060)+	−0.109 (0.060)+	−0.124 (0.048)*	−0.13 (0.049)*	−0.117 (0.043)**	−0.122 (0.049)*	−0.135 (0.052)*
Observations	499	499	126	126	246	246	246
Countries	87	87	21	21	87	87	87
R-squared	0.15	0.16	0.55	0.55	0.24		

Standard errors clustered by state in parentheses.
+ significant at 10 percent; * significant at 5 percent; ** significant at 1 percent
NOTE: ΔW10 is the change in the proportion of workers aged 15–19. ΔW20, W30, W40, W50 are the changes in the proportion of workers ages 20–29, 30–39, 40–49, and 50–59. ΔW60 is the change in the proportion of workers ages 60 and older. The dependency ratio is the proportion of the population younger than 15 and older than 64. The nonoil sample excludes the set of countries that the World Bank classifies as oil exporters.

Additional robustness checks were performed but are not presented here. One concern might be that the output data used are measured in terms of output per worker and do not take into account differences in hours worked, which may be age-specific. In general, the productivity calculations are quite crude and do not take into account many factors that would be appropriate

TABLE 2 Effect of workforce composition on total factor productivity: Cross-country regressions

Sample: Imputed W:	(1) nonoil yes	(2) nonoil yes	(3) OECD yes	(4) OECD yes	(5) nonoil no	(6) nonoil no	(7) nonoil no
W10	−4.913	−3.404	−5.85	−5.637	−4.697	−6.744	−6.149
	(1.507)**	(1.633)*	(1.074)**	(1.255)**	(1.822)*	(2.111)**	(2.292)**
W20	−0.928	−2.257	−2.165	−1.607	−1.109	−1.773	−2.099
	(1.391)	(1.157)+	(0.858)*	(1.084)	(1.796)	(1.493)	(1.549)
W30	−2.307	−2.811	−3.931	−3.625	−1.926	−1.8	−1.376
	(1.155)*	(1.121)*	(0.943)**	(0.930)**	(1.666)	(1.667)	(1.852)
W50	−0.987	−1.124	−1.447	−1.113	−1.251	−1.682	−0.367
	(1.565)	(1.554)	(0.930)	(0.921)	(1.972)	(2.249)	(2.471)
W60	−4.905	−5.46	−2.974	−2.476	−4.817	0.874	2.578
	(1.911)*	(1.704)**	(2.069)	(1.999)	(2.368)*	(4.475)	(5.158)
Dependency ratio		−2.795		1.311			
		(1.002)**		(1.209)			
Year							
1965	0.256	0.222	0.255	0.261	11.018	11.102	10.711
	(0.037)**	(0.034)**	(0.030)**	(0.034)**	(1.278)**	(1.301)**	(1.378)**
1970	0.212	0.224	0.216	0.216	0.215	0.233	0.247
	(0.040)**	(0.039)**	(0.053)**	(0.057)**	(0.043)**	(0.049)**	(0.050)**
1975	0.38	0.329	0.389	0.391			
	(0.054)**	(0.057)**	(0.058)**	(0.060)**			
1980	0.154	0.175	0.226	0.244	0.163	0.223	0.269
	(0.056)**	(0.053)**	(0.065)**	(0.069)**	(0.063)*	(0.082)**	(0.094)**
1985	0.295	0.224	0.432	0.468			
	(0.053)**	(0.059)**	(0.054)**	(0.054)**			
1990	0.004	0.022	0.234	0.291	0.007	0.033	0.098
	(0.083)	(0.077)	(0.087)*	(0.099)**	(0.095)	(0.121)	(0.135)
Observations	586	586	147	147	333	333	333
Countries	87	87	21	21	87	87	87
R-squared	1	1	1	1	0.89	0.88	0.87

Standard errors clustered by state in parentheses.
+ significant at 10 percent; * significant at 5 percent; ** significant at 1 percent
NOTE: W10 is the proportion of workers aged 15–19. W20, W30, W40, W50 are the proportion of workers ages 20–29, 30–39, 40–49, and 50–59. W60 is the proportion of workers ages 60 and older. For definitions of dependency ratio and nonoil sample, see note to Table 1.

for a careful analysis of total factor productivity. This is largely attributable to data limitations. However, some estimates can be made on the subsample of the data for which more detailed information is available. Regressions were run using data on hours worked from the OECD. Also, more detailed productivity numbers from Jorgenson (2003) are available for the G7 countries. The results from these subsamples do not contradict the base results.

These results suggest that the age structure of the workforce has a significant correlation with total factor productivity. The regressions using lagged age structure indicate that movements in productivity are not causing contemporaneous changes in age structure. Possible endogeneity of participation rates and migration is not driving the results.

Although the evidence in this section does not make a conclusive case for a causal link between demographic change and productivity growth, the results certainly suggest that such a link is likely. Many alternative explanations have been eliminated by the IV results. Any noncausal explanation would require some omitted factor that had an impact on the demographic structure in the past but that affects productivity with long lags. Given this, looking for further evidence of contemporaneous causal links seems sensible.

Implications

Cross-country productivity differences

The results of the previous section can be used to provide insight into cross-country productivity patterns. The demographic characteristics of the workforce differ greatly across countries with different income levels. Figure 1 illustrates the proportion of the workforce between the ages of 40 and 49 by groups of countries of differing income levels.

Two facts are immediately apparent. The poorer countries have a lower proportion of 40-year-old workers than the richer countries in every year. The second aspect of the graph is the trend. The wealthy countries saw a relatively static 40-year-old cohort until about 1980. From 1980 until 2000 the proportion of 40-year-olds increased dramatically. This is not true of the poor countries.

The results of the previous section lead to two obvious conclusions. First, some proportion of the income gap between rich and poor countries can be attributed to persistent differences in the age structure. Poor countries typically have younger workforces, which the results suggest lead to lower productivity. Feyrer (2007) suggests that one-quarter to one-third of the rich–poor productivity gap can be explained by steady-state demographic structure. Second, over the second half of the sample the demographically induced productivity gap has further widened.

The United States and Japan

Relative demographic movements can also inform us about relative growth rates between rich countries. The demographic composition of the Japanese workforce has differed greatly from that of the United States in the period since World War II. Figure 2 shows the number of live births in Japan and the United States in the postwar period.[9]

FIGURE 1 Workers aged 40–49 as percent of all workers by groups of countries differing in income levels

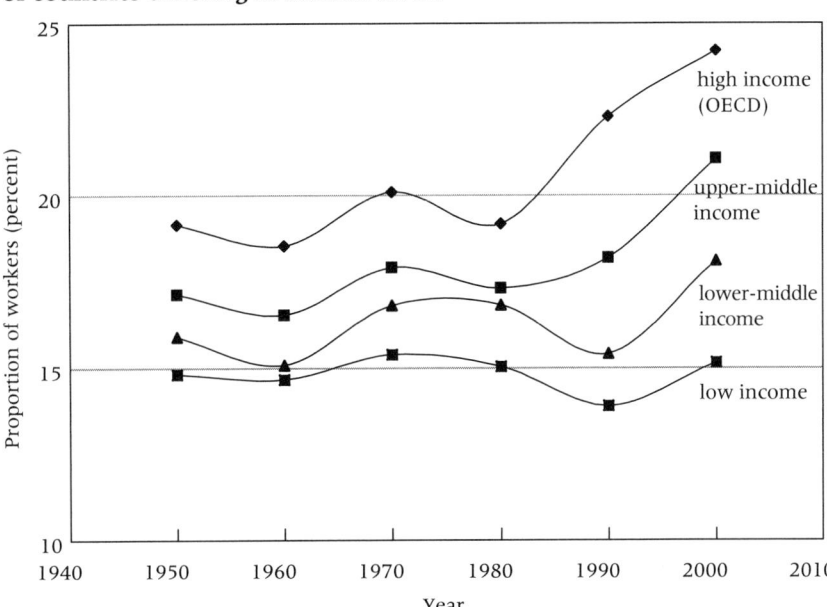

NOTE: Data are for 1995. The classifications are standard World Bank income classification codes. High income: 25 OECD countries, median GDP per worker $39,000. Upper-middle income: 14 countries, median GDP per worker $17,000. Lower-middle income: 21 countries, median GDP per worker $12,000. Low income: 26 countries, median GDP per worker $3,000.
SOURCE: ILO «http://laborsta.ilo.org».

The most remarkable feature of this graph is the degree to which US and Japanese birth rates move in opposite directions.[10] During the peak of the US baby boom (around 1960), Japan was experiencing a local minimum in births. Japan had an upsurge in births during the mid-1970s as the United States was experiencing a significant slowdown in births. Consequently the Japanese workforce has very different demographic movements than that of the United States. Japan has a steeply rising cohort of workers in their 40s from 1960 to 1980, a period when the United States saw this cohort fall in size. From 1990 to 2000 the situation reverses.

The demographic effect roughly maps to the observed growth pattern between the United States and Japan. Between 1960 and 1980, the United States was experiencing worsening demographic structure—in the sense of a shrinking proportion of workers in their 40s—and low productivity growth. Figure 3 shows the demographic effect on productivity implied by the results presented earlier in the chapter.

The model suggests that 2–3 percent of the difference between US and Japanese growth in the 1970s is correlated with demographic shifts. In the 1990s, this situation reverses. The United States saw higher productivity growth attributable to demographic change while Japan experienced declining productivity growth. Age structure is associated with a 2 percent dif-

FIGURE 2 Annual number of live births in the United States and Japan, 1920–2000

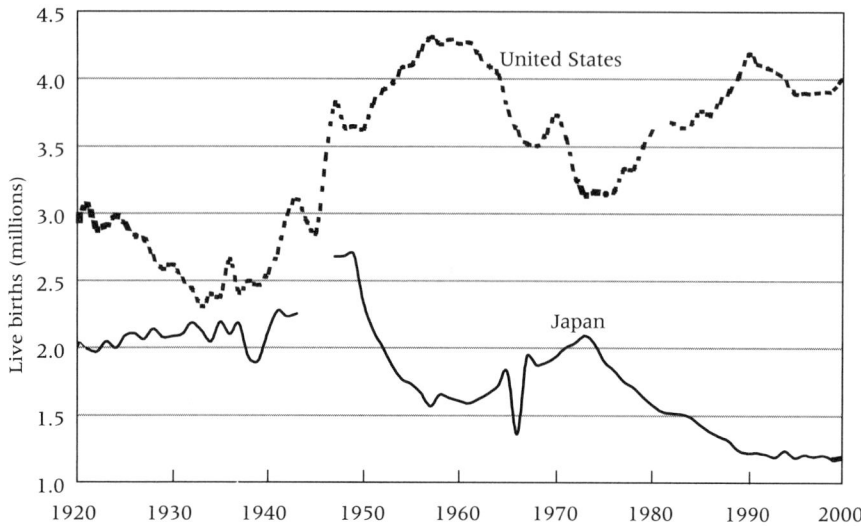

SOURCES: Vital Statistics of the United States; Japanese Ministry of Health, Labor and Welfare.

FIGURE 3 Estimated demographic effect on US and Japanese productivity growth, from the 1950s to the early 2000s

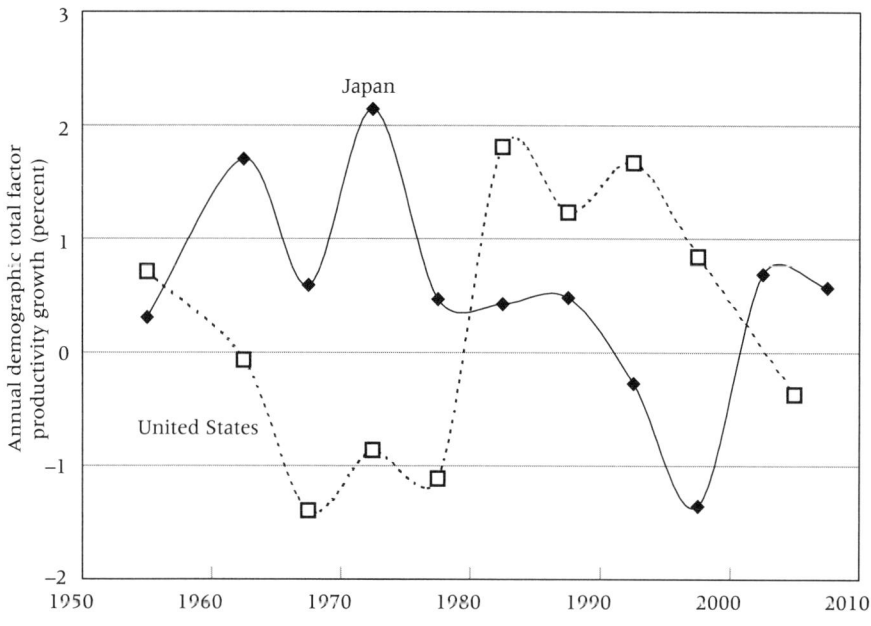

SOURCE: Author's calculations.

ferential between the United States and Japan during the 1990s. The model predicts that relative growth rates will reverse once again in the coming decade. The United States is about to enter a period of slower productivity growth while Japan should see a significant improvement in productivity growth relative to the 1990s.

Externalities

The cross-country results show that demographic structure has a significant correlation with output and productivity. This should come as no surprise since labor economists have long identified experience effects in the wages of workers. The canonical Mincer wage regression takes the following form.

$$\log(wage) = \alpha + \beta_1 * school + \beta_2 * experience + \beta_3 * experience^2 + \varepsilon. \quad (5)$$

Bils and Klenow (2000) collect a sample of these coefficients estimated for 52 countries. Using the average coefficients from their sample produces

$$\log(wage) = \alpha + 0.096 * school + 0.051 * experience - 0.00071 * experience^2. \quad (6)$$

According to these estimates, an additional year of schooling increases the wage by 9.6 percent.[11] Experience has diminishing returns, with each additional year of experience increasing the wage by some amount less than 5.1 percent.

Worker productivity rises with age up to about age 50 then falls somewhat. The Mincer evidence implies that there is about a 60 percent difference between the productivity of 20-year-old workers and 50-year-old workers. For the aggregate data, this implies that an economy with a large cohort of young workers will have lower productivity than an economy with a large cohort of older workers.[12]

The Mincer evidence is therefore relatively similar to the results presented here. However, there are very large differences in the magnitude of the effects. The Mincer evidence suggests that moving 5 percent of the population from the 20–30-year age category to the 40–50-year age category will increase wages (and output) by 1–2 percent. The evidence presented here suggests that this same demographic shift is associated with a 10–15 percent increase in output, an effect an order of magnitude larger than predicted by the Mincer evidence.

The Mincer evidence may not tell the entire story at the aggregate level, however. The micro evidence, based on wage data, only captures the private return to experience and education. The social returns may be higher than the private returns. Externalities to experience (or age) may mean that the Mincer coefficients understate the aggregate productivity effects.

The importance of externalities to education has long been emphasized, beginning with the theoretical work of Nelson and Phelps (1966). It has, however, been difficult to show empirically that these externalities exist. Panel growth regressions such as Caselli, Esquivel, and Lefort (1996) take into account country-specific productivity effects and try to deal with the endogeneity of schooling relative to output. These regressions fail to find coefficients on schooling consistent with large externalities. In a study of US states, Acemoglu and Angrist (2000) also fail to find evidence of large externalities to education. Some recent work has had more success in finding external effects of education. Aiyar and Feyrer (2002) find evidence of dynamic externalities to human capital that act over long time periods. Moretti (2004) and Bloom, Hartley, and Rosovsky (2006) find evidence of externalities to higher education at the state and city level.

The results of this chapter thus far suggest that externalities to workforce demographic composition go beyond the private return to experience. The next two sections suggest two possible channels through which social returns to the age structure might be realized. First, idea creation through inventive activity. Second, idea adoption through managerial talent and entrepreneurial activity. The first is important because the nonrival aspect of ideas increases the potential for large externalities.

Innovation

Suppose that productivity changes are driven by individuals engaged in innovative activity. The private returns to experience are unlikely to capture the full societal gains from innovation because of the inability of firms to capture the full surplus created by innovation. Many types of innovation are, by their nature, nonrival. Nonrivalry may make it particularly difficult to capture more than a small fraction of the gains of innovative activity. In many innovative industries a large proportion of productivity increases may benefit consumers far beyond the price that they pay for the product. Take as an extreme example the Google search engine. Google has almost certainly increased the productivity of academic researchers as well as the productivity of anyone else who relies on the internet for productivity-enhancing information.[13] Yet, most people have never paid any money to Google. While the creators of Google have benefited from their creation, it seems likely that their revenues represent only a small fraction of the aggregate gains in output that their invention has made possible.

Suppose that the age structure of the workforce affects the probability that an invention like Google will be created. If a country has an age structure that increases the likelihood of Google being invented, productivity will be higher for all workers. Only a small fraction of these productivity gains will be captured by the original inventors. If this hypothesis is true, then we should not be surprised that the aggregate productivity effects are much larger than the micro Mincer effects.

There is evidence that generating and implementing new ideas varies by age. Lehman (1953) finds that creative output in science and invention varies substantially by age. There is some variation among disciplines, but Lehman finds that peak productivity tends to be in the interval between ages 30 and 40. If there is indeed an age effect in idea generation, having a larger cohort of workers in the peak idea-generating ages should result in more rapid production of new ideas and new technologies. As an extreme example, consider the world of academic mathematics, where a significant portion of the innovative ideas are produced by people between the ages of 25 and 35.[14] If the world were like a mathematics department, we would expect to see more new ideas being produced in countries with a large cohort of young workers.

More recent work by economists has also found a link between age and creative performance. Galenson and Weinberg (2000) find that artistic output is related to the age of the artist. Galenson and Weinberg (2005) find that the peak years for Nobel Prize–winning economists tend to be in their 40s. Jones (2005) collects the birth dates for a sample of inventors granted patents in the NBER patent database. Figure 4 presents the age distribution of these patent grantees by year from 1975 until 1995.

While the age profile of inventors changes somewhat in response to the large underlying changes in the age distribution of the workforce as a whole, the median age of 48 does not vary by more than one year during the sample period. This is in stark comparison to the age profile of managers, which will be presented in the next section. The relatively stable distribution of the patent holders suggests that the creativity profile of inventors may be quite stable with a peak somewhere in the mid-40s. When demographic change results in a low number of workers (and therefore inventors) in this age group, it seems likely that there will be a reduction in the level of inventive activity.

This argument is essentially one of scale. More potential inventors equals more invention. While scale effects in the production of nonrival goods seem undeniable on theoretical grounds, the evidence of them in the aggregate data is harder to find. Jones (1995) argues that productivity growth has not increased despite the increase in the number of researchers. His argument relies on the decreasing returns in the search for new knowledge. Kremer (1993) suggests that over longer time horizons there is strong evidence of scale effects in knowledge production.

Over the shorter time horizons used in this study, it is not clear that raw knowledge creation explains the aggregate results, especially outside the OECD where knowledge adoption is more important. The following section examines how idea adoption might be affected by demographic change.

FIGURE 4 Distribution by single years of age of US inventors granted patents, 1975–95

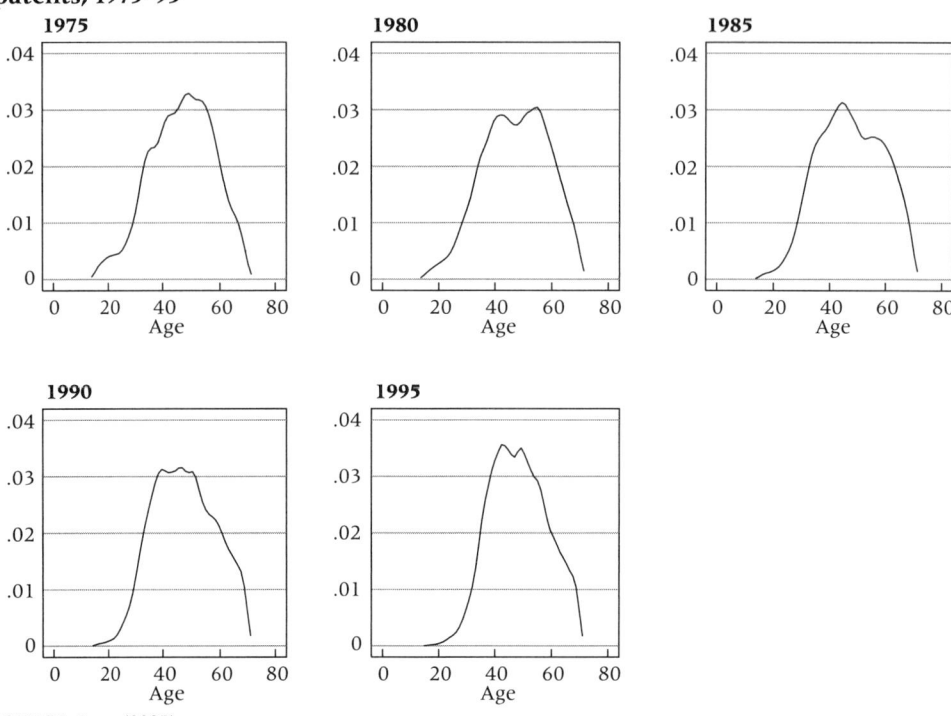

SOURCE: Jones (2005).

Idea adoption

While creative output is one potential channel through which age may affect productivity, it may not be the most relevant for cross-country comparisons. For most of the countries in the world, idea creation matters less than idea adoption. Organizations (or countries) that increase productivity by producing new ideas are different from organizations that adopt ideas generated elsewhere.

Idea creators operate at the technological frontier at all times because they define the frontier. The rate of new idea creation determines the rate of expansion of the frontier. For technology adopters, the technological frontier is a given. Nothing an adopter does affects the rate of expansion of the frontier, and adopters are always operating below the frontier. The relevant question is how far below the frontier they are operating. If age structure affects the rate of technology adoption, then favorable demographic shifts may make a country more effective at implementing ideas generated elsewhere. This allows the country to get closer to the frontier, and in the short run this means more rapid productivity growth. However, in the long run growth will be determined by the movement of the frontier, which is exogenous from the point of view of the adopter. It seems apparent that most countries in the world are technology adopters.

There is microeconomic evidence that age matters in the adoption of technology. Weinberg (2002) finds that both experience and age matter for technology adoption. Among high school graduates, technology adoption complements experience while among college graduates, technology adoption complements youth. This evidence points toward a tension between youth and experience. Since schooling tends to be concentrated early in life, young workers have the advantage of more recent human capital.[15] It may also be that younger workers are less bound by tradition and more likely to take risks. Young workers, on the other hand, lack human capital in the form of experience.

Large demographic shifts may also matter through the effect on the quality of management. Lucas (1978) suggests that the quality distribution of managers may play a large role in determining output. In the Lucas model, a firm with a manager of quality x managing n workers and k units of capital will produce the following amount of output,

$$y = xg\big[f(n,k)\big], \tag{7}$$

where $f()$ is a standard neoclassical production function, and $g[]$ has decreasing returns. The decreasing returns to $g[]$ imply that increasing the size of any given firm will reduce per worker output. This indicates that there are advantages to having smaller firms, on average. However, each firm needs to have a manager. In order to have smaller firms, there must be a larger group of managers. Assuming heterogeneity in management talent, an efficient allocation of workers into management positions will result in a talent cutoff, v. Workers with managerial talent $x>v$ will be managers and all other workers will be normal workers in firms. In order to reduce average firm size, this threshold will need to be reduced, causing a fall in overall management quality. These two competing factors result in an equilibrium number of managers.

This model would seem to apply to managerial age insofar as age affects managerial talent. We observe that young workers are much less likely to take management positions than older workers. This is probably because some amount of experience is important in managing other workers. It may also be that social constraints prevent young workers from managing older workers even if they are particularly talented. Up and out promotion systems of the sort used in the military tend to produce a structure where people are managed by someone older than themselves.

In either case, a large influx of young workers will increase the probability that a worker in one of the smaller and older cohorts will be called upon to take a management role. This suggests that the marginal manager will be less talented since there is a need to dip farther into the talent pool of the older cohorts. The Lucas model suggests that less talented managers will make all workers less productive. Indeed, one need not rely on this specific model to accept the basic argument. Any model where the quality of management has spillovers for all workers will produce similar results.

An examination of census data suggests that the entrance of the baby boom cohorts into the US workforce caused significant changes in the age structure of the management of US firms. Figure 5 shows the evolution of the age distribution of managers in the United States over time against the evolution of the workforce as a whole. The latter is shown by the dark line of the age distribution. The dashed line is the age distribution of US workers categorized as managers.

The baby boom cohorts first entered the workforce in large numbers in the 1970 census, but they were not well represented in the management workforce in that year. This is consistent with the idea that young workers are not chosen to be managers, because of their lack of experience. This implies that a worker with the necessary experience to manage was more likely to be a manager in 1970 than in 1960. The marginal manager was therefore likely to be less talented as the baby boomers entered the workforce in large numbers. By 1980 the baby boom cohorts had fully entered the workforce

FIGURE 5 Distribution by single years of age of the entire US workforce and of those categorized as managers, 1960–2000

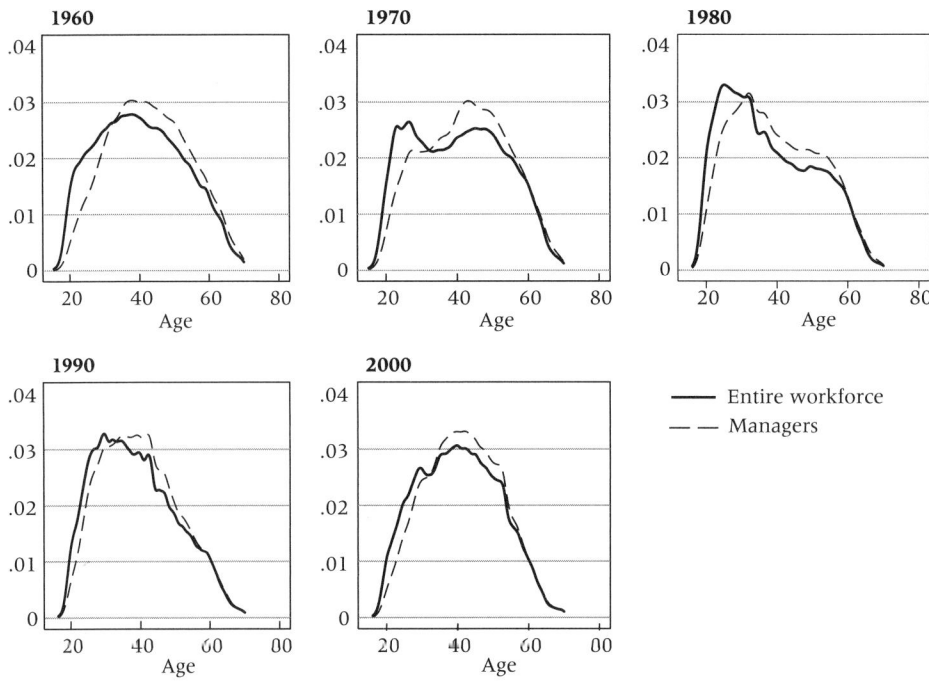

SOURCES: IPUMS; author's calculations.

but were still quite young and were proportionally under-represented in the managerial workforce. However, the overall size of the boom was such that the average age of managers fell by 4 years between 1970 and 1980 from 43 years old to 39 years old. As the mass of the boomers entered their 30s in the 1990 census, the managerial workforce began to return to its earlier shape. By 2000, when the boomers were of an age when people typically are in management, the distribution looks almost identical to the 1960 distribution. Indeed, the median age of managers in 2000 is nearly the same as in 1960.

Figure 6 shows the proportion of each age category in management job classifications over time. Over this time period there was a secular increase in the proportion of workers classified as managers, so the data have been detrended to emphasize the within-group effects.

The most striking feature of this graph is the increase in the proportion of workers classified as managers (relative to trend) from 1960 followed by a decline from 1980 until 2000. As argued earlier, when the baby boomers were young they were under-represented in the management workforce. This necessitated that a larger percentage of the older cohorts enter management roles. As the boomers aged, they began taking over the management burden generated by the size of their cohort. Between 1980 and 2000, this resulted

FIGURE 6 Proportion of US workforce categorized as managers (detrended), by age group

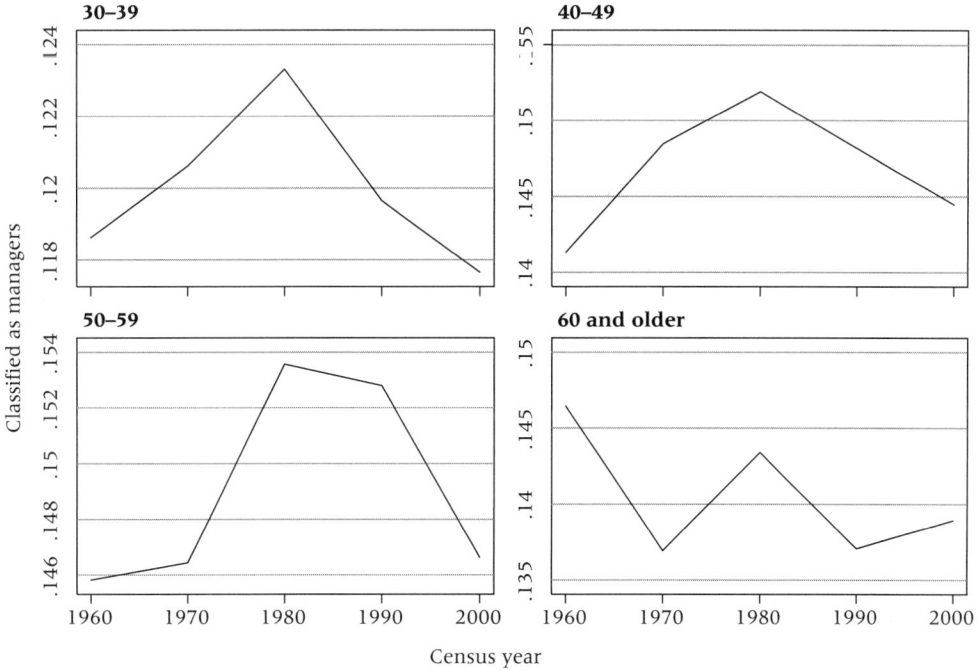

SOURCE: IPUMS, author's calculations.

in a lowering of the proportion of managers in each age cohort (relative to the time trend).

The data suggest that from 1960 until 1980 the entry of the baby boomers resulted in a lowering of marginal manager quality, while from 1980 until 2000 the baby boom's aging resulted in higher manager quality. This effect is likely magnified by the fact that the workers in the baby boom cohort were called on to manage earlier in their careers, so that by 2000 they not only had an appropriate experience level to manage other workers, but also had more specific experience as managers than other cohorts at the same age. Higher manager quality will cause higher overall productivity, potentially contributing to the aggregate results.

Tests on US state and metropolitan area data

The results presented thus far suggest that the composition of the workforce at the country level matters. If this result also holds at the US state and local level this may suggest a different set of mechanisms than a result that is confined to the country level. This section attempts to replicate the cross-country results using US state and metropolitan area data.

State and metropolitan area data on income and the demographic composition of the workforce are taken from the Integrated Public Use Microdata Series of the US census.[16] The base data is a 5 percent sample of the US census from 1960 until 2000. Population proportions are from the entire sample, while workforce proportions are from a subsample of full-time workers. Income is measured as the average hourly income of full-time workers.

While hourly income is not a perfect measure of total factor productivity, it is the best available proxy for this purpose. If we assume that workers earn their marginal product and that capital is mobile within the United States, the regional differences in wages should reflect productivity differences. The use of wages in studies of schooling externalities is common (see, e.g., Moretti 2004).

Estimation is identical to that in the cross-country sample, but the use of US data presents several challenges. One problem is that of endogenous participation rates. For example, in the United States high participation rates among teenagers may be correlated with unobservable area characteristics that drive wages downward. This source of bias can be addressed by instrumenting the workforce proportions on population proportions.

Within the United States, the workforce is highly mobile. If migration is driven by wage differentials and people of different age groups migrate differentially, the US estimations will likely reflect reverse causality. In the cross-country data, this was much less of an issue because cross-country mobility is much smaller than US cross-state and metro-area mobility. It is possible to eliminate the impact of mobility by instrumenting on lagged population data. In the cross-country data, this showed that mobility was not driving the results. The same test will be applied for the US data.

Table 3 shows the results of regressions at the state and metropolitan area level of log hourly wage on demographic proportions. Estimation is done in differences to eliminate fixed effects. Standard errors are clustered at the regional area to deal with serial correlation. Three different estimations were performed on each sample. Columns (1) and (4) were estimated using OLS. Columns (2) and (5) were estimated using IV with current population age structure as instruments. This estimation deals with the problem of endogenous participation rates. Columns (3) and (6) estimate using IV with ten-year lagged age structures as instruments.

These results are not nearly as clear as the cross-country results and are inconclusive. Point estimates and almost all significant coefficients are negative.[17] In general, the point estimates suggest that the effect of changes in the age structure is smaller at the state and MSA level than at the cross-country level. In the case of the state-level results, we cannot reject that the effect of changes in the age structure is different than at the cross-country level, at least in the IV regressions. However, the confidence intervals for the OLS regression at the state level suggest that this set of coefficients is significantly smaller than the point estimates for the cross-country regressions. All three

TABLE 3 Effect of changes in workforce composition on US wages: State and metro area, 1960–2000

Sample:	Δlog(wage)					
	(1) State OLS	(2) State IV	(3) State IV-lag	(4) MSA OLS	(5) MSA IV	(6) MSA IV-lag
ΔW15	−3.497	−3.206	−7.253	−1.967	−5.402	1.608
	(1.855)+	(11.395)	(5.806)	(0.620)**	(2.132)*	(7.551)
ΔW20	0.032	0.19	−0.827	0.273	0.529	0.388
	(0.406)	(0.826)	(1.523)	(0.184)	(0.254)*	(0.586)
ΔW30	−0.743	−0.943	−1.536	−0.135	−0.315	−0.521
	(0.546)	(1.281)	(1.194)	(0.184)	(0.308)	(0.823)
ΔW50	−1.357	−4.371	−4.773	−0.007	−0.759	−0.04
	(0.780)+	(1.229)**	(1.417)**	(0.226)	(0.443)+	(0.809)
ΔW60	−0.354	12.76	1.195	0.157	−0.451	2.88
	(1.243)	(11.843)	(1.947)	(0.327)	(2.480)	(1.795)
Observations	190	190	188	441	441	335
R-squared	0.79	0.46	0.74	0.72	0.67	0.73

Standard errors in parentheses.
+ significant at 10 percent; * significant at 5 percent; ** significant at 1 percent
NOTE: ΔW15 is the change in the proportion of workers aged 15–19. ΔW20, W30, W40, W50 are the changes in the proportion of workers ages 20–29, 30–39, 40–49, and 50–59. ΔW60 is the change in the proportion of workers ages 60 and older. MSA = metropolitan statistical area.

regressions at a lower level of aggregation, the MSA level, have coefficients that are significantly closer to zero than the cross-country point estimates.

These results suggest that the demographic effects diminish at lower levels of aggregation. This should not come as a surprise. The United States has highly integrated labor and product markets. Suppose that the increased availability of prime-age workers makes an individual plant more efficient. These efficiency gains will not necessarily be captured completely by the wages of the workers of that plant. Shareholders of the firm, who do not necessarily live in the immediate area, may reap some of the gains. If product markets are competitive, consumers will gain as a result of lower marginal costs of production. Obviously, these consumers are not necessarily located in the same geographic area as the workers and plants.

Conclusion

The results presented in this chapter show that changes in workforce age structure are strongly correlated with productivity and output. A significant portion of the productivity gap between rich and poor countries may be related to different age structures. The results also appear to capture some of the productivity divergence between poor and rich countries since 1980. In Japan and the United States over the last 40 years, the relative demographic movements are consistent with the cross-country results in productivity changes.

Given the importance of productivity in explaining cross-country income differences, this is a useful result. Demographic changes have substantial predictable time series variation that is largely exogenous to contemporaneous events, at least at the country level. Also, the regressions using lagged demographic data indicate that movements in productivity are not causing contemporaneous changes in age structure. The magnitudes of the results are much larger than one would expect from the standard labor results, suggesting that externalities play a large role.

Two possible hypotheses are suggested as mechanisms through which the age distribution might affect aggregate output. First, the productivity of innovative activity is undoubtedly related to age. However, US patent data show that the age distribution of innovators did not change substantially in the United States as a result of the entry of the baby boom cohorts into the workforce. This suggests that changes in the supply of workers who are at the prime age to innovate may have an impact on the rate of innovation.

By contrast there were substantial changes in the age distribution of managers in the United States. Initially the baby boomers were inexperienced and could not provide their own management talent, necessitating the use of less talented managers from older cohorts. As the boomers aged, they entered management ranks earlier than previous cohorts. This had the net effect of increasing the proportion of managers drawn from all age cohorts from 1960 to 1980, almost certainly lowering management quality. This trend reversed from 1980 through 2000.

Results at the US state and MSA level, while less conclusive than the cross-country results, suggest that the effect of age structure is smaller at lower levels of aggregation. This suggests that the externalities at work are stronger at higher levels of aggregation. Given the integrated product and labor markets in the United States, this is not surprising. The nonrivalry of ideas makes it likely that an age–innovation link may not be evident at the state or MSA level because the gains of inventive activity are spread out quickly with little regard to geography. For management, however, it is not hard to imagine that gains will be more (though not completely) local.

These explanations for the aggregate results are hardly exhaustive. This chapter has focused on the direct impact of the age profile on production. It is also possible that certain market demand effects matter. For example, a particular age profile might result in consumption patterns that have aggregate effects. Taxation patterns may also differ across age profiles.

Understanding the relationship between age structure and productivity is important because of the useful and predictable characteristics of age structure and because the significance of the relationship is strong. Almost every region in the world is experiencing significant demographic change. Rich countries are rapidly becoming older and most have birth rates below replacement level. Some poor countries are experiencing dramatically reduced birth rates in the wake of rapid population growth. Understanding how these changes will affect productivity over the coming decades is of crucial importance. While this study indicates a relationship between productivity and age structure, more research is needed to understand the mechanisms behind this relationship and their strengths.

Notes

I am grateful to David Bloom, Peter Klenow, Doug Staiger, and Bruce Sacerdote for their helpful comments and advice.

1 I choose to exclude W40 because the 40-year-old age group generally has the highest coefficient when included. By excluding W40, significant coefficients on the other age groups indicate that they are significantly different from the implied zero coefficient on W40.

2 Gollin (2002) shows that capital's share is roughly equal across countries.

3 The choice of coefficients follows Hall and Jones (1999), who in turn use returns to schooling data compiled in Psacharopoulos (1994). The present chapter differs in using data from a recent update in Psacharopoulos and Patrinos (2004). The differences are minor. For the first four years of schooling the return to schooling in sub-Saharan Africa, 11.7 percent, is used. For schooling from four to eight years the world average return to schooling, 9.7 percent, is used. For schooling beyond eight years the OECD return to schooling, 7.5 percent, is used. The results are not sensitive to the precise method of calculating human capital from schooling.

4 This correction is taken from UN national accounts data, as collected in Aiyar and Feyrer (2002). Because the regressions in this chapter exclude oil-exporting countries, the

corrections are quite minor and have very little impact on the results.

5 Their calculations, in turn, are based on the Penn World Tables 5 and 6. Both are available from the World Bank website «http://www.worldbank.org/research/growth».

6 The population data used in the imputation is limited to the working-age population in order to avoid contaminating the imputed data with information about dependency ratios.

7 Demographic shifts of this size, while not the norm, are present in the data. Between 1980 and 1990, the proportion of workers in the United States aged 40–49 rose by 4.6 percentage points.

8 The instrument set in these cases is restricted to the population structure of people who will be in the workforce at the end of the lag period. For example, the instruments for the 10-year lagged IV regressions are constructed from the population aged 5–54 since they will comprise the working-age population 10 years later.

9 Figure 2 shows the raw number of births and is not scaled to the size of the population. The important features of the figure are the locations of the peaks and troughs, which are more easily seen in the unscaled graph.

10 In 1966 there was a dramatic one-year downturn of almost one half million births in Japan. Apparently, 1966 was the most recent "Year of the Fire Horse." According to Japanese superstition, girls born in the year of the Fire Horse will have very unhappy lives and most likely will kill their husbands.

11 While there is cross-country variation in the coefficient estimates, the range of variation is relatively small. Bils and Klenow (2000) find coefficients on schooling as high as 0.28 (Jamaica) and as low as 0.024 (Poland). The majority of coefficients, however, fall between 0.05 and 0.15.

12 Assuming, of course, that productivity is measured in a way that does not account for differences in human capital through experience.

13 Even if you are not using the Google search engine, Google's competitors have almost certainly improved as a result of the competition.

14 Lehman (1953), p. 8.

15 Chari and Hoenhayn (1991) find that technologies diffuse slowly because technology is embedded in long-lived capital.

16 «http://www.ipums.org».

17 The exception to this is the positive and significant coefficient on 20–29-year-old workers in regression (5). Recall that one of the problems in using US state and MSA data is migration. If 20–29-year-olds are differentially likely to migrate to high-income areas, we should expect a larger coefficient on the 20–29-year-old age category. Instrumental variables regressions using lagged population data as instruments should eliminate migration as a source of bias. Doing so eliminates the positive coefficient on 20–29-year-old workers (albeit with a large standard error).

References

Acemoglu, Daron and Josh Angrist. 2000. "How large are human capital externalities? Evidence from compulsory schooling laws," *NBER Macro Annual* 2000: 9–59.

Aiyar, Shekhar and James Feyrer. 2002. "A contribution to the empirics of total factor productivity," Dartmouth College Working Paper, August.

Barro, Robert J. and Jong-Wha Lee. 2001. "International data on educational attainment: Updates and implications," *Oxford Economic Papers* 53(3): 541–563.

Bils, Mark and Peter Klenow. 2000. "Does schooling cause growth?," *American Economic Review* 90 (5): 1160–1183.

Bloom, David E., David Canning, and Jaypee Sevilla. 2004. "The effect of health on economic growth: A production function approach," *World Development* 32 (1): 1–13.

Bloom, David E., Matthew Hartley, and Henry Rosovsky. 2006. "Beyond private gain: The public benefits of higher education," in James J. F. Forest and Philip G. Altbach (eds.), *International Handbook of Higher Education*. Springer, pp. 293–308.

Caselli, F., G. Esquivel, and F. Lefort. 1996. "Reopening the convergence debate: A new look at cross-country growth empirics," *Journal of Economic Growth* 1(3): 363–389.

Chari, V. V. and Hugo Hoenhayn. 1991. "Vintage human capital, growth, and the diffusion of new technology," *Journal of Political Economy* 99(6): 1142–1165.

Easterly, William and Ross Levine. 2001. "It's not factor accumulation: Stylized facts and growth models," *World Bank Economic Review* 15(2): 177–219.

Feyrer, James. 2007. "Demographics and productivity," *Review of Economics and Statistics* 89(1): 100–109.

Galenson, David W. and Bruce Weinberg. 2000. "Age and the quality of work: The case of modern American painters," *Journal of Political Economy* 108(4): 761–777.

———. 2005. "Creative careers: The life cycles of Nobel Laureates in economics," NBER Working Paper series no. w11799. Cambridge, MA: National Bureau of Economic Research.

Gollin, Douglas. 2002. "Getting income shares right," *Journal of Political Economy* 110: 458–475.

Hall, Robert and Charles I. Jones. 1999. "Why do some countries produce so much more output per worker than others?," *Quarterly Journal of Economics* 114(1): 83–116.

Jones, Benjamin F. 2005. "Age and great invention," NBER Working Paper 11359, May.

Jones, Charles I. 1995. "R&D-based models of economic growth," *Journal of Political Economy* 103 (4): 759–784.

Jorgenson, Dale. 2003. "Information technology and the G7 economies," *World Economics* 4(4): 139–169.

Kremer, Michael. 1993. "Population growth and technological change: One million B.C. to 1990," *Quarterly Journal of Economics* 108(3): 681–716.

Lehman, Harvey C. 1953. *Age and Achievement*. Princeton University Press.

Lucas, Robert E. 1978. "On the size distribution of business firms," *The Bell Journal of Economics* 9(2): 508–523.

Mincer, Jacob. 1974. *Schooling, Experience, and Earnings*. New York: Columbia University Press.

Moretti, Enrico. 2004. "Estimating the social return to higher education: evidence from longitudinal and repeated cross-sectional data," *Journal of Econometrics* 121: 175–212.

Nelson, Richard and Edmund Phelps. 1966. "Investment in humans, technological diffusion, and economic growth," *American Economic Review* 56: 69–75.

Psacharopoulos, George. 1994. "Returns to investment in education: A global update," *World Development* 22(9): 1325–1343.

Psacharopoulos, George and Harry Anthony Patrinos. 2004. "Returns to investment in education: A further update," *Education Economics* 12(2): 111–134.

Weinberg, Bruce A. 2002. "Experience and technology adoption," Ohio State University working paper, May.

PART II.

*THE ROLE OF HUMAN
CAPITAL ACCUMULATION IN
ECONOMIC GROWTH*

Declining Mortality Among British Scientists During the Age of Enlightenment

Ryan D. Edwards

Traditional perspectives on economic growth and development usually interpret the process of mortality decline as a product of technological change. Preston (1975) famously reported that 75–90 percent of the increases in world life expectancy during the first half of the twentieth century were attributable to technological change. Historical work on the course of modern development and the demographic transition typically deduces causality based on the sequence of key events: scientific advancement starting in the seventeenth century, acceleration of population growth beginning in the eighteenth century, economic growth and the Industrial Revolution starting in the early nineteenth century, and widespread mortality decline taking hold later in the nineteenth century. While there is a range of views on how popular improvements in health and mortality decline resulted from earlier developments, the common thread is that lengthening life spans are the end result. Researchers typically assume that technological change is either fostered by the development of institutions or brought about by increases in population or in population density.

This conceptualization of increasing life expectancy as solely an output is also implicit in current perspectives on the future impacts of continued mortality decline in industrialized countries. While most of the historical gains in life expectancy at birth during the demographic transition were attributable to declines in infant and child mortality, which effectively increased productive working years, mortality improvements in advanced countries today tend primarily to lengthen life spent in retirement. Thus many view population aging as a strain on productive resources and a potential threat to future prosperity, in part because of defined-benefit public pensions (Bongaarts 2004), but also because of the structure of fiscal policy and markets (Kotlikoff and Burns 2005). To be sure, population aging is a serious issue for modern economies with extensive systems of public old-age support, especially when those systems contain strong incentives for elderly individuals to cease economically productive activity and retire regardless of whether they are productive or not. But is it clear whether population aging must necessarily be a drag on economic growth? If aging is solely an output of growth, then the chances are good that it is.

In this chapter, I argue that the traditional view of mortality decline and technological change misses an important connection between the two: that gains in adult life span can facilitate more scientific discovery. Put simply, this is an argument about the life-cycle productivity of scientists. Physical functioning naturally deteriorates as a result of aging, and so do some intellectual capabilities. But I show that scientific productivity, much of which builds directly on personal histories of prior output, does not exhibit the same deterioration with age that we see with most other types of productive activity. It is true that many breakthroughs in theoretical science are contributed by young scientists with fresh critical perspectives on established knowledge. But a large part of knowledge production and the learning of techniques is facilitated by the application and augmentation of knowledge and techniques acquired earlier. Older scientists clearly have direct access to their own stocks of knowledge, and younger scientists typically acquire their access through learning facilitated by older scientists. Examples from both modern and historical times show that older scientists are productive members of the scientific community, and the productivity of the average scientist declines much more slowly with age than that of the average worker. This pattern suggests that mortality decline, by lengthening the life spans of scientists, may stimulate knowledge production and thus raise productivity, other things equal.

Has there been any connection between increasing life spans and accelerating knowledge production over long periods of time? The traditional perspective on historical development in England assigns no role to life span extension, although Hollingsworth (1964) showed that mortality among British elites was declining prior to 1800. But population growth, typically viewed according to a Boserupian (1965, 1981) perspective as the engine for technological growth, was not steady during the early phases of scientific development. I show below that an interesting subgroup of British elites experienced early gains in mortality. Vital records data on members of the Royal Society of London show steady declines in mortality beginning with the Society's inception in 1660. Because the Society is widely seen as an important early institution in the development of empirical and deductive reasoning, these findings are telling. Mortality decline among British elites surely facilitated early knowledge production by extending the lives of those early knowledge pioneers. Exactly to what extent life span matters to scientific production is a natural next question, but I leave the answer to future efforts.

The sections that follow lay out the evidence and the argument for why longer life was probably good for early scientific development. First, I review the literature on individual productivity over the life course, and then explore scientific productivity through the life span, in both modern and historical periods. Next, I discuss contemporary theories of historical development and examine the timeline of key events in English history. I present new evidence on early increases in the life spans of Royal Society fellows and offer a reinterpretation of the historical chronology. Finally, I discuss some of the broader issues and policy implications to which these insights speak.

Productivity and age in modern economies

We perceive population aging to be costly because we view older individuals as less productive than younger individuals. In the case of old-age mortality decline, we view an additional year of life as one spent unproductively, with consumption financed by transfers or savings rather than by productive activities. Gains against infant and childhood mortality are notably different, since they increase productive years. Evidence for this simple view is shown in Figure 1, which depicts the age schedule of labor income per person in the United States during the 1990s. This locus is the schedule of age-specific productivity per living person, and to a first approximation it represents the contribution to market output by an individual at each age.[1]

For young individuals, market productivity is low because participation is near zero, but it would be low in any case. Education, which is typically

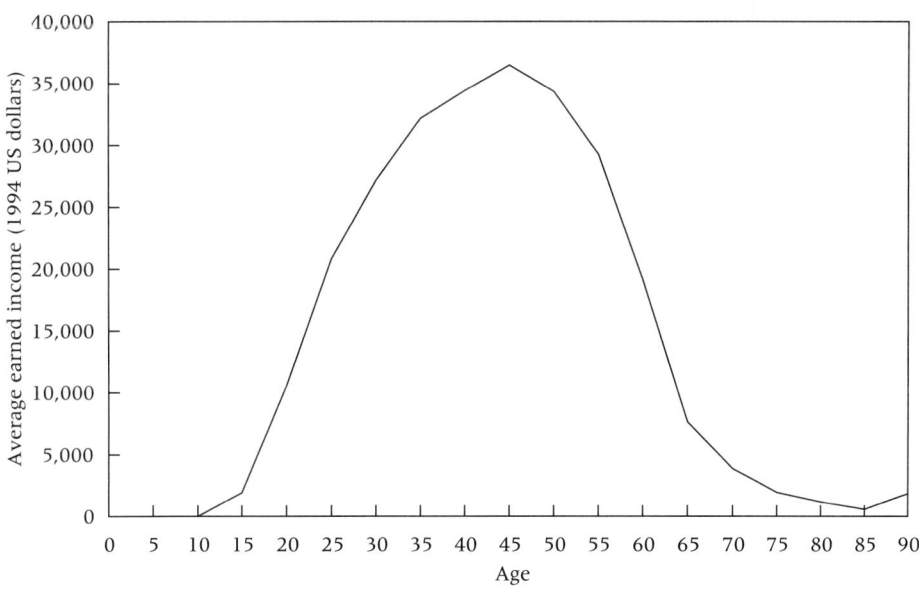

FIGURE 1 The modern age-profile of earned income

SOURCE: March Current Population Surveys, 1992–96. Data are earned income for US males (total earnings by males divided by total male population at the given age), averaged by five-year age group.

rival to labor force participation, develops mental abilities and imparts knowledge and familiarity with productive techniques. Physical development also occurs during adolescence. During the prime working years, productivity is high and growing. Participation is high, and workers hone skills with repetition while developing new techniques in order to meet challenges.

By age 65, individuals are retiring from market-based work, while a minority may continue to work and earn into later years. The retirement decision is a function of attitudes, abilities, and external circumstances. We know that public pension programs provide strong incentives for retirement (Gruber and Wise 2002), but it is also clear that many abilities degrade with age (Skirbekk 2004). The ability of individuals to produce surely does not decline as precipitously as Figure 1 depicts, but the confluence of social and economic policies, preferences, and vitality produces a steep decline in labor force participation rates and average market productivity.

Given this relationship, reductions in mortality during adult years will tend to result in more economic dependency, not an increase in productive potential. An additional person-year lived past age 65 will produce little additional market output, ceteris paribus. But is this a universal characteristic of all productive activities, or is it just true for the average wage earner?

Productivity and age in science

There are several ways in which age is likely to affect scientific productivity differently than other types of economic productivity. First, knowledge is primarily produced through mental rather than physical activity, and it tends to be very time intensive. While many key innovations in theoretical science are produced by young scientists who challenge conventional wisdom,[2] empirical knowledge is more a product of a large accumulation of interconnected ideas stored within an individual or within closely knit groups of individuals. Hammel (1983) finds these patterns in a sample of mathematicians and chemists at the University of California, while Weinberg and Galenson (2005) discuss these differences in the production of theoretical and empirical knowledge by Nobel Prize winners in economics. Older scientists may not produce as many theoretical innovations as younger mavericks, but they probably contribute disproportionately large amounts of empirical knowledge with their accumulated stocks of knowledge that are important for inductive reasoning. If a significant component of knowledge production is characterized by increasing returns to scale in time inputs, long life spans may be critical ingredients of knowledge growth.

A more pessimistic view, at least for industrialized countries today, is offered by Jones (2005). He argues that increases in the stock of all knowledge have made acquiring that knowledge more costly for young scientists, a situation that threatens to slow technological change. If the number of years spent by students to acquire an ever-expanding basic level of knowledge grows faster than life spans, the productive working years of scientists must effectively shrink. Jones reports evidence that this may be the case in the United States currently. Underlying both these views is the belief that knowledge production requires the acquisition of a person-specific stock of knowledge, which yields a stream of dividends in the form of new ideas over time. Transmission of knowledge via books, or in modern times via the Internet, is a requisite component of knowledge production, but not a substitute for the scientist's stock of knowledge. The length of a trained scientist's professional career therefore still matters for knowledge production, even if the medium of knowledge transmission improves. If individual stocks of knowledge are important, so too is the associated rate of depreciation. If the rate were high, say, during periods of rapid growth in knowledge, the benefits of a longer scientific career might appear diminished. But Weinberg and Galenson (2005) find that empirical researchers typically produce prize-winning research only later in life, after many years of inductive reasoning using accumulated knowledge. It would appear that stocks of knowledge do not rapidly depreciate, at least in the case of empirical science.

A second way in which knowledge producers are likely to be different as regards their working life spans is in their preferences for work and leisure. Scientific research is conducted by some of the most highly educated members of society, who by virtue of their education have a wide array of more lucrative career opportunities available to them other than research science. Their revealed preference suggests that knowledge production in and of itself is valuable compensation. This contrasts with prevailing views of work in many other fields, where workers see productive years as the price of consumption during retirement. Knowledge producers probably enjoy their occupations more on average and thus probably would not choose to reduce their working time as sharply with age. Institutional constraints still exist, but tenure and emeritus status generally facilitate longer productive working lives than the average.

A third point is that knowledge production directly begets more knowledge production. University researchers themselves train the next generation of researchers. The process of instruction often results in both an increase in knowledge for the students and the gaining of new perspective by the instructor, who through teaching may reevaluate conventional wisdom and identify open questions for future research.

Fourth, older scientists directly facilitate the growth and health of scientific institutions that foster further growth in knowledge. Institution building requires the focusing of many resources, chief among them being the prestige of individuals who have developed reputations as knowledgeable scientists, their advice, and their knowledge of how to build institutions. Older researchers lend external legitimacy to the development of new and existing institutions, and they can provide crucial guidance to members on achieving internal and external harmony within institutions.

The first two points describe ways in which individual scientific productivity is likely to follow a different, less rapidly declining trajectory through age than other forms of productivity. The third and fourth points describe components of value added by older scientists that are more difficult to capture in traditional measures. These can be termed spillover effects so as to capture how these particular impacts of older scientists are likely to be felt by many entities other than the scientist. Contributions of older scientists to the development of institutions, for example, is a particularly elusive topic. For brevity, I examine simple measures of the individual productivity of scientists and not the spillovers, which I leave to future work.

Scientists in the United States today

The National Opinion Research Center conducts a biennial Survey of Doctorate Recipients (SDR) on behalf of the US National Science Foundation and National Institutes of Health. The SDR contains data on career development for 40,000 doctorate recipients in the sciences and engineering. Figure 2 displays average scientific productivity among doctorate recipients in the United

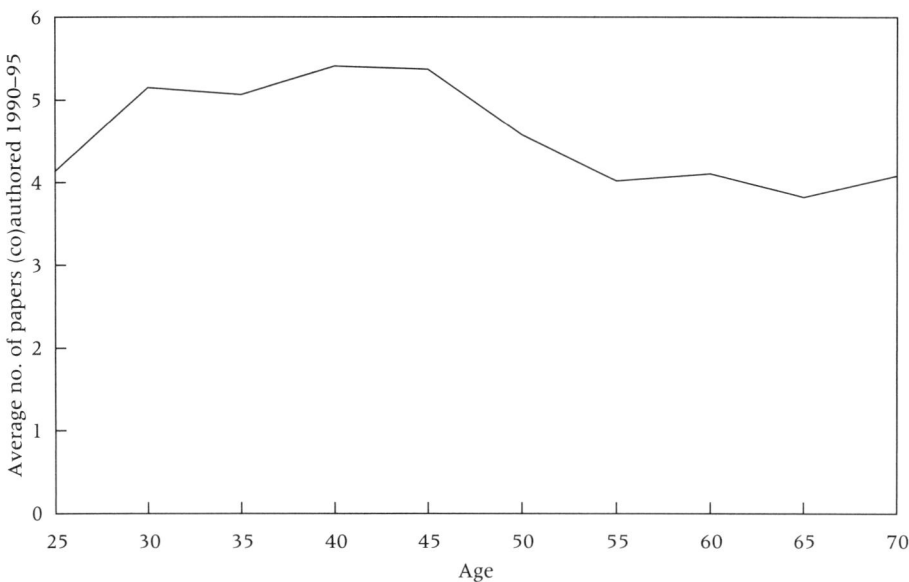

FIGURE 2 Individual scientific productivity in the United States, 1990–95

NOTES: Data are the number of journal articles authored or coauthored between 1990 and 1995, averaged over five-year age groups. Age 25 is an open-ended group of individuals younger than age 29; age 30 is ages 30–34, etc.; and age 70 refers to ages 70 and older.
SOURCE: 1995 Survey of Doctorate Recipients, National Science Foundation.

States as measured by journal articles authored or coauthored between 1990 and 1995.

A decline in average productivity after age 45 is apparent in Figure 2, but the decline is not large. On average, doctorate recipients aged 65 and older published four journal articles over this five-year period, while those aged 30–45 had a little over five new published articles. Viewed relative to age profiles of earnings or hours worked across all occupations, such as displayed in Figure 1, the decline in research productivity through age appears quite small. Rather, research productivity even at ages 70 and older, which typically are retirement years for the general population, remains high on average among scientists.

The measure of productivity I use in Figure 2 is meant to be illustrative, and it does not value output particularly well. Being an author or coauthor says nothing about actual contributions made to the published research, and we do not know the quality of the research. If there were trends by age in either of these unmeasured characteristics, an age profile of valuable scientific production might be different from what is shown in Figure 2. Weinberg and Galenson (2005) value the contributions of Nobel Laureates in economics by counting citations, revealing that empirical thinkers often produce prize-winning research around age 60, while theoretical thinkers tend to do so earlier, by age 40. The SDR data show that among a representative sample of all doctorate recipients in many disciplines, a cruder measure of scientific output is remarkably flat. The common finding is that older scientists remain productive.

Scientists in the Royal Society of London in 1660

I obtain a remarkably similar picture using data on scientific activity from a completely different time period and setting. Hunter (1982) examines the meeting minutes of the Royal Society of London, a scientific organization in Britain begun in 1660 that played a vital role in the development of empirical scientific knowledge (Hall 1991). The Society was founded by a small group of natural philosophers wishing to promote experimental learning of the type proposed and developed by Francis Bacon, who had died in 1626. Early members included Christopher Wren, the architect and astronomer, and Robert Boyle, the first modern chemist. The Royal Society quickly expanded to around 200 members and in later years would include such notables as Sir Isaac Newton and Charles Darwin. Members in good standing served for life, and many of the early members were aristocrats with few direct ties to science other than sponsorship. Still, the Royal Society is widely seen as a key institution that fostered the nascent growth of empirical knowledge and techniques. Like academies of science in other countries, it remains active today and has nearly 1,300 members.

Examining the minutes of the Society, Hunter assigns a qualitative ranking to the activity of Society members as indicated by the mentioning of their meeting interventions. For each member, Hunter also charts the trend in participation over time. I translate these qualitative groups into ordinal rankings, spread them over the life of the member according to Hunter's observations in time, and take averages of the index by age in order to produce a cohort-based age profile of productivity.

The resulting schedule measures the intensity of participation in Society meetings through age. In one clear sense, it is not as good a measure of productivity as we could obtain from publications data if they were available. Meeting interventions probably vary in quality much more than published works. In modern times, attending meetings of official societies may reflect the lack of anything better to do rather than time spent productively. But a key purpose of the Royal Society was to present and discuss scientific experiments (Hall 1991). Meeting participation was undoubtedly the mechanism for much early scientific development, so a measure of the intensity of participation is an entirely appropriate index of scientific productivity during this early period. And Hunter provides an ordinal scale of activity, not a binary measure of whether or not the individual was present. Although expulsion from the Society was rare and lifetime membership was standard, consistently absent fellows were removed from the rolls entirely. The index measures activity, not just presence.

Figure 3 plots the age profile of Hunter's index averaged over the lives of 74 early members. The figure shows that average activity at meetings peaked between ages 30 and 50 for these individuals. But the decline in activity with age is not particularly large, about half of one qualitative category. Advancing age apparently did little to reduce the participation at meetings of early Royal Society members who survived.

In contrast to the sharply humped age schedule of economic productivity per person shown in Figure 1, the age profiles of scientific productivity per doctorate holder in Figure 2 and per Royal Society member in Figure 3 are both relatively flat. Age does not appear to be synonymous with the lack of production in scientific fields. Following the thought experiment, this suggests that expansions in adult life spans among scientists may result in more productive scientists and more scientific productivity, other things equal.

To investigate this hypothesis, I examine historical trends in scientific discovery and development in preindustrial England alongside demographic data on members of the Royal Society. I preface my inquiry with a review of the literature on the origins of modern economic growth. One of the unanswered questions is how early scientific development took hold, and I find that trends in mortality among early scientists provide new insights, given the shape of the age profile of scientific productivity.

FIGURE 3 Activity among fellows of the Royal Society of London, 1661–1700

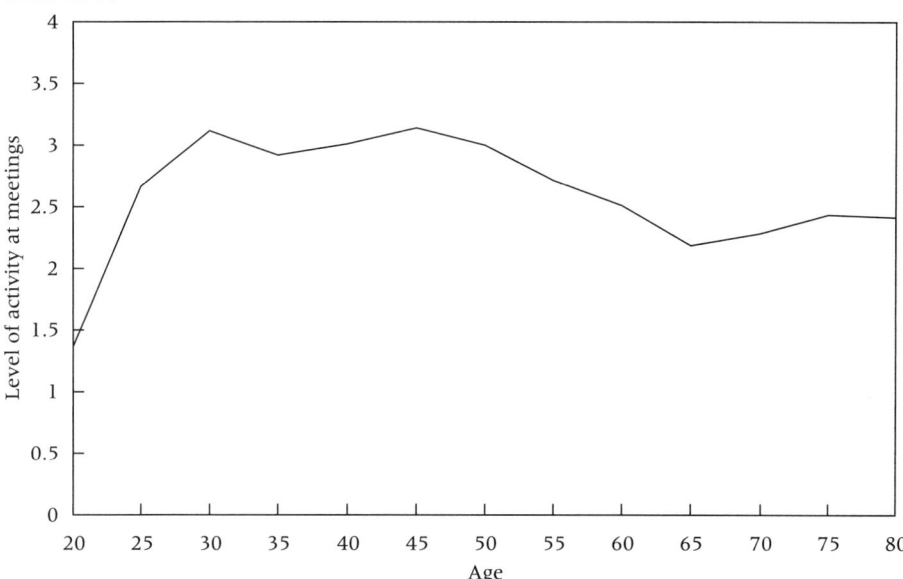

NOTES: Ordinal rankings of activity are scored as 1–6 with 1 being inactive; 2 barely active; 3 slightly active; 4 fairly active; 5 active; and 6 very active. The data are averaged over five-year age groups and cover 74 fellows inducted between 1661 and 1663. A small fraction of them resigned or were expelled and are included in the denominator.
SOURCE: Hunter's (1982) characterization of fellows' activity based on meetings minutes.

Unanswered questions about historical development

The determinants of economic growth remain a perennial topic of inquiry. Modern theories of development typically focus on the role of population growth and density in providing incentives for technical innovation, in the spirit of the classic work by Boserup (1965, 1981) on agricultural technology and the incentives to innovate conveyed by population density.[3] Subsequent efforts in this vein include Lee (1988), Tsoulouhas (1992), Kremer (1993), Galor and Weil (2000), and Jones (2001).

At first glance, the sequence of historical events appears to fit the Boserupian perspective quite well. The Industrial Revolution followed a large increase in population size and density in western Europe, typically attributed to a reduction in crisis mortality, such as from famines (Wrigley and Schofield 1981; Wrigley et al. 1997), or to a reduction in chronic malnutrition (Fogel 2004). Population grew by about 50 percent over the course of the eighteenth century, while mortality rates for the population as a whole remained stable at high levels, with e_0 averaging about 40 years. After this growth in population, income per capita accelerated rapidly, rising at an annual rate of 1.2 percent after 1820, up from about 0.05 percent since 1000 CE (Maddison 2001).

After the Industrial Revolution, life spans also began to increase at a roughly linear rate. Oeppen and Vaupel (2002) find increases in female life expectancy of about 0.25 years per year since 1840. Whether these major improvements in population health were caused by the Industrial Revolution or achieved in spite of it, or whether they were not directly associated with economic development at all, is a matter of much debate. A related question is whether increases in life expectancy actually represented improvements in health and reductions in morbidity, as we often assume. McKeown (1976) posited that increases in income brought about by the Industrial Revolution led directly to the improvements in nutrition that fostered gains in health and life expectancy, a view similar to that of Fogel (2004). Szreter (1997) concurs with the timing but disagrees on the causality, preferring instead to attribute importance to concerted efforts in public health and the political will necessary to engender them. Meanwhile, Preston (1975) clearly prefers to characterize the force behind mortality decline, at least in the twentieth century, as technological progress and not income at all. When life spans expand through improved medical treatment, the surviving population may in fact become more frail depending on the nature of the illness and treatment (Alter and Riley 1989). Based on trends observed among Union Army veterans in the United States, Fogel (2004) argues that reductions in morbidity have accompanied declines in mortality, at least from the nineteenth into the twentieth century.

Easterlin (1995), adopting a view similar to Preston's, suggests a reinterpretation of the timing of historical events. He perceives both the Industrial Revolution and the Mortality Revolution, which refers to the epidemiological transition of the late nineteenth and early twentieth centuries, as twin products of a much earlier revolution in scientific thought. The earlier period is commonly referred to as the Age of Enlightenment, and it is typically defined as spanning the seventeenth and eighteenth centuries. As measured by numbers of scientific publications, the production of scientific knowledge in England and Europe as a whole was indeed growing rapidly during this early period (Tsoulouhas 1992; Easterlin 1995). Easterlin's line of reasoning has clear merit but raises the question of what engendered and facilitated the revolution in scientific thought.

A Boserupian view attributes technological development to population growth or density. But population growth was not stable during the period in question, whereas technological change was proceeding steadily. Figure 4 plots English population size as reported by Tsoulouhas (1992) based on Wrigley and Schofield (1981). Population growth was indeed rapid prior to 1650 but then entered a period of relative stagnation, leaving total population essentially stable until 1740. Meanwhile, basic scientific advancement and

FIGURE 4 The population of England, 1550–1830

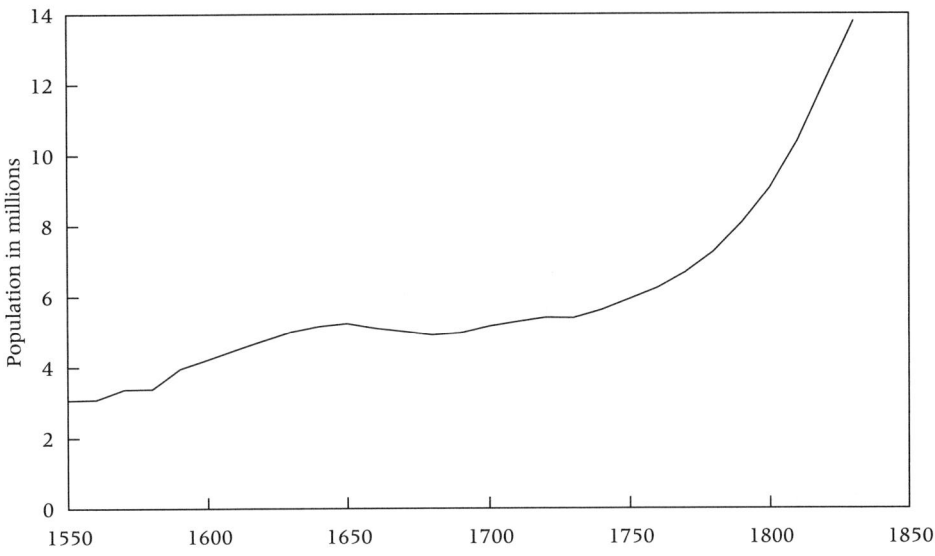

SOURCE: Tsoulouhas (1992).

innovation in production techniques were growing more steadily. Figure 5 plots two of Easterlin's data series on scientific development together with Tsoulouhas's series on agricultural production techniques using a log scale. Tsoulouhas's data are noisy, and I have superimposed a simple trend line. Although the growth rates of the three series are different, all show steady increases. Taken together, these data suggest that scientific development was well underway during the seventeenth century, prior to the period of sustained population growth starting in the eighteenth century. Although these patterns do not refute the Boserupian view, they raise the question of whether other factors may have influenced early growth in science.

What else might have led to early scientific development, if not just population growth? Acemoglu et al. (2005) emphasize the role of trans-Atlantic trade in promoting institutional changes in western Europe that later facilitated economic growth. Exposure to world markets probably revealed gains to innovations in thought, and also led to the rise of the merchant class, property rights, and constraints on the powers of monarchies. The founding of the Royal Society of London in 1660 occurred not long after the restoration of a weakened British monarchy. The French analogue to the Society, the Académie des Sciences, was founded six years later by the powerful Louis XIV.

Many modern theories of economic growth attach importance to the role of institutions in general. Hall and Jones (1999) find that institutions and

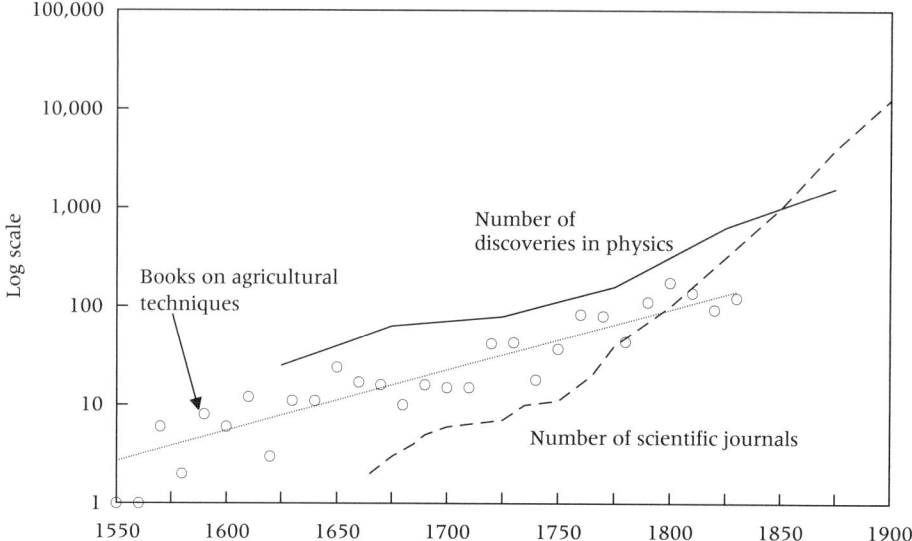

FIGURE 5 Scientific knowledge and production techniques 1550–1900

NOTES: The dotted line is a simple trendline fitted to the data on books on agricultural techniques, which are shown by the circles. The data are graphed on a base-10 logarithmic scale.
SOURCES: Tsoulouhas (1992), Easterlin (1995).

infrastructure are key in explaining modern cross-sectional differences in income per capita between rich and poor countries. Early scientific institutions certainly were vital as well. The Royal Society of London played a key role in the development of modern empirical science, and the same was true of scientific societies elsewhere in Europe during this period. Education is another potential focal point, although widespread increases in education occurred much later than the Enlightenment. But Boucekkine et al. (2003) explore urban educational attainment in seventeenth- and eighteenth-century Europe, and they find that early improvements in urban mortality coincided with increases in education. Their results echo the work of Hollingsworth (1964), who discovered early mortality improvements among aristocratic families in England before 1800.

The synchronous timing of these disparate strands—preindustrial mortality declines among urban populations and aristocrats, institutional development, and growth in scientific knowledge—prompts the question of how they may be linked. Vital statistics drawn from the records of the Royal Society of London indicate that mortality rates among its members were declining throughout its history. That is, the life spans of early scientists were steadily lengthening at the same time as scientific development was proceeding apace, while overall population size was stagnant.

Mortality decline among early British scientists

With nearly 350 years of continuous existence and more than 8,000 members since its inception, the history of the Royal Society of London provides a unique look at how life spans among scientists and associated elites have evolved since 1660. The Society has collected vital statistics on its members and made them conveniently accessible through its website, along with a selection of biographical information. Records on dates of birth, induction, and death facilitate the analysis of mortality among this select group of scientists. Induction into the Society is of course conditional on survival to the age of induction, which has averaged between 40 and 50 years and has risen steadily during the life of the Society. As a result, I examine adult mortality conditional on reaching the age at induction.

To my knowledge, this study is the first to examine the life spans of early scientists alongside trends in scientific development. I focus on members of Britain's Royal Society because their vital statistics are as readily available as are indicators of knowledge production in Britain, courtesy of Tsoulouhas (1992) and others. In a separate study, Leridon (2004) examines the demography of France's Académie des Sciences, with a focus on trends in the composition of the society and the average age of members in particular. That study addresses scientific productivity only indirectly, as an implicit outcome associated with the average age of the group. Leridon documents an inexorably rising average age of Académie members after 1840, which he attributes to secular declines in mortality above age 60 beginning then.

Figure 6 plots the natural logarithm of period mortality rates among Royal Society fellows in ten-year age groups from 30 to 79 against time, using data up until the middle of the twentieth century. The picture is one of fairly steady declines in all age-specific mortality rates over the entire period, although considerable temporal fluctuation is apparent in all five series. Rates of decrease are greater at younger ages, a relatively consistent pattern in mortality decline. Still, the figure shows that even 60–69-year-olds enjoyed persistent decreases in mortality rates, although fellows over 70 experienced more static mortality. Annual rates of decline in mortality rates averaged around 0.34 percent, which halves a rate in about 200 years. By comparison, rates of mortality decline averaged around 1 percent per year in the United States during the twentieth century. Fellows aged 30–39 saw their mortality rates fall from around 2 percent in 1660 to 1 percent by 1860, while those aged 50–59 saw declines in rates from 4 percent to 2 percent, and fellows aged 60–69 experienced a decline from 9 percent to 4.5 percent.

These gains in mortality rates resulted in steady increases in remaining life expectancy. Figure 7 shows average years remaining in the sample by age at induction at six points in time. Increases averaged about 0.03 years of remaining life for every year of time during this period. These findings

FIGURE 6 Log mortality rates among fellows of the Royal Society of London since 1660

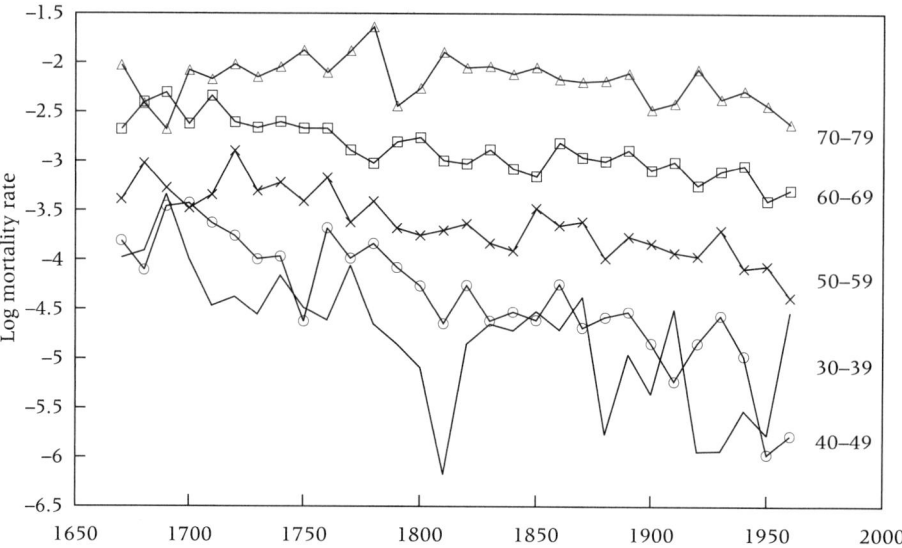

NOTE: The data are period mortality rates constructed using ten-year age groups observed over ten years of time and then logged.
SOURCES: Royal Society (2004) and author's calculations.

FIGURE 7 Average years of life remaining by age at induction in the Royal Society of London

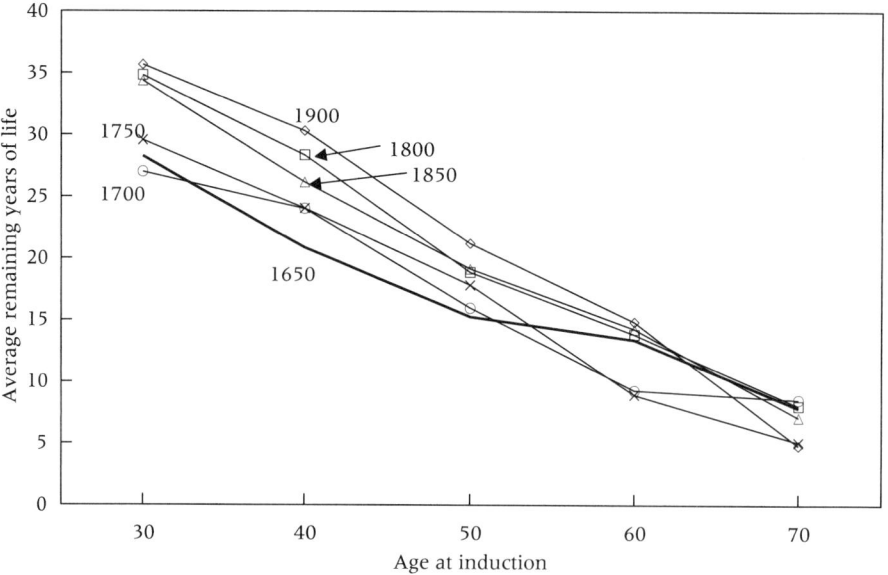

NOTE: Curves show cohort life expectancies: average years remaining on the y-axis by age at induction on the x-axis at six points in time.
SOURCE: Royal Society (2004) and author's calculations.

mirror those of Hollingsworth (1964), whose cohort life tables based on the British Peerage during the same period also imply average annual increases in adult life expectancies of roughly 0.03 years.

In his examination of the much smaller French Académie des Sciences, which averaged only about 20 members prior to 1800, Leridon (2004) reports the average age at death among members by calendar year from 1666 to the present. This is the appropriate measure for analysis of the group, but not for the individuals within. For easier comparison, I calculate the average age at death for Royal Society members by year of death and graph the results in Figure 8, alongside the average age at induction, which Leridon also provides for French Academy members in his Figure 3a. The top line shows the average age at death fluctuating around a linear trend of 0.07 year per year. This is considerably faster than Leridon's series, which is noisier around an upward trend of about 0.025 per year. The latter also shows less clear direction prior to 1840, which is consistent with Leridon's interpretation of the timeline.[4] To be sure, Figure 8 reveals the same components of graying in the Royal Society that Leridon finds in the Académie des Sciences: the average ages at induction and death are both increasing. But we also see declines in mortality and expansions in adult life spans for Royal Society members far earlier than 1840.

FIGURE 8 Average age at death and average age at induction, fellows of the Royal Society of London

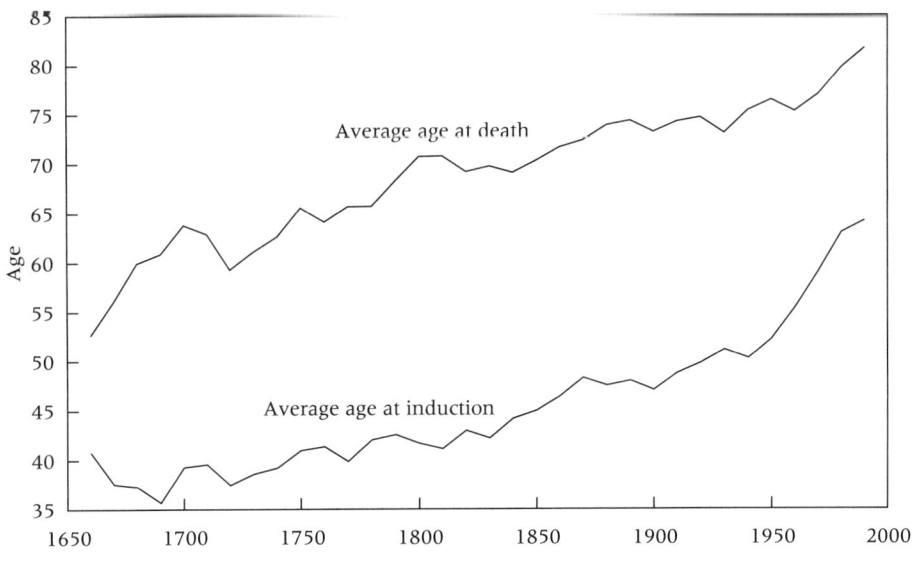

NOTE: The top line shows the average age at death among those dying by decade of death. The bottom line shows the average age at induction by decade of induction.
SOURCE: Royal Society (2004) and author's calculations.

The timing of these early increases in life expectancy among scientists is clearly of interest. While mortality among the general population remained high at preindustrial levels until the nineteenth century, members of the Royal Society were experiencing steady declines in mortality throughout its entire history. How do these mortality declines among scientists fit into the timeline of key events in English preindustrial history that we have established thus far?

A new view of the chronology of preindustrial events

Trends in period life expectancy afford a clearer picture of historical trends in mortality than do the cohort and group rates we have examined up to now. Using the mortality rates depicted in Figure 6, I construct period life expectancy at age 40, e_{40}, for Royal Society members starting in 1670. Wrigley et al. (1997) provide age-specific mortality rates for both sexes combined in England between 1640 and 1800, from which I then calculate e_{40}. Hollingsworth (1964) reports age-specific mortality for birth cohorts of the British peerage separately by sex, from which I derive period rates and period e_{40} starting in 1625. Males and females in this group of aristocrats experienced similar e_{40} during the period, with an initial female disadvantage of one to three years disappearing by about 1750 and becoming an advantage by 1850.

Figure 9 plots these three series of period e_{40} for different British groups on the same axes. Adult life spans among the peerage, shown by the dashed line, were considerably shorter than among the general population, shown by the thick line. This is the well-known urban penalty: communicable diseases could spread more easily in dense cities than in rural areas, and the aristocracy spent much of their time in cities (Johansson 1999). Life expectancy at age 40 among Royal Society fellows is higher than either of these series, and it exhibits rapid growth prior to 1800. Between 1670 and 1920, the average annual increase, measured by the slope of a least-squares regression line, was 0.045 years. Adult life spans among the peerage also expanded rapidly after 1675, which Johansson attributes to innovative medical practices and improved hygiene, of the type advocated by Francis Bacon. Before 1820, these increases averaged 0.047 year per calendar year. By comparison, e_{40} was also increasing among the general population of England, but the pace was slower, perhaps because of a relative lack of access to new techniques or a distrust of them. During the sample period shown, the average annual increase in e_{40} for English men and women was 0.027.

Were these early increases in adult life expectancy accompanied by declines in morbidity? We have indirect evidence that they were, at least for scientists: the relatively flat age profile of meeting participation intensity shown in Figure 3. Johansson (1999) reports many innovations in treating

FIGURE 9 Period life expectancy at age 40, e_{40}, for Royal Society fellows, males in the British peerage, and population of England (both sexes)

SOURCES: The thin solid line plots period life expectancy at age 40, e_{40}, for Royal Society fellows, constructed using the period mortality rates depicted in Figure 6. The thick solid line shows period e_{40} for all English men and women, based on mortality rates provided by Wrigley et al. (1997). The dashed line shows period e_{40} for males in the British peerage, based on cohort mortality rates presented by Hollingsworth (1964) transformed into period rates. Male and female e_{40} were roughly the same in the Hollingsworth data.

chronic diseases among the British aristocracy during this early period, which also suggests concomitant declines in morbidity.

During this early period, infant and youth mortality remained quite high, hence life expectancy at birth showed little upward trend. This is why demographers have traditionally dated the escape from the Malthusian trap as occurring around the time of early industrialization and not before. But this focus on adult life spans, and on the lifetime productivity of scientists, prompts a revisitation of the historical timeline. The top panel of Figure 10 plots the same e_{40} series for Royal Society Fellows. Circles plot actual data points, while the solid line is a least-squares fit of the series over the time period shown. The middle panel depicts the natural logarithm of Tsoulouhas's series on agricultural techniques, the same series that appeared in Figure 5. Data points are shown by x's, with a least-squares trend line superimposed. The bottom panel shows the same series on English population seen in Figure 4, beginning in 1650.

Figure 10 shows that e_{40} among scientists was growing linearly during this early period, at around 0.06 year per year, while publications on agricultural techniques were increasing at about 1.5 percent per year. Population growth did not begin its sustained increase until 1740, having waned

FIGURE 10 Period life expectancy at age 40, e_{40}, for Royal Society fellows, number of publications on agricultural techniques, and population in England, before 1830

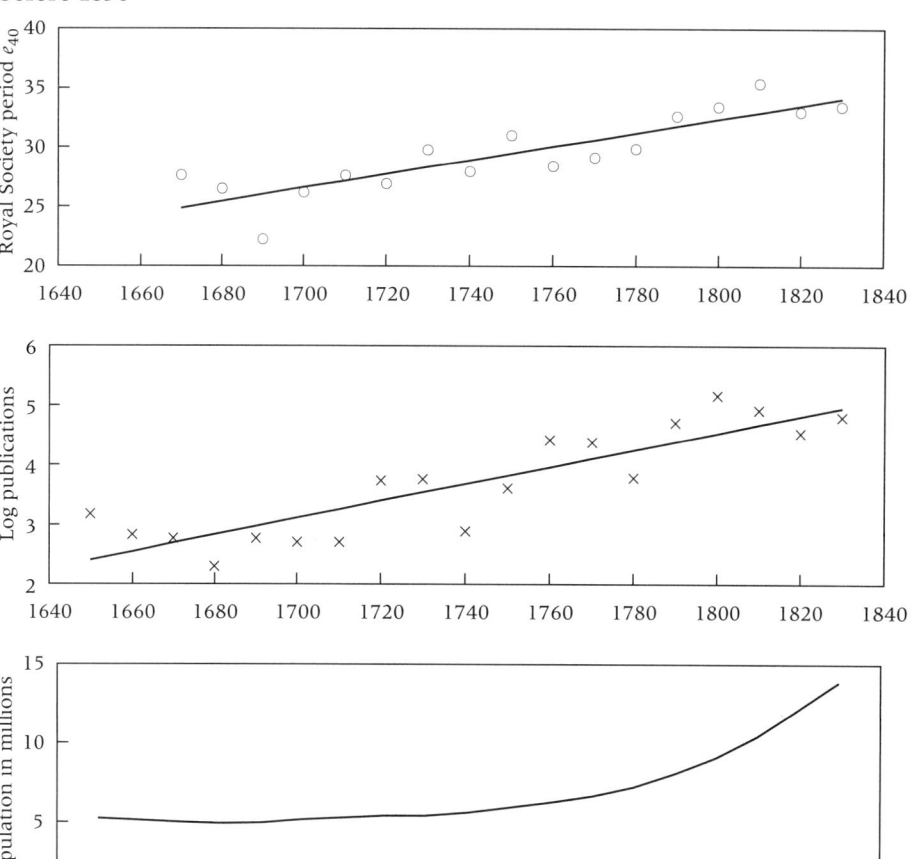

NOTES: The top panel shows period life expectancies at age 40, e_{40}, for Royal Society fellows, constructed using the period mortality rates depicted in Figure 6. Data points are shown by circles, with a least-squares trendline superimposed. The middle panel depicts the logarithm of new publications on agricultural techniques, a data series representing technology compiled by Tsoulouhas. The same series appears in Figure 5. Data points are shown by x's, with a least-squares trendline superimposed. The bottom panel depicts English population in millions, also supplied by Tsoulouhas. The same series appears in Figure 4.
SOURCES: Tsoulouhas (1992), Royal Society (2004), and author's calculations.

considerably around 1640 as a wave of infectious disease spread through England. While traditional theories emphasize the role of population growth in technological growth, this timeline suggests that increasing life spans of scientists preceded population growth and more closely accompanied technological change.

If the productivity of scientists does not decline with age, then expansions in adult life spans among scientists should result in greater scientific productivity. Early declines in adult mortality among scientists and among the

FIGURE 11 Views of the historical record and causality

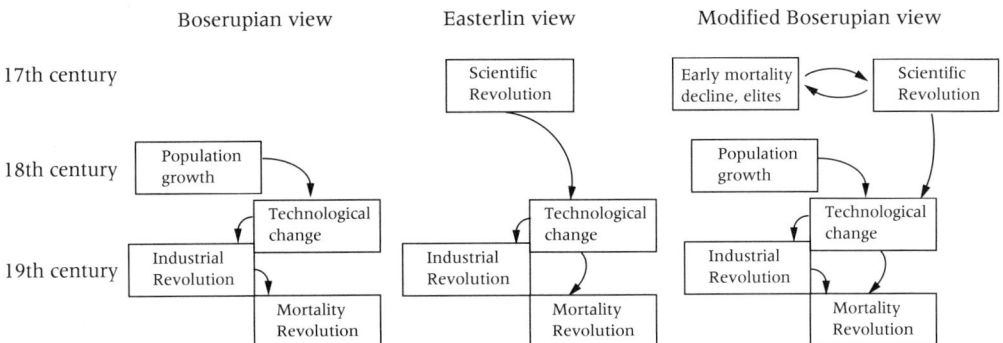

peerage were presumably caused by some prior cause, and it seems reasonable to assume that improvements in the scientific understanding of disease indeed produced them and came first. This is a modification of the standard view of the link between knowledge and mortality. But the new perspective I propose is that scientists enjoyed the fruits of their own labor, living longer to produce yet more knowledge, and so the cycle continued.

In Figure 11, I summarize several competing views of the historical sequence of events and the causal progression leading to the modern period of steady mortality decline and economic growth. Each of the three columns in the graphic depicts major events in order from the earliest at the top to the latest at the bottom. The leftmost portion of the figure depicts the standard Boserupian view, in which population growth ignites technological change, which is followed by economic growth and then mortality decline. In the middle of the figure is the Easterlin view, in which the Scientific Revolution fosters both the Industrial Revolution and the Mortality Revolution. The middle graphic is taller, reflecting Easterlin's belief that the causal impetus behind both developments began earlier.

The new hybrid view advanced here is depicted on the right side of Figure 11 and labeled "Modified Boserupian." Preindustrial decreases in mortality among elites, and among scientists in particular, facilitate Easterlin's Scientific Revolution. The modified Boserupian view allows population growth to affect technology, which in turn stimulates the Industrial and Mortality Revolutions. The new view remains undecided about the relative importance of the Industrial Revolution and technological change in explaining the Mortality Revolution.

Discussion

It is widely recognized that the discovery and application of new technologies are responsible for most of the robust growth in life expectancies enjoyed since the dawn of the modern era. In this chapter, I have laid out the case for an augmented view, in which this growth in technology may be self-sustaining. When improved knowledge fosters lengthened life, scientists can enjoy longer and more productive working careers, facilitating more innovation that helps lengthen life, and so the cycle continues.

This view begins with the observation that life-cycle productivity among scientists does not appear to decline rapidly with age, in contrast to what is found in other sectors of the economy. We also hypothesize that longer life spans allow scientists to invest their most precious resource, time, in greater allotments to projects that may exhibit increasing returns. The training of new scientists, the building of institutions through accumulated prestige and experience, and other spillover effects may further increase the benefits to knowledge production contributed by increasing life spans.

Patterns of mortality among members of the Royal Society of London reveal large and steady improvements in adult life spans among early scientists during a crucial period in the development of empirical scientific thought. Hollingsworth (1964) first recognized this pattern of preindustrial mortality decline, in his case among British nobility widely defined. But previous research has largely ignored this dynamic in interpreting the flow of preindustrial history, concentrating instead on the role of population growth in facilitating development of new knowledge and production techniques. This analysis joins Boucekkine et al. (2003) in offering a reinterpretation that takes account of early developments in life expectancy. These early mortality declines among scientists and elites are certainly overshadowed by postindustrial trends in population health, which were of unprecedentedly large scale. The fruits of mortality decline became much more widely distributed after the epidemiological transition beginning in the late nineteenth century, and for obvious reasons we tend to be more concerned with broad-based improvements in population health.

But we are also interested in a broader view of how large-scale improvements in public health can be conceptualized, and the evidence I present suggests that isolated gains against mortality among the elite may sometimes be important in this regard. It is therefore striking that recent research on the distribution of mortality decline across socioeconomic groups suggests widening disparities (Schalick et al. 2000). These are clearly cause for concern, but one is also tempted to ponder the similarities with historical trends, which also exhibited great inequality in the access to mortality decline, at least in Britain. Do modern patterns presage another major mortality revolution, for example? Are long-run social returns to temporary inequalities a pattern in development or more an aberration? These are questions for future investigators to address.

Future research should also explore how life spans and the production of ideas and techniques may be related in modern economies, both industrialized and developing. It appears that a large portion of differences in economic well-being between rich and poor countries is attributable not to observable differences in factories, equipment, labor supply, or education, but to how those inputs are combined to produce output (Hall and Jones 1999). Knowledge production, along with other concepts like social capital, infrastructure, and institutions, feeds directly into that residual category of production factors that consist of ideas, techniques, and productive environments. If reducing adult mortality spurs knowledge production, development policies that target adult mortality may add to the productive potential of the macroeconomy while directly raising individual well-being by improving health. This argument is similar to one found in the development literature today, in which there is debate regarding whether better health improves economic growth (Bloom and Sachs 1998; Acemoglu et al. 2003). But scientific production in developing economies is very different from physical production there, and it is also different from scientific production in advanced economies, either in the past or at present.

My results also bear implications, albeit weak ones, for the impacts of population aging in industrialized countries. Cutler et al. (1990) find that trends in labor productivity among industrialized countries since 1960 suggest that population aging and labor shortages may result in more rapid productivity growth. The mechanism my results suggest, namely more older but productive scientists as a result of population aging, is completely different, but the relatively more positive outlook is similar. If longer adult life spans result in more scientific productivity, the costs of population aging may be somewhat offset. But historical relationships between increases in the life spans of scientists and scientific production may not be easily repeated. We do not know whether further mortality declines at advanced ages will produce life years that are as scientifically productive as produced by prior mortality declines at adult ages. Industrial structures in advanced economies today are quite different than during historical periods. But a trend toward producing ideas and services rather than physical goods probably bodes well for the future of aging societies, since older workers are more likely to remain productive in ideas and services.

Notes

Preparation was supported by NIA grant T32 AG000244 during my time as a postdoctoral scholar in the study of aging with the RAND Corporation. I wish to thank Ronald Lee, Shripad Tuljapurkar, and seminar participants at RAND and the Vienna Institute of Demography for helpful comments.

1 The schedule is based on cross-sectional data and is therefore analogous to a quantity in a period rather than a cohort life table.

2 That major theoretical innovations are attributable to young maverick scientists seems to be especially true in the physical sciences, as pointed out by Lehman (1953) and Levin and Stephan (1991), among others.

3 The argument as to why population growth may spur innovation can proceed in several ways. Increased population density strains the ability of traditional production techniques to sustain the population. Produc-

ers then face heightened incentives to innovate and expand food output, and, if they are successful, their actions break the system out of a Malthusian population trap. Another perspective is that there are fixed costs to conducting innovative activity. With more people among whom to spread those costs, innovation becomes cheaper and is increased. Population density may also simply facilitate more rapid spreading of ideas between individuals.

4 It remains unclear whether mortality declines among French elites and scientists really began later than they did in Britain. The small sample size that Leridon relies on in his examination of the Académie des Sciences may obscure these early trends prior to 1800.

References

Acemoglu, Daron, Simon Johnson, and James Robinson. 2003. "Disease and development in historical perspective," *Journal of the European Economic Association* 1(2–3): 397–405.

———. 2005. "The rise of Europe: Atlantic trade, institutional change, and economic growth," *American Economic Review* 95(3): 546–579.

Alter, George and James C. Riley. 1989. "Frailty, sickness, and death: Models of morbidity and mortality in historical populations," *Population Studies* 43(1): 25–45.

Bloom, David E. and Jeffrey D. Sachs. 1998. "Geography, demography, and economic growth in Africa," *Brookings Papers on Economic Activity* 2: 207–295.

Bongaarts, John. 2004. "Population aging and the rising cost of public pensions," *Population and Development Review* 30(1): 1–23.

Boserup, Ester. 1965. *The Conditions of Agricultural Growth: The Economics of Agrarian Change Under Population Pressure*. New York: Aldine.

———. 1981. *Population and Technological Change: A Study of Long-Term Trends*. Chicago: University of Chicago Press.

Boucekkine, Raouf, David de la Croix, and Omar Licandro. 2003. "Early mortality declines at the dawn of modern growth," *Scandinavian Journal of Economics* 105(3): 401–418.

Cutler, David M., James M. Poterba, Louise M. Sheiner, and Lawrence H. Summers. 1990. "An aging society: Opportunity or challenge?," *Brookings Papers on Economic Activity* 1: 1–56.

Easterlin, Richard A. 1995. "Industrial revolution and mortality revolution: Two of a kind?," *Journal of Evolutionary Economics* 5(4): 393–408.

Fogel, Robert W. 2004. *The Escape from Hunger and Premature Death, 1700–2100*. Cambridge: Cambridge University Press.

Galor, Oded and David N. Weil. 2000. "Population, technology, and growth: From Malthusian stagnation to the demographic transition and beyond," *American Economic Review* 90(4): 806–828.

Gruber, Jonathan and David Wise. 2002. "Social security programs and retirement around the world: Micro estimation," *NBER Working Paper* 9407.

Hall, Marie Boas. 1991. *Promoting Experimental Learning: Experiment and the Royal Society 1660–1727*. Cambridge: Cambridge University Press.

Hall, Robert E. and Charles I. Jones. 1999. "Why do some countries produce so much more output per worker than others?," *Quarterly Journal of Economics* 114(1): 83–116.

Hammel, E. A. 1983. "The productivity of chemists and mathematicians at the University of California: An age/cohort analysis," *U.C. Berkeley Program in Population Research Working Paper* No. 11.

Hollingsworth, T. H. 1964. "The demography of the British peerage: Supplement," *Population Studies* 18(2).

Hunter, Michael. 1982. *The Royal Society and Its Fellows, 1660–1700: The Morphology of an Early Scientific Institution*. Chalfont St. Giles, Bucks, England: British Society for the History of Science.

Johansson, S. Ryan. 1999. "Death and the doctors: Medicine and elite mortality in Britain from 1500 to 1800," *Cambridge Group for the History of Population and Social Structure Working Paper Series* No. 7.

Jones, Benjamin F. 2005. "Age and great invention," *NBER Working Paper* 11359.

Jones, Charles I. 2001. "Was an Industrial Revolution inevitable? Economic growth over the very long run," *Advances in Macroeconomics* 1(2): 1–43.

Kotlikoff, Laurence J. and Scott Burns. 2005. *The Coming Generational Storm: What You Need to Know about America's Economic Future.* Cambridge, MA: MIT Press.

Kremer, Michael. 1993. "Population growth and technological change: One million BC to 1990," *Quarterly Journal of Economics* 108(3): 681–716.

Lee, Ronald. 1988. "Induced population growth and induced technological progress: Their interaction in the accelerating phase," *Mathematical Population Studies* 1(3): 265–288.

Lehman, Harvey C. 1953. *Age and Achievement.* Princeton, NJ: Princeton University Press.

Leridon, Henri. 2004. "The demography of a learned society: The Académie des Sciences (Institut de France), 1666–2030," *Population-E* 59(1): 81–114.

Levin, Sharon G. and Paula E. Stephan. 1991. "Research productivity over the life cycle: Evidence for academic scientists," *American Economic Review* 81(1): 114–132.

Maddison, Angus. 2001. *The World Economy: A Millennial Perspective.* Paris: OECD Development Centre.

McKeown, Thomas. 1976. *The Modern Rise of Population.* New York: Academic Press.

Oeppen, Jim and James W. Vaupel. 2002. "Broken limits to life expectancy," *Science* 296: 1029–1031.

Preston, Samuel H. 1975. "The changing relationship between mortality and level of economic development," *Population Studies* 29(2): 231–248.

Royal Society. 2004. Lists of Royal Society Fellows 1660–2004. Available at http://www.royalsoc.ac.uk.

Schalick, Lisa Miller, Wilbur C. Hadden, Elsie Pamuk, Vincente Navarro, and Gregory Pappas. 2000. "The widening gap in death rates among income groups in the United States from 1967 to 1986," *International Journal of Health Services* 30(1): 13–26.

Skirbekk, Vegard. 2004. "Age and individual productivity: A literature survey," in Gustav Feichtinger (ed.), *Vienna Yearbook of Population Research 2004.* Vienna: Austrian Academy of Sciences Press, pp. 133–153.

Szreter, Simon. 1997. "Economic growth, disruption, deprivation, disease, and death: On the importance of the politics of public health for development," *Population and Development Review* 23(4): 693–728.

Tsoulouhas, Thefanis C. 1992. "A new look at demographic and technological changes: England, 1550 to 1839," *Explorations in Economic History* 29(2): 169–203.

Weinberg, Bruce A. and David W. Galenson. 2005. "Creative careers: The life cycles of Nobel laureates in economics," *NBER Working Paper* 11799.

Wrigley, E. A., R. S. Davies, J. E. Oeppen, and R. S. Schofield. 1997. *English Population History from Family Reconstitution 1580–1837.* Cambridge: Cambridge University Press.

Wrigley, E. A. and R. S. Schofield. 1981. *The Population History of England 1541–1871: A Reconstruction.* Cambridge: Harvard University Press.

Demographic, Economic, and Institutional Factors in the Transition to Modern Growth in England: 1530–1860

Raouf Boucekkine
David de la Croix
Dominique Peeters

Economic growth, understood as an increase in the gross domestic product over a long period of time, is a contemporaneous phenomenon. As clearly explained in Maddison (2001), humanity was caught in a long-lasting trap of economic stagnation until the nineteenth century. This premodern period was accompanied by even more dire demographic conditions: according to Maddison's estimates, the size of the world population remained almost constant in the first millennium CE, and life expectancy at birth was below 50 years until the beginning of the twentieth century.

For European countries, premodern times are traditionally associated with successive mortality crises related to wars, famines, and epidemics. Essays by Platt (1996) on England and Herlihy (1997) on Western Europe have stressed the structural changes induced by the bubonic plague in the late medieval ages. However, since Wrigley and Schofield (1989), the view that a unitary premodern demographic regime preceded the industrial revolution has been seriously undermined, especially in the case of England.[1] Births, marriages, and mortality in England sharply fluctuated in the two centuries before the industrial revolution, and the variations cannot be fully attributed to mortality crises. While mortality decline contributed significantly to population growth in England, its effect was clearly overshadowed until 1820 by rising fertility driven notably by increased nuptiality. Another major conclusion to draw from Wrigley and Schofield's careful empirical work on England is that historical mortality crises show a low correlation with food scarcity and, thus, with the standard of living of the population.

Yet several issues remain unresolved. Even if we agree with the demographic scenario above, the ultimate challenge is to incorporate it into a more global analysis of the transition to modern growth and to identify the economic and demographic mechanisms involved. The demographic determinants have been increasingly emphasized in the development literature (see Lee 1979 and McNicoll 2003). Unified growth theory, a recent stream of economic growth literature, surveyed by Galor (2005), emphasizes the role of demographic change in the transition to the modern economic growth regime. This chapter highlights the role of population density in the economic development of England during the period 1530–1860. Because industrial revolutions rely on innovation and the adoption of new technologies requires a certain density of educated people, population density and literacy are likely to be key variables in the development process. Indeed, the rise in literacy and education in the pre-industrial era may have initiated the process leading to the English industrial revolution. Cipolla (1969) argues that improvements in literacy favored the industrial revolution in more than one way. Literacy increased the ranks of skilled workers in those fields in which such workers were specifically required, and, more generally, it made more people adaptable to new circumstances and receptive to change. In times of rapid technological progress, literate workers assimilate new ideas more readily.

Higher educational achievement might have been triggered by several economic and demographic factors. We distinguish three of them. First, technological progress increased labor productivity and wage rates in the modern sector and thereby increased the return to investment in education. Facing better income prospects in this sector, households would invest in education to benefit from the higher returns. This view is defended, among others, by Hansen and Prescott (2002) and Doepke (2004). Second, improvement in adult longevity is another explanation for the rise in literacy. Although, according to Wrigley and Schofield (1989), mortality decline is not the main engine of population growth in pre-industrial England, increased longevity is potentially an important determinant of literacy: longer lives increase the returns to investment in education, inducing longer schooling, according to the well-known Ben-Porath (1967) mechanism. Recent papers by Boucekkine, de la Croix, and Licandro (2003) and Nicolini (2004) argue that lower mortality induced higher investment in human capital and physical capital at the time of the industrial revolution, paving the way to future growth. Clark (2005a), however, remarks that, if demographic transition and industrial revolution are the two great forces that lead to modern growth, the latter did not lead to fertility decline until over 100 years after its onset. He explores the difficulties in trying to uncover the underlying connection between them.

A third possibility is drawn from various authors who stress that the rising density of population may have played a role in fostering the rise in literacy and education. Higher density can lower the cost of education through facilitating the creation of schools. Fujita and Thisse (2002) provide a textbook treatment of this effect. A representative empirical study by Ladd (1992) shows that a small increase in density lowers the costs of providing services, at least at very low levels of population density. Externalities can also be generated by denser population. For Kremer (1993), high population density spurs technological change. Galor and Weil (2000) and Lagerloef (2003) argue for "population-induced" technological progress. Population needs to reach a threshold for productivity to accelerate.

In this chapter we propose a new framework to disentangle the effects of three factors on literacy and economic growth in England: technological progress, mortality decline, and population density. We look at the linkages between literacy, school establishment, and income growth and evaluate the role of each. In our model, the length of schooling is chosen by individuals who maximize lifetime income, which depends on future wages, longevity, and the distance to the nearest school. Then, the number and location of educational facilities is determined, either chosen by the optimizing state or following a free entry process (market solution). Higher population density makes it optimal to increase school density, opening the possibility to attain higher educational levels.

In our model, two sectors coexist: a traditional sector with constant productivity, and a modern sector with exogenously rising productivity. The remuneration of workers in the modern sector depends on their human capital level. Therefore the transition to this modern sector depends on both technological evolution and education. A denser population induces a higher educational level, which promotes the transition to the modern sector.

Wrigley (1988) provides a more elaborate narrative of the industrial revolution. A traditional sector, called "organic economy," based on agricultural goods, eventually evolves into a more productive sector, an "advanced organic economy," thanks to animal power. Such a regime is not sustainable, however, because of a fixed land supply and decreasing marginal returns. England's good fortune, argued Wrigley, was to have abundant coal resources, which made possible the transition to a "mineral-based economy," in which industries (producing iron, pottery, or glass) could be operated without significant pressure on land, permitting an escape from decreasing returns. The mineral-based economy opened the door to a series of innovations (notably in energy and power production) that elevated productivity and real wages far above the levels allowed by the agricultural economy. Wrigley provides empirical support to his story, especially based on investment data over the period studied.

Our modeling of the traditional and modern sectors is much more stylized than Wrigley's description. It captures, however, a central message in the latter: the transition to a modern economy represents primarily an escape from decreasing returns. While in Wrigley this transition is made possible by the much broader set of technological opportunities allowed by the mineral-based economy, in our model it is additionally favored by human capital accumulation, itself boosted by increasing population density.

The next section sets forth the demographic, economic, geographic, and institutional structures of our theoretical model. The third section describes the data and the experimental methodology we use to disentangle the effects of the three aforementioned factors—technological progress, mortality decline, and population density—on literacy and growth. The fourth section displays the findings, and the final section offers concluding comments.

Theory

To assess the development mechanisms just outlined, we first build a theoretical model with the relevant demographic, economic, institutional, and geographic ingredients. The mathematical details, including rigorous proofs of the claims in this section, can be found in Boucekkine, de la Croix, and Peeters (2007).

The demographic structure

We consider an economy populated by overlapping birth cohorts. Individuals belonging to cohort t, that is individuals born at date t, have an uncertain life span: their probability of reaching age a is given by the survival function:

$$m_t(a) = \frac{e^{\beta_t a} - \alpha_t}{1 - \alpha_t}$$

where α_t and β_t are two numbers (for fixed t). This survival function was introduced by Boucekkine, de la Croix, and Licandro (2002). If α_t and β_t satisfy $\alpha_t > 1$ and $\beta_t > 0$, then the survival function is concave, that is, the probability of death increases with age and there is a maximum age A_t that an individual can reach. This parameter configuration allows the function $m_t(a)$ to accurately represent the empirical adult survival laws and has the advantage of being analytically tractable. The maximum age is obtained by solving $m_t(A_t)=0$ and is equal to

$$A_t = \frac{\log(\alpha_t)}{\beta_t}.$$

Note that a higher longevity of individuals belonging to cohort t corresponds to larger α_t and/or lower β_t. Finally, for the sake of simplicity, we do not explicitly model fertility and instead assume the initial size of each cohort to be given exogenously. If that size, for the cohort born at t, is ζ_t, then its size at any subsequent time $z \in [t, t+A_t]$ is given by $\zeta_t m_t(z-t)$, reflecting attrition through time. The demographic processes α_t, β_t, and ζ_t for varying t, are estimated using English data for the period 1530–1860.

The economic structure

To account for the role of technological advances in the transition to modern growth, we postulate two distinct production sectors in the economy, a traditional and a modern sector. The latter is subject to technological progress, inducing rising productivity over time (at a positive rate, say, γ_t at time t), while the former has a constant productivity level. If workers are paid at their productivity level, as we postulate in our model, then the modern sector will become more attractive over time, eventually yielding a full transition to the modern sector. This way of modeling the transition follows Hansen and Prescott (2002).

Such a sharp transition is not realistic, however; the process is much more gradual and much less mechanistic than outlined above. To generate a more realistic picture, we need to account for human capital formation. Historically, human capital accumulation and its associated literacy improvements have taken place gradually, and this pace is likely to be crucial in determining the actual shape of the transition to modern growth. To incorporate this feature, we model both the supply and demand sides of human capital. The supply side, developed in the next section, builds on the idea that school creation depends on attendance rates, which in turn are determined by population density.

The demand side mechanism originates in a further difference between the two production sectors. Individuals working in the traditional sector have a productivity level, and thus a remuneration level, that are independent of their level of human capital. In contrast, the remuneration of workers in the modern sector is not only determined by their (exogenously) rising productivity, it is also determined by their level of human capital. Thus, there is a complementarity between human capital and technological progress in the development process: for technological innovations to be exploited to their full potential, skilled workers are imperative.[2] In particular, we take the view that technological progress and human capital interact in a multiplicative way, so that the remuneration of a given worker at time t is the product of his or her human capital and technological progress at t. This is consistent with a modern-sector technology producing an output Y_t from the multiplicative interaction of the level of technology or productivity, say $\exp\{\gamma_t t\}$, and the stock of human capital available in the economy, say H_t:

$$Y_t = \exp(\zeta_t t) H_t.$$

This makes the development process much more complex, since human capital formation is costly. We assume that going to school involves a transportation cost, which is proportional to the distance to the nearest school, and the payment of tuition fees. From the English Schools Inquiry Commission (1868a)[3] we learn that boys could attend a city school from distances up to

20 miles, and with travel times of more than one hour in the morning and in the evening (on foot, ponies, or donkeys). Concerning tuition fees, we know from historical surveys (see again the Schools Inquiry Commission) that schools were funded through income from an endowment and through fees paid by the students' parents. Fees were imposed in order to supplement the endowment, and parents were willing to pay fees, provided they were not excessive and the education provided was of acceptable quality.

Within such a framework, an individual may not find it optimal to go to school. The cost incurred during schooling time can only be paid back (via wages from the modern sector) after this time. There is no guarantee that lifetime earnings allowed by schooling net of school costs are superior to the lifetime revenue that could be directly extracted from the traditional sector. An individual in our framework might choose not go to school for many reasons. The reasons could be demographic. Where life expectancy is markedly low for cohort t (which corresponds to a low parameter α_t and/or a high parameter β_t in the model), the returns to schooling are likely to be discouraging, given the expected very short remuneration period. The reasons could be technological. The expected pace of technological progress, denoted by γ_t in our model, might be too slow, which would also induce low returns to schooling. Finally, institutional reasons related to the organization and location of schools might yield the same outcome: the absence of schools in the neighborhood and/or prohibitively high tuition fees are very strong barriers to schooling.

As a consequence, the decision to attend school and the resulting schooling time depend on demographic, technological, geographic, and institutional conditions. These conditions change over time, and schooling decisions are therefore likely to vary from one cohort to another. Moreover, there is no reason to believe that all individuals in a cohort will make the same schooling decisions. To allow for within-cohort variation, we postulate that individuals in the same cohort may differ in their location and in their innate abilities. For simplicity, however, a given individual stays at his or her location permanently. In the pre-industrial era, the main reason for households to move was to reach regions with better employment opportunities or higher wages. In our theoretical model, the same technologies are available everywhere, hence the main migration engine is shut down. We postulate that innate abilities are distributed according to a unimodal distribution. We use the log-normal distribution in our experimental studies.

This completes the demand side of human capital. Within the same cohort, other things equal, only the most gifted and those located closest to schools will attend school. In other words, there exists a threshold value for innate ability, such that individuals with an ability above (or below) the threshold will go to school (or remain uneducated). Naturally, this threshold value of ability increases when tuition fees, the distance to the nearest school, or the alternative remuneration in the traditional sector goes up. The threshold ability value is also sensitive to demographic and technological conditions: a higher life expectancy or faster technological progress should lower the threshold. For individuals above the threshold, the duration of schooling time can be longer or shorter depending on the same technological, demographic, and institutional conditions, for the same plausible reasons. Longer life expectancy, faster technological progress, or closer schools induce a longer duration of schooling and therefore a higher human capital level. And of course, other things equal, more-gifted individuals go to school for a longer time.

We now turn to the supply side of human capital, the school creation part of our theory.

The geographic and institutional structure

Location theory is a field of research that draws on economic geography and operations research. Its purpose is to model, formulate, and solve problems of siting facilities in order to supply goods and services to a spatially dispersed population. The recent survey by ReVelle and Eiselt (2005) gives a bird's-eye view of the topic and its abundant literature, while the reader can refer to Daskin (1995), among others, for a more in-depth presentation. One of the core models of location theory is the Simple Plant Location Problem (in short SPLP), which can be formulated as follows. Assume a geographically dispersed population with known demands for a certain commodity that is made available at facilities to be created. Opening a facility involves incurring a fixed cost, while distributing the commodity entails transportation costs. The problem is to determine the number, locations, and respective market areas of the facilities in order to minimize total cost, defined as the sum of the transportation costs to the clients and the fixed opening costs. The SPLP captures one of the essential features of economic geography: the tradeoff between transportation costs and economies of scale. The former favor the multiplication of facilities; the latter, expressed by the fixed costs, tend to restrict their number.

In this section, we use an extension of the SPLP to build a theory connecting the creation of schools to population density. We choose a simple geographical setting: a circle of unit circumference. We assume that, at every point of time, the cohort of the newborn generation is uniformly spread along the circle and has the same distribution of abilities at every location. Clearly, such a representation is inconsistent with actual population patterns, since there are strong disparities in density between urban and rural areas, between cities of different sizes, and even within cities. Nonetheless, we argue this is a minor point in our setting: rural population accounted for more than 80 percent of England's total population by the end of the period we consider. We suppose that every point on the circle can accommodate a school and that schools are identical in their characteristics (same services, same quality, same reputation, etc.). It follows that a pupil will attend the closest school. Moreover, the results of the preceding section allow us to determine the demand for schooling arising from each point on the circle as a function of the distance to the nearest school. Given the hypothesis on the dispersion of the population, it is obvious that schools will be optimally located if they are evenly spaced. Hence, for a given number of facilities, we can determine the literacy rate of the population, the total amount of fees paid by the pupils, and the total transportation costs. Accordingly, the school location problem is reduced to the single question: how many schools (or classrooms) will be founded at every date t to educate the newborn cohort?[4] But this entails the formulation of an objective function.

To model the school creation process, one must examine the relevant institutional arrangements at work in the period considered. And in particular, one needs to clarify the objectives pursued by school founders at that time. According to the Schools Inquiry Commission (1868a), the picture is far from uniform. Three types of schools can be distinguished: endowed schools, private schools, and proprietary schools.

Endowed schools usually have some income from funds permanently appropriated to the school. Even in this category, schools vary widely in character and history. Some are part of large charitable foundations, others are run by the Church. Private schools are typically the property of their (head) teacher. They "owe their origin to the operation of the ordinary commercial principle of supply and demand," according to the Schools Inquiry Commission (1868a). They provide more individual care and teaching, but the Schools Inquiry Commission finds much fault in the quality of these schools. Commissioners noted that "A really large and flourishing school is of course a marketable commodity, and sometimes sells well. But it is always a dangerous purchase for a stranger. ... when the school declines the house is let for a shop or a private residence, and the master betakes himself elsewhere." And also "Considered commercially, few descriptions of business seem to require less capital than the keeping of a private day school of the second order. A house is taken, a cane and a map of England bought, an advertisement inserted, and the master has nothing more to do but teach. It is not likely that schools established at so slight a cost should have buildings well adapted to purposes of education." These two quotes stress the commercial nature of private schools. The third type of school is the proprietary school. It too is private property: it belongs to a body of shareholders. This type of school is more recent, dating from the 1820s.

Because we have no information on the composition of English schools by type, we posit two different forms of institutional arrangement. In the first, denoted CP for central planning, the optimal number of classrooms is determined by a central authority every year, by maximization of aggregate profits of the education sector, reflecting that "the purpose of schools was never to save those from paying who could afford to pay," as noted by the Schools Inquiry Commission (1868a). The return yielded from building a school in a given area is roughly the difference between the tuition fees paid by the individuals in the catchment area of the school who decide to educate themselves or their children, and the cost of building and/or operating a classroom.[5] The link between school creation and population density is therefore clear. Since the profitability of a school mainly depends upon tuition revenues, the size of the population in the catchment area of the school should be a major determinant of school creation.

Our second institutional arrangement is market-based, denoted MA, in which we assume that the density of schools results from a free entry process: schools are created as long as they earn a net profit. This models the functioning of private schools described above. It can readily be shown that MA is equivalent to a model where a central authority maximizes aggregate attendance (for example, for religious reasons). In that case, it would create as many schools as possible, subject to a non-negative profit condition.

Population size is a major determinant of school creation because the main source of a school's revenues, tuition fees, depends on this demographic variable. This is true for both institutional arrangements CP and MA. No school is viable below a certain threshold of population size (or of cohort size, ζ_t, in our model). When the newborn population is low, the school creation or set-up costs are unlikely to be covered, hence no schools are created. Once the population reaches a threshold value, many schools may be created at once. The process by which illiteracy is eliminated is thus initiated by a jump. After this initial jump, the process takes place much more smoothly over time depending on the evolution of population density and of the attendance rate at schools of the successive cohorts, which in turn depends on the demographic, technological, and geographic factors outlined above.

We now apply our theory to England over the years 1530–1860 in order to disentangle the salient characteristics and determinants of the English development process.

Data and methodology

We first describe our sources with some key descriptive statistics over the period of interest. Then, we give an overview of the chosen experimental setting and an outline of how the data have been brought into the theoretical framework detailed in the previous section (the so-called calibration step).

The data

Literacy. Figure 1 shows the evolution over time of literacy rates (average of men and women) for England as estimated by Cressy (1980). It suggests that

FIGURE 1 Literacy levels for men and women combined: England, 1530–1860 (percent of adult population)

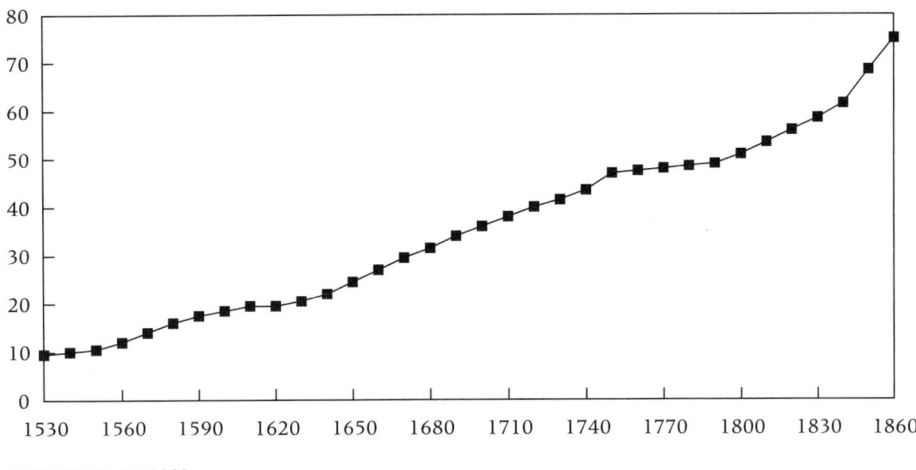

SOURCE: Cressy 1980.

improvements in literacy started as early as the sixteenth century. The steady rise from 1580 to 1760 is notable.

Technological progress. Technological progress, captured in our model by the productivity growth rate γ_t, increases the attractiveness of the modern sector and should therefore stimulate schooling. We derive the data on productivity growth from Clark (2001). As illustrated by Figure 2, productivity gains in England started to accelerate in the beginning of the nineteenth century. Consequently, the technological factor cannot account for the higher literacy rates achieved two centuries before any significant gain in productivity. The search for alternative demographic and institutional explanatory factors continues.

Demography. The demographic trends in England over the period considered are taken from the detailed historical studies of Wrigley and Schofield (1989) and Wrigley et al. (1997). We need detailed demographic information to identify the time series of parameters α_t and β_t of the survival function postulated earlier and to estimate the size of the successive birth cohorts, ζ_t. These time series are crucial in determining the schooling decisions taken by the individuals in our theoretical set-up.

Survival rates and changes in population size can be extracted from the studies cited above. Figure 3 presents the survival rate to age 40 among individuals surviving to age 5 years. It ignores infant mortality swings in order to concentrate on mortality during the active years of life. Adult longevity was first stagnant and then declined over the period 1600–1700, probably because of the urban penalty associated with the rapid growth of cities.

FIGURE 2 Total factor productivity: England, 1530–1860 (index, 1860 =100)

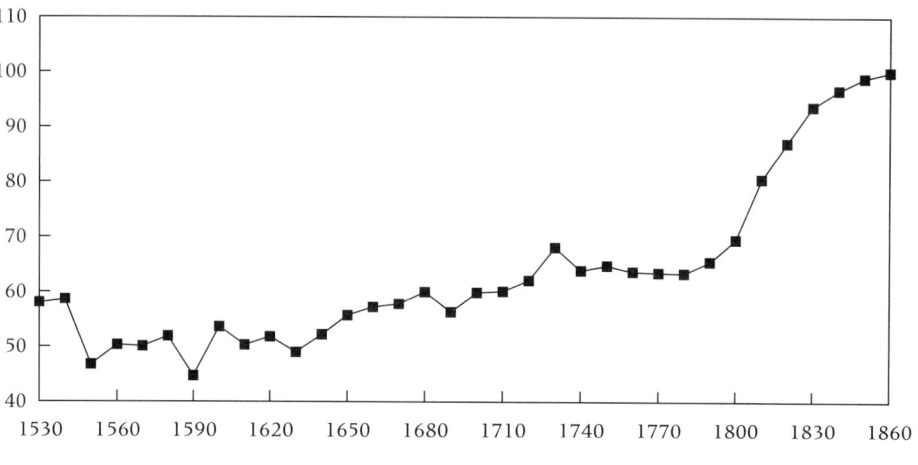

SOURCE: Clark 2001.

During this period of high mortality, literacy rose continuously, as seen in Figure 1.

We consider the population aged 5 years and older, because it coincides with the concept of population in our model. Figure 4 shows that population rose rapidly in the sixteenth and nineteenth centuries, while the seventeenth century was a period of demographic stagnation. The corresponding swings in crude birth rates are plotted in Figure 5. Rises in population size in the sixteenth century, together with high (but declining) birth rates, correspond to the first wave of improvement in literacy.

FIGURE 3 Survival beyond early childhood: Number of survivors at age 40 per 1,000 individuals at age 5: England, 1530–1860

SOURCE: Wrigley et al. 1997.

FIGURE 4 Population aged 5 and older: England, 1530–1860

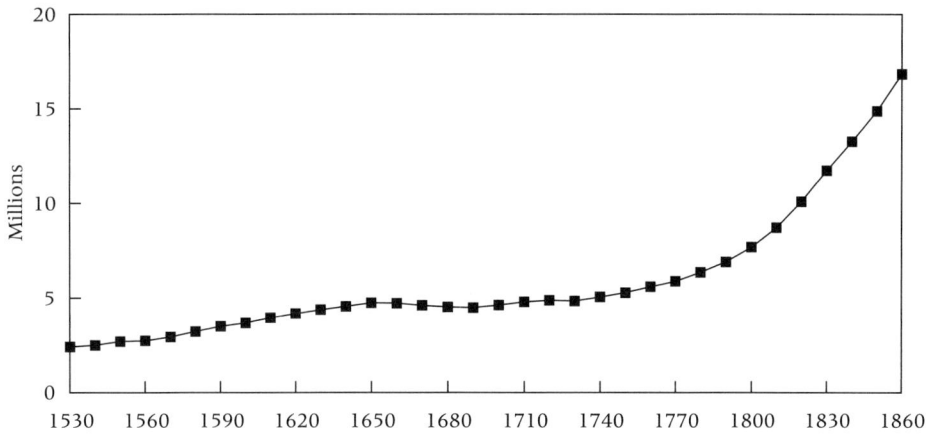

SOURCE: Wrigley et al. 1997.

School creation. We collected data on school creation from the appendix to the reports of the Schools Inquiry Commission (1868b). Two lists of schools are provided, together with their dates of establishment. The "endowed grammar schools" taught a mixture of Latin and practical skills to sons of the middle class and the lesser elite (list in the Schools Inquiry Commission). The "endowed non-classical schools" were products of the Charity School Movement, offering Protestant socialization and basic skills to the worthy poor. According to Cressy (1980), although short-lived private schools are omitted from the list, a check against other sources proves the Commission's work to

FIGURE 5 Crude birth rate: England, 1530–1860 (per 1,000 population)

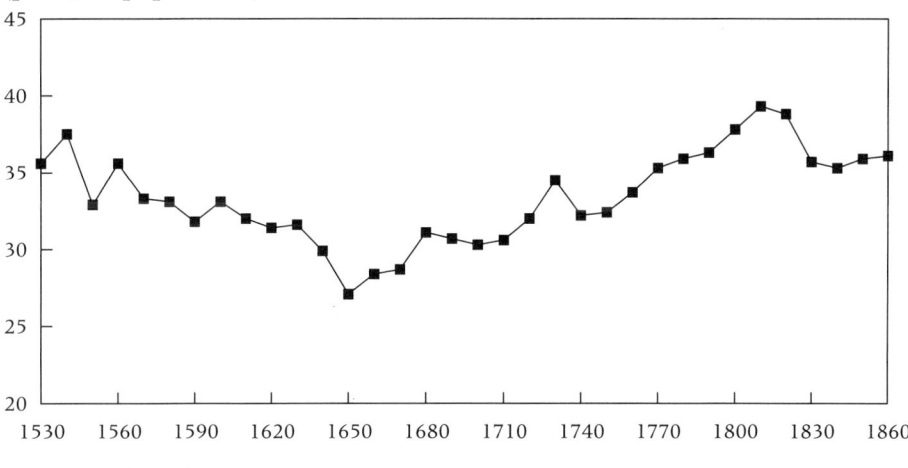

SOURCE: Wrigley et al. 1997.

TABLE 1 School creation by decade

	Endowed grammar schools	Endowed non-classical schools		Endowed grammar schools	Endowed non-classical schools
1100–1499	23	2	1680–89	31	75
1500–09	9	2	1690–99	25	81
1510–19	8	2	1700–09	23	188
1520–29	13	0	1710–19	24	287
1530–39	8	0	1720–29	23	279
1540–49	36	0	1730–39	12	152
1550–59	47	10	1740–49	9	91
1560–69	44	7	1750–59	4	93
1570–79	31	2	1760–69	3	128
1580–89	19	14	1770–79	7	84
1590–99	26	13	1780–89	8	99
1600–09	41	18	1790–99	6	106
1610–19	42	27	1800–09	3	87
1620–29	27	33	1810–19	1	125
1630–39	31	38	1820–29	3	64
1640–49	15	33	1830–39	4	36
1650–59	42	45	1840–49	6	9
1660–69	34	58	1850–59	9	4
1670–79	38	67			

SOURCE: Schools Inquiry Commission 1868b.

be reliable. We use these lists to compute the number of schools created per decade. These data are presented in Table 1.

Methodology

To assess the relative importance of the demographic, technological, and institutional factors in the English transition to modern growth, we take the following steps.

Step 1, calibration of a benchmark model. We first enter the data into our theoretical model. To this end, we need to specify the institutional arrangements in the education sector. We start with scenario CP, with a central authority determining the optimal number of classrooms as well as the level of the tuition fee so as to maximize profits. This is our benchmark case. We will study in further steps how the results are altered if we switch to maximizing aggregate attendance. Calibration of the benchmark model requires estimation of the three demographic processes, α_t, β_t, ζ_t, and the process of productivity growth, γ_t. It also requires setting the values of some parameters for which we lack accurate information, including productivity in the traditional sector, transport costs, and the discount factor. An extensive analysis of robustness will be conducted later on these parameters.

Step 2, counterfactual experiments. Of the four exogenous processes in our economy, α_t, β_t, ζ_t, and γ_t, the first two represent mortality factors, the third is a measure of cohort size (determined mainly by fertility net of infant mortality), and the fourth is a measure of technological progress. To evaluate the importance of each of these factors in accounting for literacy and economic growth, we run counterfactual experiments: for example, if we seek to evaluate the extent to which technological progress can explain the observed historical evolution of literacy and growth, we let this factor play in isolation, which amounts to solving our calibrated model with constant α_t, β_t, and ζ_t, and with the estimated technological progress, γ_t, as the unique active force. Repeating the same exercise for each factor permits an assessment of the relative importance of each in explaining the observed transition to modern growth.

Step 3, robustness analysis. The results obtained from the counterfactual experiments are conditional upon the calibrated model. A minimal requirement to test the scientific validity of the results is to conduct extensive robustness analysis, which in our case means not only performing a sensitivity analysis with respect to the values of some parameters but also checking how the results are altered if we move to the alternative institutional arrangement (MA), maximizing aggregate attendance.

Before presenting our main findings from the counterfactual experiments and robustness analysis, we describe the calibration procedure of the benchmark model.

Calibration

The four exogenous processes, α_t, β_t, ζ_t, and γ_t, should be made explicit. We assume that all four processes follow a polynomial function of time. Polynomials of order 3 are sufficient to capture the main trends in the data.

For the survival function processes, α_t and β_t, the parameters of the polynomial are chosen by minimizing the deviation from the survival functions estimated by Wrigley et al. (1997). These survival functions apply to ages 5–85 years, and accordingly have been normalized to 1 at age 5 (hence excluding the effect of early child mortality). The parameters of the process for ζ_t are chosen so as to minimize the difference between the total population implied by our model and the observed level of population aged 5 and older. Finally, the parameter of exogenous technological progress γ_t is set to follow the estimated level of total factor productivity in Figure 2.

In a second step, we select a log-normal distribution for abilities, say the function $g(\mu)$ where μ stands for ability, which is commonly used to approximate the actual distribution of innate characteristics. We next choose jointly four parameters in order to satisfy four conditions on endogenous variables, implied by the data. Since we have little information to calibrate these parameters, we choose values that give a reasonable benchmark scenario. The four parameters are: the variance of $g(\mu)$; the transportation cost (in this benchmark calibration, we assume that the transportation cost is indexed on technological progress); the set-up cost; and the productivity or remuneration in the traditional sector. The four conditions are: ten schools in 1820 (there are 3,000 schools in our database in 1820, so the scale of the model is 1/25); the level of literacy in 1820 (55 percent); the change in literacy over the period 1540–1820; and a skill premium of 60 percent on average over the period for seven years of education (according to van Zanden 2004 this was the premium received by skilled craftsmen after seven years of apprenticeship).

Findings

We first summarize the properties of the benchmark model and then present the results of the counterfactual experiments and sensitivity exercises.

Benchmark simulation

The two first bars in Figure 6 report measured ("own estimation") and simulated ("baseline") school density. Each bar represents the change since 1530. The baseline change in the density of schools results from the decision process of the central school authority in the institutional arrangement CP, or central planning. Both the measured and the simulated density of schools increase monotonically. The simulation underestimates school creation in the eighteenth century and overestimates it in the nineteenth century but manages to capture well the overall trend. The literacy rate, presented in Figure 7, follows closely the creation of schools. Estimated literacy rises steadily over the period, while for the baseline simulation there is an initial increase prior to 1600, reflecting the creation of the first schools; this is followed by a period of slower growth and, after 1700, by a second period of rapid growth.

The density of schools and the level of literacy are fully consistent with the estimated data. A precise mapping is not obtained, but this is unsurprising in that literacy data cover the ability to sign a marriage register, not school attendance. Notice also the role of expectations: the sharp acceleration at the end of the period is related to the anticipation by households of strong productivity gains in the modern sector in the nineteenth century.

Figure 8 displays gross domestic product per capita. The height of the bar is proportional to the change in GDP per capita since 1530. Recall that output in the modern sector is postulated to be the product of the level of technology (or productivity) and aggregate human capital. The former in-

FIGURE 6 Cumulative changes in school density since 1530: Baseline and counterfactuals isolating the roles of mortality, cohort size, and productivity in turn

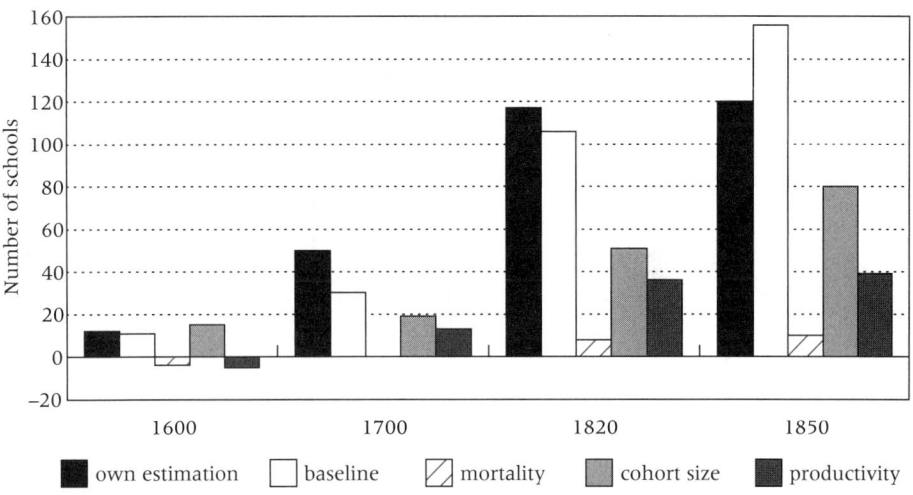

SOURCE: Simulation of our model.

put can be immediately extracted from the already-estimated productivity growth process γ_t. The latter input corresponds to the total stock of human capital of all generations that are currently at work in the modern sector: this implies an exact accounting of all individuals in all co-existing cohorts who

FIGURE 7 Cumulative changes in literacy rate since 1530: Baseline and counterfactuals isolating the roles of mortality, cohort size, and productivity in turn

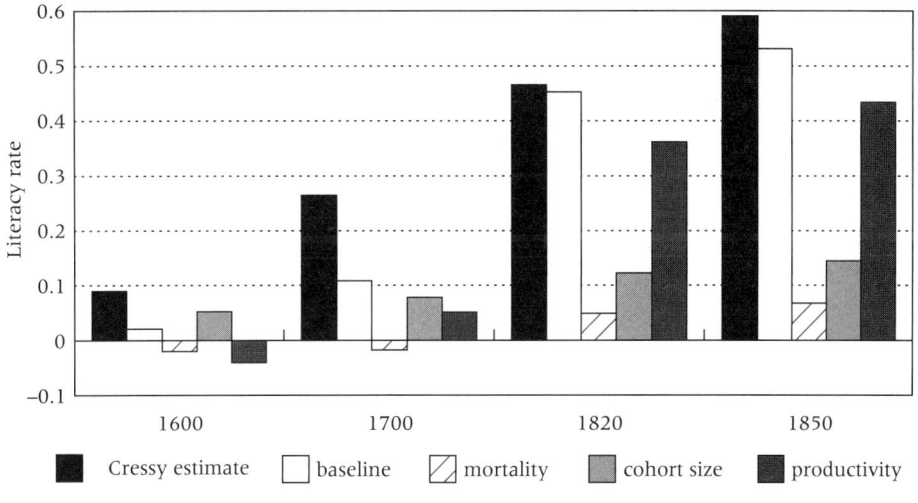

SOURCE: Simulation of our model.

FIGURE 8 Cumulative change in GDP per capita since 1530: Baseline and counterfactuals isolating the roles of mortality, cohort size, and productivity in turn

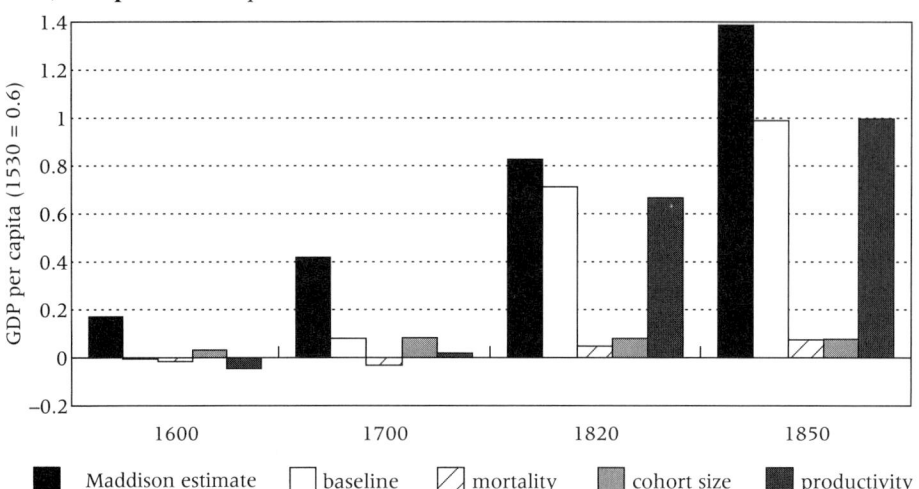

SOURCE: Simulation of our model.

attend school. Finally we can compute total GDP as the sum of production in the traditional and modern sectors minus the transportation cost minus the set-up cost of schools. According to the baseline there is a period of no growth after 1530, because the economy has to pay the transportation costs of students and the set-up cost of schools but does not yet benefit from better-educated workers. The seventeenth century is characterized by very low growth—too low compared to Maddison's data. After this stagnation period, growth starts accelerating after 1700 to reach 0.7 percent per annum at the end of the eighteenth century.

Our GDP numbers should be interpreted as the income generated by the accumulation of human capital and by productivity growth, without any effect from the accumulation of physical capital. The difference between Maddison's estimate and the baseline simulation can be attributed to physical capital accumulation, which is absent from our model.

Counterfactual experiments

In a first experiment we hold cohort size and technological progress constant over the period; this allows us to isolate the role of mortality. Since mortality declines very late in England (see comparable data on Geneva and Venice in Boucekkine, de la Croix, and Licandro 2003), it does not exert a positive influence before the eighteenth century. The bar "mortality" in the figures represents the hypothetical change in school density, literacy, and GDP per capita if mortality was the only factor in play. If mortality improvements were the only driving force of the industrial revolution, no school would have been created before 1700 and the literacy rate would have increased by only 6.8 percent by 1850. Compared to the baseline simulation, mortality improvements explain 6.5 percent of total school creations over the period 1530–1850, 12.8 percent of improvements in literacy, and 7.5 percent of growth of income per capita.

Next we run a simulation holding both mortality and technological progress constant. Only cohort size ζ_t varies, reflecting all changes in population that are not due to mortality. In this simulation we observe that the rise in population can explain both school creation in the sixteenth century and the early rise in literacy. In the seventeenth century, however, population stagnates and school creation stops. In the end, the rise in cohort size explains a majority of school creations over the period 1500–1850, 27.5 percent of improvements in literacy, and 7.8 percent of income growth per capita.

In a third simulation both mortality and cohort size are held constant, and only technological progress is variable. In this simulation we observe that technological progress cannot explain the timing of school creation and literacy improvements, but it explains a major part of the changes at the end of the period.

These results display a neat picture of the English transition to modern economic growth. First, the counterfactual analysis highlights the fact that neither increases in productivity nor mortality decline can explain the establishment of schools in the sixteenth century at the high rate documented in Table 1. Only the rise in cohort size can account for it. Second, technological progress is the predominant engine of the growth rate of GDP, while increases in longevity play a small role. These results need to be corroborated by sensitivity tests, which we conduct next.

Robustness analysis

We provide a robustness analysis of changes in some of our key hypotheses. For each experiment, we recalibrate the parameters such that the model matches the four conditions on endogenous variables described earlier.

In the benchmark calibration, transportation costs are indexed on technological progress. This assumption is probably too pessimistic because transportation costs no doubt declined relative to other costs in the eighteenth century.[6] To evaluate the importance of this assumption, we ran a simulation in which the transportation cost was not indexed on productivity; as a consequence, the relative importance of this cost diminished in the eighteenth century and the rise in literacy became more important. We recalibrated the model under this assumption. The new baseline with non-indexed transportation costs yields very similar results, showing that the previous analysis remains valid whether or not transportation costs are indexed on productivity.

Another assumption we test concerns the growth of productivity after 1860. In the baseline, we assumed that households anticipate correctly the growth of future productivity (1 percent per year). This creates an incentive to accumulate more human capital. To assess the importance of this mechanism, we ran a simulation where households suppose that productivity will stay at a constant level beyond 1860 (i.e., they consider that the industrial revolution is a temporary phenomenon). This change in assumption does not require any modification in the calibration. Results show that the effect of lower expectations is quite small.

In another robustness test, we set a lower value of the risk-free interest rate, assuming a rate of 3 percent per year instead of 5 percent. The other parameters need to be adjusted. A lower interest rate gives an incentive for households to invest in more education, so we need higher transportation costs to match the observed education investment. The number of schools is very close to the baseline, while literacy increases faster in the beginning of the period. Using 3 percent as an interest rate would bring our simulated literacy closer to the estimate by Cressy for the beginning of the period.

The robustness analysis indicates that the results on literacy and economic growth are little affected by changes in the parameters. This conclusion, however, does not extend to the parameter measuring productivity in the traditional sector, w^h. If for example we index w^h on productivity in the modern sector, A_t, there is no way to choose the parameters so as to fulfill our four conditions relating endogenous variables to data, and in particular the rise in literacy over the period. In fact, the non-indexation of w^h is the main mechanism through which technological progress plays a role in the model. If we shut down this channel by indexing w^h, we reduce drastically the role of technological progress, and we are left with the two other factors, mortality and cohort size, which together explain about 40 percent of the observed rise in literacy.

We also investigate the robustness of the results to the assumption about the institutional arrangement. We ran simulations for the MA arrangement in which schools are created in a decentralized way as long as profit opportunities exist. Comparing CP to MA, we reach two conclusions. First, the timing of the take-off for school creation does not vary across models; in both cases it starts as early as 1540. Second, the density of schools increases much faster with the market solution than with a central authority. This very rapid rise entails important fixed costs for the economy, slowing down growth compared to the central authority case. The model with the market solution therefore does not perform as well as the model with a central authority in reproducing the acceleration in growth during the early nineteenth century because the former would imply the creation of too many schools.

Finally, one issue that is potentially important but very complex involves the modeling of spatial structure. In our formulation, space is modeled as a circle, with schools spread evenly along its circumference. This is a one-dimensional model of location. In real life, of course, the English countryside is two dimensional. To see whether the predictions of the one-dimensional space can be transposed to a more realistic set-up, let us consider the infinite plane. There are basically two ways of covering the plane with regular shapes of the same size: squares and hexagons. It is well known from the literature on central place theory (see, e.g., Beckmann 1968) that the latter is more efficient than the former, hence we will consider an infinite covering of the plane with hexagons of the same size. The relevant descriptor for our problem is the density of centers, that is, the number of centers in a unit area. An equivalent descriptor is the edge length of the hexagon. Consider the simple case where all children have to attend school and there is free entry for school creation. Then it can be shown that the density of schools is a linear function of the density of population, exactly as it is in the one-dimensional case. The relationship between the number of schools and population density is linear whatever the dimensionality of the space.

This result prompts two additional comments. First, in the one-dimensional world, the average travel distance is linearly related to the number of schools, implying that the average travel distance falls in proportion to the inverse of population density. However, in the two-dimensional world, the average travel time is proportional to the reciprocal of the square root of population density. Whether this affects our estimation of the importance of changing population density in explaining rising schooling is an open question. Recent papers in the optimal location literature (see, e.g., Morgan and Bolton 2002) have provided estimates in some special cases. Using their results in a simple example, we find that if the number of schools in the two-dimensional world doubles, then the average distance decreases by a factor of 0.267, while, in the one-dimensional world, doubling the number of schools decreases the average distance by a factor of 0.25. Hence, the difference between 1/density and 1/(square root of density) is compensated by a scaling factor that makes the difference between the two worlds acceptable. In the more complex model, the discrepancy will depend, among other things, on whether tuition fees are set lower to attract students from more distant places in the two-dimensional space.

Second, while space is generically two dimensional, most of human activities at any time have been organized along certain principal routes. Our circular representation of space could well fit such an organization, and that is precisely why it is so frequently adopted in economic geography.

Conclusion

In this chapter, we developed a theoretical model with the main demographic, economic, and institutional factors traditionally considered to be crucial in the transition to modern economic growth. We provided a formal link between population density and the provision of schools, that is, given economies of scale, higher density allows one to reduce the cost of education per capita and to increase the level of human capital. This is in agreement with the literature on agglomeration economies (see, e.g., Duranton and Puga 2004 and Henderson 2005).

We applied our theory to England over the period 1530–1860. Using a calibrated version of our model, we measured the impact of mortality, cohort size, and technological progress on school density, literacy, and economic growth through a set of counterfactual experiments. We found that one-third of the rise in literacy over the period 1530–1850 can be directly related to the effect of cohort size, while one-sixth is linked to higher longevity, and one-half to exogenous total factor productivity growth.

Some concluding remarks are in order. First, one has to mention the reduced role of mortality decline relative to other factors in explaining England's development over the period studied. This is at odds with studies on other countries (see, e.g., Boucekkine, de la Croix, and Licandro 2003) but is not so surprising if we have in mind Wrigley and Schofield's study described in the introduction. Because we rely on this study to calibrate the demographic components of the model, it is a fortunate outcome of our simulations that mortality declines do not play the major role. Second, while the model used is properly calibrated to capture the main observed demographic and technological characteristics of the English transition, it is built on several simplifying assumptions that can, we hope, be relaxed in future work to bring the model closer to reality. Including physical capital accumulation and human capital externalities should be the next steps. Working with a two-dimensional representation of space and determining whether it really matters compared to the one-dimensional space used here would also be a desirable extension.

Notes

Boucekkine and de la Croix acknowledge financial support from the Belgian French-speaking community (Grant ARC 03/08–235 "New macroeconomic approaches to the development problem") and the Belgian Federal Government (Grant PAI P5/21, "Equilibrium theory and optimization for public policy and industry regulation").

We thank T. Lindh and B. Malmberg for their comments on an earlier draft and D. Cressy for providing useful information on English schools prior to the industrial revolution.

1 England is not an exception, though: Ireland and Holland, for example, share some historical demographic trends with England, notably the preeminent role of fertility compared to mortality in the acceleration of population growth in the mid-eighteenth century. Sweden and France exhibit a completely different picture.

2 Note that we are invoking this complementarity argument at the implementation stage of innovations; it is even more obvious if one has in mind the prior research and development stage giving rise to innovations.

3 The Schools Inquiry Commission of 1867–68, appointed by the British Parliament, was in charge of a survey on the state of education. The appendix to the 24-volume report

contains a list of endowed schools in England and Wales with their formation dates ranging from the twelfth century to 1860.

4 Here we take the view that classrooms are specific to cohorts. In particular, they are assumed to be closed when the last person of cohort t graduates.

5 This set-up and operating cost can be seen as being net of the possible endowment.

6 Culp and Smith (1989) mention that in *The Wealth of Nations*, Adam Smith reviewed eighteenth-century public attitudes toward two new forms of wealth creation: "forestalling" and "engrossing." Both activities had become possible only as transportation costs dropped.

References

Beckmann, Martin. 1968. *Location Theory*. Random House.
Ben-Porath, Yoram. 1967. "The production of human capital and the life-cycle of earnings," *Journal of Political Economy* 75(4): 352–365.
Boucekkine, Raouf, David de la Croix, and Omar Licandro. 2002. "Vintage human capital, demographic trends and endogenous growth," *Journal of Economic Theory* 104: 340–375.
———. 2003. "Early mortality declines at the dawn of modern growth," *Scandinavian Journal of Economics* 105(3): 401–418.
Boucekkine, Raouf, David de la Croix, and Dominique Peeters. 2007. "Early literacy achievements, population density and the transition to modern growth," *Journal of the European Economic Association* 5:183–226.
Cipolla, Carlo. 1969. *Literacy and Development in the West*. Baltimore: Penguin Books.
Clark, Gregory. 2001. "The secret history of the Industrial Revolution," UC Davis, mimeo.
———. 2005a. "Human capital, fertility, and the industrial revolution," *Journal of the European Economic Association* 3: 505–515.
———. 2005b. "The long march of history: Farm wages, population and economic growth, England, 1209–1869," *Economic History Review* 60(1): 97–136.
Cressy, David. 1980. *Literacy and The Social Order: Reading and Writing in Tudor and Stuart England*. Cambridge: Cambridge University Press.
Culp, Christopher and Fred Smith. 1989. "Speculators: Adam Smith revisited," *The Freeman* vol. 39, no. 10, available from «http://fee.org».
Daskin, Marc. 1995. *Network and Discrete Location: Models, Algorithms and Applications*. New York: John Wiley and Sons.
Doepke, Matthias. 2004. "Accounting for fertility decline during the transition to growth," *Journal of Economic Growth* 9(3): 347–383
Duranton, Gilles and Diego Puga. 2004. "Micro-foundations of urban agglomeration economies," in Vernon Henderson and Jacques-François Thisse (eds.), *Handbook of Regional and Urban Economics*, Volume 4. Amsterdam: North-Holland, pp. 2063–2117.
Fujita, Masahisa and Jacques-François Thisse. 2002. *Economics of Agglomeration*. Cambridge: Cambridge University Press.
Galor, Oded. 2005. "From stagnation to growth: Unified growth theory," *Handbook of Economic Growth* 2005: 171–293.
Galor, Oded and David Weil. 2000. "Population, technology, and growth: from the Malthusian regime to the demographic transition and beyond," *American Economic Review* 90(4): 806–828.
Hansen, Gary and Edward Prescott. 2002. "Malthus to Solow," *American Economic Review* 92(4): 1205–1217.
Henderson, Vernon. 2005. "Urbanization, economic geography, and growth," in Philippe Aghion and Steven Durlauf (eds.), *Handbook of Economic Growth*. Amsterdam: North-Holland, pp. 1543–1591.

Herlihy, David. 1997. *The Black Death and the Transformation of the West*. Cambridge, MA: Harvard University Press.

Kremer, Michael. 1993. "Population growth and technological change: One million BC to 1900," *Quarterly Journal of Economics* 108(3): 681–716.

Ladd, Helen. 1992. "Population growth, density and the costs of providing public services," *Urban Studies* 29 (2): 273–295.

Lagerloef, Nils-Petter. 2003. "From Malthus to modern growth: can epidemics explain the three regimes?," *International Economic Review* 44(2): 755–777.

Lee, Ronald. 1979. "Introduction: Population growth, economic development and social change in Europe, 1750–1970," in W. R. Lee (ed.), *European Demography and Economic Growth*. London: Croom Helm, pp. 10–26.

Maddison, Angus. 2001. *The World Economy – A Millennial Perspective*. Paris: OECD, Development Centre Studies.

McNicoll, Geoffrey. 2003. "Population and development: An introductory view," Policy Research Division Working Paper no. 174. New York: Population Council.

Morgan, Frank and Roger Bolton. 2002. "Hexagonal economic regions solve the location problem," *The American Mathematical Monthly* 109(2): 165–172.

Nicolini, Esteban. 2004. "Mortality, interest rates, investment, and agricultural production in 18th century England," *Explorations in Economic History* 41(2): 130–155.

Platt, Colin. 1996. *King Death: The Black Death and Its Aftermath in Late-Medieval England*. Toronto: University of Toronto Press.

ReVelle, Charles and Horst Eiselt. 2005. "Location analysis: A synthesis and survey," *European Journal of Operational Research* 165: 1–19.

Schools Inquiry Commission. 1868a. *Report of the Commissioners*. Volume 1. London: George E. Eyre and William Spottiswoode.

———. 1868b. *Tables*. Volume 21. London: George E. Eyre and William Spottiswoode.

van Zanden, Jan Luiten. 2004. "The skill premium and the Great Divergence," IISG/University of Utrecht, mimeo.

Wrigley, E. A. 1988. *Continuity, Chance and Change: The Character of the Industrial Revolution in England*. New York: Cambridge University Press.

Wrigley, E. A., R. S. Davies, J. E. Oeppen, and R. S. Schofield. 1997. *English Population History from Family Reconstitution: 1580–1837*. Cambridge: Cambridge University Press.

Wrigley, E. A. and R. S. Schofield. 1989. *The Population History of England, 1541–1871: A Reconstruction*. Cambridge, MA: Cambridge University Press.

The Population Dynamics of Human Capital Accumulation

WOLFGANG LUTZ
ANNE GOUJON
ANNABABETTE WILS

This chapter presents a method for modeling the dynamics of changes in human capital as measured by educational attainment. The methodological basis for this approach, known in demography as multi-state methods, was developed in the 1970s at the International Institute for Applied Systems Analysis (IIASA). Originally developed for the simultaneous projections of the populations of subnational regions with migration between them, these methods can be applied to modeling virtually all subsets of the population as defined by relatively stable criteria. They are hence appropriate for modeling the dynamics of the subpopulations as defined by educational attainment levels. Over recent years researchers associated with IIASA have successfully applied the methods to human capital projections in selected countries and major world regions. Until now, however, there has not been an effort to study the feasibility of making such projections by level of educational attainment on a regular basis for virtually all countries. That is the main purpose of this exercise.

When studying education trends at the macro-level of society, it is essential to distinguish between stocks and flows. We use the following terminology: Education is the process (flow) through which people gain skills and knowledge. The stock of educated people with such skills and knowledge is referred to as human capital. Under this definition, education as measured by enrollment or completion rates contributes to the accumulation of human capital stock, which is measured by the educational attainment of the adult population. There is an important time lag: today's human capital stock is a result of education over the past decades. Since education is mostly attained at a young age, changes in the human capital of the adult population have a large momentum. Current education efforts influence the adult population only at the margin. We will show that these effects of specific near-term education efforts on longer-term changes in human capital, as measured by educational attainment or years of schooling in the adult population, can be accurately and comprehensively described using demographic methods.

In this chapter we study only formal education. Every human society has developed systems to educate their young members. These systems differ widely across cultures in methods, content, and duration of education. Focusing on formal education does not imply that informal learning processes are unimportant. Learning processes before school, parallel to school, and after finishing school can be essential, but it is difficult to obtain internationally consistent empirical information about them.

Even in the restricted context of formal education it is difficult to categorize and quantify the multi-dimensional issue of content and quality of education. Various series of international learning assessments[1] have found wide variation in the performance of pupils from different countries on standardized tests (for an excellent summary, see UNESCO 2004). Nonetheless, for internationally comparative studies, it is easier to simply measure the length of education, because here one can refer to a universal metric, namely the years spent in formal education. Another closely related but not identical metric refers to the widely available international attainment standards of primary, secondary, and tertiary education. In this study school levels and grades are our metrics of education, but the methodology can be applied to years of schooling attained as well. The large International Adult Literacy Survey (IALS) found that the length of schooling was the most accurate predictor for a complex array of reading and math skills, suggesting that our measure of education, school level, is a reasonable first proxy (OECD 2000).

This analysis is a step in the effort to develop reliable projections of human capital across countries. We also argue that the accuracy of population projections in general can be improved through the explicit inclusion of education because education levels in particular affect fertility and child mortality. The latter claim is based on the following. Over decades of research and across many countries, studies have found that mothers with higher education have fewer children, and those children are less likely to die. Our reasoning is that this relationship will continue into the future. Up to a certain limit, the more the mother's education level improves, the lower the levels of fertility and child mortality will be. Hence, taking account of the mother's education allows one to make a more reliable prediction of fertility and mortality trends. In other words, if education indeed captures an important source of otherwise unobserved heterogeneity in population dynamics, then population projections become more realistic by explicitly including education in the projection models in a similar way to what is usually done with age and sex. The gains resulting from this are systematically addressed in Lutz, Goujon, and Doblhammer-Reiter (1999).

The following section discusses why it is important to model the dynamics of education and human capital accumulation for reconstructing the past and in particular for forecasting. Next, we present the appropriate demographic multi-state method for doing so. We then present illustrative applications to three countries: Guinea, Nicaragua, and Zambia. Our discussion of the results includes a consideration of the impacts of better education on child mortality. We conclude with a recommendation for next steps.

Why it is important to forecast education and human capital

Forecasting education will be considered an important task if (1) the educational composition of the population has been found to matter for the wellbeing of individuals and countries, and (2) significant benefits for planning are to be gained by studying not only the past and current educational structure, but also the likely future educational structure. These two separate questions are addressed sequentially.

Education matters for economic growth

A large body of literature on the relevance of education goes beyond the dominant focus on its importance for economic growth—for example, on education and development (Sen 1999), on education and fertility (Bledsoe et al. 1999), on education and mortality and health (Alachkar and Serow 1988). At the aggregate level it has been argued that education lowers the risk of conflict (Collier and Hoeffler 2000), and the noneconomic individual- and societal-level benefits of better education are generally considered to be substantial and far reaching. Some of the impacts in the fields of health, mortality, and fertility are discussed later in this chapter with specific examples.

The main focus in studying the benefits of education has been its effect on income growth (Haddad et al. 1990; Barro and Lee 1993, 2000; Barro and Sala-i-Martín 1995; Castelló and Doménech 2002; Psacharopoulos and Patrinos 2002). Here one typically encounters an interesting puzzle. While there is overwhelming empirical evidence that, at the individual level, investments in education result on average in higher income, the findings at the macro level are less clear (e.g., Pritchett 2001; Bils and Klenow 2001). Particularly when studying the effects of increases in mean years of schooling on GDP growth rates, regressions on cross-sectional datasets show differing results, largely depending on the model specification and especially on the educational indicator used (Coulombe, Tremblay, and Marchand 2004; Cohen and Soto 2001; De la Fuente and Doménech 2000; Krueger and Lindhal 2001). A close reading of the literature shows that the chosen indicators of educational attainment at the macro level are often crude and do not consider the full educational attainment distribution by age and sex. The macroeconomic studies generally lump together adults of all ages (15+ or 25+). Since the dynamics of change in the different age-specific human capital indicators follow very different patterns, as will be shown below, this lumping makes it difficult to interpret the roles of specific causal mechanisms in inducing economic growth. The relationship of education to economic growth may be clearer if we can take into account the age composition of education in the labor force. Better age-specific indicators of human capital allow for the calculation of models with greater age precision.[2]

The general lack of attention to age-specific aspects of human capital in the dominant economic literature is probably due to the absence of a comprehensive dataset that provides such detailed information in a consistent manner across countries and time for a large number of countries. Using multi-state methods for projecting human capital, Lutz et al. (2007) produced a systematic reconstruction of populations of 120 countries by age, sex, and level of educational attainment from 1970 to 2000 (covering 93 percent of the world's population). Unlike the empirical data available from UNESCO and earlier reconstructions (Barro and Lee 1993; De la Fuente and Doménech 2002; Cohen and Soto 2001), this new dataset jointly produced by IIASA and the Vienna Institute of Demography (VID) gives the full educational attainment distributions for four categories (no education, primary, secondary, and tertiary education) by five-year age groups in five-year intervals and with definitions that are strictly comparable across time. Based on empirical distributions of educational attainment by age and sex for the year 2000, the method moves backward along cohort lines, while explicitly considering the fact that men and women with different education have different levels of mortality. The resulting dataset allows for new estimates of the impact of age-specific human capital growth on economic growth. Some first analyses that chose selected, well-established economic growth equations and applied them independently to both the Barro and Lee dataset and to our new IIASA/VID dataset showed promising results in the sense that the IIASA/VID data produced consistently significant positive coefficients for improvements in human capital on economic growth. In particular, the age-specific analysis seems to add to the explanatory power of the economic growth models in that the growth in the human capital of younger adults (aged 20–39 years) matters more than that of older adults, while (not surprisingly) that of pension-age men and women turns out to be irrelevant (Crespo Cuaresma and Lutz 2007).

If further systematic analyses based on this newly reconstructed human capital dataset result in significant and stable patterns of coefficients for age-, sex-, and educational-attainment-level-specific effects on economic growth, then the human capital projections described here may also provide the basis for new population- and human-capital-based economic growth projections in the future.

Human capital forecasts benefit planning

What is to be gained from forecasting education and human capital? Here we distinguish four functions of forecasting: a) planning, b) orientation, c) realistic target setting, and d) motivation for near-term investments that produce only long-term benefits.

a) In terms of specific government *planning* in the field of education, the time horizon tends to be relatively short (not longer than 5–10 years). In this context the forecasting of the student and teacher populations is more relevant than the changing educational composition of the general adult population. Planners need to know where scarce resources should be allocated, for example, in a process of planned rapid educational expansion in pursuit of the Millennium Development Goals (MDG) in education. In countries with still rapidly growing numbers of children (which even under declining fertility rates are the result of the population momentum caused by increasing numbers of potential mothers), improvements in enrollment rates are a challenge in terms of both recruiting and training the teachers and expanding the infrastructure, including school buildings. Decisions about whether to invest in adult literacy programs can be influenced by forecasts that show, for example, whether adult education programs (such as those in India) have demonstrable economic benefits. Detailed forecasts of schooling, including measures of pupil numbers, intake, promotion, and repetition, as well as assumptions on infrastructure and teacher training, can give guidance for the planning of resource allocation.

b) On the aggregate level, the expected changing educational composition of the total population gives essential guidelines for strategic *orientation* and longer-term planning. The longer-term human capital outlook is an important factor in thinking about a country's future or even about changing geopolitical balances. For instance, the likelihood that over the next two decades China alone will have more working-age people with secondary and tertiary education than all of Europe and North America combined (see Lutz and Goujon 2001) has implications for long-term economic, geopolitical, and strategic planning. It can also be informative to compare the longer-term human capital potentials of different countries in a similar way, just as it was useful to compare the trends in the Human Development Index. The structure of the population by age, sex, and education could also be related to other pertinent indicators, such as the General Entrepreneurship Monitor, an international database measuring the extent of individual entrepreneurship within countries and its effect on business start-ups. Businesses can use projections of human capital to inform their decisions for long-term investments in particular countries.

c) *Target setting* has become a prominent feature of education strategies. But the targets do not always reflect the fact that changes in the educational composition of the population have great momentum and improvements cannot take place overnight, even in the presence of strong political will and good funding. Aside from adult literacy campaigns and on-the-job training programs, education takes place at young ages; it takes decades for the improved education of the young to result in significant improvements for the total adult population. Since this momentum follows strict demographic regularities, it can be precisely quantified using demographic methods. But many politically driven educational targets in the past did not reflect knowledge about this momentum and were at times not only unrealistic but simply unachievable. For example, in a series of global conferences during the 1990s, the goal of halving female illiteracy was officially proclaimed (with changing target years, most recently 2015). But the education projections by Lutz and Goujon (2001) clearly demonstrate that at the global level, even under the most optimistic scenario, improved literacy of the young does not allow this goal to be reached until around 2030 because of the persistence of illiteracy among the elderly. Moreover, after 2030 the goal would automatically be achieved at current enrollment rates (i.e., without further efforts) because the illiterate elderly will die off and the more educated young will take their place. An educational goal that is not achievable for the stated time horizon, but later will be achieved without any change to current enrollment rates, is pointless. Models of education projection that explicitly quantify the dynamics of change along cohort lines can help to produce more appropriate targets.

d) Long-term human capital projections can also *provide a rationale for short-term investments* in education. In the short run, investments in education can suffer from government policies aimed at budget consolidation, as has been the case with many so-called structural adjustment programs. Those have been harsh on the education sector and have led to a decline or to slower growth in education spending (Ferreira 1996; SAPRIN 2004), which in turn curbs a country's human capital development. Human capital projections that demonstrate quantitatively—and also visually in the form of educational age-pyramids—how short-term improvements in enrollment translate into longer-term improvements in the educational composition of the adult population can serve a powerful role in convincing governments that indeed the return to their investments will come, but with a significant lag.

The above reasons, in our view, offer strong support for efforts to forecast education and human capital. In fact, two institutions have begun such efforts on a large scale. IIASA is producing alternative projection scenarios for 120 industrialized and developing countries that include four categories: no education, primary, secondary, and tertiary education. The Education Policy and Data Center (EPDC) in Washington, DC has made human capital forecasts for 78 transitional and developing countries (Wils 2007). So far, these are one-time efforts, but, we argue, there is good reason to make them ongoing for all countries in the world.

What to project? Mean years of schooling versus educational attainment

Before discussing the demographic multi-state methods that we use, it is worth comparing the strengths and weaknesses of the two most often used quantitative indicators of human capital: mean years of schooling and educational attainment. Mean years of schooling is an indicator of the human capital stock of a given population in a given year. This indicator can also be measured for separate age groups. The data on mean years of schooling typically come from censuses and surveys. Since many of these sources do not directly ask for the number of years a person has attended school, but rather ask for the highest education that the person has completed, this information often needs to be converted into years of schooling by assuming average study times for certain educational attainments. Also the issue of grade repetition rates, which tend to be very high in several developing countries, complicates the direct measurement and interpretation of mean years of schooling.

An obvious advantage of mean years of schooling as an indicator of human capital stock is that it comes in the form of a single number that can be easily compared and is easy to plug into regression equations. Its disadvantage is that, as an average, it hides the underlying distribution, which in the case of education may be very important. Two countries that have the same mean number of years of schooling for the adult population may have very different educational attainment distributions—one with small, highly educated elites in the midst of an uneducated majority, and another where broad segments of the population have intermediate education levels. The consequences of these two different education regimes on poverty and economic growth as well as on health and mortality may differ significantly. The policy debate about the best mix of efforts for primary, secondary, and tertiary education can only be informed by studies that explicitly consider these different categories. For this reason we use the full distribution of educational attainment by age and sex (typically using four categories). The same method as described here can be used to make even more detailed projections of the population, by grade completed, for example.

Figure 1 illustrates the kind of educational attainment data by age and sex that we use in our model. It gives the education and age pyramid for Singapore in 2000. Four levels of education are indicated: no formal education, primary, secondary, and higher education (equivalent to tertiary education). As a comparison to this approach, Figure 2 shows the mean years of schooling for the entire adult population aged 25 and older. Obviously, it contains much less information than Figure 1.

Figure 1 clearly shows the speed of educational expansion over past decades, when, within only one generation, Singapore's education system moved from that of a poor developing country to that of a highly advanced

FIGURE 1 Age pyramid by level of formal education, Singapore, 2000

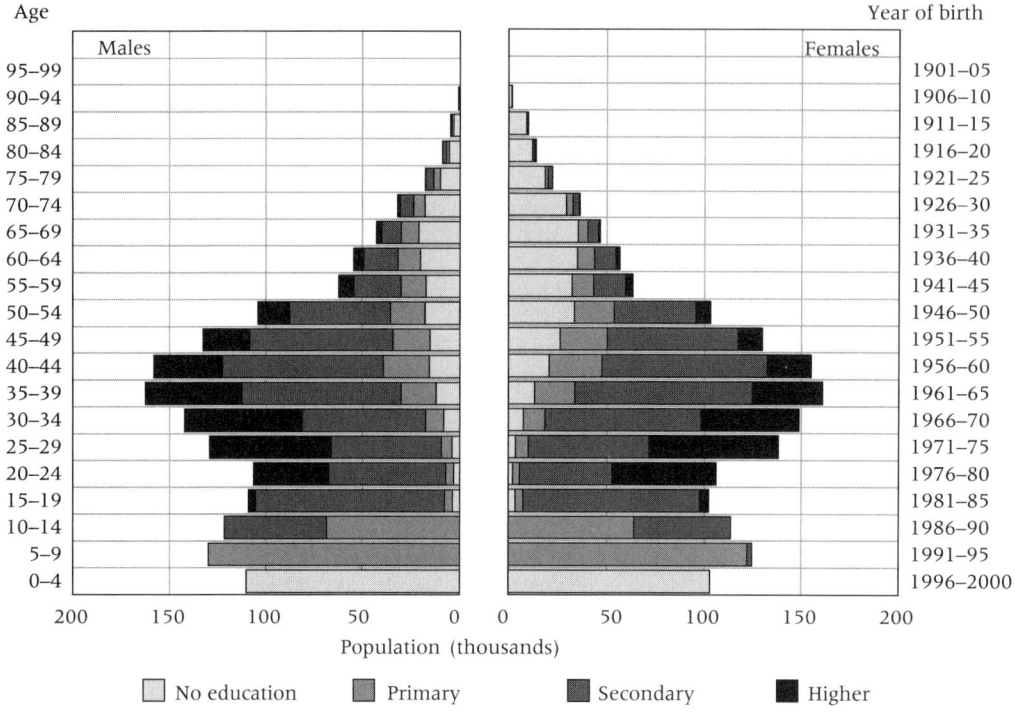

SOURCE: Lutz and Scherbov 2004.

FIGURE 2 Mean years of schooling of the population aged 25 and older, Singapore, 1970–2000

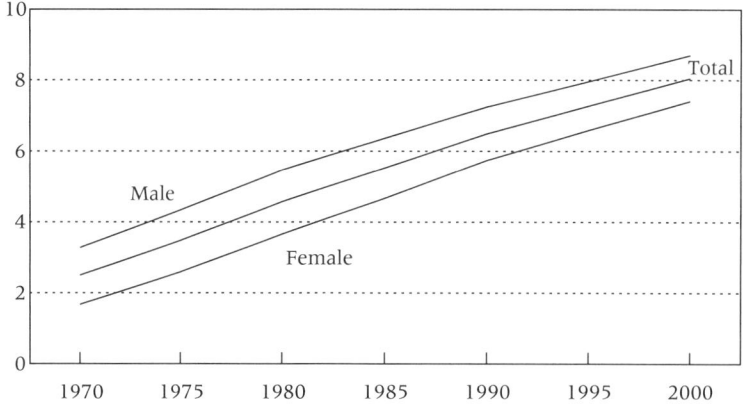

SOURCE: Lutz et al. 2007.

society. More than half of all women born before 1945 had no formal education. They are now aged 60 and above. But of all young women aged 20–25 today, more than half have already had some tertiary education, among the highest levels in the world. Figure 1 also shows the progress of educational improvement in Singapore, where the expansion of primary education was soon followed by a rapid expansion of secondary education, with the rise of tertiary education being a more recent phenomenon. All of these developments, which may matter greatly for the specific course of economic growth, are hidden when looking only at mean years of schooling as plotted in Figure 2.

While the empirical distribution of the level of education by age and sex, particularly if the information is available for several points in time, can be used to analyze the consequences of changes in educational composition, the task at hand is to project such complete age pyramids by level of education into the future.

Methods for forecasting the educational composition of the population

Past efforts

The increasing awareness of the importance of human capital in development has stimulated several attempts to estimate and project the educational composition of the population. Estimates of past human capital have generally relied on population censuses or, when not available, cumulated enrollment ratios or illiteracy rates (Mankiw, Romer, and Weil 1992; Romer 1989; Ahuja and Filmer 1995; Dubey and King 1994; Kyriacou 1991; Nehru, Swanson, and Dubey 1993; Psacharopoulos and Arrigada 1986, 1992). The most widely used datasets of human capital estimates, produced for the period 1960–2000, are from Barro and Lee (1993, 2000). They rely on census data and show their results for educational attainment by school level and average number of years of schooling (total and by level) for a large number of countries. However, the datasets provide the estimates for only two broad age groups, 15+ and 25+.

Ahuja and Filmer (1995) have taken the estimates of past human capital further by developing a method for projection. They take existing United Nations population projections and superimpose on them an educational distribution estimated for two broad age groups (6–24 and 25+) from given sets of enrollment ratios and UNESCO enrollment projections. Similar to Nehru, Swanson, and Dubey (1993), they use the so-called perpetual inventory method, which sums total school enrollment over long time series and then converts these into estimates of educational attainment of the adult population. Because such long time series are rarely available, this method involves much back projection based on numerous assumptions. Ahuja and Filmer then project the educational composition (for four educational groups) for a large number of developing countries by taking the existing UN population projections and superimposing trends of educational change on them.

Concurrent with the above efforts, starting in the late 1980s a group of researchers at IIASA, led by Wolfgang Lutz, began to make simultaneous projections of population and educational attainment, using the multi-state projection method developed a decade earlier by Andrei Rogers (1975) to account for migration. The multi-state approach was first applied to human capital projections in a study of future development options in Mauritius (Lutz 1994), Cape Verde (Wils 1996), the Yucatan Peninsula (Lutz, Prieto, and Sanderson 2000), Botswana (Sanderson, Hellmuth, and Strzepek 2001), Namibia (Sanderson et al. 2001), and Mozambique (Wils et al. 2001). Yousif, Goujon, and Lutz (1996) applied this methodology to project the population of six North African countries by age, sex, and education. Further case studies include projections for India at the state level (Goujon and McNay 2003), for some countries in the Arab region (Goujon 2002), for Southeast Asia (Goujon and K.C. 2006), and for Egyptian governorates (Goujon et al. 2007). Lutz, Goujon, and Doblhammer-Reiter (1999) evaluated the power of this approach, presenting it to a broader forecasting community. More recently, the method has been applied to produce the first global-level (for 13 world regions) projections by age, sex, and educational attainment to 2030 by Lutz and Goujon (2001) and by the EPDC (Wils 2007) for 78 developing countries. It is currently being applied to 120 countries by IIASA.

Another education projection tradition has focused on school enrollment. In the past decades, UNESCO, the World Bank, and some government ministries developed models to project school enrollment and the resources required for the projected pupils.[3] The demographic input of these models is typically limited to a projection of the population of school-entry age. A given fraction of these children is assumed to enter first grade, and enrollment in subsequent grades is based on tracking the flows of promotions, repetitions, and dropouts. While these models have been used for planning purposes and have been particularly useful as negotiation tools, the models end when pupils graduate; therefore, they have not been used to project the impact of changing enrollment on human capital. A model recently developed at the EPDC, however, has combined enrollment projections with the human capital projections as discussed here.

Demographic multi-state projection methods

The multi-state projection method applied here is now a standard ingredient in the toolbox of mathematical demographers around the world, but it is not yet well known among scholars outside that narrow circle. It is based on a multi-dimensional expansion of the life table (increment-decrement table) and of the traditional cohort-component method of population projection (Rogers 1975; Keyfitz 1985). The multi-state model is based on a division of the population by age and sex into any number of "states," which were originally geographic units with the movements between the states being migration streams. But a state can also reflect any other clearly defined subgroup of the population, such as groups with different educational attainment, with the movements then becoming educational transition rates. The projection of human capital stocks by age and sex is an ideal example of the application of the multi-dimensional cohort-component model, because education tends to be acquired at young ages and then simply moves along cohort lines.[4] Change in the educational composition of the total population is then caused by the depletion (through mortality) of less-educated cohorts and the entry of more-educated younger cohorts. But the multi-state model can also incorporate dynamic feedbacks, by using the fact that fertility, mortality, and migration are closely associated with education. Women with more education tend to have significantly lower fertility, lower maternal and child mortality, and greater longevity. A change in the educational composition of the population of young women will, hence, have direct impacts on the total number of births, even if fertility within each educational group does not change.

The multi-state methodology is typically described in terms of equations with matrices indexed by age, sex, state, and time. The mathematics is complicated because it has to consider competing risks, for example, accounting for the fact that individuals are simultaneously exposed to the risks of dying and of moving to another state. Since the method is comprehensively documented in the literature cited above, a simple description will suffice here.

The population of each age and sex category is divided into four distinct groups according to educational attainment. Fertility, mortality, and migration thus have four age- and sex-specific schedules, one for each educational group. In addition, there must be three sets of age- and sex-specific educational transition rates, that is, the age-specific intensities for young men and women to move, for example, from the category of primary educational attainment to secondary attainment. Theoretically, the model can handle transitions at any age, including, for example, more education through adult education campaigns. Educational transitions discussed in this chapter are limited to those below age 25. In the projections presented here, alternative scenarios pertaining to these educational transition rates are defined.

The multi-state model can also be extended to accommodate any number of states, for example, educational attainment by single grades, school intake by single-year age of entry, as well as promotion, repetition, dropouts, and graduation. Promotion rates are educational transition rates to higher grades in this more extended version. Repetition is nontransition and can be accommodated by assuming that a certain portion of each grade remains in that grade, but moves up one age category. Dropouts and graduation are transitions from in-school states to post-school states and can be grade specific. This extension to include the grade-states and transitions within the school system is used in the EPDC modeling exercise referred to earlier. The advantage of such a model is that it can more realistically track the complex flows that lead to adult educational attainment; and it can be an education-sector planning and advocacy tool.

Education projections for 13 world regions

Lutz and Goujon (2001; Goujon and Lutz 2004) recently produced the first global projections of the population by age, sex, and education to 2030 for 13 world regions. They consider three scenarios for future educational attainment. Education-specific fertility, mortality, and migration assumptions are the same for all three scenarios, but the projections have different population outcomes based purely on different assumptions for educational transitions. The Constant scenario assumes that currently observed educational transition rates (corresponding to current enrollment rates) remain unchanged over the projection period. This scenario results in a better-educated population in all regions because of past improvements in education—reflected in better education of the younger age groups—even in Africa. The ICPD scenario assumes that it will be possible to meet the targets defined at the 1994 International Conference on Population and Development in Cairo, which include a closing of the gender gap in schooling and universal primary education. The American scenario assumes that enrollment rates prevailing in 2000 in Northern America will be reached in all world regions by 2020 (this implies big rises in tertiary education in many regions). Lutz and Goujon's results show that even under the most optimistic enrollment scenarios, the educational attainment of the adult population will not have changed very significantly by 2030 because of the great momentum of human capital formation.

Such human capital projections illustrate the changing educational composition of the population, which is significant not only for individual development and a nation's institutional and economic performance, but also for the relative weights, productivity, and competitiveness of major world markets. In this context it is useful to look at absolute numbers of workers by skill levels rather than at the proportions discussed above. Figure 3 compares four of the economic mega-regions of the future (Europe and North America together, China, South Asia, and sub-Saharan Africa) in terms of trends in the size of the working-age population (age 20–65) by educational attainment. The data presented are taken from the American scenario. At present China clearly has the largest total working-age population of these four regions, but its educated population (secondary and tertiary together)

FIGURE 3 Population aged 20–65 years (in millions) by level of education, according to the American scenario for four mega-regions, 2000–30

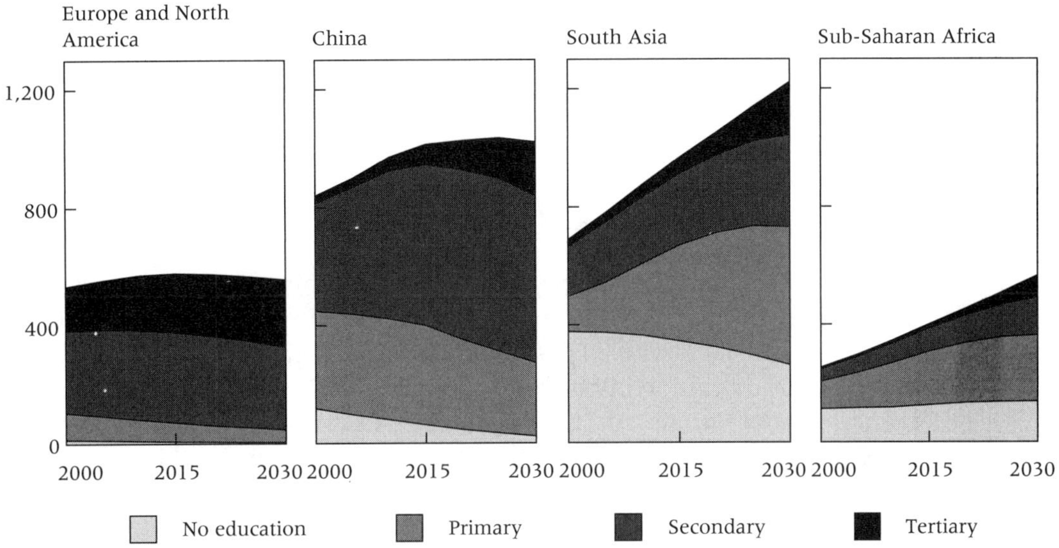

SOURCE: Lutz and Goujon 2001.

is still smaller than that of Europe and North America combined. In terms of the secondary- and tertiary-educated working-age population, South Asia is far behind, with less than half the size of that same population in Europe and North America, or in China.

Over the next 20 years, South Asia is expected to surpass China in terms of the total size of the working-age population. But in terms of the educational composition of the population, the difference between the two regions will be striking. In China in 2030, 73 percent of the working-age population will have secondary or tertiary education, compared with only 40 percent in South Asia. The main reason for this divergence lies in the differences between the two regions in investment in primary and secondary education over the last two decades. Of the four major world regions, Europe and North America will continue to have the highest educational levels of the working-age population, but, in terms of absolute numbers of educated people, this region will clearly fall behind China. China's working-age population with secondary education or higher is likely to increase from 390 million in 2000 to 750 million in 2030, while that of Europe (without the former Soviet Union) and North America together will increase only from 430 million to 510 million in 2030. These significant future changes in the numbers of skilled workers are likely to have far-reaching consequences for the weights in the global economic system. In sub-Saharan Africa, low human capital associated with past neglect of education systems and enormous present pressure on them pose significant limits to the prospects for social and economic development. In 2000, only 19 percent of the population in the 20–65 age group had a secondary education or more. Although this percentage will almost double to 36 percent in 2030 according to the American scenario, sub-Saharan Africa will still be far from converging to other regions' levels of educational attainment.

Multi-state human capital projections for Guinea, Nicaragua, and Zambia

Guinea, Nicaragua, and Zambia were chosen for this exercise because they pose different challenges in terms of data availability[5] and exemplify different educational conditions. These countries are also the focus of a number of international education initiatives. Nicaragua and Zambia have high rates of primary school enrollment. Nicaragua has had consistent and high rates of growth in secondary school enrollment as well, while in Zambia secondary school enrollment for males has stagnated for some time. Guinea has very low enrollment rates and, at present rates of growth, is still decades away from universal primary education (Wils, Carrol, and Barrow 2005). For all three countries, recent Demographic and Health Surveys (DHS) provide high-quality and detailed information.

As a part of the effort to identify and project trends, it is instructive to look at the consequences of past education policies and outcomes. Figure 4 shows the population pyramids for Guinea, Nicaragua, and Zambia in years around 2000, which will be used as the starting point for the human capital projections. The population with no schooling is shown in the lightest, innermost shading. Moving outward along each bar to ever-darker shades are those with primary, secondary, and tertiary education. Hidden within the primary school attainment group are the many people who did not complete the primary cycle, but only attended one or two years of school—generally too little time to learn basic literacy skills in countries with weak education systems (see UNESCO 2006, for example).

As the age pyramids show, the educational attainment of Guinea lags far behind that of the other two countries, with a large portion of even the youngest cohorts never having attended school. Closer inspection will show that the portion without schooling is higher among females (69 percent) than among males (44 percent). In both Zambia and Nicaragua most adults, from age 15 on, have been to school, but in Nicaragua the proportions of adults with secondary and tertiary education are higher than in Zambia. In Zambia men have more education than women, while in Nicaragua the educational attainment of young women is higher than that of young men.

Table 1 shows the educational attainment for four broad age groups. Besides the disadvantage for most groups of women, the table shows that in

FIGURE 4 Population age pyramids showing educational attainment in Guinea, Nicaragua, and Zambia, ca. 2000 (population in thousands)

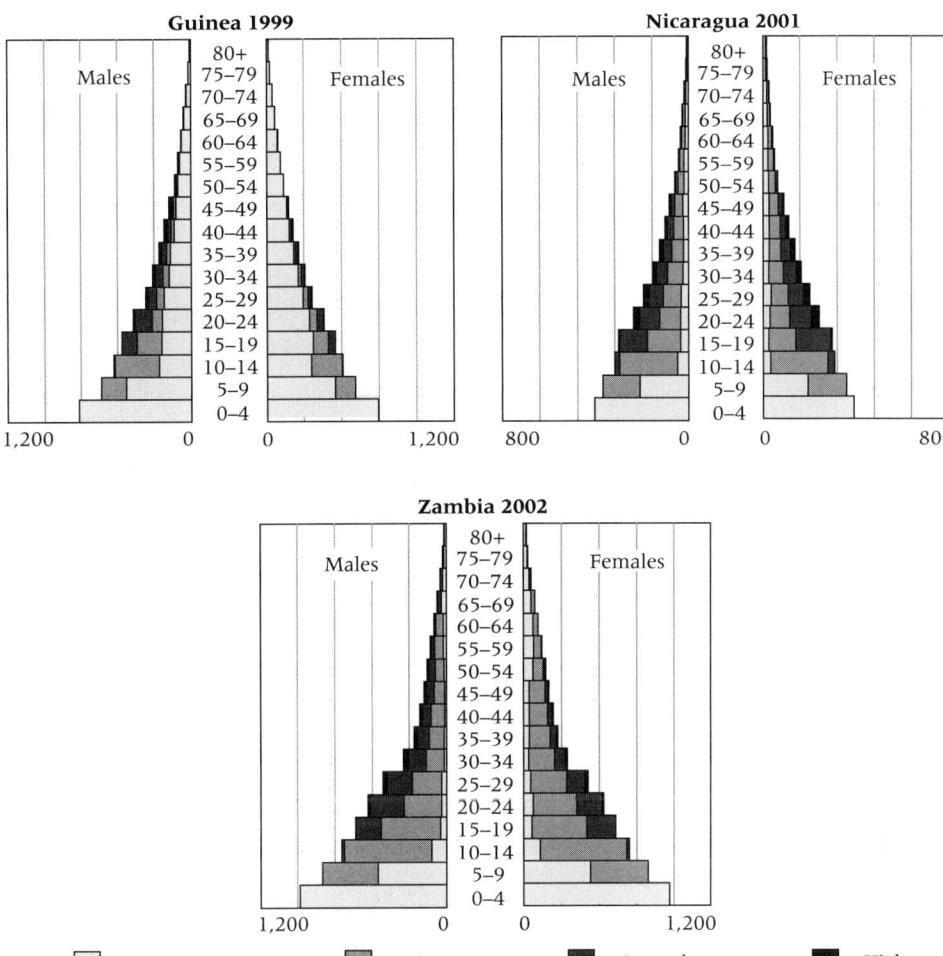

SOURCES: *DHS Guinea 1999; DHS Nicaragua 2001; DHS Zambia 2002.*

all three countries, among adults who went to primary school, only 30–60 percent in all age groups and both sexes continued on to secondary school. The table also shows the clear decline in the proportion of adults with no education for younger age groups in Guinea and Nicaragua, as well as a stagnation for the same indicator in Zambia. Conversely, the attainment of secondary education rises with younger age groups up to the cohort aged 20–24 years. The attainment of primary education or more has risen most in Guinea, albeit starting from the lowest base. Attainment at the tertiary level seems to be stagnating in all three countries for both males and females.

TABLE 1 Educational attainment for four broad age groups by country (in percentage)

	Males				Females			
	None	Primary	Secondary	Higher	None	Primary	Secondary	Higher
Guinea 1999								
15–19	44	34	22	0	69	21	10	0
20–24	51	17	30	2	75	12	11	1
25–34	58	17	18	6	80	10	6	2
35+	77	8	7	7	91	3	3	2
Nicaragua 2001								
15–19	12	48	38	2	8	40	50	3
20–24	14	38	36	11	11	36	38	14
25–34	17	41	30	12	15	39	33	13
35+	33	41	17	9	35	41	16	8
Zambia 2002								
15–19	6	66	28	0	9	59	31	0
20–24	6	48	43	4	12	54	32	3
25–34	6	44	41	8	11	57	27	5
35+	14	50	27	8	37	50	10	3

SOURCES: *DHS Guinea 1999; DHS Nicaragua 2001; DHS Zambia 2002.*

Initial conditions for projections

Projections of educational attainment require data specifying initial conditions. The experience of IIASA and EPDC has shown that the necessary data are available for many countries for a recent year, and human capital projections have been made for over 90 countries and regions so far.

The starting-year data consist of information on population, fertility, mortality, and migration, all by sex, age, and education level, and rates of transition between education levels. These numbers can be obtained from household surveys, population censuses, and United Nations estimates. More-detailed projections of education by grade require enrollment, repetition, and dropout rates by grade and sex, and are usually obtained from Ministry of Education publications.

The population by age and sex for the three countries is taken from United Nations (2002) estimates and projections. The education structures originate from the DHS implemented in Guinea (1999), Nicaragua (2001), and Zambia (2002) and were superimposed on the estimates of the population. Four education groups were considered—no education, primary education, secondary education, and higher education[6]—but one can choose any combination of education levels depending on the research needs and data available. The advantage of choosing only four education categories is

TABLE 2 Measured and estimated total fertility rates by education and country, ca. 2000 and average 2000–05

	Guinea		Nicaragua		Zambia	
	DHS 1999	Estimated for 2000–05	DHS 2001	Estimated for 2000–05	DHS 2002	Estimated for 2000–05
No education	5.9	6.0	5.7	5.7	7.4	6.8
Primary	4.8	5.6	4.9 (1–3) 3.8 (4–6)	4.2	6.5	6.2
Secondary	3.5	4.7	2.7	2.7	3.9	4.0
Higher		3.0	1.5	1.7		3.3
Total	5.5	5.8	3.6	3.6	5.9	5.6

SOURCES: Authors' calculations based on United Nations (2002); *DHS Guinea 1999; DHS Nicaragua 2001; DHS Zambia 2002.*

practicality. It reduces the amount of data and assumptions necessary. The initial education values for a selection of age groups and education levels are given in Table 1.

All estimates of fertility levels by education were taken from the DHS. These education-specific DHS fertility rates were then adjusted so that the total average fertility levels were equal to the United Nations 2000–2005 estimates (see Table 2).

Infant (below one year) and young child (ages one to four years) mortality rates by mother's education also come from the DHS. Table 3, which aggregates infant and child mortality, shows that a child's chances of survival are highly correlated with mother's level of education. These rates were used to estimate differential mortality levels by level of education for the whole population of the three countries using the United Nations software package for mortality measurement (Mortpak Lite).[7] For Zambia, because of the country's HIV epidemic, we decided to take the mortality rates provided by the United Nations (which reflect the specific age profile of AIDS mortality) and scale them up or down with the educational differentials found through the Mortpak procedure. The resulting total life expectancy is equivalent to the United Nations total.

TABLE 3 Under-five mortality rates ($_5q_0$) per 1,000 live births by mother's level of education by country

	Guinea	Nicaragua	Zambia
No education	204	72	198
Primary	162	43	177
Secondary	104	26	121
Higher		19	
Total	195	45	168

SOURCES: *DHS Guinea 1999; DHS Nicaragua 2001; DHS Zambia 2002.*

TABLE 4 Initial educational transitions in 2000–2005 (proportions moving from one educational category to the next) by age, sex, and country

Transitions in 2000–05		Males					Females				
From:	To:	5–9	10–14	15–19	20–24	25–29	5–9	10–14	15–19	20–24	25–29
Guinea											
No educ.	Primary	0.28	0.40				0.23	0.22			
Primary	Secondary		0.06	0.36				0.05	0.22	0.06	
Secondary	Higher			0.08	0.07	0.14			0.02	0.14	
Nicaragua											
No educ.	Primary	0.43	0.75	0.24			0.46	0.75	0.26		
Primary	Secondary		0.15	0.41				0.21	0.50		
Secondary	Higher			0.29	0.24				0.30	0.23	
Zambia											
No educ.	Primary	0.45	0.71	0.46			0.46	0.67	0.58		
Primary	Secondary		0.05	0.31	0.23			0.05	0.36		
Secondary	Higher			0.05	0.12	0.07			0.05	0.09	0.08

SOURCE: Authors' calculations based on *DHS Guinea 1999*; *DHS Nicaragua 2001*; *DHS Zambia 2002*.

In all three countries net emigration rates influence the development of the population. To estimate migration flows by education, we took the total net number of migrants provided by the United Nations and applied a typical migration age schedule. The total migrants were distributed proportionally over the education groups. In this way, migration affects the population by age, but does not affect the education structure.

The four education state projections require three sets of educational transition probabilities by sex and by five-year age groups: the transition from no education to primary education, from primary to secondary education, and from secondary to higher education. The base-year transitions were estimated from the educational attainment levels provided by the DHS data. The resulting initial transition probabilities are shown in Table 4. The transitions to primary school were lowest in Guinea and roughly equal in Nicaragua and Zambia. Transitions to secondary school were also lowest in Guinea. Male transitions to secondary school were equal in Nicaragua and Zambia, but for females they were lower in Zambia than in Nicaragua. In fact, more girls than boys made the transition to secondary school in Nicaragua (a pattern typical of many Latin American countries). How this has come about and how the pattern will affect the status of women in Nicaragua in the coming decades is worth exploring for lessons regarding women's equality in education.

Scenarios

The projections of the total population by level of education presented below have a 30-year time horizon. For the demographic variables fertility, mortality, and migration, only one demographic scenario was defined for each country, which replicates as closely as possible the medium variant of the UN population projections for these countries (United Nations 2002). But because fertility, mortality, and migration are stratified by education categories, and weights of the education categories change over time, the assumed trends in fertility and mortality had to be defined carefully so that the weighted average in the Constant scenario comes close to the total assumed in the UN projections.[8] All the demographic assumptions are shown in Appendix Table 1.

The trends in fertility differentials by education over time were modeled so that by a certain distant date the population in all education categories would have converged to the same low level of fertility. This convergence assumption is consistent with the assumption that the role of education as a factor of heterogeneity in fertility decisionmaking diminishes once the process of education diffusion has been completed (Jejeebhoy 1995). However, the assumed date of convergence is far in the future (after 2050) so that by 2030, in all three countries, significant education differentials still exist.

As in the case of fertility, the principle of convergence was also applied to mortality differentials. However, as observed in a few studies in developed countries (Doblhammer 1997; Huisman et al. 2002), education remains a strong determinant of mortality patterns, even at very high levels of life expectancy. Therefore, the convergence date was set to the end of the twenty-first century, and significant life expectancy differentials by education remain throughout the projection period.

The total migration trends to 2030 are taken from the migration assumptions of the United Nations (2002) and are proportionally distributed over the sex and education groups. In this way, migration is taken into account but does not upset the weights of the different education categories in the country.

Education scenarios

Three education scenarios were chosen to illustrate three stylized stories of progress in education. The stories are the same for the three countries, although the implementation levels are different depending on the specific country situation.

A: Constant Enrollment scenario: Under this scenario, the transition rates to primary school, from primary to secondary school, and from secondary to higher education are maintained at constant levels throughout the projection period. This scenario is artificial, but it shows the progress already embedded in the educational structure of today—the education momentum. Despite constant transition rates, the adult education levels improve as a result of recent improvements in education as younger and better-educated cohorts replace the older cohorts.

B: Trend scenario: Here it is assumed that the rate of change in the rate of transition to primary school and to secondary school as observed over past decades continues into the future. The trend is calculated based on the levels of primary school attainment of subsequent cohorts, using information from all age groups of the adult population but giving greater weight to the younger groups. For example, primary school attainment in Guinea increased from 36 percent among men aged 40–44 (who attended primary school approximately 30 years ago when they were 10 years old) to 42 percent among men aged 30–34, and further to 48 percent among 20–24-year-old males. This trend is assumed to continue following a logarithmic curve up to 2020. A similar approach of cohort extrapolation was applied for projections in 73 countries by Wils, Carrol, and Barrow (2005).

Using Zambia as an example, Figure 5 shows the educational attainment of past birth cohorts, who were aged 20–24 years and older at the time of the DHS survey, as well as the assumed trend for educational attainment of future birth cohorts. To translate these birth-cohort attainments into educational transition rates during schooling, it is assumed that primary school entry occurs on average at age 10, and secondary school entry occurs on average at age 15. In this way, the primary school attainment of the birth cohort of 1975 is an indication of the transition into primary school in 1985.

C: Millennium Development Goal (MDG) scenario: This scenario is tailored to Goals 2 and 3 set by the MDGs in terms of education.[9] We assume that full gender equity will be achieved for all levels of education by 2010–15. Intake to primary school is assumed to be complete, but since we do not model

FIGURE 5 Past and assumed future trends for primary and secondary education attainment in Zambia by birth cohort

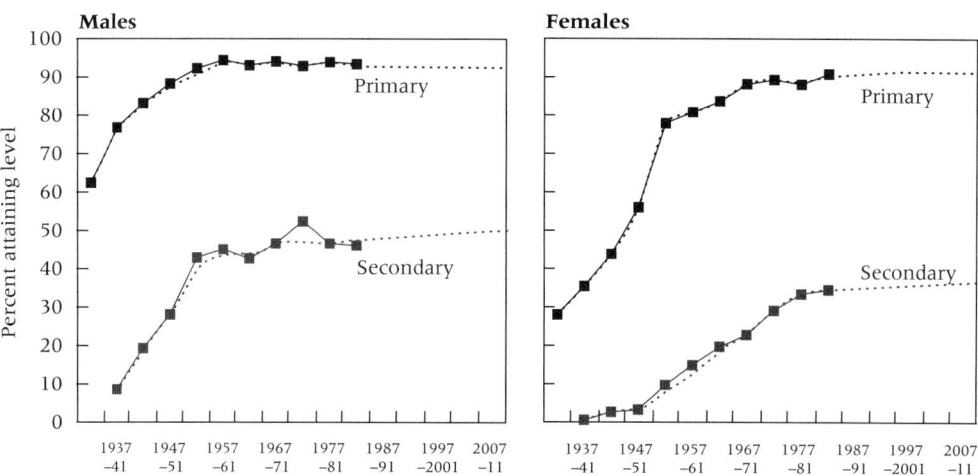

SOURCES: Authors' calculations; *DHS Zambia 2002.*

completion, there can be no explicit assumptions about it. However, we approximate higher completion by assuming further increases in the transition to secondary and higher education for both males and females. The education assumptions for Guinea, Nicaragua, and Zambia are summarized in Appendix Table 2.

Country-specific results

The results of the scenarios along with the 2000 values for Guinea, Nicaragua, and Zambia are shown in Figure 6 and in the age pyramids of Appendix Figures 1–3. (The percentages given in the discussion below are taken from the underlying projection estimates.)

Guinea is an example of a country where the consequences of neglect in educational investment will be detrimental to long-term development. The absolute number of persons with no education will continue to increase until 2020 under the most favorable scenario (MDG) and for the whole projection period under the other two scenarios. Only an aggressive adult education campaign can address this issue. The momentum of past education neglect will continue to have an effect over the next decades. However, there is some modest progress. The portion of the population aged 15–64 with no education starts at almost 70 percent in 2020; by 2015 it is 55 percent in all three scenarios. This progress comes from changes already embedded in the education structure of the population. The implementation of higher intake or grade promotion does not make any appreciable difference to the composition of Guinea's labor force before 2015, at which time the children who were affected by the changes finally enter the labor force. Even then it is not until well into the 2020s that real differences are noticeable. The proportion with no education has fallen significantly only by 2030. Women account for 56 to 58 percent of the population with no education during the projection period across all scenarios.

In Zambia, some progress is similarly embedded in the labor force, despite recent stagnation in educational attainment (see Figure 5). Even in the Constant scenario, the share of the no education group in the population aged 15–64 will decline from 13 percent in 2000 to 8 percent in 2030. The share of the primary and secondary education group will increase from 83 to 88 percent. The Trend scenario shows that more people will have secondary education, the proportion rising from 29 percent in 2000 to 39 percent in 2030. This proportion would go as high as 47 percent if the MDG scenario were implemented. Once again, one has to be mindful of the issue of the quality of education attained, and Zambia has problems with retention levels, very much like Guinea. Also, women remain disadvantaged. Under the Trend scenario and the Constant scenario, women will make up more than 50 percent of the combined no education and primary education group aged 15–64, but

FIGURE 6 Population of Guinea, Nicaragua, and Zambia aged 15–64 by level of education, 2000–30, according to the Constant, Trend, and MDG scenarios (in millions)

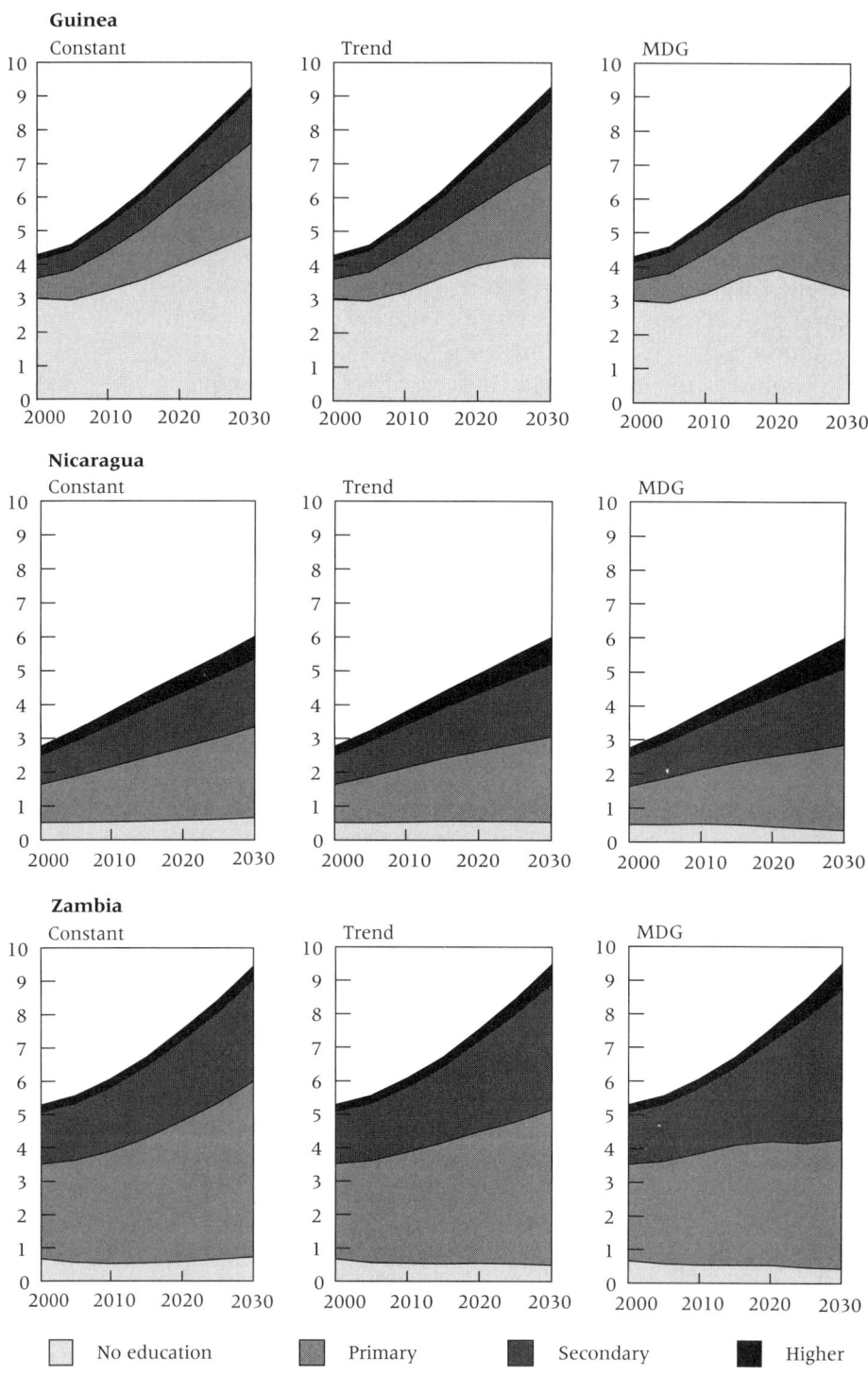

SOURCE: Authors' calculations

only 43 to 44 percent of the secondary and higher education group. Under the MDG scenario, the proportion of women in these more highly educated groups would be 47 percent.

Figure 6 shows that the educational attainment levels of Nicaragua and Zambia are quite similar. One main difference is the shape of the overall population pyramid (see Appendix Figures 2 and 3). Zambia has barely started its transition to lower fertility levels, whereas Nicaragua is advanced. In 2030, the proportion of the labor force in the no education category in Nicaragua should be between 6 and 11 percent, depending on the scenario (from a level of 18 percent in 2000). In 2030, according to the Trend scenario, 36 percent of the labor force should have secondary education and 13 percent tertiary education, which makes up almost 50 percent of the working-age population. The MDG scenario would bring a small change compared to the Trend scenario to 38 percent with secondary and 15 percent with tertiary education. Quite astonishing in Nicaragua is the advantage that women have in terms of higher education. They represent between 50 and 55 percent of those with secondary or higher education.

Education and the demographic window of opportunity The notion of the "demographic window" has gained prominence in the economic literature. As birth rates fall and the elderly population remains small, the total dependency ratio declines, offering the opportunity for rapid economic growth and further investments in education and infrastructure. This time is also seen as a unique opportunity for countries to invest in their future human capital by increasing educational enrollment (see Pool 2004; Bloom and Canning 2003). In this section we discuss the extent to which the demographic window exists in our three countries.

Figure 7 shows the total dependency ratios over time for Guinea, Nicaragua, and Zambia in the Trend scenario. Nicaragua has the lowest dependency ratios of the three countries and will remain in that position during the whole projection period. After 2005, Guinea and Zambia will enter a period of declining dependency ratios that will last at least until the end of the projection period. This projected decline in the total dependency ratio will make it easier for these two countries to expand their educational enrollment ratios through two distinct mechanisms. First, the absolute yearly increase in the number of children at the age of entering school will grow less rapidly than in the past. Second, the demographic window can be expected to contribute positively to economic growth, thus allowing countries to invest more in education. Here one can also expect a virtuous reinforcing mechanism by which more investments in education will lead to still more rapid fertility decline and hence to smaller cohorts of children to be educated and possibly more economic growth, allowing a further increase in enrollment rates.

Summary of country-specific results. The methodology of multi-state forecasting by level of education has been illustrated for Guinea, Nicaragua, and

FIGURE 7 Total dependency ratio of Guinea, Nicaragua, and Zambia, 2000–30, Trend scenario (population aged 0–14 and 65+ per 1,000 population aged 15–64)

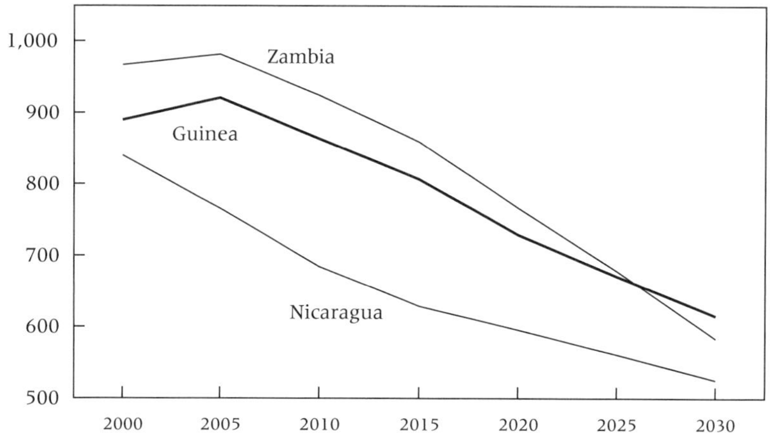

NOTE: Choice of scenario does not affect the level of the dependency ratio for the 30-year projection period; for clarity only one scenario is shown.
SOURCE: Authors' calculations.

Zambia, three countries with different data challenges and at different stages of demographic and human capital development.

In the starting year 2000, Guinea is the least developed of the three countries in terms of education. More than half of the adult population is without any formal education, and more than 90 percent of the female population above age 35 has no education. For the younger age groups, recent improvements in enrollment show somewhat higher proportions with education. The fertility of uneducated women in Guinea is twice as high as that for women with higher education. Given the recent improvements in educational transition rates (enrollment) for both girls and boys in Guinea, the Trend scenario is much closer to the MDG scenario than to the Constant scenario. But the consequences of the previous neglect of education will not be easily overcome. The projections illustrate clearly that by 2030 even the optimistic assumptions of the Trend and MDG scenarios will scarcely have affected the educational attainment of the adult population above age 25. Only in the more distant future, perhaps by 2050, will the difference between the Constant and the two optimistic scenarios make a marked difference in terms of improved human capital of the adult population.

Nicaragua in 2000 has much better starting conditions. More than 80 percent of young men and women have been to school. The sex differentials are also very small for higher education. Fertility in Nicaragua has fallen to around 3.5 births per woman, with large differentials and highly educated women having below replacement-level fertility. Interestingly, the Trend scenario for primary education is not so different from the Constant scenario, since the country's educational efforts date back some time and recent efforts have not gone much beyond them. For secondary and higher education, the Trend scenario is close to the MDG scenario. In terms of projection results, the differences between the three scenarios are not very big, all of them showing a fairly well-educated, but still rapidly growing, population. The more optimistic scenarios make a visible difference with respect to the number of young adults with secondary and higher education.

Zambia has higher male education among the adult population than Nicaragua in 2000, but female human capital lags behind. Zambia also saw recent improvements in enrollment, which result in a rather optimistic Trend scenario that is not so different from the MDG scenario. Even gender equity in education has improved markedly over the past years. Fertility is still high (around 5.6 births per woman) and educational fertility differentials are sizable. The projections for 2030 show a significant increase for the population with secondary education under the Trend and MDG scenarios. As a result of high fertility, the total population will still grow significantly, even though AIDS is claiming a high toll.

The policy dimension

Alternative paths to improving educational attainment

One of the challenges in the interpretation of educational attainment scenarios lies in estimating what kinds of education flows—namely, intake, promotion, and repetition—will generate the overall transitions. Education policy can affect education flows but not the stock of human capital; therefore, for policy, it is useful to examine what kinds of school flows can lead to the educational attainment scenarios outlined above.

We use the combined, multi-state educational enrollment and educational attainment model recently developed by the Educational Policy and Data Center. In the simulations, promotion and intake rates are set to reproduce the Constant, Trend, and MDG scenarios for educational attainment. That means, for example, that to replicate an increase in the transition from primary to secondary school, promotion rates throughout primary school are set to increase, leading to higher survival to the last primary grade, and, from there, a higher transition to secondary school.

The resulting school intake and average promotion rates are shown in Table 5. One of the interesting results is that to achieve the higher human capital outcomes of the MDG scenario, the percentage point improvements in intake and average promotion rates are not large and look achievable.

In Zambia, the MDG scenario requires 100 percent intake as opposed to the Trend values of 93 and 91 percent for males and females respectively, an

TABLE 5 Intake rates and average primary school promotion rates in 2000 and the rates required in 2020 to reproduce the stylized Constant, Trend, and MDG scenarios, by sex and country (in percent)

	Guinea				Nicaragua				Zambia			
	Intake by age 15		Average primary promotion		Intake by age 15		Average primary promotion		Intake by age 15		Average primary promotion	
	M	F	M	F	M	F	M	F	M	F	M	F
2000	57	40	63	61	90	89	79	83	93	91	88	87
2020												
Constant	57	40	63	61	90	89	79	83	93	91	88	87
Trend	95	95	62	59	100	100	85	88	93	91	89	90
MDG	100	100	72	74	100	100	87	88	100	100	92	93

NOTE: M = males; F = females
SOURCE: Authors' calculations.

increase of less than 10 percentage points over 15 years. The average promotion rates would have to be only 3 percentage points higher than today.

In Nicaragua, the Trend scenario is already close to the MDG scenario. Both the Trend and the MDG assume 100 percent intake by 2020. The Trend scenario assumes that secondary attainment rises from 39 and 48 percent in 2000 (male and female respectively) to 57 and 66 percent in 2020. To obtain those primary and secondary attainment levels, intake rises to 100 percent by 2020, and the promotion rate rises to 85 and 88 percent (male and female). The MDG scenario would assume a small improvement to 87 and 88 percent promotion rates.

Guinea faces the biggest challenge in moving up from the Trend to the MDG scenario. There the Trend scenario assumes that primary intake rises to 95 percent by 2020. However, it calls for secondary education to rise only marginally, resulting in a growing primary–secondary gap. In the Trend scenario, average promotion rates in primary school would actually decline slightly from 63 and 61 percent for males and females to 62 and 59 percent by 2020. (These very low promotion rates are partly due to very high average grade repetition rates of around 25 percent.) To reach the MDG goals, the promotion rates would have to rise to 72 and 74 for males and females respectively. This is a big task for makers of education policy.

MDG goals—The impact of full intake versus full primary completion

One of the MDG goals for education is full primary school completion for all children by 2015. For many countries, this implies raising not only intake rates but also promotion and retention rates. The goals are very different in terms of policy—the first being a question of access to schools, the second more a question of school quality and family resources needed to keep children in school. Which will contribute more to increases in educational attainments, raising intake rates or raising retention rates? In this section we compare the effects of intake and retention improvements in two scenarios: MDG-Intake, where intake for a country rises to 100 percent but retention remains constant; and MDG-Completion, where intake rates are constant and primary retention is 100 percent (all children who enter primary school complete the cycle). For the sake of brevity, the results shown here are for Nicaragua only, but they are similar for Guinea and Zambia. The scenarios assume that raising intake and reducing dropout are achieved through measures that do not affect school quality, so in each scenario the human capital value of primary and secondary education is the same. In reality, quality may rise or fall, depending on how the policies for complete intake or zero dropout are implemented.

The primary and secondary net enrollment rates (NER)[10] according to the MDG-Intake and the MDG-Completion scenarios for Nicaragua are shown in Figures 8a and 8b with the Constant scenario for comparison. Under the Constant scenario, primary NER would be 74 percent (0.74) in 2015; with MDG-Intake it would be 81; and with the additional zero dropout in MDG-Completion, NER would be 76 by 2015. Secondary NER by 2015 would be 24 in the Constant scenario; 26 with the MDG-Intake scenario; and 32 with the MDG-Completion scenario. It appears that higher school retention makes a big difference to secondary NER, but much less to primary. This outcome occurs for two reasons. One, many children in Nicaragua enter school above age for grade; therefore, their higher retention in primary school occurs when they are beyond the official primary school age, hence they are not counted in NER. Second, primary NER benefits from incremental effects of higher retention, while secondary NER benefits from the accumulated effects of zero dropout in all six primary grades.

What is the impact of these different MDG scenarios on adult educational attainment? Figure 8c shows the proportion of adults aged 15–64 with some secondary education in the three scenarios. Figure 8d shows the absolute number of young adults aged 15–34 with complete secondary education. The beneficial impact on adult secondary education of the full intake rate is small because most children in Nicaragua are already entering school. The MDG-Completion scenario has a major impact on the proportion of young adults with complete secondary education.

The investment return for achieving the MDG-Completion scenario comes in the increases in the proportion of the adult population with secondary schooling. As more children finish primary school and (assuming constant transition rates to secondary) proceed to secondary school, the ranks of well-educated young adults swell. From about 2010 onward, the line for secondary attainment in the MDG-Completion scenario departs sharply upward from

FIGURE 8 Net enrollment rates (NER) at the primary and secondary levels, proportion of adults aged 15–64 with some secondary schooling, and proportion of adults aged 15–34 with complete secondary schooling for Nicaragua, 2000–30, for the Constant, MDG-Intake, and MDG-Completion scenarios

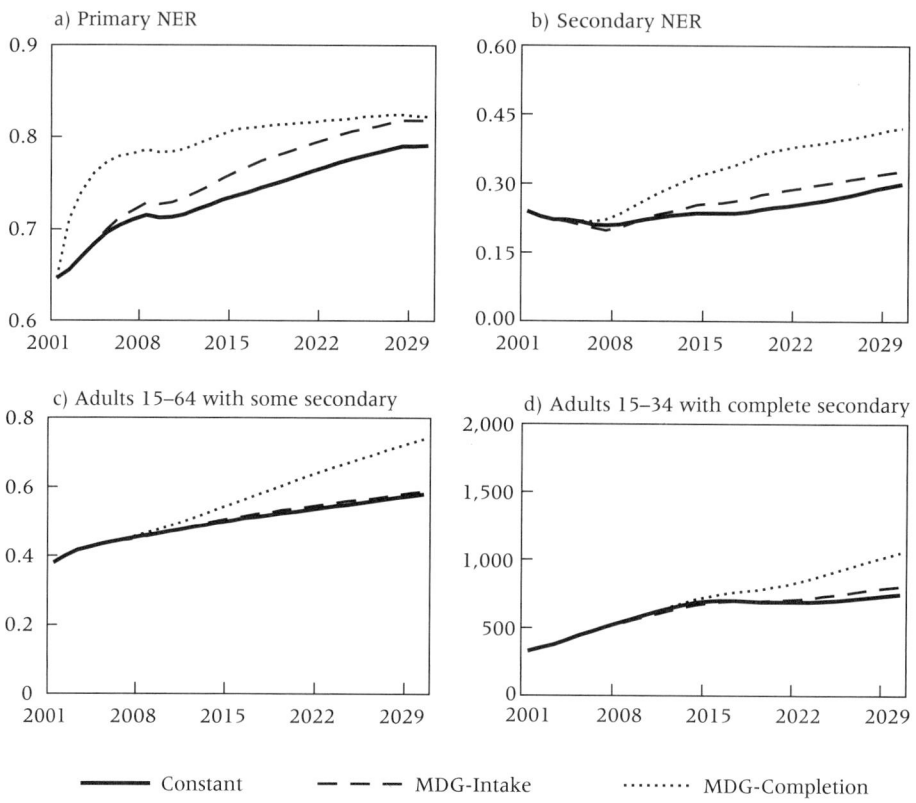

SOURCE: Authors' calculations.

the other scenarios. In fact, raising the promotion rates has a much bigger impact on adult educational attainments than raising intake rates. The reason is that an improvement in promotion and retention affects all those who are already in school, whereas the effect of higher intake rates begins at first grade and must work its way up through all the grades of the school system.

Conclusions and outlook

This analysis demonstrates both the importance and the feasibility of producing country-level projections of the population by age, sex, and educational attainment. It illustrates the benefits of this method by considering the full and detailed age and education distribution of the population and by demonstrating that persons with different educational attainment tend to have significantly different fertility, mortality, and migration levels.

We provide detailed education projection studies for three countries, Guinea, Nicaragua, and Zambia. These three specific applications demonstrate the feasibility of conducting such human capital projections, even for countries with imperfect databases. The assessment of the DHS data for these countries (provided in the appendixes of the DHS reports) shows that their quality is sufficient for the necessary base data on educational attainment, fertility by education, and child mortality by mother's education.

The three case studies show impressive examples of the momentum of improvements in human capital stock. Even the scenarios that assume the very optimistic path of being able to meet the MDG educational goals of full intake and gender equality do not in the short run produce a human capital stock of the working-age population that is much different from that in the scenario which assumes constant enrollment rates over time. Larger human capital stock differentials begin to show up after two or three decades. A projection for Nicaragua that assumes changing promotion rates to 100 percent in the primary grades begins to improve human capital earlier, within a decade, largely because promotion affects those already in school. The case studies also demonstrate that past improvements in education, which are reflected in today's distribution of education by age, will continue to improve the human capital stock over the coming years, even if no additional efforts in expanding enrollment are made. This significant momentum of improvements in human capital stock is very important to keep in mind when setting political targets and when studying the costs and benefits of investments in education.

Finally, in the context of the mid-term review of the Millennium Development Goals, we have shown that systematic studies of past, current, and future educational attainment by age and sex can make vital contributions to understanding the dynamics by which many of the MDG indicators change over time. It seems to us that using the methods described here has more justification than using the simplistic method of drawing a line between the starting point and the goal set for 2015 and then using this line as the basis to judge whether individual countries lie above or below the MDG target path.

This study primarily addresses the population dynamics of improvements in human capital in developing countries. Most of these countries are also aging in the sense that the mean age of the population and the proportions above age 60 are increasing over time. Yet these populations are still very young and generally have a long way to go before they reach the proportions elderly currently observed in industrialized countries.

The methods of human capital projections described here apply to all populations. Improvements in human capital are critical for all countries, irrespective of whether they are in the early or late stages of demographic transition. More work is needed to understand to what degree a further improvement in the educational levels of industrialized societies can help to compensate for the feared negative consequences of population aging and even population decline. There will be fewer young people, but they could be better educated and hence more productive.

APPENDIX TABLE 1 Demographic assumptions for Guinea, Nicaragua, and Zambia by level of education

	Guinea				Nicaragua				Zambia			
Indicator	No educ.	Primary educ.	Sec. educ.	Higher educ.	No educ.	Primary educ.	Sec. educ.	Higher educ.	No educ.	Primary educ.	Sec. educ.	Higher educ.
Total fertility rate												
2000–05	6.0	5.6	4.7	3.0	5.7	4.2	2.7	1.7	6.8	6.2	4.0	3.3
2025–30	3.4	3.2	2.3	1.8	3.5	2.7	2.0	1.7	4.3	3.8	2.4	2.1
Average 2000–05		5.8				3.6				5.6		
Life expectancy at birth (years)												
Males												
2000–05	46.7	51.5	55.5	55.5	62.7	68.2	72.8	74.5	30.7	32.7	36.0	36.0
2025–30	56.6	60.2	62.7	62.7	69.5	74.0	75.0	76.2	40.5	42.3	45.0	45.0
Females												
2000–05	48.3	53.3	59.0	59.0	67.5	72.7	76.7	78.3	30.6	32.3	36.0	36.0
2025–30	57.7	61.2	65.9	65.9	75.6	78.6	79.1	80.2	39.2	40.0	44.0	44.0
Net number of migrants (thousands)												
Males 2000–05	−148	−42	−31	−11	−9	−12	−7	−2	−14	−33	−19	−4
Females 2000–05	−190	−26	−12	−3	−9	−12	−7	−2	−20	−36	−12	−2
Males 2005–10	0	0	0	0	−8	−12	−6	−2	−10	−23	−13	−2
Females 2005–10	0	0	0	0	−8	−11	−7	−2	−14	−25	−8	−1
Males 2025–30	0	0	0	0	−6	−13	−8	−3	−1	−1	−1	0
Females 2025–30	0	0	0	0	−6	−12	−9	−3	−1	−1	−1	0

SOURCE: Authors' calculations.

APPENDIX TABLE 2 Final educational transitions in 2025–30 by scenario by age, sex, and country

Transitions			Males					Females				
From:	To:	Scenario	5–9	10–14	15–19	20–24	25–29	5–9	10–14	15–19	20–24	25–29
Guinea												
No education	Primary	Constant	.28	.40				.23	.22			
		Trend	.95					.95				
		MDG	1*					1*				
Primary	Secondary	Constant		.06	.36				.05	.22	.06	
		Trend		.39	.23				.31	.13		
		MDG		.50*	.20*				.50*	.20*		
Secondary	Higher	Constant			.08	.07	.14			.02	.14	
		Trend			.08	.12	.14			.02	.25	
		MDG			.22*	.21*	.10*			.22*	.21*	
Nicaragua												
No education	Primary	Constant	.43	.75	.24			.46	.75	.26		
		Trend	.52	.91	.30			.53	.87	.30		
		MDG	1*					1*				
Primary	Secondary	Constant		.15	.41				.21	.50		
		Trend		.18	.50				.24	.59		
		MDG		.20*	.54*				.20*	.54*		
Secondary	Higher	Constant			.29	.24				.30	.23	
		Trend			.35	.29				.36	.28	
		MDG			.38*	.32*				.38*	.32*	
Zambia												
No education	Primary	Constant	.45	.71	.46			.46	.67	.58		
		Trend	.93					.91				
		MDG	1*					1*				
Primary	Secondary	Constant		.05	.31	.23			.05	.36		
		Trend		.49					.45			
		MDG		.53*					.53*			
Secondary	Higher	Constant			.05	.12	.07			.05	.09	.08
		Trend			.05	.15	.07			.05	.13	.08
		MDG			.07*	.18*	.10*			.07*	.18*	.10*

* By 2015
NOTE: For comparison, the figures for the Constant scenario in 2025–30 are the same as the base-year transitions.
SOURCE: Authors' calculations.

APPENDIX FIGURE 1 Guinea: Population projections by education, according to the Constant, Trend, and MDG scenarios, 2000–30 (population in thousands)

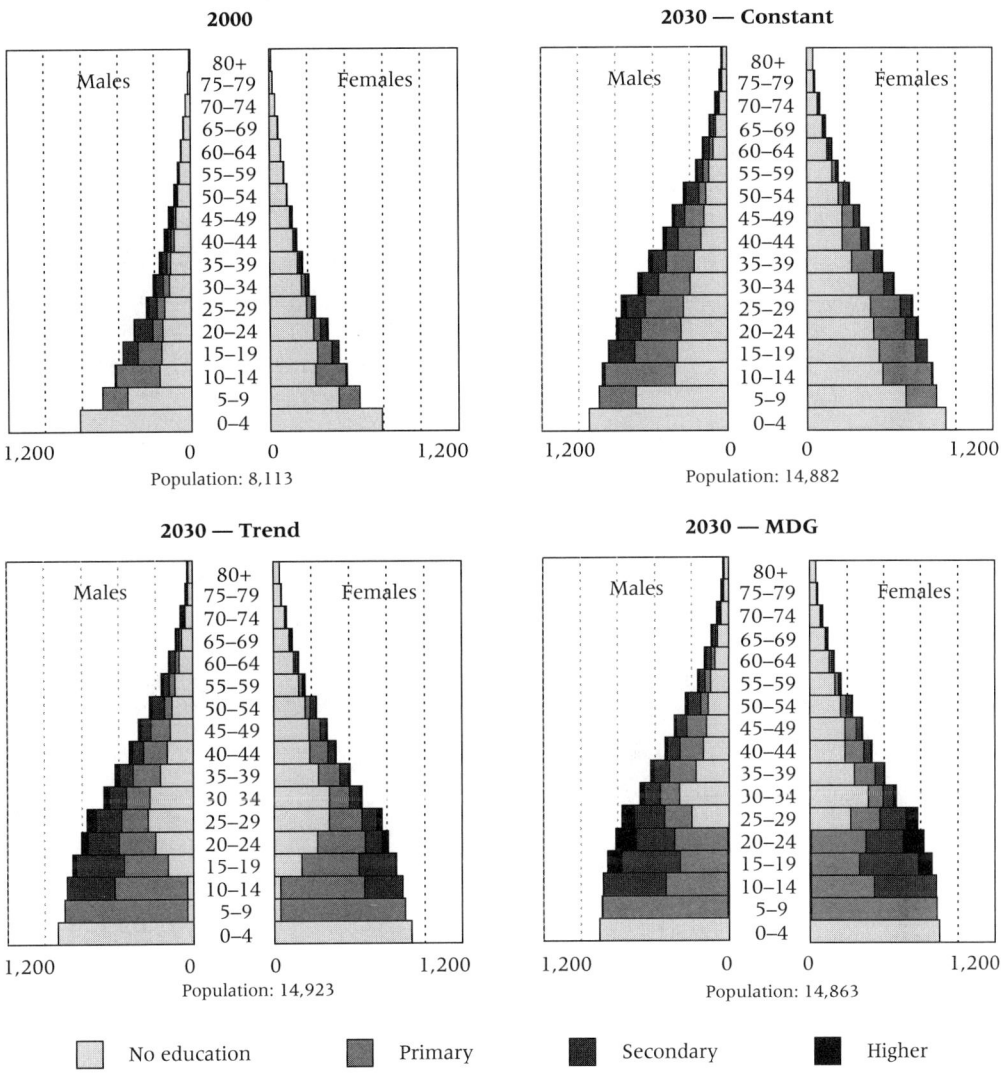

SOURCE: Authors' calculations.

APPENDIX FIGURE 2 Nicaragua: Population projections by education, according to the Constant, Trend, and MDG scenarios, 2000–30 (population in thousands)

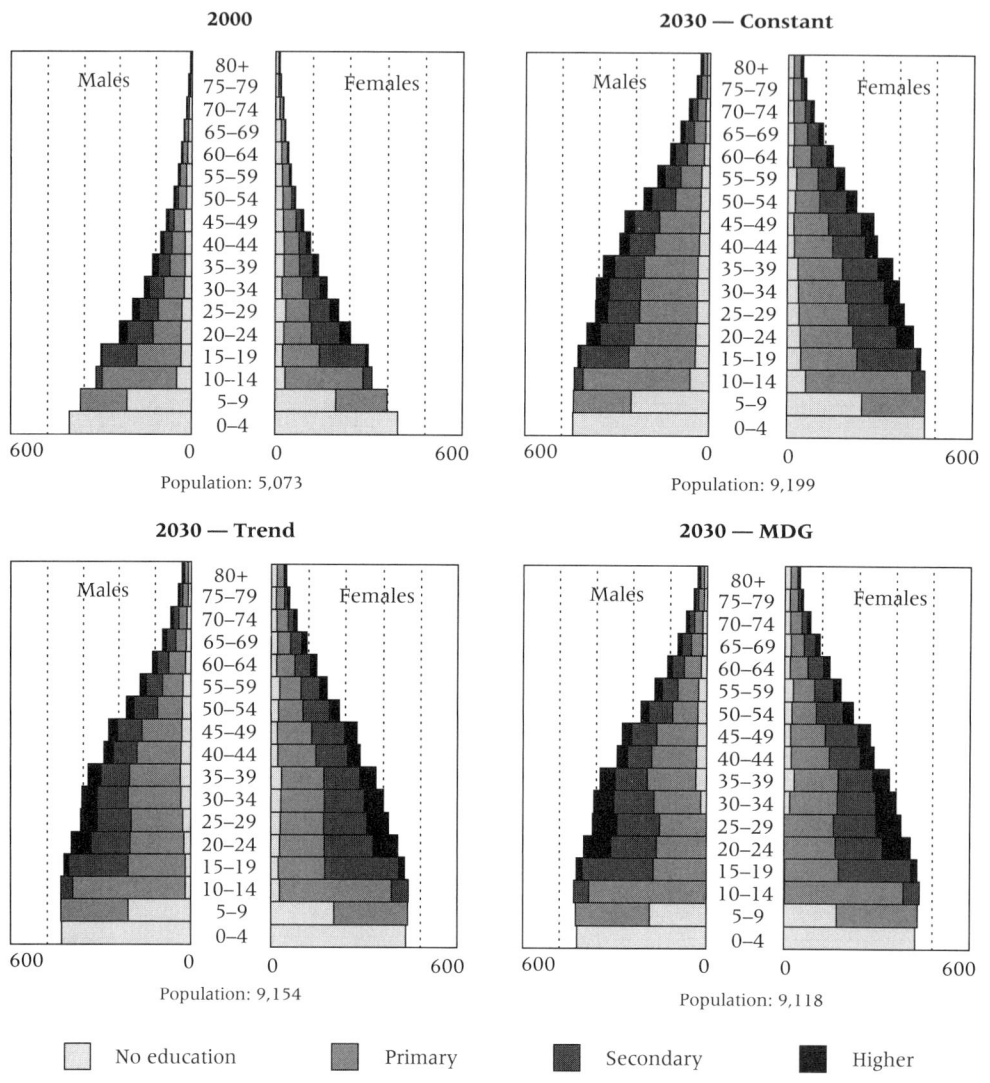

SOURCE: Authors' calculations.

APPENDIX FIGURE 3 Zambia: Population projections by education, according to the Constant, Trend, and MDG scenarios, 2000–30 (population in thousands)

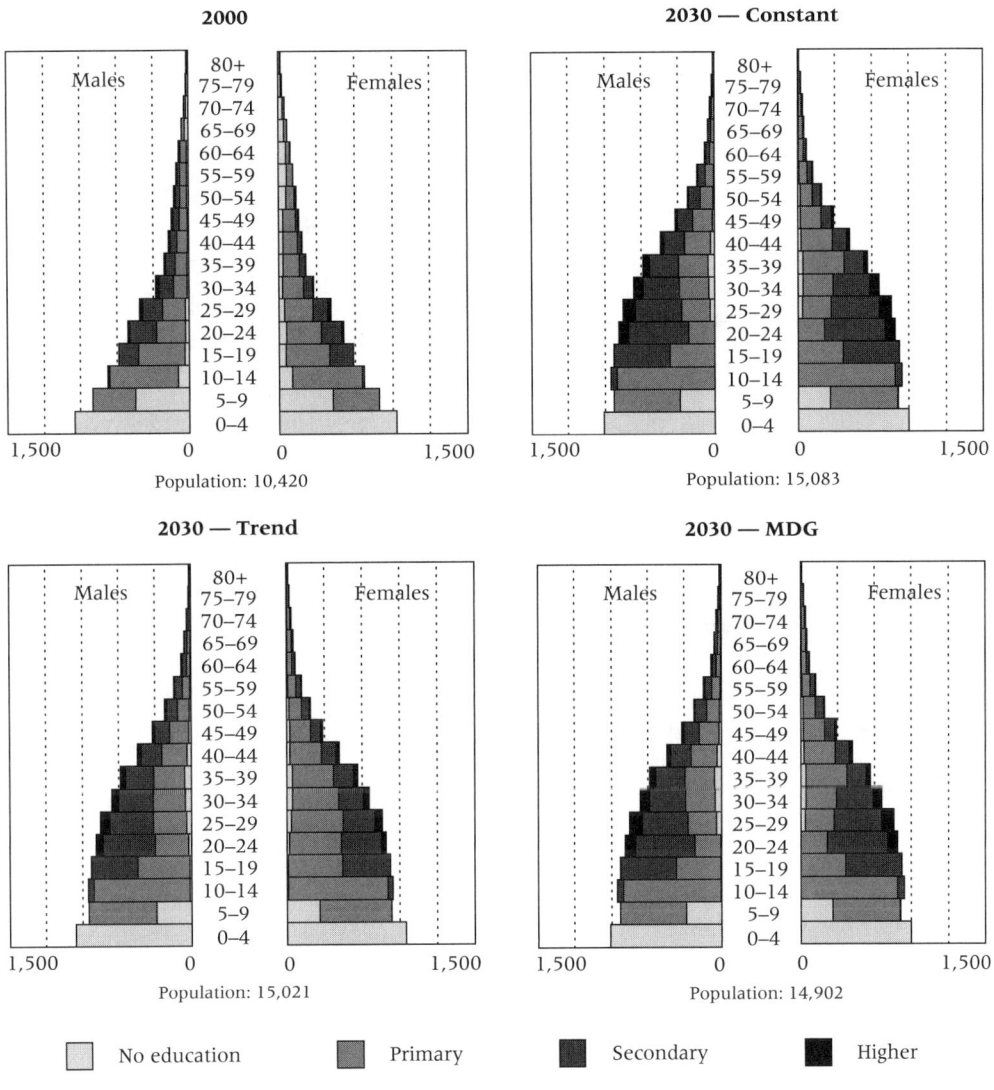

SOURCE: Authors' calculations.

Notes

The research presented in this chapter was supported in part by the World Bank.

1 Among these assessments are TIMSS, the Trends in International Mathematics and Science Study, available at «www.timss.bc.edu»; PIRLS, the Progress in International Reading Literacy Study, available at «www.timss.bc.edu»; PISA, the Programme in International Student Assessment, at «www.pisa.oecd.org»; SACMEQ, the Southern and Eastern Africa Consortium for Monitoring Educational Quality, at «www.sacmeq.org»; LLECE, Laboratorio Latinoamericano de Evaluación de la Calidad de la Educación, at «www.llece.unesco.cl».

2 A similar problem of lacking age detail applies to the aggregate indicator of life expectancy that is frequently used in regressions aimed at explaining economic growth. Demographic analysis shows that, depending on the level of life expectancy, improvements in this indicator result either from a decline in child mortality or from declines in old-age mortality. These are two very different phenomena when it comes to assessing their possible effects on personal investment strategies and consequently on economic growth.

3 Examples of two UNESCO models are the EFA Projection Model (EFAPM), which is being applied in a number of Asian countries (UNESCO 2003), and the SIMEDUC model (Duvieusart 1991). National models have been developed for Nicaragua (Porta 2004) and Uganda (Moses and Golladay 2004).

4 The model could also take into account the family education background of children so that there would be feedback from parents' education on their children's schooling. It has been tested experimentally in Lutz and Goujon (2001) but is not applied in this chapter.

5 Recent data are available from sample surveys but not from the census, at least for Guinea and Nicaragua where the last censuses were conducted in 1996 and 1995. Also the data on the education sector are less than complete, and the data on mortality and migration by level of educational attainment are also deficient.

6 "No education" for all three countries refers to those who never went to school or finished less than one year of primary schooling. Primary education for all three countries includes those who finished one or more years of primary, but no secondary education. Primary schooling in Guinea and Nicaragua is six years; in Zambia it is seven years; and in all three countries the official age to start school is seven. Secondary education for all three countries includes both junior and senior or upper secondary school, and vocational secondary school. Tertiary education includes all post-secondary levels (including, for example, teacher academies, agricultural schools, etc.).

7 First we used the BESTFT function to find the life table to best fit the probabilities of dying for age groups 0–1 and 1–4 years given as an input, and then we constructed a life table based on those age-specific probabilities of dying using the procedure LIFTB. The total life expectancies at birth resulting from these age-specific probabilities of dying were different from the estimates provided by the United Nations. For Guinea, we applied the differential found through the Mortpak procedures to the UN life expectancy, in order to obtain new life expectancy by education. The life expectancies of the secondary and higher education groups were further adjusted (five years for males and four years for females) in order to be closer to the total life expectancy provided by the United Nations.

8 The choice that the projection assumptions should follow those of the UN is not obligatory. In fact, a useful feature of such multi-state projections is that the changing weights of education categories in the population affect the aggregate fertility, mortality, and migration assumptions and produce different aggregated projections as compared to single-state projections.

9 MDG Goal 2 aims at achieving universal primary education, ensuring that by 2015 all children will be able to complete a full course of primary schooling. Goal 3 aims at promoting gender equality and the empowerment of women by eliminating gender disparity in primary and secondary education, preferably by 2005, and at all levels of education no later than 2015.

10 Primary net enrollment rate = (number of children of primary school age in primary school) / (number of children of primary school age).

References

Ahuja, V. and D. Filmer. 1995. "Educational attainment in development countries: New estimates and projections disaggregated by gender," Washington, DC: The World Bank, mimeo.

Alachkar, A. and W. J. Serow. 1988. "The socioeconomic determinants of mortality: An international comparison," *Genus* 44(3–4): 131–151.

Barro, R. and J. W. Lee. 1993. "International comparison of educational attainment," *Journal of Monetary Economics* 32: 363–394.

———. 2000. *International Data on Educational Attainment. Updates and Implications*. NBER Working Paper 7911. Cambridge, MA: National Bureau of Economic Research.

Barro, R. and X. Sala-i-Martín. 1995. *Economic Growth*. New York: McGraw-Hill.

Bils, M. and P. Klenow. 2001. "Does schooling cause growth?," *American Economic Review* 90(5): 1160–1183.

Bledsoe, C. H., J. B. Casterline, J. A. Johnson-Kuhn, and J. G. Haaga. 1999. *Critical Perspectives on Schooling and Fertility in the Developing World*. Washington, DC: National Academy Press.

Bloom, D. and D. Canning. 2003. "How demographic change can bolster economic performance in developing countries," *World Economics* 4(4): 1–14.

Castelló, A. and R. Doménech. 2002. "Human capital inequality and economic growth: Some new evidence," *The Economic Journal* 112 (March): 187–200.

Cohen, D. and M. Soto. 2001. *Growth and Human Capital: Good Data, Good Results*. OECD Development Centre Technical Papers 179. Paris: Organisation for Economic Co-operation and Development.

Collier, P. and A. Hoeffler. 2000. *Greed and Grievance in Civil War*. Policy Research Paper 2355. Washington, D. C.: The World Bank.

Coulombe, S., J.-F. Tremblay, and S. Marchand. 2004. *International Adult Literacy Survey; Literacy Scores, Human Capital and Growth Across Fourteen OECD Countries*. Catalogue No. 89–552-MIE. Ottawa, Ontario: Statistics Canada.

Crespo Cuaresma, J. and W. Lutz. 2007. *Human Capital, Age Structure and Economic Growth: Evidence from a New Dataset*. Interim Report IR–07–011. Laxenburg, Austria: International Institute for Applied Systems Analysis.

De la Fuente, A. and R. Doménech. 2000. *Human Capital in Growth Regressions: How Much Difference does Data Quality Make?* OECD Economics Department Working Papers 262. Paris: Organisation for Economic Co-operation and Development.

DHS Guinea 1999. Direction Nationale de la Statistique [Guinea] and Macro International, Inc. 2000. *Enquête Démographique et de Santé, Guinée 1999*. Calverton, MA: Direction Nationale de la Statistique and Macro International, Inc.

DHS Nicaragua 2001. Instituto Nacional de Estadísticas y Censos [Nicaragua], Ministerio de Salud [Nicaragua], and DHS+/ORC Macro. 2002. *Encuesta Nicaragüensede Demografía y Salud 2001*. Calverton, MA: Instituto Nacional de Estadísticas y Censos, Ministerio de Salud, and DHS+/ORC Macro.

DHS Zambia 2002. Central Statistical Office [Zambia], Central Board of Health [Zambia], and ORC Macro. 2003. *Zambia Demographic and Health Survey 2001–2002*. Calverton, MA: Central Statistical Office, Central Board of Health, and ORC Macro.

Doblhammer, G. 1997. *Socioeconomic Differentials in Austrian Adult Mortality: A Study Based on Linked Census and Deaths Records for the Years 1981/1982*. Ph.D. Thesis. Vienna, Austria: Sozial- und Wirtschaftswissenschaftliche Fakultät, Universität Wien.

Dubey, A. and E. King. 1994. "A new cross-country education stock series differentiated by age and sex." Washington, DC: The World Bank, typescript.

Duvieusart, B. 1991. *SIMEDUC 1.1 A Simulation Model for Educational Development*. Working Document. Paris: UNESCO.

Ferreira, M. L. 1996. *Poverty and Inequality During Structural Adjustment in Rural Tanzania*. Policy Research Working Paper No. 1641. Washington, DC: The World Bank.

Goujon, A. 2002. "Population and education prospects in the Arab region," in I. Serageldin (ed.), *Human Capital: Population Economics in the Middle East*. Cairo: The American University in Cairo Press, pp. 116–140.

Goujon, A. and S. K.C. 2006. *Past and Future of Human Capital in Southeast Asia: From 1970 to 2030*. VID Working Paper 07/2006. Vienna: Vienna Institute of Demography, Austrian Academy of Sciences.

Goujon, A. and W. Lutz. 2004. "Future human capital: Population projections by level of education," pp. 121–157 in W. Lutz, W. C. Sanderson, and S. Scherbov (eds.), *The End of World Population Growth in the 21st Century: New Challenges for Human Capital Formation and Sustainable Development*. London: Earthscan.

Goujon, A. and K. McNay. 2003. "Projecting the educational composition of the population of India: Selected state-level perspectives," *Applied Population and Policy* 1(1): 25–35.

Goujon, A., H. Alkitkat, W. Lutz, and I. Prommer. 2007. *Population and Human Capital Growth in Egypt: Projections for Governorates to 2051*. Interim Report IR–07–010. Laxenburg, Austria: International Institute for Applied Systems Analysis.

Haddad, W. D., M. Carnoy, R. Rinaldi, and O. Regel. 1990. *Education and Development Evidence for New Priorities*. World Bank Discussion Papers 95. Washington, DC: The World Bank.

Huisman, M., A. E. Kunst, O. Andersen, J.-K. Borgan, C. Borrell, G. Costa, P. Deboosere, G. Desplanques, A. Donkin, S. Gadeyne, J. Kytir, C. Minder, E. Regidor, T. Spadea, T. Valkonen, and J. P. Mackenbach. 2002. "Socio-economic inequalities in mortality in Europe among elderly people," Sedha Project, unpublished.

Jejeebhoy, S. 1995. *Women's Education, Autonomy, and Reproductive Behaviour: Experience from Developing Countries*. Oxford, UK: Clarendon Press.

Keyfitz, N. 1985. *Applied Mathematical Demography*. 2nd Edition. New York: Springer Verlag.

Krueger, A. and M. Lindhal. 2001. "Education for growth: Why and for whom?," *Journal of Economic Literature* 39–4: 1101–1136.

Kyriacou, G. A. 1991. "Level and growth effects of human capital: A cross-country study of the convergence hypothesis," New York: Department of Economics, New York University, mimeo.

Lutz, W. (ed.). 1994. *Population-Development-Environment: Understanding Their Interactions in Mauritius*. Berlin: Springer Verlag.

Lutz, W. and A. Goujon. 2001. "The world's changing human capital stock: Multi-state population projections by educational attainment," *Population and Development Review* 27(2): 323–339.

Lutz, W., A. Goujon, and G. Doblhammer-Reiter. 1999. "Demographic dimensions in forecasting: Adding education to age and sex," in W. Lutz, J. W. Vaupel, and D. A. Ahlburg (eds.), *Frontiers of Population Forecasting*, supplement to Volume 24, 1998, *Population and Development Review*. New York: The Population Council, pp. 42–58.

Lutz, W., A. Goujon, Samir K.C., and W. Sanderson. 2007. "Reconstruction of populations by age, sex and level of educational attainment for 120 countries for 1970–2000," *Vienna Yearbook of Population Research 2007*, pp. 193–235.

Lutz, W., L. Prieto, and W. Sanderson (eds.). 2000. *Population, Development, and Environment on the Yucatán Peninsula: From Ancient Maya to 2030*. Research Report RR–00–14. Laxenburg, Austria: International Institute for Applied Systems Analysis.

Lutz, W. and S. Scherbov. 2004. "Probabilistic population projections for Singapore and Asia," *Innovation* 5(1): 44–45.

Mankiw, N. G., D. Romer, and D. N. Weil. 1992. "A contribution to the empirics of economic growth," *Quarterly Journal of Economics* 107(2): 407–437.

Moses, K. and F. Golladay. 2004. "Recent Uganda experiences strategic projections—EPDC workshop," paper presented at the Maps to the Future Workshop on Making Education Projections for Policy, Washington, D. C., Education Policy and Data Center, 12 July.

Nehru, V., E. Swanson, and A. Dubey. 1993. *A New Database on Human Capital Stock: Sources, Methodology and Results*. Policy Research Working Paper 1124. Washington, DC: The World Bank.

OECD. 2000. *Literacy in the Information Age: Final Report of the International Adult Literacy Survey.* Paris: Organisation for Economic Co-operation and Development / Statistics Canada.
Pool, I. 2004. "Of 'demographic dividends,' 'windows of opportunity' and development: Age-structure, population waves and cohort flows," paper presented at CICRED Seminar on Age-structural Transitions: Population Waves, Disordered Cohort Flows and the Demographic Bonus, Paris, 23–26 February.
Porta, E. 2004. "Nicaragua sectoral education model," paper presented at the Maps to the Future Workshop on Making Education Projections for Policy, Washington, DC, Education Policy and Data Center, July 12, 2004.
Pritchett, L. 2001. "Where all education has gone," *The World Bank Economic Review* 15(3): 367–391.
Psacharopoulos, G. and A. M. Arrigada. 1986. "The educational composition of the labor force: An international comparison," *International Labor Review* 125(5): 561–574.
———. 1992. "The educational composition of the labor force: An international update," *Journal of Educational Planning and Administration* 6(2): 141–159.
Psacharopoulos, G. and H. A. Patrinos. 2002. *Returns to Investment in Education: A Further Update.* Policy Research Working Paper WPS2881. Washington, DC: The World Bank.
Rogers, A. 1975. *Introduction to Multiregional Mathematical Demography.* New York: John Wiley.
Romer, P. M. 1989. *Human Capital and Growth: Theory and Evidence.* NBER Working Paper 3173. Cambridge, MA: National Bureau of Economic Research.
Sanderson, W. C., B. Fuller, M. E. Hellmuth, and K. M. Strzepek. 2001. *Namibia's Future. Modeling Population and Sustainable Development Challenges in the Era of HIV/AIDS.* IIASA Executive Summary. Laxenburg, Austria: International Institute for Applied Systems Analysis.
Sanderson, W. C., M. E. Hellmuth, and K. M. Strzepek. 2001. *Botswana's Future. Modeling Population and Sustainable Development Challenges in the Era of HIV/AIDS.* IIASA Executive Summary. Laxenburg, Austria: International Institute for Applied Systems Analysis.
SAPRIN (Structural Adjustment Participatory Review International Network). 2004. *The Policy Roots of Economic Crisis and Poverty: A Multi-country Participatory Assessment of Structural Adjustment.* London: Zed Books.
Sen, A. 1999. *Development as Freedom.* Oxford: Oxford University Press.
UNESCO. 2003. "Development of EFA planning simulation model," presentation at the meeting in Bangkok, Thailand, November 24–29, 2003. Available at «http://www.unescobkk.org/aims/documents/Planning%20Tools.pdf».
———. 2004. *Education for All: The Quality Imperative.* EFA Global Monitoring Report, 2003/4. Paris: UNESCO.
———. 2006. *2006 EFA Global Monitoring Report—Literacy for Life.* Paris: UNESCO.
United Nations. 2002. *World Population Prospects: The 2002 Revision.* New York: United Nations.
Wils, A. 1996. *PDE-Cape Verde: A Systems Study of Population, Development, and Environment.* Working Paper WP–96–009. Laxenburg, Austria: International Institute for Applied Systems Analysis.
———. 2007. *Window on the Future: 2025—Projections of Education Attainment and Its Impact.* Washington, DC: Academy for Educational Development.
Wils, A., B. Carrol, and K. Barrow. 2005. *Educating the World's Children: Patterns of Growth and Inequality.* Academy for Educational Development Special Report. Washington, DC: Academy for Educational Development.
Wils, A., M. da Costa Gaspar, M. E. Hellmuth, M. Ibraimo, I. Prommer, and E. Sebastiao. 2001. *Mozambique's Future. Modeling Population and Sustainable Development Challenges.* IIASA Executive Summary. Laxenburg, Austria: International Institute for Applied Systems Analysis.
Yousif, H. M., A. Goujon, and W. Lutz. 1996. *Future Population and Education Trends in the Countries of North Africa.* Research Report RR–96–11. Laxenburg, Austria: IIASA.

# PART III.
PRODUCTIVITY STUDIES AT VARIOUS LEVELS OF ANALYSIS

Age and Productivity Potential: A New Approach Based on Ability Levels and Industry-Wide Task Demand

Vegard Skirbekk

I propose a framework to estimate the relation between age and productivity potential (a work performance measurement based on cognitive and non-cognitive skills and the labor market importance of these skills). This is done to show that the age–productivity curve is not necessarily static but can vary with changing labor market requirements. By basing the analysis on age variation in individuals' abilities and the changing importance of these abilities in the labor market, focus is given to the causes of age differences in productivity.

Using a dynamic causal approach, I focus on issues that have been neglected in earlier investigations. Earlier studies have seldom investigated why productivity varies by age. Nor have they considered that the shape of the age–productivity profile can change over time. Previous research has failed to develop a general model of the interrelationship of age and productivity. Conclusions on age-performance variation based on piece-rate samples or supervisors' ratings can be biased, as they tend to come from a very limited set of occupations. Analyses of employer–employee datasets are also usually restricted in terms of industries (for example, they often do not consider service industries).

The investigation overcomes some of these shortcomings by focusing on the potential causes of age differences in productivity. I estimate how the determinants of productivity vary by age and the relative importance of these determinants in the labor market, using ability tests and estimates of the relative importance of the abilities in the labor market. These estimates suggest that job performance follows an inverted U-shaped curve, increasing in the initial labor market years and decreasing toward the end of one's career. The shape and peak of the curve varies over time according to changes in the labor market demand for abilities. Given that experience has a reasonably strong effect on productivity, the peak productivity potential occurs in ages 35–44 years.

The attempt to understand how causal factors affect the shape of the age–productivity curve could provide a better understanding of how productivity varies over the lifecycle under different circumstances. This work may be best understood as a framework for understanding the influence of some of the causal factors that determine age variation in job proficiency and for assessing how changing labor market demands shift the shape of the age–productivity curve.

Age–productivity literature review

Evidence from both employment shifts between industries and changes in the relative wage levels of unskilled and skilled employees suggests that there has been an increase in the demand for cognitive abilities over a long period of time (Acemoglu 2002; Dickerson and Green 2002; Goldin and Katz 1998; Howell and Wolff 1991; Juhn et al. 1993; Phelps Brown, and Hopkins 1955; Spitz 2004). In modern societies, where physical strength has lost much of its importance, cognitive skills can be the best predictor of productivity (Hanushek and Kimko 2000; Schmidt and Hunter 1998; Tyler et al. 2000).

For the purpose of correctly estimating the age–productivity profile and how it changes over time, it is necessary to consider the possible effect of changing labor market conditions on the role of experience in productivity. Long experience on the job can improve older workers' productivity relative to that of younger workers. Studies show that older employees use more efficient working strategies (De la Mare and Shepherd 1958; Salthouse 1984). At some point, however, further experience no longer improves job performance. Ilmakunnas et al. (2004) assess a broad sample of Finnish manufacturing employees and find that job duration improves productivity for only up to 3.8 years, while Ericsson and Lehmann (1996) argue that it takes roughly 10 years to achieve expert competence in games and situations where strategic and analytic competence is important. The 10-year estimate is supported by findings from a variety of job domains, ranging from livestock evaluation and x-ray analysis to scientific performance in medical and natural sciences (Econ 1998; Lehman 1953; Lesgold 1984; Phelps and Shanteau 1978; Raskin 1936).

Increasing emphasis is likely to be put on the ability to acquire new knowledge in a rapidly changing workplace. This could have an adverse effect on the relative productivity of senior employees, as the speed and efficiency of learning decrease with age (Rybash et al. 1986; Smith 1996). In industries that have a high rate of skill-biased technological change, or where technological shocks render acquired competencies obsolete, early retirement is common (Bartel and Sicherman 1993; Ahituv and Zeira 2000), and workers are assessed to be most productive at relatively young ages (Dalton and Thompson 1971).

Previous studies have measured age–productivity profiles by using supervisors' ratings, production records, or employer–employee panels (for surveys, see Warr 1994 and Skirbekk 2004). The most common measurement of age–productivity profiles is the comparison of supervisors' ratings. Studies on age and productivity, which tend to be based on managers' ratings, find little or no relationship between the assessment score and the age of the employee (Hunter and Hunter 1984; McEvoy and Cascio 1989). However, estimates based on this approach may be upward biased since supervisors could inflate evaluations of senior employees as an acknowledgment of past achievements as well as out of loyalty (Salthouse and Maurer 1996). Moreover, a firm's best employees receive promotion, while inefficient employees may lose their jobs, and the resulting selectivity by age can lead to bias in the estimates.

Studies based on production records are more objective as they are based on output measures such as the number of items produced within a given time. A US Department of Labor study, based on a broad selection of industries, compared output between individuals of different ages. The authors found that performance increased until the age of 35, before declining until the age of retirement. However, the slope of the decline was not steep: productivity declined by only 14 percent in the men's footwear industry, and 17 percent in the household furniture industry (US Department of Labor 1957). Further analyses of the performance of manual workers (Mark 1957; Kutscher and Walker 1960) also found declines from the middle of the working life.

Analyses of employer–employee datasets study the impact of the age structure of a firm's labor force on the firm's output. Studies such as Hægeland and Klette (1999), Crépon et al. (2002), and Ilmakunnas et al. (2004) found that the productivity levels of older workers tend to be lower than those of their younger counterparts. However, the difficult procedure of isolating the age structure from the other factors that affect the firm's output can induce errors. Moreover, since most of these studies are based on cross-sectional evidence, they do not reveal whether a young age structure is the result rather than the cause of the firms' success.

Productivity for exceptional performers, including scientists and writers, also suggests an inverted U-shaped productivity function, where productivity tends to peak from ages 20 to 40 (Jones 2005; Lehman 1953; Simonton 1997). However, the peaks differ according to the type of discipline and whether long experience or innovative thinking is more important, and Simonton (1997, p. 72) finds that peak productivity for historians is 12 years later than for mathematicians.

While productivity tends to reach its peak in mid-career, wages often increase throughout the career. Across the OECD, seniority-based wage systems are negatively related to employment opportunities for workers in the 55–64-year age group (OECD 2006). Lazear (1979) and Hutchens (1989) argue that the differences between age-earning profiles and age–productivity profiles can be explained by firms' wish to create loyalty to the firm and by uncertainty about new workers' true productivity levels.

In settings with few labor regulations and without seniority-based wage systems, age-earnings profiles may reflect differences in performance. A study by Boot (1995) examines the age-earnings profiles of British workers in the first half of the nineteenth century, a period characterized by a laissez-faire labor market with few regulations. For the physically demanding work that is examined, male wages peak in the early 30s and decrease substantially from around 40 years of age. Lazear and Moore (1984) studied wage profiles by examining the difference between the age-earnings profile of the self-employed and that of salaried workers. They found that the earnings of the former group (where wages are likely to be closer to productivity) show a relatively flat age profile, while the earnings of salaried workers increase throughout their career.

The age–productivity curve based on causal, time-varying determinants

The aim of the current study is to provide estimates for a framework to measure productivity potential by age. Rather than studying static output measures of productivity, we focus on time-variant causal factors. This is done by using data on age-specific supply of abilities (cognitive and noncognitive test scores). These data on abilities across age groups are weighted with a measure of time-variant labor market demand. An estimate of work experience and how it affects the productivity of workers from different age groups is also taken into account.

A key feature of the method used is the separation of the factors that increase productivity from those that decrease it. Experience boosts productivity and makes workers more effective. However, getting older is also associated with reductions in the performance level of several work-related abilities. At younger ages, the productivity-enhancing effect of longer experience is more important than the decrease in ability levels. The net effect is productivity increase. For senior workers, however, additional experience no longer affects job performance, and productivity is reduced according to the decline in ability levels.

An outline of this framework is given in Figure 1. The figure shows the combined impact on productivity of experience (which raises performance for the first years) and other productivity input factors (which would typically decrease performance with advancing age). The productivity slope first increases as a result of experience and crystallized abilities and later declines as fluid abilities are reduced at the latter half of the working life.

Variation between individuals tends to be greater than variation across age groups, as indicated by the parallel curves in experience and productivity

FIGURE 1 Stylized diagram of factors influencing age–productivity profiles

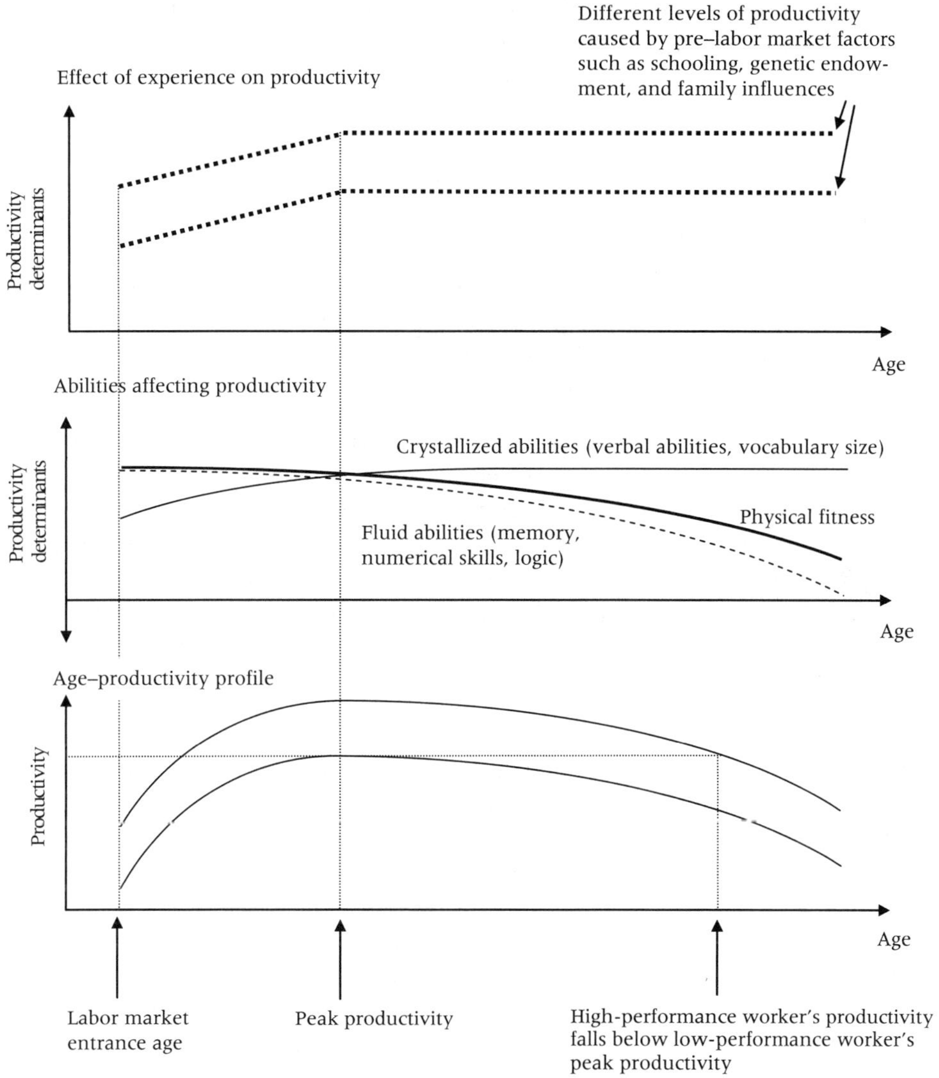

in Figure 1. Schooling, genetic endowment, and family influence are some of the key factors that determine individual performance variation.

Factors affecting productivity: Work-related abilities

Illustrative data on the age-specific supply of abilities can be taken from the General Aptitude Test Battery (GATB), a workforce survey carried out by the US Department of Labor (the data are presented in Avolio and Waldman 1994). The GATB consists of detailed ability scores from 16,134 white American male and female workers with a wide range of educational and professional backgrounds. The subjects are aged 16–74 years, but those above age 65 years were excluded from the present study.

The model includes the abilities for which there is knowledge about relative labor market importance. The relative labor market demand for five abilities is provided by Autor et al. (2003), who estimate how the demand for work tasks has changed over the period 1960–98 in the US labor market. The "matching" of the supply and demand for numerical ability, managerial ability, clerical perception, finger dexterity, and manual dexterity is given in Table 1.

A description of the abilities used, partly based on the description of GATB abilities by Hartigan and Wigdor (1989), follows.

Numerical ability. This measures the extent to which arithmetic and advanced mathematics are required in the occupation and the speed and accuracy with which an individual is able to perform such tasks. Numerical abilities and quantitative skills are relevant for a large number of professions, ranging from accounting to engineering. Several studies have documented the labor market importance of mathematics and have identified a close association between numerical skills and wage levels (Mitra 2002; Murnane et al. 1995).

Managerial ability. This measures the extent to which interpersonal and communication skills, managerial skills, and nonroutine communication are needed in the workplace and the extent to which a person is able to understand the meaning of words and language. This ability is relevant for most jobs, particularly where communication, transmitting knowledge, and making strategic decisions are central occupational tasks. Managerial skills are often required in the labor market, and various measures of verbal aptitude are closely associated with income levels (e.g., IALS 2001). Increases in managerial ability at younger ages are due to an increase in verbal aptitude, as suggested from the GATB survey. Thereafter, it is unaffected by age, as found in Colonia-Willner (1998).

TABLE 1 Matched ability supply and demand

Supplied ability	Demanded ability
Numerical ability	GED math
Managerial ability	Direction, control, and planning of activities
Clerical perception	Set limits, tolerances, or standards
Finger dexterity	Finger dexterity
Manual dexterity	Eye-hand-foot coordination

SOURCES: Supplied ability: General Aptitude Test Battery, Avolio and Waldman 1994. Demanded ability: Dictionary of Occupational Titles, Autor et al. 2003.

TABLE 2 Age-specific ability levels, values relative to 25–34-year-olds

Age	Numerical ability	Managerial ability	Clerical perception	Finger dexterity	Manual dexterity	Experience
16–19	−0.30	−0.17	0.14	0.05	0.16	−0.40
20–24	−0.11	0.00	0.17	0.10	0.35	−0.40
25–34	0.00	0.00	0.00	0.00	0.00	0.00
35–44	−0.39	0.00	−0.28	−0.40	0.05	0.27
45–54	−0.63	0.00	−0.55	−0.92	−0.49	0.27
55–65	−0.85	0.00	−0.80	−1.42	−0.94	0.27

DATA SOURCES: Avolio and Waldman 1994; Colonia-Willner 1998; Ericsson and Lehmann 1996; OECD 1999; and own calculations.

Clerical perception. This is the ability to discriminate and perceive relevant detail in visual and tabular stimuli. This ability is relevant for routine clerical tasks, including to check for errors or to transcribe.

Finger dexterity. This is a measure of the accuracy and speed with which one can manipulate small objects with hands and fingers. It shows how well one is able to use one's hands and to carry out repetitive movements over time. It is relevant, for example, for shoemakers or typists.

Manual dexterity. This is the ability to coordinate hand and foot movement. This measure is important in occupations that require coordination and physical agility (e.g., fire-fighters). The GATB age-specific test scores for these abilities are presented in Table 2. Consistent with findings elsewhere (Blum et al. 1970; Schaie 1996), crystallized abilities (important in, for example, managerial ability) are the least affected by age, while fluid abilities (such as memory span and mental quickness) tend to decline substantially with age.

Demand for abilities

To estimate the labor market value of the different abilities, I use estimates for how the importance of different job tasks has changed over time (see Autor et al. 2003). The data are considered appropriate for this study since they present the level and change of task demands for all employees. The task demand data are matched with the data on age-specific supply of abilities, as shown in Table 1.

Autor et al. (2003) analyze how task input for total US employment has evolved during 1960–98. They use data that describe the average task input required by labor in the economy based on definitions from the Dictionary of Occupational Titles (US Department of Labor 1972), and they merge these with data from population censuses to describe how the job structure is changing over time. The labor input of all American workers from more than 450 job categories in ages 18–64 is examined. By combining data on both

FIGURE 2 Importance of abilities (0–10 scale), 1998

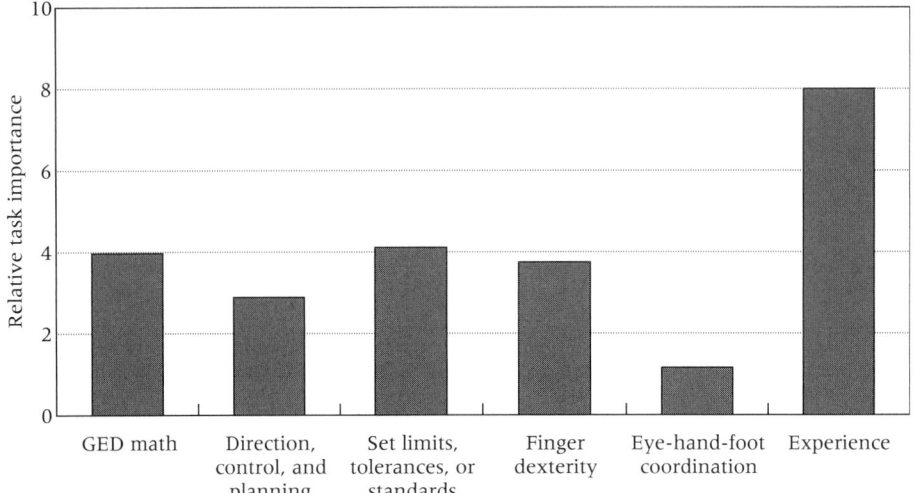

SOURCES: Autor et al. 2003, Golini et al. 2004, and own calculations.

the skill intensity and composition of employment structures with within-job estimates, Autor et al. produce estimates on the extent to which each task input changes over time on an economy-wide scale.

In addition to the five abilities discussed above, I include an estimate of experience in the model. Experience is calculated in a similar way to the other abilities, where age-specific supply is measured relative to the 25–34-year-old workers. No direct evidence exists on the importance of experience in the labor market. I assume that experience is rated as highly important, which is in line with surveys on employers' valuation of workers' skills where experience is ranked as the most important trait (see, e.g., Golini et al. 2004), and I assign it the value 8 on a scale from 0 to 10.

The relative importance of these abilities in the United States in 1998 is shown in Figure 2, and the changes in their relative importance between 1960 and 1998 are given in Table 3. I chose the time period 1960–98 because data from this period allow us to look at recent and past patterns in the demand for

TABLE 3 Importance of abilities (0–10 scale)

Ability	1960	1970	1980	1990	1998
GED math	3.61	3.72	3.76	3.87	3.97
Direction, control, and planning	2.40	2.40	2.46	2.68	2.89
Set limits, tolerances, or standards	4.53	4.70	4.61	4.40	4.11
Finger dexterity	3.78	3.90	3.90	3.83	3.75
Eye-hand-foot coordination	1.37	1.29	1.24	1.17	1.16
Experience	8.00	8.00	8.00	8.00	8.00

SOURCES: Autor et al. 2003, Golini et al. 2004, and own calculations.

abilities. I use the five task categories to assess changing labor market demand for the five abilities described in Table 1.

Experience

The length of experience that the different age groups have is calculated from responses to the question: "How much experience (in years and months) have you had in your present occupation? Include time with both your present and previous employers" (Avolio and Waldman 1994).

I use Ericsson and Lehmann's (1996) estimate that the productivity-enhancing effect of experience reaches its maximum at ten years. Members of the age group 20–24 years are categorized as having no job experience, since the average person in this group is below the average age of labor market entrance. In 1996, the median age of labor market entrance was 22.9 years (OECD 1999). The average worker in the 25–34-year group had 6.0 years of experience (with a standard deviation of 5 years), taking into account age-specific labor force participation rates. Individuals aged 35–65 had acquired the maximum productivity-enhancing effect of experience of at least 10 years.

Method

The productivity measurement is based on the cognitive and non-cognitive ability levels at different ages and on the labor market relevance of these abilities. Each ability's impact on the productivity level is determined by the demand for the ability in the labor market. This may be a strong assumption, since many jobs are not affected by ability variation unless, for example, the ability level drops below a certain threshold. Therefore I later relax this assumption.

I start by postulating the equation for the age-specific supply of abilities.

$$\hat{a}_{X,S,g} = \frac{\overline{a}_{X,S,g} - \overline{a}_{X,S,\text{25-34 year olds}}}{\sigma(a_{X,S,\text{25-34 year olds}})} \quad (1)$$

In equation 1, $\hat{a}_{X,S,g}$ is the estimate for the supply, S, of ability X for age group g. The mean ability score for those aged 25–34 years is subtracted from the average ability score for each age group, and the difference is divided by the standard deviation of ability X for the 25–34 age group. Thus, $\hat{a}_{X,S,g}$ expresses the ability level in ability X of an average individual from age group g in relation to the mean of the age group 25–34 years, as a proportion of the standard deviation. The values of $\hat{a}_{X,S,g}$ are presented in Table 2.

$$\hat{a}_{X,D(t)} = \frac{a_{X,D(t)}}{\sum_X a_{X,D(t)}} \quad (2)$$

Equation 2 gives the estimate for the demand for ability X at time t. Dividing the importance of ability X, $a_{X,D(t)}$, by the sum of all task scores, $\sum_X a_{X,D(t)}$, gives a measurement of the relative importance of task input X in the economy, $\hat{a}_{X,D(t)}$. The values for the relative demand are given in Table 3 and shown in Figure 2.

$$\hat{a}_{X,g,t} = \hat{a}_{X,S,g} \cdot \hat{a}_{X,D(t)} \tag{3}$$

In equation 3, the supply of each ability by age group g is multiplied by its demand at time t. This equilibrium index, $\hat{a}_{X,g,t}$, is used to give an estimate of the market value of each age group's share of ability X.

$$\hat{a}_{g,t} = \sum_X \hat{a}_{X,g,t} \tag{4}$$

Equation 4 shows that $\hat{a}_{g,t}$ is the sum of the equilibrium index scores. The variable $\hat{a}_{g,t}$ is the *productivity potential index*, an aggregate equilibrium index, for age group g at time t. If one of the abilities is in less demand than the others, its impact on the productivity potential index is lower.

To illustrate how the productivity potential index is constructed, assume an average person from the 55–65-year age group works in an occupation that requires 50 percent numerical abilities and 50 percent finger dexterity. An average person from this age group scores 85 percent of a standard deviation below the 25–34-year-old mean on numerical abilities, and 142 percent lower on finger dexterity. This means that the person from the 55–65 age group has a productivity potential index score that is 114 percent of a standard deviation below the average of the 25–34-year-olds. Should there be more demand for numerical abilities, the productivity potential of the senior employees would increase relative to that of younger individuals, as numerical abilities decline less than finger dexterity.

Assume a given productivity index level is needed, γ_t, and when $\hat{a}_{g,t} > \gamma_t$, the impact of a higher productivity potential on job performance is reduced. This situation is given in equation 5, where the variable $P_{g,t}$ represents the adjusted productivity index. The indicator function, $I_{(-\infty,\gamma_t)}(\hat{a}_{g,t})$ is 1 when $\hat{a}$ is between $-\infty$ and γ_t, and 0 otherwise.

$$P_{g,t} = I_{(-\infty,\gamma_t)}(\hat{a}_{g,t})\hat{a}_{g,t} + I_{[\gamma_t,\infty)}(\hat{a}_{g,t})\left[\beta(\hat{a}_{g,t} - \gamma_t) + \gamma_t\right] \tag{5}$$

The coefficient β is positive but below 1, and the lower it is, the stronger is the reduction in the adjusted productivity index.

Results: Productivity potential by age

The estimates of the age–productivity index, based on equation 4, are shown in Figure 3. Productivity potential continues to increase until around age 40 years, when the productivity-reducing effect of lower ability levels outweighs

FIGURE 3 Index of productivity potential, by age, based on US data on job abilities, 1960 and 1998

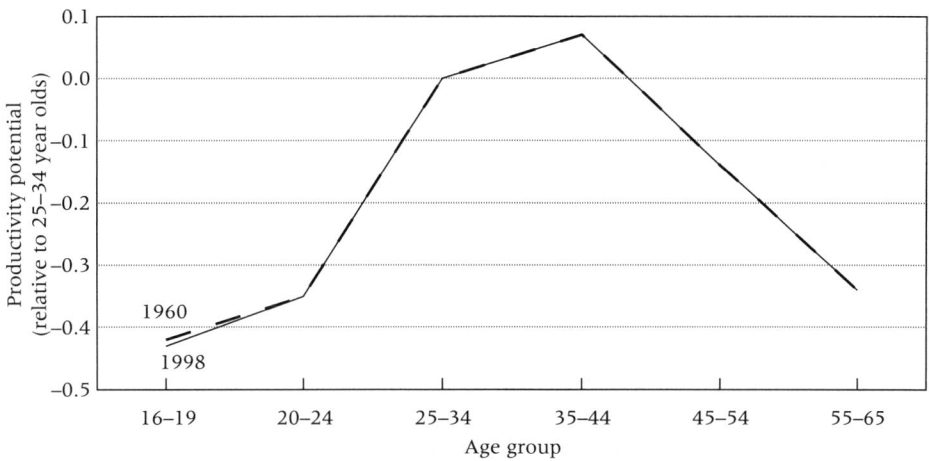

SOURCE: Own calculations.

the productivity gains from long experience. Thereafter, productivity declines linearly until retirement age. The 55–65-year-olds' productivity potential is 0.34 standard deviations lower than that of 25–34-year-olds, although they still have a productivity potential above that of those age 24 years and younger. The effect of changing labor market demand, with an increasing importance of managerial abilities, is very slight.

Figure 4 shows the effect of variation in the labor market importance of experience. If experience should play no role (which is not likely to be

FIGURE 4 Index of productivity potential, with high and low importance of experience

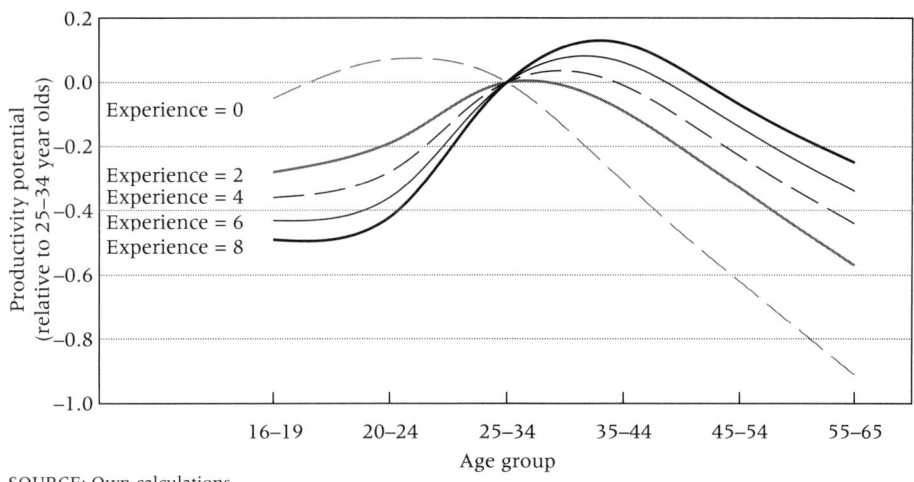

SOURCE: Own calculations.

FIGURE 5 Index of productivity potential by age, given that ability requirements are basic

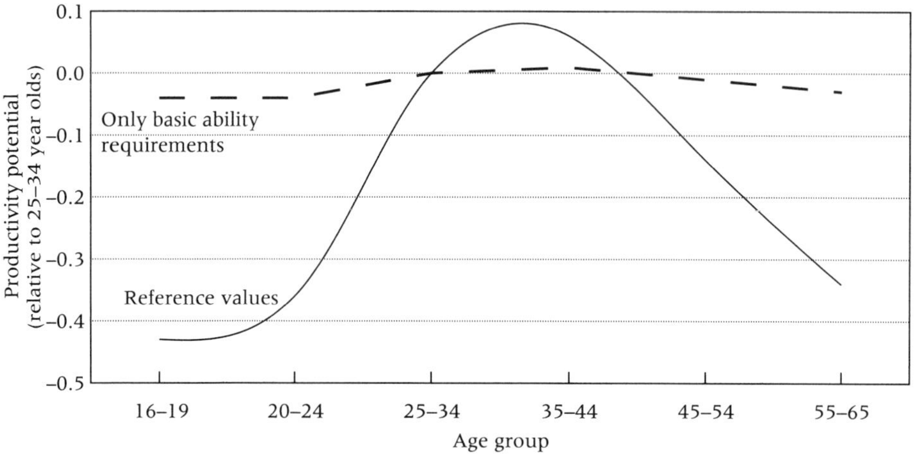

[Graph showing productivity potential (relative to 25–34 year olds) on y-axis from −0.5 to 0.1, and age groups (16–19, 20–24, 25–34, 35–44, 45–54, 55–65) on x-axis. Dashed line labeled "Only basic ability requirements" stays near 0.0. Solid curve labeled "Reference values" is hump-shaped, starting near −0.43 at 16–19, peaking around 0.08 at 35–44, declining to −0.34 at 55–65.]

SOURCE: Own calculations.

realistic as experience matters in almost all professions), productivity peaks for age groups 20–24. The more experience matters for labor market performance, the later productivity peaks, and increases the productivity of senior workers relative to the productivity of the younger age groups. However, the age–productivity profile is always hump-shaped.

Figure 5 shows productivity potential by age when ability requirements are basic, based on equation 5. This could apply to simple or light work, where

FIGURE 6 Estimates of hypothethical professions where only "management-communication" skills or "estimations-analytical" skills matter

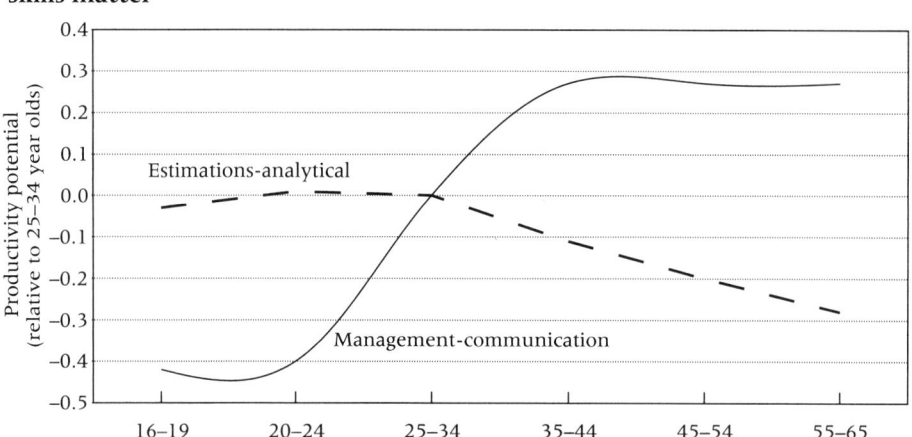

SOURCE: Own calculations.

TABLE 4 Productivity potential estimates for Figures 3 through 6, values relative to 25–34-year olds

	16–19	20–24	25–34	35–44	45–54	55–65
Figure 3						
1960 productivity potential	–0.42	–0.35	0.00	0.07	–0.14	–0.34
1998 productivity potential	–0.43	–0.35	0.00	0.07	–0.14	–0.34
Figure 4						
Experience high importance	–0.49	–0.42	0.00	0.12	–0.07	–0.25
Experience no importance	–0.05	0.07	0.00	–0.31	–0.62	–0.91
Figure 5						
Reference values	–0.43	–0.36	0.00	0.06	–0.14	–0.34
Only basic ability requirements	–0.04	–0.04	0.00	0.01	–0.01	–0.03
Figure 6						
Management-communication	–0.42	–0.40	0.00	0.27	0.27	0.27
Estimations-analytical	–0.03	0.01	0.00	–0.11	–0.20	–0.28

only basic cognitive and non-cognitive ability levels are needed. One observes only very moderate productivity differences by age, as shown by the adjusted productivity index (dashed line).

Figure 6 shows the productivity profile where the only skills that matter are those that increase or are stable with age, namely managerial ability and experience (solid line); in this case productivity potential increases up to ages 35–44 and remains stable thereafter. For the case where only clerical and numerical skills matter (dashed line), productivity decreases from ages 25–34. Although these scenarios are somewhat unrealistic since other abilities also matter in most professions, these scenarios could reveal the type of professions where comparative advantages are evident for older and younger workers.

The values for Figures 3 to 6 are shown in Table 4.

Discussion

Earlier studies on the relation between age and job performance tend to neglect the causes of productivity differences as well as the impact of changing labor market demands. The present study estimates the productivity potential by weighing age-specific ability levels against the labor market demand for these abilities.

Basing the estimates on the causes of productivity differences permits estimation of the impact of structural changes in the labor market. The age–productivity profile is found to vary over time in accordance with changing labor market needs. Assuming a reasonably strong effect of experience, I estimate that productivity peaks for the 35–44-year age group.[1] If the demand for experience falls, the productivity peak shifts toward younger ages. Conversely, if the minimum ability requirement should drop over time, age differences in productivity would decrease.

This approach contains several simplifications that could bias the results: 1) It is arduous, if not impossible, to take all individual job-related abilities into account. Moreover, one cannot postulate exact functions for how changes in labor market demand determine the shape of the age–productivity curve. This means that my approach is necessarily restricted to include only a few of the factors that determine job performance. 2) Estimating the supply of experience from different age groups, and how this relates to labor market performance is subject to particular challenges. Identifying the average length of experience that is beneficial to job performance is difficult, and the need to rely on strong assumptions can decrease the validity of the estimates. 3) The factors for which information on labor market demand exists are similar, but not identical, to the abilities that are supplied, which means that the matching procedure may lead to estimation errors. 4) Creating a productivity potential by matching the supply of abilities with the demand for these abilities is not the same as measuring actual job performance. In spite of these weaknesses, this approach gives a general understanding of why age should matter for productivity and outlines the shape of the age–productivity curve in various circumstances.

The estimations of the productivity profile reflect the tendency for job performance on average to decrease in the latter half of the working life, given almost any calibration of the model. The sole exceptions would be those in which only basic ability requirements are needed or in which the abilities that decrease with age are not important to work performance. In other cases, the age–productivity curve is likely to be hump-shaped.

Age–productivity profiles where productivity drops from mid-working life can contrast with a late peak in the age-earnings curve. Age-earnings profiles can stem from seniority-based earnings schedules rather than from productivity increases over the life cycle. In effect, it will be more costly for the firm to employ older individuals as compared to younger ones. Therefore, population aging decreases the firm's profits and creates incentives to abolish the use of seniority-based wage systems. Accelerating technological progress could represent an additional factor that could shift the peak of age-earnings schedules toward younger ages, because it can increase the demand for workers who learn and adjust fast, abilities that young individuals tend to have in greater supply than older ones. This can imply that the shape of the age-earnings schedules will increasingly resemble the shape of the age–productivity curve. The implication, in some professions, could be a decrease in the relative wages of senior workers.

Notes

Support and comments from Sara Grainger, Alexia Prskawetz, Heiner Maier, Dorothea Rieck, and participants at the December 2004 Population Aging and Economic Productivity symposium in Vienna are gratefully acknowledged.

1 A productivity peak in the late 30s and early 40s is in line with several previous studies, including Davies and Sparrow (1985), and slightly older than the "age of achievement peak" identified by Lehman (1953).

References

Acemoglu, D. 2002. "Technical change, inequality, and the labor market," *The Journal of Economic Literature* XL(1): 7–72.

Ahituv, A. and J. Zeira. 2000. "Technical progress and early retirement," CEPR Discussion Paper no. 2614.

Avolio, B. J. and D. A. Waldman. 1994. "Variations in cognitive, perceptual, and psychomotor abilities across the working life span: Examining the effects of race, sex, experience, education, and occupational type," *Psychology and Aging* 9(3): 430–442.

Autor, D. H., F. Levy, and R. Murnane. 2003. "The skill content of recent technological change: An empirical exploration," *Quarterly Journal of Economics* 118(4): 1279–1334.

Bartel, A. P. and N. Sicherman. 1993. "Technological change and retirement decisions of old workers," *Journal of Labor Economics* 11(1): 162–183.

Blum, J. E., L. F. Jarvik, and E. T. Clark. 1970. "Rate of change on selective tests of intelligence: A twenty-year longitudinal study of aging," *Journal of Gerontology* 25: 171–176.

Boot, H. M. 1995. "How skilled were Lancashire cotton factory workers in 1833?," *Economic History Review* XLVIII(2): 283–303.

Crépon, B., N. Deniau, and S. Perez-Duarte. 2002. "Wages, productivity and worker characteristics: A French perspective," Mimeo, INSEE.

Colonia-Willner, R. 1998. "Practical intelligence at work: Relationship between aging and cognitive efficiency among managers in a bank environment," *Psychology and Aging* 13(1): 45–57.

Dalton, G. W. and P. H. Thompson. 1971. "Accelerating obsolescence of older engineers," *Harvard Business Review* 49(5): 57–67.

De la Mare, G. C. and R. D. Shepherd. 1958. "Ageing: Changes in speed and quality of work among leather cutters," *Occupational Psychology* 32(3): 204–209.

Dickerson, A. and F. Green. 2002. "The growth and valuation of generic skills," mimeo, Department of Economics, Keynes College, University of Kent.

Econ. 1998. "Arbeidsmarkedspolitikken overfor eldre arbeidssøkere" (Labour market policies toward elderly job seekers). Report for the Ministry of Local Government and Regional Development, *Econ Report* No. 98/97, Oslo, Norway.

Ericsson, K. A. and A. C. Lehmann. 1996. "Expert and exceptional performance: Evidence of maximal adaption to task constraints," *Annual Review of Psychology* 47: 273–305.

Goldin, C. and L. F. Katz. 1998. "The origins of technology-skill complementarity," *Quarterly Journal of Economics* 113: 693–732.

Golini, A. et al. 2004. "Demographic trends, aging and labour: The work of the young elderly: is there willingness and possibility? Two Italian surveys among people and firms." Manuscript, Rome University.

Hægeland, T. and T. J. Klette. 1999. "Do higher wages reflect higher productivity? Education, gender and experience premiums in a matched plant-worker data set," in J. L. Haltiwanger, J. R. Spletzer, J. Theeuwes, and K. Troske (eds.), *The Creation and Analysis of Employer–Employee Matched Data*. Amsterdam: North Holland.

Hanushek, Eric A. and Dennis D. Kimko. 2000. "Schooling, labor-force quality, and the growth of nations," *American Economic Review* 90(5): 1184–1208.

Hartigan, J. and A. K. Wigdor. 1989. *Fairness in Employment Testing*. Washington, DC: National Academy Press.

Howell, D. and E. N. Wolff. 1991. "Trends in the growth and distribution of skills in the US workplace, 1960–1985," *Industrial and Labour Relations Review* 44 (3): 486–502.

Hunter, J. E. and R. F. Hunter. 1984. "Validity and utility of alternative predictors of job performance," *Psychological Bulletin* 96: 72–98.

Hutchens, R. 1989. "Seniority, wages and productivity: A turbulent decade," *Journal of Economic Perspectives* 3(4): 49–64.

IALS (International Adult Literacy Survey). 2001. *Literacy, Numeracy and Labour Market Outcomes in Canada*. Ottawa: Statistics Canada.

Ilmakunnas, P., M. Maliranta, and J. Vainiomäki. 2004. "The role of employer and employee characteristics for plant productivity," *Journal of Productivity Analysis* 21: 249–276.

Jones, B. 2005. "Age and great invention," NBER Working Paper Series No. 11359, National Bureau of Economic Research, Cambridge, MA.

Juhn, C., K. M. Murphy, and Brooks Pierce. 1993. "Wage inequality and the rise in returns to skill," *Journal of Political Economy* 101(3): 410–442.

Kutscher, R. E. and J. F. Walker. 1960. "Comparative job performance of office workers by age," *Monthly Labor Review* 83(1): 39–43.

Lazear, E. P. 1979. "Why is there mandatory retirement?," *Journal of Political Economy* 87(6).

Lazear, E. P. and R. L. Moore. 1984. "Incentives, productivity, and labor contracts," *The Quarterly Journal of Economics* 99(2): 275–296.

Lehman, H. C. 1953. *Age and Achievement*. Princeton, NJ: Princeton University Press.

Lesgold, A. 1984. "Acquiring expertise," in J. Anderson and S. Kosslyn (eds.), *Tutorials in Learning and Memory: Essays in Honor of Gordon Bower*. New York: Freeman, pp. 31–60.

Mark, J. A. 1957. "Comparative job performance by age," *Monthly Labor Review* 80: 1467–1471.

McEvoy, G. M. and W. F. Cascio. 1989. "Cumulative evidence of the relationship between employee age and job performance," *Journal of Applied Psychology* 74(1): 11–17.

Ministry of Health. 2004. "Longer life, better health? Trends in health expectancy, New Zealand 1996–2004," Wellington: Ministry of Health.

Mitra, A. 2002. "Mathematics skill and male–female wages," *Journal of Socio-Economics* 31(5): 443–456.

Murnane, R. J., J. B. Willett, and F. Levy. 1995. "The growing importance of cognitive skills in wage determination," *Review of Economics and Statistics* LXXVII(2): 251–266.

OECD. 1998. "Work force ageing: Consequences and policy responses," *Maintaining Prosperity in an Ageing Society: The OECD Study on the Policy Implications of Ageing Working Paper*, AWP 4.1.

———. 1999. "Thematic review of the transition from initial education to working life: Final comparative report," *Directorate for Education, Employment, Labour and Social Affairs. Education Committee*, DEELA/ED (99) 11, pp. 319–322.

———. 2006. *Live Longer, Work Longer: A Synthesis Report*. Paris: OECD.

Oeppen, J. and J. Vaupel. 2002. "Broken limits to life expectancy," *Science* 296 (10 May).

Olshanksy, S. J. et al. 1991 "Trading off longer lives for worsening health," *Journal of Aging and Health* 3: 194–216.

Phelps, R. and J. Shanteau. 1978. "Livestock judges: How much information can an expert use?," *Organizational Behavior and Human Performance* 21: 209–219.

Phelps Brown, E. H. and S. V. Hopkins 1955. "Seven centuries of building wages," *Economica* 22: 195–206.

Raskin, E. 1936. "Comparison of scientific and literary ability: A biographical study of eminent scientists and men of letters of the nineteenth century," *Journal of Abnormal and Social Psychology* 31: 20–35.

Rybash, J. M., W. Hoyer, and P. A. Roodin. 1986. *Adult Cognition and Ageing*. New York: Pergamon Press.

Salthouse, T. 1984. "Effect of age and skill in typing," *Journal of Experimental Psychology: General* 113: 345–371.

Salthouse, T. and T. J. Maurer. 1996. "Aging, job performance and career development," in J. E. Birren and K. W. Schaie (eds.), *Handbook of the Psychology of Aging*, 4th ed. San Diego: Academic Press, pp. 353–364.

Schaie, K. W. 1996. *Intellectual Development in Adulthood: The Seattle Longitudinal Study*. New York: Cambridge University Press.

Schmidt, F. L. and J. E. Hunter. 1998. "The validity and utility of selection methods in personnel psychology: Practical and theoretical implications of 85 years of research findings," *Psychological Bulletin* 124(2): 262–274.

Simonton, D. K. 1997. "Career productivity: A predictive and explanatory model of career trajectories and landmarks," *Psychological Review* 104(1): 66–89.

Skirbekk, V. 2004. Age and individual productivity: A literature survey," in G. Feichtinger (ed.), *Vienna Yearbook of Population Research*. Vienna: Verlag der Österreichischen Akademie der Wissenschaften.

Smith, A. D. 1996. "Memory," in J. E. Birren and K.W. Schaie (eds.), *Handbook of the Psychology of Aging*, 4th ed. New York: Academic Press, pp. 236–247.

Spitz, Alexandra. 2004. "Are skill requirements in the workplace rising? Stylized facts and evidence on skill-biased technological change," ZEW Discussion Paper no. 04–33, Mannheim.

Tyler, J. H., R. J. Murnane, and J. B. Willett. 2000. "Do the cognitive skills of school dropouts matter in the labor market?," *Journal of Human Resources* 35(4): 748–754.

United Nations. 2005. *Population Projections by Age and Sex*. New York: UN.

US Department of Labor. 1957. "Comparative job performance by age: Large plants in the men's footwear and household furniture industries," Bulletin no. 1223, Washington, DC.

———. 1972. *Handbook for Analyzing Jobs*. Washington, DC: Manpower Administration.

Warr, P. 1994. "Age and employment," in H. Triandis, M. Dunnette, and L. Hough (eds.), *Handbook of Industrial and Organizational Psychology*, 2nd ed. CA: Consulting Psychologist Press, pp. 485–550.

Charting the Economic Life Cycle

RONALD LEE
SANG-HYOP LEE
ANDREW MASON

The shape of the demographic life cycle is of fundamental interest, which demographers recognize through extensive efforts to estimate, describe, and interpret the age-shapes of fertility, mortality, marriage, divorce, and migration. These age-shapes are influenced by biology, culture, economic constraints, and individual choice. Similarly, the shape of the economic life cycle is of fundamental interest in its own right, and this shape is influenced by the same set of factors. Here we are primarily concerned with the estimation and description of the basic economic life cycle and some illustrative comparisons of how it differs across countries and over time within countries in recent years.

The life cycle is a longitudinal concept, referring to the passage through life of an individual or a generation. It is most properly examined using longitudinal data. Nonetheless, data limitations and the desire for measures that reflect current conditions often lead demographers to employ cross-sectional measures such as the period total fertility rate and period life expectancy, and for the most part we also will be examining cross-sectional data in our exploration of the economic life cycle. When we speak of the economic life cycle we refer to these cross-sectional age patterns. Later we discuss how their shapes have changed over time. Demographers have analyzed how changes across generations in the shape of longitudinal age profiles can distort cross-sectional measures (tempo and quantum effects), and it would no doubt be revealing to analyze economic age profiles from this perspective as well.

Economic behavior over the life cycle can be summarized by the amount consumed at each age and by the amount produced through labor at each age. One sort of economic dependency occurs when consumption exceeds labor earnings,[1] a condition that distinguishes periods in childhood and old age. From this point of view, an older person is economically dependent even if he or she has accumulated claims on output that more than offset his or her consumption, claims that could take the form of entitlements to transfers or ownership of assets. Often the economic life cycle is treated in a highly stylized fashion. Dependency ratios and similar age structure variables, for example, capture only the broadest features of the economic life cycle, and quadratic functions smooth out details of the age patterns. Our goal here is to measure the life cycle in comprehensive detail. However, we have not attempted to take time use into account, so such important issues as the time spent by parents caring for their children, or time spent caring for elderly relatives, are not covered here.

Individual consumption or production by age is seldom calculated, because attention naturally turns toward more disaggregated measures such as wages, labor force participation rates, hours worked, or household expenditures. Although per capita consumption and production may seem like crude measures, they summarize and incorporate the influences of many factors that may have contradictory or complementary effects on the economic life cycle.

Demographic age profiles for fertility and mortality are of interest because they describe a basic aspect of human behavior. But they are also important because they can be applied to a population age distribution to calculate the number of births and deaths occurring in a period. Such a calculation requires the assumption, seldom made explicit, that variations in the population age distribution and in the age profiles of fertility and mortality are independent. The Easterlin Hypothesis asserts the contrary: that an unusually large age group will experience unusually low fertility. Similarly, an unusually large share of young children in the population might, in some contexts, be expected to cause mortality of young children to be higher. The assumption of independence makes it possible to generate numbers, but various feedback processes render the calculations suspect.

Concerns of the same sort arise when age schedules of consumption and production are applied to population age distributions to generate levels of aggregate consumption and labor earnings, which we call expected consumption and expected labor earnings. When the population age distribution changes, it alters the ratio of expected earnings to expected consumption, called the support ratio.[2] There has been recent interest in the demographic dividend, which occurs during a sustained period of improving support ratios associated with the demographic transition and which is estimated using age profiles of per capita consumption and labor earnings of the sort described above. As with fertility and mortality, however, such calculations are undermined when there is feedback from the population age distribution to the age profiles of consumption and labor earnings. For example, there is ample reason to expect an unusually large cohort to experience reduced earnings (Easterlin 1978 and a large subsequent literature).[3]

Just as broad changes in aggregate economic dependency may be illuminated by age profiles of consumption and labor earnings in general, more specific consequences of changing population age distributions can be illuminated using per capita age profiles for more specific kinds of consumption, production, or other economic behaviors, but always in reference to population-level age group averages rather than conditional on participation. Examples include the demand for housing (Mankiw and Weil 1989; McFadden 1994), stock market fluctuations (Poterba 2005), saving rates (Modigliani 1988; Mason 1987, 1988; Cutler et al. 1990), interest rates, and impending fiscal problems (Lee and Edwards 2001, 2002). As always, such disaggregation carries its own hazards, since there may be substitution across subcategories such as publicly provided health care or education, and private expenditures on these, and the overall patterns of change may be obscured.

The estimates presented here draw upon a number of studies being carried out as part of a larger study of the economic life cycle and the reallocations systems—primarily through saving and public and familial transfers—that respond to the economic life cycle. A system of accounts, called National Transfer Accounts (NTA), is being developed that is consistent with National Income and Product Accounts but provides much-needed age data (Mason et al., forthcoming). The methodology for constructing estimates is discussed briefly in this chapter, and more detailed information is available on the project website, www.ntaccounts.org.

We begin by discussing the conceptual background for our estimates and then discuss our methods of estimation. We present estimates of the consumption and labor income age profiles for a number of countries. Next we consider the two sets of age profiles in relation to one another. In the final empirical section we discuss the changing shapes of the age profiles over two decades for the United States and Taiwan.

Conceptual background

Individuals versus households

Age profiles of consumption and production are viewed from an individual, rather than a household, perspective in this chapter. In economies where formal-sector employment dominates, measuring production (or earnings) for individuals is relatively straightforward. In traditional settings, where employment is informal and production is often organized within a family enterprise, estimating production by age for individuals is difficult. In any setting, allocating consumption to individuals is a challenging task, because most expenditure data are collected for households rather than individuals. Moreover, some goods are jointly consumed or involve increasing returns to scale so that allocating consumption to individuals inevitably involves arbitrary rules.

From the household perspective, production and consumption are attributes of households, varying with age of the household head. Constructing production and consumption profiles is more straightforward, but tradeoffs are involved. The first is that the effects of co-resident children and elderly on household consumption and production profiles must be explicitly modeled or—as is often the case—neglected altogether. Indeed, a large share of all societal income redistribution occurs within households and would therefore be invisible to accounting on a household basis. The second is the difficulty of translating changes in population age structure into changes in the age structure of household heads and household membership (Lee 1980).

Here we opt for the individual perspective, but irrespective of the methodology employed, the age patterns of consumption and production are central to understanding the role of population in the macroeconomy.

Forces shaping age profiles of consumption

A large body of theory and empirical research in economics addresses the age–time trajectory of consumption chosen by individuals. In the absence of intergenerational transfers, the expected present value of consumption must be no greater than that of labor earnings over the life cycle. With perfect foresight about future labor earnings, taxes, survival, discount rates, and other relevant information, with perfect credit markets, and with typical assumptions about how consumption affects utility, standard life cycle theory concludes that consumption will increase exponentially with age along the optimal path at a rate equal to the discount rate less the rate of time preference. Because this optimal path typically differs from the age trajectory of labor earnings, individuals borrow and lend at the market rate of interest to achieve the desired consumption path.

The real world circumstances of individuals violate each of these assumptions, and a large literature explores the consequences. The ability of individuals to borrow is often limited by their current net worth, credit cards aside. Future wages are unknown given uncertainty about the macroeconomy, career success, and health, for example. Intergenerational transfers are pervasive. An individual's consumption is funded by his parents until the age of economic independence, which may not come until after age 20. Consequently adults must allocate a substantial portion of their income to consumption by their children. In most contexts, elderly people live and consume in the household of an adult child. Thus an individual's consumption may be governed by at least three different budget constraints over the life cycle, depending first on the resources of parents, then on personal resources, and finally on resources of children. Marriage, divorce, and widowhood further complicate the situation. Bequests, which are highly uncertain in timing and amount, also alter the available resources. Some scholars have questioned the value of the life cycle model altogether and have proposed alternatives (Carroll 1992; Carroll and Summers 1991; Deaton 1991).[4]

Many problems are inherent in estimating individual consumption. Fertility and the age pattern of consumption may be jointly determined, in the sense that parents may choose to have fewer children because they want to invest more resources in each of them, as in the quantity–quality theory of fertility (Becker and Lewis 1973). Only a fraction of household consumption is assignable to individuals, even conceptually. Much is joint consumption of public goods, as when a family watches television. Some consumption comes in the form of in-kind transfers from the government for health care, education, food, housing, or energy assistance, and these transfers are chosen through the political process and subject to a government budget constraint.

Public and private consumption

The consumption side of the economic life cycle depends on both public and private consumption, but their relative importance is not easily judged. Many public programs target particular age groups for in-kind transfers: education for the young, health care for the elderly. Other public programs, such as pension programs, family allowances, or unemployment benefits, provide cash rather than in-kind transfers. These programs lead to increases in private rather than in public consumption, affecting the economic life cycle indirectly. An additional complexity is that public consumption may crowd out private consumption with little effect on the composition or age pattern of total consumption. Thus, the public–private breakdown of consumption provides useful and suggestive information, but it is by no means definitive about how public policy influences the age pattern of total consumption.

The importance of public consumption varies substantially across countries (Table 1). In general, public consumption as a share of total consumption rises with per capita income, but demographic and institutional factors play critical roles. Public spending on health and education rises more sharply with income than does combined public spending, suggesting that age targeting is more important in high-income countries. The relationship between the level of economic development and public consumption holds to some extent for the five countries compared below. Public consumption as a share of total consumption was smallest in Indonesia and Thailand and largest in France and the United States. Pubic spending on health is highest in France and the United States, countries with both higher income and older populations. Public spending on education is high in France and the United States, but also in Thailand, which has lower income but a relatively large school-age population. The substantial variation among the five countries compared in Table 1 stands out, suggesting the importance of country-specific institutional factors.

TABLE 1 Government share of final consumption expenditure, 2000, selected countries and countries of the world by per capita income

Country (per capita GDP)	Government share of final consumption expenditure (%)		
	Total	Health	Education
Indonesia ($2,807)	9.6	0.8	2.0
Thailand ($5,846)	16.5	3.1	7.9
Taiwan ($14,114)	19.3	0.3	3.9
France ($23,225)	29.8	9.1	7.4
United States ($31,338)	23.8	6.4	5.8
Per capita GDP			
Less than $1,000	15.6	2.2	3.0
$1,000–4,999	16.1	2.9	4.5
$5,000–9,999	20.7	4.6	5.9
$10,000 or more	25.4	7.1	7.0

NOTES AND SOURCES: Per capita GDP is purchasing power parity adjusted using 1995 prices. Source is World Bank *World Development Indicators 2004*, except for Taiwan for which source is Directorate General of Budget, Accounting, and Statistics, *Statistical Yearbook of Taiwan 2004* and Mason et al., forthcoming. For the United States, Medicare and Medicaid expenditures are included in public health spending.

Forces shaping the age profiles of labor income

Standard economic theory views work as a tradeoff between the utility of leisure and the utility of the consumption that increased work allows. An individual at each age chooses to work that number of hours which equates the marginal utility gained through these wages to the marginal utility lost from reduced leisure time. Experience, health, vitality, and other factors that vary over the life cycle affect the productivity of labor and, therefore, its wage value. But they also influence the utility of leisure. Variations with age in the competing demands on time at home—for example due to childrearing—also affect the opportunity cost of work. At some ages, the optimal choice may be not to work at all. In theory, with perfect credit markets, these decisions made at different ages are all closely linked over the life cycle. One can choose not to work and yet to consume at age 27, for example, by borrowing based on earnings anticipated at age 52 with due account taken of discount rates and survival probabilities. In addition to entering the labor force or staying at home, individuals may spend time investing in their human capital through education or training, thereby raising their future earnings. Once working, they may devote some time to maintaining or upgrading skills, or they may let them decline. Work experience itself tends to raise productivity and wages.

As with consumption, the real world is more complex. Credit markets are imperfect. Workers do not have complete flexibility in choosing their hours. Institutions may constrain wages to rise with age through seniority systems, regardless of productivity. The productivity of labor, and therefore wages, will depend on macroeconomic conditions that are outside the control and foresight of an individual. Public pension programs may be unexpectedly instituted or terminated, altering the life cycle budget constraint and perhaps introducing strong incentives to retire from the labor force or return to work. Changes in tax policies may alter the tradeoff between work and leisure. Unemployment may thwart individual plans, and age discrimination or mandatory retirement may prevent older people from finding work.

Aside from these contextual factors, it appears that individual productivity varies by age. Skirbekk (2003) reviews a dozen studies, concluding that they point to an inverse U-shaped individual productivity profile, with significant decreases taking place from around age 50. There are a number of reasons for declining productivity at older ages. A large body of literature supports the view that mental abilities decline during adulthood (Maitland et al. 2000; Verhaegen and Salthouse 1997). Poor physical and mental health is also strongly related to early retirement (Quinn et al. 1990; Bound 1991; Dwyer and Mitchell 1999). Rapid technological progress has an uneven influence on skills and competencies by age (Autor et al. 2003). Rapid changes in educational systems might also give middle-aged and younger workers a competitive advantage over their older counterparts.

All of these factors can vary over time and between countries, leading to differences and changes in the way earnings vary with age. Perhaps most important, however, are the decisions made by three demographic groups. First, many teenagers and young adults are extending their time in school and delaying their entry into the labor force as returns to education rise. Second, many women are increasing the time spent in the labor force as rates of childbearing have declined and labor market opportunities have improved. Third, older men are withdrawing from the labor force at a younger age as incomes have risen and pensions have become available.

Methods for constructing consumption profiles

Consumption consists of private and public components. Age patterns of private consumption have been much more extensively analyzed, but public consumption—the consumption of in-kind transfers from the public sector—is important to developing a full picture of the life cycle of consumption.

Private consumption

Private consumption by age is particularly difficult to estimate because, for the most part, we have data only at the level of the household. Consumer expenditure surveys provide information on household-level consumption expenditures. Many studies have addressed the problem of allocating these consumption expenditures between adults and children, typically as part of an effort to estimate the costs of children. Much less is known about the allocation of household consumption between prime-age adults and the elderly. This issue is not important in societies where the elderly live independently, because their consumption can be directly observed. In societies where multigenerational living arrangements are common, the issue is an important one.

The general approach taken in the literature is based on some measure of the consumption utility of the adults in a household. With such a measure, we can ask by how much the total consumption of a household with one additional child would have to be increased in order to restore the adults' consumption utility to its original level. The size of the increase measures the cost of that incremental child.

The Engel method uses the share of the household budget spent on food as the measure of adult welfare. It has been used extensively (Espenshade 1984), but it is also widely criticized on conceptual grounds. The difficulty with the method is that children may be more intensive consumers of food than are adults. If so, families with more children would spend a larger share of their budgets on food in part because their per capita real income is lower, but also because the household's preferences are tilted toward food. Thus, children would appear to reduce parents' welfare more, and therefore to cost more, than is actually the case. The consensus among researchers is that Engel's method yields an upward-biased estimate of the cost of children. On a priori grounds we can only say that Engel's method will generally yield a biased result (Deaton 1997).

In the Rothbarth method, the welfare metric is the level of spending on goods that are consumed mainly by adults, usually taken to be tobacco, alcohol, and adult clothing. The Rothbarth method does not suffer from the same problem as Engel's method because these adult goods are not consumed by children. The Rothbarth method, however, must assume that the presence of children in the household has no direct effect on the utility that adults derive from consuming their adult goods. Children must affect adult consumption of these goods only because they reduce the amount parents can spend on themselves. If the presence of children induces parents to smoke and drink more because of stress, for example, the Rothbarth method underestimates the cost of children, and vice versa. Views vary as to whether or not this assumption is plausible.

Several practical difficulties with the Rothbarth method limit its application. First, in some instances the only adult goods available are tobacco and alcohol. Expenditure on these goods is insensitive to income, owing to their addictive characteristics. Furthermore, in some societies alcohol and tobacco are rarely consumed. Second, the method cannot be used to allocate consumption among adults of different ages, and it is often contaminated by the presence of older children, who may also consume the adult goods. This leads to an underestimate of the cost of these children. While the Rothbarth method cannot be used to estimate expenditures for the elderly, the Engel method can be used to estimate age profiles of consumption for all ages, but the flaws in the method make it relatively unattractive.

Estimates are often reported in the form of equivalence scales, which express the consumption going to different ages relative to that of a prime-age adult. These scales are often called Equivalent Adult Consumer scales, or EAC. These scales have been estimated for many countries, both developing and developed, using the Engel and Rothbarth methods. It would be useful to address several questions. First, are the available methods robust? Do they yield plausible estimates of child costs when applied in varying contexts? Second, do the available methods suggest similar or substantially different equivalence scales when applied to the same data? If similar, the biases identified in the literature may be tolerable in practical applications. Third, does the comparison of estimates using the same method across countries or time yield useful information about changes or differences in child costs?

Despite the extensive literature on equivalence scales, it is not yet clear to what extent these questions can be answered. Table 2 reports estimates of equivalence scales for Indonesia based on the 1996 socioeconomic survey (Indonesia, 1996 round of SUSENAS; Maliki 2005). Results from three methods are reported—the Engel method, the Rothbarth method, and Ray's demographic method, a variant of the Engel method that uses budget shares for several expenditure items rather than just food. The Rothbarth method was estimated using tobacco and adult clothing to represent adult goods.[5] The results are not reassuring. The one consistent finding is that children consume less than adults. The Engel method and the Ray method both yield high estimates for children. The Rothbarth method yields very low estimates, with children under five having a negative cost. The age pattern also varies across methods. Costs decline with age according to the Engel method, increase with age according to the Rothbarth estimates, and are non-monotonic according to the Ray method.

If the Engel method is upward biased and the Rothbarth method is downward biased, then the true value would lie somewhere in between.

TABLE 2 Alternative estimates of equivalence scales by age of children, Indonesia, 1996

Method	0–4	5–9	10–14	Notes
Engel	0.87	0.72	0.62	
Rothbarth	<0	0.06	0.32	Cigarettes
Rothbarth	<0	0.22	0.64	Adult clothing
Ray	0.88	0.91	0.83	

SOURCE: Maliki (2005) and authors' calculations.

However, it cannot be conclusively demonstrated that the true value in fact lies between the two estimates.

These difficulties have led us to adopt a simple and transparent approach to allocating consumption to household members. First, we allocate education and health expenditures to members using a method similar to one employed by Attanasio et al. (1999). We regress total household education expenditures on the number of household members in each age group enrolled in school and the number of household members not enrolled, with the intercept suppressed. Private health expenditures are allocated using a similar regression approach, using numbers of household members in each age group as regressors. For some age groups, private health spending might be very low and estimated coefficients may sometimes be negative. To avoid this occurrence, health spending can be constrained to be non-negative.

Second, other household consumption is allocated to individuals using an ad hoc allocation rule. The allocation rule is based on an extensive review of the literature and follows the view of Deaton (1997) that an ad hoc approach to child costs is probably the preferred approach, given problems of the Engel and Rothbarth methods. He suggests that children aged 0–4 years be counted as 0.4 of an adult, children aged 5–14 be 0.5, and children 15 and older be 1. We employ a more continuous, but similar equivalence scale, which is equal to 1 for adults aged 20 or older and declines linearly from unity at age 20 to 0.4 at age 4 and below.

In some cultural contexts there might be other special expenditures specific to an individual in the household, such as a dowry for example, that are itemized in the expenditure survey. According to our methods, the dowry would be a transfer received by the bride at the specific age at which it is given. Of course there are ambiguities, such as whether the dowry is a transfer to the groom, to the groom's family, or to the bride. There might be a corresponding bride price paid by the groom, which would be treated similarly. Any effect of the dowry or bride price on consumption might occur over many years. This transfer would be averaged across all individuals at this age in the survey, including the majority who did not receive a dowry or bride price. A dowry may have been funded in part by earlier reductions in schooling for the girl in question. This would be reflected in a longitudinal survey that included information on the school enrollment of the girl in question. In cross-sectional data, this girl's earlier experience would not be available. Other younger girls in the survey would have reduced schooling in anticipation of their own dowries, however, and they would represent the dowry recipient's earlier reduced schooling. In this way, the cross-section should capture even subtle longitudinal patterns to a considerable extent.

Using these methods, we estimate consumption for each individual in each household in the sample. We average across all the individuals in the survey of a given age to construct age schedules of private expenditures on education, health, and other items. Often expenditures are underreported in surveys, so some further adjustment of the age profiles may be desirable to make them consistent with reliable national-level control totals for total private expenditures on health, education, and the balance of total private consumption. National Income and Product Accounts (NIPA) and other reliable public statistical sources provide suitable control data. In this way, the profiles can be made consistent with NIPA in general and with private and government final consumption expenditure in particular.

Public consumption

Public transfer programs are classified according to the following list of 11 expenditure categories—Public goods and services; Congestible goods and services; Health; Education; Sickness and disability; Old age; Survivors; Family and children; Unemployment; Housing; and Other. This classification scheme is based on the United Nations COFOG (Classification of Functions of Government) System. COFOG was developed by the UN to harmonize the accounting of government expenditures among the member nations.

Our approach is to assign the benefits to the individual for whom the government intends them. For example, an educational voucher might be provided by the government to the parents of school-age children. In this case, the benefits are assigned to the children who are receiving the education, not to the parents who received the voucher. In some cases the government may provide a single cash payment to an adult in the household on behalf of all household members. In this case, each household member is assigned his or her share of this benefit.

For estimation, we would like to know the cost of the service provided to the individual by the government. Survey data are unlikely to include such costs, but they can be calculated from administrative data. For example, in the United States, Medicare administrative data such as the Current Beneficiary Survey contain information on the medical costs of individuals. These data can be used to derive age profiles of costs of Medicare benefits.

If we lack information on the actual costs incurred for services to individuals, then we obtain information on program use. For example, hospital admissions data by age are used to develop an age profile of medical costs. If we lack information on program use, then the minimum data we need is program participation—for example, school enrollment rates by age. We can improve our estimate by using public school enrollment rates rather than general enrollment rates, which include public and private schooling. We can further improve estimates by disaggregating by grade level of schooling since costs may differ substantially by grade level.

Many public goods and services are not targeted to particular age groups. We allocate these equally to all members of the population.

Methods for constructing age profiles of labor income

We are interested in labor income at a given age averaged across all members of the population at that age. This is not the usual concept of an age-earnings profile, which would typically be calculated conditional on being in the labor force and perhaps even conditional on working full time, year round. Our measure will include non-workers in the denominator, so it can vary across age because labor force participation varies across age, because annual hours worked per participant vary across age, or because earnings or productivity per hour varies across age. Our profiles are also averages across sex.

We measure labor income as the sum of earnings, fringe benefits, other labor income, and a share of entrepreneurial (self-employment) income. While estimating earnings is straightforward using individual survey data, estimating self-employment income is not, except in the cases of Taiwan and the United States, where self-employment income is provided on an individual basis and individual labor income is estimated directly as described above. The most difficult problem in our estimation is posed by unpaid labor: some young children, older people, and prime-age women in developing countries work as unpaid family workers in family-based enterprises.

Estimating the labor portion of self-employment income

The National Transfer Accounts are designed to be consistent with NIPA totals when weighted by population and summed. The labor income of the self-employed is not reported separately in NIPA. Rather the operating surplus of unincorporated businesses or mixed income, as it is called in NIPA, includes returns both to capital and to workers who are not paid employees. Gollin (2002) considers three methods for estimating the portion of mixed income that is a return to labor: (1) attributing all mixed income to labor; (2) attributing a share to labor equal to the share of labor income for the rest of the economy; and (3) imputing to the self-employed the labor income of employees. He finds that the first of these methods clearly overstates the labor income of the self-employed. The other methods yield an average labor share that varies from 0.654 to 0.686 depending on the method and sample used. The labor shares in high- and low-income countries are very similar. Thus, the simple method of allocating two-thirds of mixed income to labor is consistent with the best available evidence on this issue.

We have done a sensitivity analysis using different sharing rules such as 0.85 instead of two-thirds. This did not affect the labor income profile substantially, suggesting that errors in the estimates of total labor income due to the two-thirds rule are not important.

The NIPA estimates may sometimes involve important errors, which, along with other difficulties in estimating self-employment income and the value of unpaid family labor, may mean that this aspect of labor income in our accounts is sometimes less accurate than other elements, particularly in poor developing world economies.

Estimating self-employment labor income by age

For most countries discussed here, household surveys report mixed or self-employment income for the household, whereas we require estimates for individuals. But the surveys also report which individuals in the household engaged in unpaid family labor. We combine these two sources of information to estimate self-employment labor income for individuals in each household. We assume that within a household, the labor income for reported unpaid family workers by age is proportional to the labor income by age of *employed* workers in the total sample, reflecting both hours supplied and marginal product per hour. For each household we then calculate the constant of proportionality that implies a total of self-employment labor income for the household that matches our estimate of that total, that is two-thirds of reported self-employment income.

This provides an estimate of self-employment labor income by age for each individual in each household in the survey. Averaged across all the individuals in the sample, including those who did not provide unpaid family labor, it provides an age profile of self-employment labor income for the population. This age profile is then adjusted proportionately so that in combination with the age distribution of the total population it implies a number equal to two-thirds of the NIPA total for self-employment income.

These steps were used to create the self-employment component of the labor income age profiles. For purposes of comparison, we normalize each curve by dividing it by the unweighted average labor income for ages 30–49. This age range was chosen to exclude younger ages, which might be affected by educational enrollments, and older ages, which might be affected by retirement. We have also smoothed the raw age profiles for graphical presentation.[6]

Before moving to results, we note that the profiles presented here represent the current best estimates of consumption and labor income for the countries included. Our estimates of these profiles continue to change over time as we refine them in various ways. For example, future profiles for the United States will incorporate more-detailed data on consumption by the institutionalized population. This will change the estimated shape of consumption somewhat, especially at the oldest ages with large proportions living in nursing homes. This leads to a more gradual increase in consumption at older ages followed by a more sudden jump as the proportion in nursing homes accelerates with age. While we do not expect this or other improvements to alter the basic conclusions drawn here, it should be noted that work to improve profile estimates is ongoing.

We now consider the estimated age profiles that result from application of these methods.

Results for consumption

We note a striking contrast between the cross-sectional age profiles of total consumption for Taiwan and the United States, as shown in Figures 1a and 1b. In the United States, consumption rises by 150 percent from birth to the early 20s; in Taiwan the corresponding increase is only 67 percent. In the United States, consumption rises by a further 67 percent from the early 20s to age 90, whereas in Taiwan there is virtually no increase at all over this age range. In total, consumption more than quadruples from birth to age 90 in the United States, while in Taiwan it grows by only 77 percent.

To be sure, these cross-sections are a poor guide to the longitudinal changes for actual generations, which in Taiwan have been exceptionally rapid as we will see later, whereas in the United States they have been relatively slow. Nonetheless, these age profiles do tell us about the age gradient in consumption in any given year, and this gradient is flat in Taiwan for adult ages, and is steeply sloped across all ages in the United States. We believe that the family support system for the elderly in Taiwan, which contrasts with public sector transfers for the elderly in the United States, lies behind this difference.

Age targeting of public consumption is less important in Taiwan than in the United States. Public education targets school-age children with a noticeable effect on their total consumption, but public education is relatively less important in Taiwan. Note, however, that private education consumption is very high and that total spending on education is higher in Taiwan than in the United States relative to labor income. Taiwan relies on national health insurance to fund health care spending. Taiwan's National Health Insurance program (NHI) was introduced in 1995 and by 1998 accounted for 4.7 percent of total consumption as compared to 6.4 percent for US Medicare and Medicaid. The elderly consume only modestly more health care services financed through NHI than do the young in Taiwan, whereas the US program is largely limited to those aged 65 and older.

Figure 2 charts the age profile of public consumption relative to average public consumption for all persons aged 0 to 85 in the United States, Taiwan, Indonesia, Thailand, and France. To make the estimated profiles more easily comparable, we have divided each age schedule by the unweighted average of per capita public consumption at each age over the range 0 to 85. Thus, a value of 0.5 at some age implies that a person at that age consumes half

FIGURE 1a Per capita private and public consumption, by sector, United States, 2000

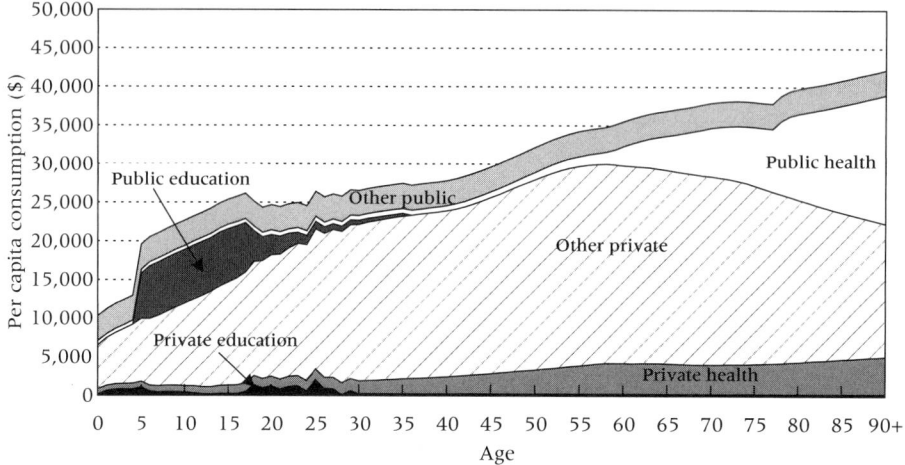

FIGURE 1b Per capita private and public consumption, by sector, Taiwan, 1998

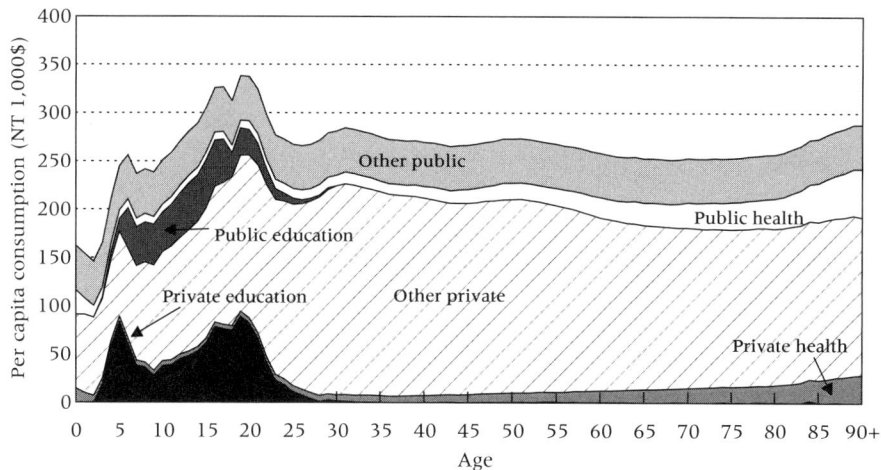

SOURCE: Authors' calculations.

the annual amount averaged over the first 86 years of life (assuming perfect survival). In the absence of any age targeting, the profile would equal 1 at all ages. The extent of age targeting is most easily judged by comparing values for those in the 30–59 age groups. Judged in this way, the United States and France target public consumption the most, while Indonesia targets public consumption the least. The extent of targeting in Thailand is similar to that in France, however, and the extent of Taiwan's targeting is similar to Indonesia's. Again, there is danger in looking at components of consumption as compared with total consumption, because public and private consumption may be close

FIGURE 2 Age profile of per capita public consumption, selected countries

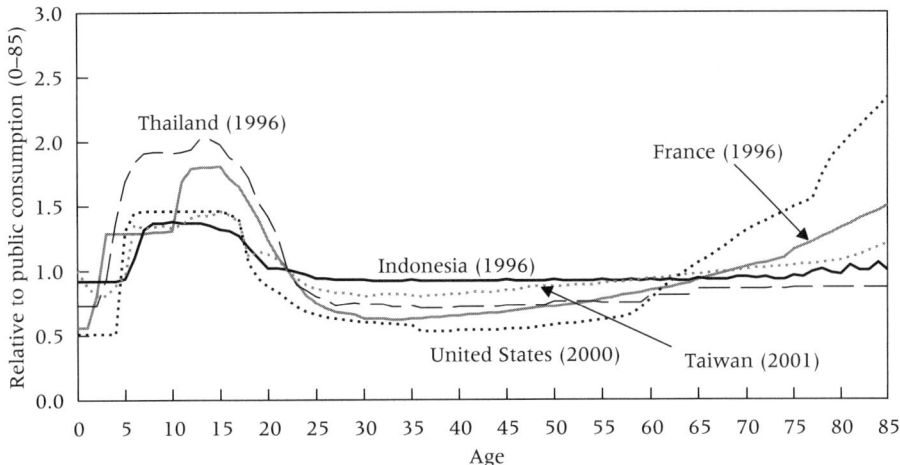

SOURCES: France (1996): Stephane Zuber, National Transfer Account Estimates for France, Economic Aspects of Population Aging Workshop Report, 35th Summer Seminar on Population, East-West Center, Honolulu, Hawaii, June 2004. Indonesia (1996): Maliki, personal communication, 2006. Taiwan (2001): Authors' calculations. Thailand (1996): A. Chawla (2007), "A comparative study of the economic lifecycles and support systems of Thailand and Taiwan," Department of Economics, University of Hawaii at Manoa. United States (2000): Authors' calculations.

substitutes. For example, France emphasizes public funding for education more than Taiwan does.

The age profile shows us the relative age orientation of public consumption in each country. The US and French programs target the young and the old. In the case of France, the allocation is roughly balanced, with the young and the old receiving similar levels of public consumption. In the United States, the program is biased more toward the elderly, particularly those aged 75 and older. In Taiwan, Indonesia, and Thailand the programs are dominated by consumption by the young to the extent that they are age targeted at all. In Indonesia age targeting is quite limited as compared to Taiwan or Thailand.

Private consumption

Most consumption is private rather than public, and in many important areas—food, housing, and clothing, for example—the private sector dominates. The public sector is also crucial, particularly in education and health. In some instances, the overall shape of the consumption profile differs significantly from that of the private sector, as we saw for the elderly in the United States. By and large, however, it is private consumption that shapes the consumption side of the life cycle equation.

Estimates of private consumption profiles are presented for four countries in Figure 3. These estimates are based on the standard NTA methodol-

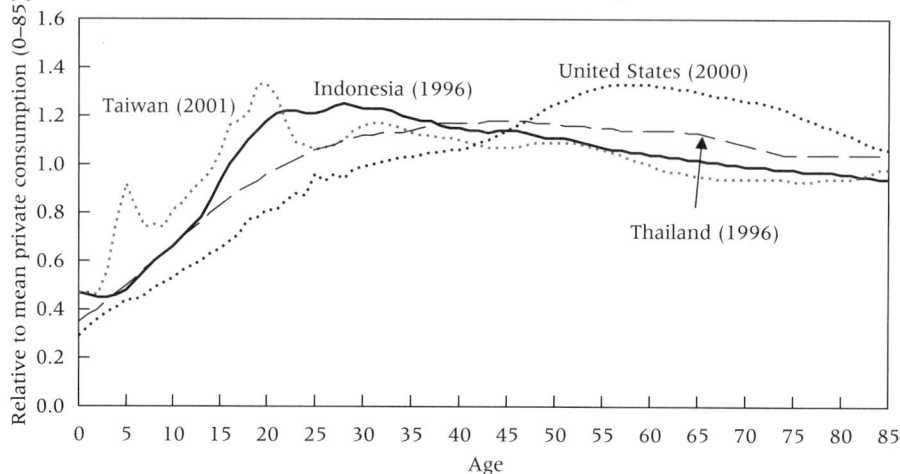

FIGURE 3 Age profile of per capita private consumption

SOURCES: Indonesia (1996): Maliki, personal communication, 2006. Taiwan (2001): Authors' calculations. Thailand (1996): A. Chawla (2007), "A comparative study of the economic lifecycles and support systems of Thailand and Taiwan," Department of Economics, University of Hawaii at Manoa. United States (2000): Authors' calculations.

ogy, hence the differences across countries are not due to the use of different methods or to different allocation rules within households.

Two distinctive patterns are apparent in Figure 3. The Asian profiles are more or less similar. Consumption rises rapidly with age from a value of about 0.4 among newborns to a value of 1 for those in their mid to late teens. For prime-age adults consumption ranges from the lifetime mean to 30 percent higher than the mean among younger adults. Private consumption among adults declines gradually with age. For those aged 65 and older, consumption varies from a high of about 10 percent above the lifetime mean to a low of about 5 percent below the lifetime mean.

Two other features of the Asian profiles are notable. One is the sharp increases among children, especially in Taiwan, that reflect private spending on education. The second is a pronounced generation-length cycle in the Taiwan consumption data. This is a Chayanov cycle that reflects the variation in per capita household income in multi-generation families as their age composition changes (Lee and Kramer 2002). The peaks of the consumption profile correspond to ages at which two generations—those in their late 20s and late 50s—are employed.

The US pattern is quite different from the Asian. Relative consumption by children is consistently lower than in the three Asian cases. Consumption by newborns at 0.27 is particularly low, which bears further investigation in light of the importance of consumption at this age to subsequent child development. While young adults have relatively high consumption in the Asian cases, this is not true in the United States. Those in their early 20s are consuming below the lifetime US mean. Private consumption continues to increase with age in the United States, reaching a peak at about 35 percent above the lifetime mean in the late 50s. Thereafter consumption declines with age and at a faster clip than in the Asian cases. By age 85, US private consumption is about 10 percent above the lifetime mean, which is somewhat higher than in the Asian countries.

What accounts for the differences in these age patterns? Consider consumption by children, which is tied to consumption by their parents. Consumption by children is low in the United States because children live in households that have low levels of consumption. The connection between consumption by adults of childrearing age and children is far from one-to-one, however. First, the rate of childbearing obviously matters. If parents have more children, then per capita consumption by both parents and children will be depressed. Second, the relationship between fertility and income matters. If low-income (low-consumption) adults have high fertility, then consumption by children will be depressed. Third, the variance of childbearing matters. If the variance is high, a larger percentage of children will live in large families with lower per capita consumption than if the variance is low.

Next consider adult consumption. One possible explanation for the difference between the US and Asian cases is that the age profiles of consumption are influenced by the age profiles of current labor income. Consumption by young adults (and their children) may be lower in the United States relative to older adults because young adults earn less relative to older adults in the United States as compared to Asia. We will see later that labor income peaks at a younger age in these three Asian countries than in the United States, but this explains a relatively small part of the difference in consumption patterns. A final explanation is that private intergenerational transfers are much more important in the Asian countries than in the United States. A much higher percentage of Asians live in multi-generation households, pool their budgets, and share standards of living.

Private education

A potentially important explanation for the high level of private consumption of children and young adults in the Asian cases is a strong commitment to education. Private spending on private education by age was estimated directly for each country using the standard NTA methodology described above. A broad measure of education is used that includes preschool costs and tutoring where it is available. The values are normalized by dividing by the average consumption of an adult aged 30 or older.

Emphasis on education is often mentioned as a key ingredient in East Asian economic success. Private spending on education is very high in Taiwan,

FIGURE 4 Private education consumption by age

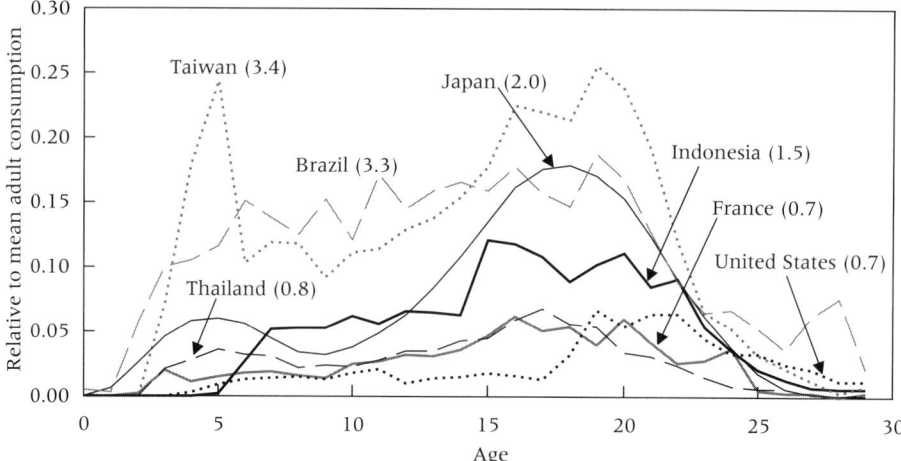

NOTE: Values in parentheses are the sums of the age-specific education values for each country.
SOURCES: Brazil (1996): Turra and Queiroz (forthcoming). France (1995): Stephane Zuber, National Transfer Account Estimates for France, Economic Aspects of Population Aging Workshop Report, 35th Summer Seminar on Population, East-West Center, Honolulu, Hawaii, June 2004. Indonesia (2001): Maliki, personal communication, 2006. Taiwan (1998): Authors' calculations. Thailand (1998): A. Chawla (2007), "A comparative study of the economic lifecycles and support systems of Thailand and Taiwan," Department of Economics, University of Hawaii at Manoa. United States (2001): Authors' calculations.
Japan (1999): Ogawa and Matsukura (forthcoming) and Maliki, personal communication, 2006.

as shown in Figure 4, and in South Korea (not shown). Spending on children ages 16–18 in Japan is high, and a substantial part of this expenditure is devoted to *Juku*—private tutoring that prepares students for college entrance examinations. High spending on private education is not confined to East Asia—private spending in Brazil rivals that in Taiwan. However, three of the four countries with the highest private spending on education are Asian.

Private spending on education per child is summarized by the sum up to age 29, which gives the total expenditure per child in terms of years of adult consumption. In Brazil and Taiwan this measure shows 3.3 and 3.4 years of mean adult consumption, respectively. Lifetime spending is much less in the other countries for which estimates are available. In Japan, 2.0 years of adult consumption are devoted to education; in Indonesia 1.5; in Thailand 0.8; and in the United States and France 0.7.

Summarizing

In many respects the United States and Taiwan represent polar cases with respect to cross-sectional consumption profiles. Ignoring some details discussed above, the Asian countries for which estimates are presented have similar private consumption profiles, lower levels of public spending, and public sectors that emphasize education more and health less. The evidence is far too fragmented, however, to suggest the existence of a general Asian pattern.

The differences and similarities between the age profiles of consumption for the United States and Taiwan are summarized in Table 3. The values are constructed for a synthetic cohort subject to the period survival rates from the 1985–89 US life table and the per capita age profiles for the United States and Taiwan. The mean age of consumption is younger in Taiwan than in the United States by 5.4 years. This is significant because the demand for life cycle saving or transfers arises from the difference between the average age of consumption and the average age of earning. Other things equal, a higher average age of consumption implies a greater demand for wealth.

What accounts for this large difference between countries? One can formally answer the question using the data in Table 3 and decomposition techniques, because the mean age is equal to the weighted sum of the mean ages of the components where the weights are the consumption shares. Here we take a more informal approach.

First, consider private versus public consumption. In both sectors, the mean age of consumption is lower in Taiwan than in the United States. The difference is 5.2 years for private consumption and 4.7 years for public consumption.

Second, education can have a large effect on the mean age of consumption. Because the mean age of education consumption is so different from the average age of total consumption, increases in the share of education lead to a relatively large effect on the overall mean. In both the United States and Taiwan, the mean age of education consumption is more than 25 years less than the mean age of consumption. The high level of private education spending in Taiwan reduces both the mean age of private consumption and the mean

TABLE 3 Summary of per capita consumption profiles, United States 2000 and Taiwan 1998

	United States		Taiwan	
	Share of total	Mean age	Share of total	Mean age
Total consumption	100.0	45.5	100.0	40.1
Private consumption	76.4	45.7	73.1	40.5
Education	1.4	16.8	5.9	15.1
Health	8.0	50.5	3.5	50.0
Other	67.0	45.7	63.6	42.3
Public consumption	23.6	43.3	26.9	38.6
Education	5.2	13.9	3.6	15.0
Health	7.0	67.2	6.0	50.0
Other	11.4	39.5	17.3	39.5

NOTE: Mean ages are calculated for a stationary population age distribution based on the US period life table for 1985–89 and therefore do not reflect differences in population age distribution across countries.

age of total consumption. The effect on the mean age of total consumption is partially offset by the higher level of public consumption of education in the United States.

Third and clearly of great importance is the effect of high public spending on the health of the elderly in the United States, which is similar in magnitude to the share of public spending for health at all ages in Taiwan, resulting in a mean age of consumption in the United States that is 17 years higher. Private spending on health is much less important in Taiwan than in the United States, and the mean ages are similar.

Finally, not to be overlooked is other private consumption. The difference in the mean ages is 3.3 years. This is an important difference given that other private consumption accounts for roughly two-thirds of total consumption in both Taiwan and the United States. By itself this accounts for more than two years of the difference in the mean ages of total consumption. It underlines the significant difference in private consumption between the United States and Asian countries described above. Differences in education spending and health spending do not, by themselves, explain why private consumption favors the young in Taiwan and the old in the United States.

Cross-sectional estimates of labor income

For all eight economies shown in Figure 5 the age profiles of labor income have the familiar inverse U-shape. However, the figure also shows large differences in the importance of labor income at younger and older ages relative to the prime working ages and in the age of peak income.

In the Philippines, where income is relatively low and agricultural and informal employment dominates, 9.8 percent of income is earned after age 65, a share 12 times greater than in France and four times greater than in Taiwan (see Table 4). These measures abstract from demographic differences because they are conditional on survival—that is, the cross-section is treated as a synthetic cohort assumed to survive until age 85. The elderly share of income does not vary strongly with development. The income of the elderly is quite high in the Philippines and Indonesia, but it is also relatively high in the United States, Japan, and Thailand. The elderly share is extremely low in France.

There are also large differences at younger ages. In the three poorer countries, the average labor income per 16-year-old is six times the average labor income in the four richer countries (including Taiwan), where each is measured relative to average income at ages 30–49. In all the poorer countries, more than 2 percent of lifetime labor income accrues to those aged 20 and under, whereas in all the richer countries including Taiwan, this share is less than 2 percent and is mostly close to 1 percent. In Thailand the share is 4.2 percent, more than four times the share in France. A similar pattern holds for the share age 25 and under.

FIGURE 5 Per capita labor income profile

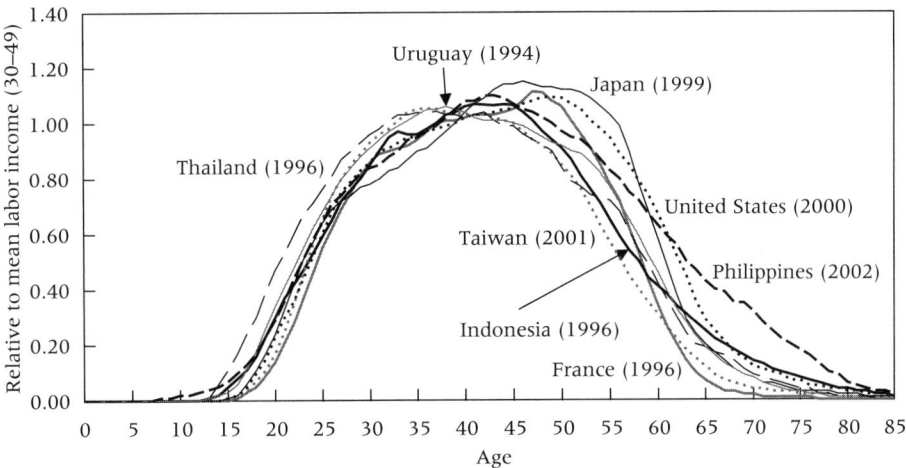

SOURCES: France (1996): Stephane Zuber, National Transfer Account Estimates for France, Economic Aspects of Population Aging Workshop Report, 35th Summer Seminar on Population, East-West Center, Honolulu, Hawaii, June 2004. Indonesia (1996): Maliki, personal communications, 2007. Taiwan (2001): Authors' calculations. Thailand (1996): A. Chawla (2007), "A comparative study of the economic lifecycles and support systems of Thailand and Taiwan," Department of Economics, University of Hawaii at Manoa. Uruguay (1994): Marisa Bucheli, personal communications, 2007. United States (2000): Authors' calculations. Philippines (2002): Marjorie Pajaron, personal communications, 2007. Japan (1999): Ogawa and Matsukura (forthcoming), and Maliki, personal communication, 2006.

Comparisons like these across rich and poor countries with very different cultures and institutions may provide crude or misleading information about how development influences labor income profiles. We can supplement the cross-sectional age profiles with longitudinal data from Taiwan and the United States. The labor income of those aged 15–29 relative to those aged 30–49 dropped by 70 percent in Taiwan between 1978 and 2001 and by 20

TABLE 4 Summary of per capita earnings profiles, 8 countries

	Mean age	Peak age	Share 25 and under	Share 20 and under	Share 65+
Indonesia (1996)	43.0	41	8.9	2.5	5.5
Philippines (2002)	45.3	43	8.4	2.3	9.8
Uruguay (1994)	42.0	38	9.9	2.5	2.6
Thailand (1996)	40.9	37	13.0	4.2	3.3
Taiwan (2001)	41.4	36	8.2	1.2	2.3
France (1996)	42.4	47	6.4	0.9	0.8
Japan (1999)	43.9	46	7.7	1.1	3.0
US (2000)	44.3	49	7.2	1.6	5.0

NOTE: Mean ages are calculated for a stationary population age distribution based on the US period life table for 1985–89 and therefore do not reflect differences in population age distribution across countries. The shares and mean ages are calculated from unsmoothed data, while the peak ages are calculated from smoothed data.

percent in the United States between 1982 and 1997 (Figure 6), consistent with the cross-sectional association of labor income at younger ages in relation to development.

The age at which income peaks varies from 36 to 49—a difference of 13 years. This peak age is associated with the level of development. It is highest in the three most advanced economies, the United States, Japan, and France, with peaks between ages 47 and 49. Income in Indonesia, Thailand, Uruguay, and the Philippines peaks between 37 and 43. Surprisingly, Taiwan has the youngest peak at age 36, which calls for further investigation.

A detailed explanation of why earnings peak later in high-income than in low-income countries is not pursued here, but a range of explanations is possible and the patterns are intriguing. Earnings rise fastest (in cross-section) with age in the lower-income countries, even though ample research shows that wages rise faster (longitudinally) in industrial countries for those with more education. In Japan, the seniority wage system ties wages closely to experience, and the country's age-earnings profile is the highest during the late 40s to the 50s. The share of earnings of the elderly is broadly consistent with findings of studies on the effects of pension and tax systems on labor incentives (Gruber and Wise 1999, 2001). As expected, the earnings shares of the elderly in Taiwan, the United States, and Japan are high compared to their shares in France.

Considering the consumption and earning profiles together

So far, we have been considering consumption and earnings separately. It is also interesting to consider them together, for it is together that they determine the periods of economic dependency and the roles of intergenerational transfers. Table 5 summarizes and compares consumption and labor income profiles for four countries. The upper panel reports the two crossing points, the youngest age and oldest age at which labor earning exceeds total consumption, and the span of years between these. The ages at the first crossing point are remarkably similar, all between 23 and 26 years, which might appear to be surprisingly high. It is important to keep in mind that consumption here includes in-kind transfers from the government, including a per capita share of "Other public" which includes such items as the military, roads, sewer systems, government-funded research, and so on. Also, some young adults are living in their parents' households and consuming based on a pooled household budget.

The other crossing ages are also clustered tightly, with the elderly becoming net consumers between ages 55 and 58 in the four countries. The corresponding net producing ages span 31 years for the United States and 32 years for the other three countries. These features of the economic life cycle

TABLE 5 Comparisons of labor income and consumption age profiles, selected countries

	Indonesia (1996)	Taiwan (2001)	Thailand (1996)	United States (2000)
Crossing ages for consumption and labor income				
First age	26	24	23	26
Last age	58	56	55	57
Span	32	32	32	31
Mean ages based on US stationary population				
Consumption	41.2	40.1	41.7	45.5
Labor income	41.0	41.4	40.9	44.3
Difference	0.2	−1.4	0.8	1.2

NOTE: Crossing ages identify the ages between which labor income exceeds consumption. Estimates are calculated for a stationary population age distribution based on the US period life table for 1985–89 and therefore do not reflect differences in population age distribution across countries.

can differ because of varying amounts of capital income versus labor income; differing levels of saving; differing enrollment in higher education; short-run economic fluctuations; differences in public policy and social systems; and higher or lower support ratios, which will raise or lower the whole consumption profile relative to the labor earnings profile across countries. We have not yet tried to parse the specific factors responsible for the differences shown in the table.

It is also interesting to compare the average ages of consumption and production for a synthetic cohort in these countries. Table 5 shows average ages of consumption and labor income based on the per capita labor income and consumption profiles of each country, weighted by the US survival rates (so differences in population age distribution have no direct effect on these averages). The differences between these average ages indicate the direction and distance of reallocations of income across ages within a synthetic life cycle, assuming a zero discount rate.

We find that these reallocations are minutely upward—really essentially neutral—in the United States, where the average age of consumption is 45.5 years and the average age of earning is 44.3. Even smaller reallocations upward are observed in Thailand at 0.8 years and Indonesia at 0.2 years. Taiwan shows a small downward reallocation by 1.4 years. There is little difference in the mean age of labor earning or consumption across the three Asian countries, but the mean ages of both labor earnings and consumption are several years later in the United States. The consumption difference for the United States is doubtless due in part to the important role of Medicare expenditures on the elderly. The labor income cause is harder to isolate.

Changes in consumption and labor income over time

Time series of private consumption and labor income age profiles have been estimated to this point only for Taiwan, from 1976 to 2003, and for the United States, from 1980 to 2000. A comparison of these two economies is quite interesting for a variety of reasons, particularly because of the great difference in their rates of economic growth. Here we examine the rates of growth by age. We leave the examination of cohort trends for another occasion.

Figure 6 plots the average annual growth in real private consumption and labor income at each age. To remove the effects of short-term fluctuations, the estimates are based on five-year centered moving averages of the age profiles. Labor income for persons aged x in year t is the average of labor income of persons aged x for years $t-2$ to $t+2$. The time series are thereby reduced to 1978–2001 for Taiwan and to 1982–97 for the United States. The growth rates are presented only for ages 15 and older, since those who were younger had no significant labor income in either economy. If these growth rates were constant across age, it would indicate that the age profiles were not changing shape over these periods.

It should come as no surprise that the growth rates for both private consumption and labor income at most ages in Taiwan are higher than in the United States. For Taiwan, the age profiles of consumption and labor income increased at annual real rates of 6.1 percent and 2.6 percent per year, respectively. The age profiles of consumption and labor income in the United States

FIGURE 6 Annual real growth of private consumption and labor income by age, Taiwan 1978–2001, United States 1982–97

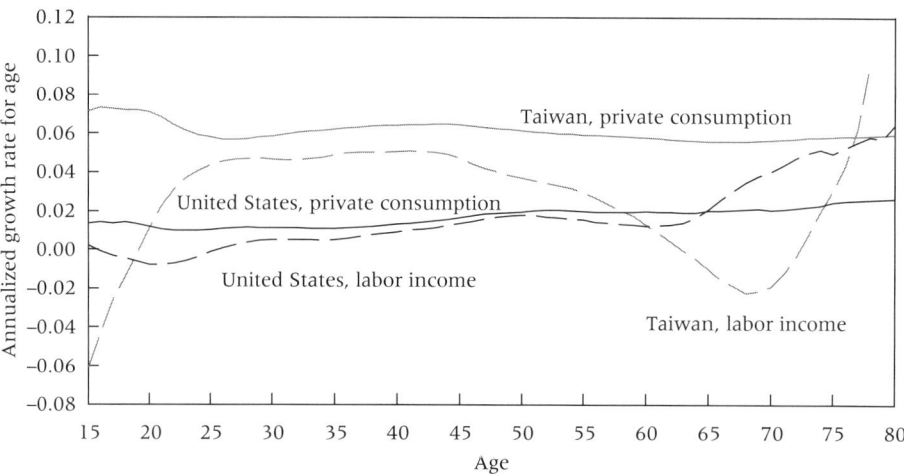

SOURCES: Taiwan (2001) and United States (2000): Authors' calculations.

shifted upward at real annual rates of 1.6 percent and 1.4 percent.[7] Growth in Taiwan was strong; in the United States it was moderate.

The stability of the age profile of private consumption in Taiwan is remarkable. Consumption of persons in their 40s and the very young grew somewhat faster than average. Consumption by those in their late 60s and early 70s grew somewhat slower than average. Overall, however, there is virtually no generational shift in consumption in Taiwan during this period. The lack of change is all the more surprising given the many other dramatic changes in Taiwan—for example, rapid economic growth and large changes in age structure. We believe that this sustained equality across adult ages reflects resource sharing within coresidential households, in contrast to the nuclear families of the United States.

The consumption profile growth rates for the United States increase steadily from the mid-30s to the oldest ages. The range is substantial in comparison with the average US growth rate during this period, and reflects the trends in private consumption that helped to produce the striking consumption pattern shown in Figure 1a.

The labor income growth rates vary more with age than the consumption growth rates in both economies, more so in Taiwan than in the United States. Certain features are common to both economies. The slowest growth was at the youngest ages—among teenagers in Taiwan and 20-year-olds in the United States. The most rapid growth was at older ages—those in their mid-70s and older in Taiwan and those in their mid-60s and older in the United States. At the highest ages, labor income in both economies is relatively low, and a large percentage increase does not translate into a large absolute increase. In Taiwan, the labor income of adults near conventional retirement age grew much more slowly than the labor income of younger adults.

The simple correlation between the growth rates of private consumption and labor income across ages is 0.87 in the United States and –0.11 in Taiwan. This does not suggest a strong relationship, but reflects in part the inclusion of age groups (the young and the old) for which labor income is relatively unimportant. If we consider only those aged 21 to 60 years, the simple correlation increases to 0.89 in the United States and 0.29 in Taiwan. This suggests that current earnings are to some extent driving private consumption, but variations in consumption growth also exhibit considerable independence from variations in labor income.

Conclusions

Understanding the economic life cycle—how it varies and why—is important in its own right, but is also critical to understanding how changes in population age structure influence many features of the macroeconomy. There have been few previous efforts, however, to estimate how consumption and production of individuals vary over the entire life span. Very little research has sought to estimate consumption profiles for a society from cradle to grave (in a cross-sectional sense), including both public and private transfers, as we seek to do in this chapter. A number of technical difficulties, some of which are described above, create substantial hurdles to such an enterprise.

We have presented estimates of labor earnings and consumption for a wide range of contemporary economies, including mature economies, rapidly growing economies, and low-income countries, from the West and from the East. The estimated cross-sectional age profiles of labor income are broadly similar, and their hump shape is consistent with our expectations. There are striking contrasts, however, in the timing of earnings over the life cycle, with the peak age ranging from 36 years in Taiwan to 49 in the United States.

The consumption profiles reveal even more striking contrasts, starting with the flat age profile of total consumption in Taiwan and the steeply rising one for the United States, which we believe reflect the extended family versus the state as the primary locus of transfers to the elderly. Profiles for private consumption are also quite variable, with Taiwan peaking early at age 20 years and the United States rising until its late peak at 58 years. In Taiwan, Indonesia, and Thailand, consumption declines after the 20s or 30s. Private expenditures on education show wide variations, with unusually high expenditures in some Asian countries. Because of possible public–private substitutions, it is questionable to assign causality to either type of consumption for differences in total consumption, but it is hard to avoid noticing that without public spending on Medicare and institutional Medicaid in the United States, total consumption would decline after age 58, whereas, with such spending, it rises strongly.

Considering the consumption and earnings profiles together, we are surprised by the short period of life during which individuals produce more than they consume, only around 31–32 years in the United States, Taiwan, Indonesia, and Thailand. The brevity of this phase contrasts sharply with high life expectancy, approaching 80 years in the United States and Taiwan.

We have also looked at two decades of change in the United States and Taiwan. The stability of the Taiwan consumption profile is remarkable in light of the country's extraordinary economic growth, and we attribute this stability to the extended family. In the United States we find that consumption at older ages has been rising over time faster than in childhood, increasing the steepness of the life cycle consumption gradient.

Many important questions remain to be explored, and we look forward both to broadening the analysis to include the experience of more countries and to deepening it by probing the causes of the differences we observe.

Notes

Research for this chapter was funded by two grants from the National Institutes of Health, NIA R01 AG025488 and R37 AG025247. The authors are grateful to other project participants for use of their estimates for other countries and to Tim Miller, Mun-Sim Lai, Comfort Sumida, An-chi Tung, and Avi Ebenstein for their help with calculations and to Ann Takayesu for assistance with the manuscript.

1 Throughout this chapter, we use interchangeably the expressions "labor income" and "labor earnings," even though "labor earnings" has a narrower technical meaning. Both terms are used to mean total labor compensation, including employer-provided benefits and an estimate of labor's share of self-employment income.

2 For example, Cutler et al. (1990) estimate support ratios for the United States from 1950 to 2050. The inverse of the support ratio is the Chayanov ratio. Chayanov (1966 [1925]) used standardized age profiles of production and consumption to form ratios of expected consumers to expected producers at the household level. Such ratios are now known as "Chayanov ratios" (see Lee and Kramer 2002). Later Lorimer (1967) developed some of the same ideas.

3 The effect of a small change in population age structure on the macro-economy can be decomposed into two additive components: the effect of the change in population age structure weighted by the initial age profiles of production and consumption (or other items of interest) and the induced changes in the shapes of these age profiles weighted by the initial population age distribution (Lee 1997). The first effect is compositional or mechanical and the second behavioral.

4 Also see Attanasio et al. 1999, which provides support for the life cycle model.

5 Although alcohol is not illegal in Indonesia, the population is predominantly Islamic. Thus, alcohol is not an appropriate variable.

6 Smoothing was performed on the log of population-weighted age-specific averages using SUPSMU in the R statistical package. Smoothing spans were determined on an ad hoc basis. Any ages with a profile value of zero because of survey assumptions were left out of the smoothing calculation and set to zero after smoothing. For example, when a survey only covers ages 14 and above, all values below 14 were set identically to zero.

7 Values are calculated using survival weights to calculate average private consumption and labor income and are explained in more detail above.

References

Attanasio, O. P., J. Banks, C. Meghir, and G. Weber. 1999. "Humps and bumps in lifetime consumption," *Journal of Business and Economic Statistics* 17(1): 22–35.
Autor, D. H., F. Levy, and R. J. Murnane. 2003. "The skill content of recent technological change: An empirical exploration," *Quarterly Journal of Economics* 118(4): 1279–1334.
Becker, G. S. and H. G. Lewis. 1973. "On the interaction between the quantity and quality of children." *Journal of Political Economy* 18(2): S279–S288.
Bound, J. 1991. "Self-reported versus objective measures of health in retirement models." *The Journal of Human Resources* 26(1): 106–138.
Carroll, C. D. 1992. "The buffer-stock theory of saving: Some macroeconomic evidence," *Brookings Papers on Economic Activity* CXII(1): 1–56.
Carroll, C. D. and L. H. Summers. 1991. "Consumption growth parallels income growth: Some new evidence," in B. D. Bernheim and J. B. Shoven (eds.), *National Saving and Economic Performance: A National Bureau of Economic Research Project Report*. Chicago: University of Chicago Press, pp. 305–343.

Chayanov, A. V. 1966 [1925]. *The Theory of Peasant Economy,* translated by D. Thorner et al. Homewood, IL: R.D. Irwin.

Cutler, D. M., J. M. Poterba, L. Sheiner, and L. Summers. 1990. "An aging society: Opportunity or challenge?," *Brookings Papers on Economic Activity* (1): 1–56.

Deaton, A. 1991. "Saving and liquidity constraints," *Econometrica* 59: 1221–1248.

———. 1997. *The Analysis of Household Surveys: A Microeconomic Approach to Development Policy.* Baltimore: Johns Hopkins University Press.

Deaton, A. and C. H. Paxson. 1997. "The effects of economic and population growth on national saving and inequality," *Demography* 34(1): 97–114.

Dwyer, D. S. and O. Mitchell. 1999. "Health problems as determinants of retirement: Are self-rated measures endogenous?," *Journal of Health Economics* 18(2): 173–193.

Easterlin, R. A. 1978. "What will 1984 be like?," *Demography* 15 (November): 397–432.

Espenshade, T. 1984. *Investing in Children: New Estimates of Parental Expenditures.* Washington, DC: The Urban Institute Press.

Gollin, Douglas. 2002. "Getting income shares right," *Journal of Political Economy* 110(2): 458–474.

Gruber, J. and D. A. Wise. 1999. "Introduction and summary," in J. Gruber and D. A. Wise (eds.), *Social Security and Retirement around the World.* Chicago: The University of Chicago Press, pp. 437–474.

———. 2001. "An international perspective on policies for an aging society," *NBER Working Papers* W8103.

Indonesia, Central Bureau of Statistics. National Socio-Economic Survey (SUSENAS, survey year of 1996).

Lee, Ronald D. 1980. "Age structure, intergenerational transfers and economic growth: An overview," in George Tapinos (ed.), *Revue Economique: Special Issue on Economic Demography* 31(6): 1129–1156.

———. 1997. "Population dynamics: Equilibrium, disequilibrium, and consequences of fluctuations," in M. R. Rosenzweig and O. Stark (eds.), *Handbook of Population and Family Economics,* vol. 1B, Chapter 19, pp. 1063–1115.

Lee, R. and R. Edwards. 2001. "The fiscal impact of population change," in J. S. Little and R. K. Triest (eds.), *Seismic Shifts: The Economic Impact of Demographic Change.* Federal Reserve Bank of Boston Conference Series, no. 46.

———. 2002. "The fiscal effects of population aging in the US: Assessing the uncertainties," in J. M. Poterba (ed.), *Tax Policy and Economy.* NBER, MIT Press, 16: 141–181.

Lee, R. and K. Kramer. 2002. "Children's economic roles in the Maya family life cycle: Cain, Caldwell, and Chayanov revisited," *Population and Development Review* 28(3): 475–499.

Lorimer, Frank. 1967. "The economics of family formation under different conditions," *Proceedings of the World Population Conference, Belgrade, 1967*: 92–95.

Maitland, S. B., R. C. Intrieri, K. W. Schaie, and S. L. Willis. 2000. "Gender differences and changes in cognitive abilities across the adult life span." *Aging, Neuropsychology, and Cognition* 7(1): 32–53.

Maliki. 2005. *Three Essays on Education and Intergenerational Transfers,* Ph.D. dissertation, Department of Economics, University of Hawaii.

Mankiw, N. G. and D. N. Weil. 1989. "The baby boom, the baby bust, and the housing market," *Regional Science and Urban Economics* 19(2): 235–258.

Mason, A. 1987. "National saving rates and population growth: A new model and new evidence," in D. G. Johnson and R. D. Lee (eds.), *Population Growth and Economic Development: Issues and Evidence.* Social Demography series. Madison: University of Wisconsin Press, pp. 523–560.

———. 1988. "Saving, economic growth, and demographic change," *Population and Development Review* 14(1): 113–144.

Mason, A., R. Lee, A. Tung, M. Lai, and T. Miller. Forthcoming. "Population aging and intergenerational transfers: Introducing age into national accounts," in D. Wise (ed.), *Devel-

opments in the Economics of Aging. National Bureau of Economic Research: University of Chicago Press.

McFadden, D. 1994. "Demographics, the housing market, and the welfare of the elderly," in D. Wise (ed.), *Studies in the Economics of Aging*. Chicago: The University of Chicago Press and NBER, pp. 225–285.

Modigliani, F. 1988. "Measuring the contribution of intergenerational transfers to total wealth: Conceptual issues and empirical findings," in D. Kessler and A. Mason (eds.), *Modeling the Accumulation and Distribution of Wealth*. Oxford: Oxford University Press, pp. 21–52.

Ogawa, N. and R. Matsukura. Forthcoming. "The role of older persons' changing health and wealth in an aging society: The case of Japan," *United Nations Population Bulletin*.

Poterba, J. M. 2005. "The impact of population aging on financial markets," in Gordon H. Sellon, Jr. et al. (eds.), *Global Demographic Change: Economic Impact and Policy Challenges*. Kansas City: Federal Reserve Bank of Kansas City, pp. 163–216.

Quinn, J. F., R. Burkhauser, and D. A. Myers. 1990. *Passing the Torch: The Influence of Economic Incentives on Work and Retirement*. Kalamazoo, MI: W.E. Upjohn Institute for Employment Research.

Skirbekk, Vegard. 2003. "Age and individual productivity: A literature survey." *MPIDR Working Paper* 2003-028, Max Planck Institute for Demographic Research, Rostock.

Turra, C. and B. Queiroz. Forthcoming. "Before it's too late: Demographic transition, labor supply and social security problems in Brazil," *United Nations Population Bulletin*.

Verhaegen, P. and T. A. Salthouse. 1997. "Meta-analyses of age-cognition relations in adulthood: Estimates of linear and nonlinear age effects and structural models," *Psychological Bulletin* 122(3): 231–249.

Wang Feng and Andrew Mason. Forthcoming. "Demographic dividends and prospects for development in China," *United Nations Population Bulletin*.

Zuber, S. 2004. "National Transfer Account Project" «http://www.schemearts.com/proj/nta/».

Productivity Consequences of Workforce Aging: Stagnation or Horndal Effect?

BO MALMBERG
THOMAS LINDH
MAX HALVARSSON

A growing population in which every successive cohort is larger than the preceding one will, in general, be characterized by a youthful, *progressive* age structure. This relation between cohort growth and age structure is not only valid for the total population but also for the working-age population. Positive cohort growth rates lead to an age profile dominated by young adults, whereas negative cohort growth rates give a dominance of older adults.

In this chapter we address the question of how such changes in the age composition of the working-age population affect productivity growth. Two hypotheses are relevant. The first one is based on productivity measurement at the individual level. Here, most studies indicate that labor productivity peaks somewhere between 30 and 50 years of age. This suggests that a prime-age workforce would be more productive than either a young- or old-age workforce.

The second hypothesis is based on the experience of the Horndal steel plant in central Sweden. Between 1927 and 1952 this plant experienced a mean annual growth rate in productivity of 2.5 percent in spite of the fact that no major investments were undertaken (Genberg 1992). The first economist to discuss the Horndal effect was Erik Lundberg (Lundberg 1961). Later, it formed an important part of Kenneth Arrow's learning-by-doing argument (Arrow 1962). A key aspect of the Horndal story is that the steelwork had an older workforce. In 1930, more than a third of the workers at the Horndal steelworks were above age 50 years, compared to only one-in-five of all nonagricultural male workers in Sweden. In 1950 almost half of the workers at Horndal were above 50, compared to one-in-four among nonagricultural male workers in general. The Horndal experience, thus, suggests that workforce aging is not a problem for productivity. To the contrary, an aging workforce was compatible with rapid increases in labor productivity through a learning-by-doing effect.

The existence of two competing, but not mutually exclusive, hypotheses on the effect of workforce aging on productivity clearly calls for a more thorough empirical study based on micro data. Although the two hypotheses are competing, both may be true and conclusions regarding the productivity of an aging workforce in the aggregate are not as obvious as they may seem. Different age groups substitute for or complement each other, and the effect of other production factors should also be considered. Thus, the aggregate effect is not necessarily a simple summation of the productivity of the age groups. The most productive combination of different age groups at the plant level may have other properties than would be indicated by the sum of individual productivities. Here, however, the focus is on whether the age combination at the plant level is primarily determined by the individual characteristics of the workers, making physically more productive young workers the natural choice, or by Horndal, learning-by-doing, effects on productivity, making older workers an important building block of efficient production.

In this study we use a panel of employer–employee matched data from Statistics Sweden covering 1985–96. Plant-level data are from the Swedish Manufacturing and Mining Surveys and contain information about sector, number of white-collar and blue-collar employees, value of output, and value added. Employee data are from the Regional Labour Market Statistics (previously ÅRSYS) database at Statistics Sweden and contain information on the age and education of individuals employed in Swedish manufacturing and mining establishments. By matching these two datasets, we have been able to obtain measures of the age and educational composition of the workforce of the establishments.[1]

The strength of these data is the combination of employee data, output data, and several observations for each plant. This allows us not only to compare the productivity levels of plants with different age and educational structures. Thanks to the panel structure, we can also control for possible plant-specific effects and, in addition, use lagged variables as instruments for potentially endogenous measures of current age structure.

If the hypothesis based on individual-level productivity measures is correct, we should expect plants with a high share of prime-age workers to be the most productive. On the other hand, if the Horndal hypothesis is valid, then workforce aging at the plant level should nevertheless be associated with increasing productivity.

Earlier studies using employer–employee matched datasets have to a large extent focused on a comparison between the age profile of earnings and the age profile of estimated productivity, with the purpose of testing the seniority wage hypothesis that wages for the elderly are higher than their marginal productivity. Notwithstanding the relevance of this issue, we argue that the productivity profile as such is of considerable importance in view of the aging of the labor force that will characterize many countries in the next 10–20 years. Therefore, we focus on the productivity issue and refrain from looking at earnings profiles.

The next section presents the results from OLS regressions relating plant-level productivity to age structure and educational levels in the pooled data. In the third section we introduce plant-level fixed effects based on the argument that the productivity levels of a plant are strongly influenced by quasi-fixed factors such as basic design and machinery set-up. The fourth section presents the results from an instrumental variable regression that controls for the possibility of endogeneity bias in the estimates of aging effects. The fifth section contains a complementary analysis of workforce age structure in start-up plants and plants that are closing down. Finally we discuss the implications of our results.

Estimated model

The estimates presented below are, at this stage, not based on an explicit theoretical model. Instead, the aim of the specifications is to answer the empirical question of how labor productivity at the plant level, measured by value added per employee, is related to the age composition of the labor force without imposing any given theoretical structure. Throughout, we use a log specification, that is, log value added per employee as dependent variable and log of the age variables. This limits problems related to asymmetric sample variations, given the highly skewed shape of the distribution of per worker value added. Moreover, using logs makes it possible to include all the age shares in spite of the fact that the non-logged values add to one. This has the advantage of simplifying interpretation.

Two specifications of age effects have been used. First, an age share model where the workforce has been divided into three age groups: less than 30 years, 30–49 years, and 50 and older. This division is in essence arbitrary, but it corresponds roughly to the earliest part of working life, prime-age working life, and later working life. Moreover, it corresponds to a division that we have been using consistently in a number of studies of age effects on the economy (Lindh and Malmberg 1998, 1999, 2007a, 2007b). One difference, however, is that the 50+ group here also includes people above age 65, because they are too few to allow a separate analysis.

The only explicit control variable we report here is mean length of education. This variable is based on an assumption on the education length of people with primary, secondary, and tertiary education. No other control variables are reported, since our aim is not to provide any comprehensive

TABLE 1 Descriptive statistics for the matched employer–employee plant sample over the period, Sweden, mining and manufacturing industry, 1985–96

Variable	Observations	Mean	Std. Dev.	Min	Max
Value added per employee (1,000 SEK/year)[a]	95,443	78.93	62.91	0.017	2,313
Education (years)	95,443	10.95	0.8	9	15
Mean age (years)	95,443	39.61	4.87	23.23	63.57
Employees (number/plant)	95,443	82.80	275	1	12,881
Share ≤29	95,443	0.30	0.157	0	0.957
Share 30–49	95,443	0.46	0.137	0	0.955
Share ≥50	95,443	0.24	0.143	0	0.955

[a] 1968 producer price.

explanation of the general development of productivity but rather to focus on the two competing hypotheses above. To avoid problems related to omitted variable bias, fixed effects have been used to account for the influence of unmeasured and unobserved variation across plants.

The Swedish Manufacturing and Mining Surveys (SMMS) provide data on somewhere between 9,000 and 12,000 establishments depending on the year, while the annual Regional Labour Market Statistics (ÅRSYS/RAMS) contain data for 550,000–750,000 individuals employed within mining and manufacturing in the month of November. After merging the data sources we end up with 8,000–9,000 establishments in each year, with a stable average of about 80 employees per plant for the years 1985–96.

Table 1 displays descriptive statistics for the total merged sample. Value added, education, and mean age are all expressed as averages—education and mean age in years, and value added as thousands of SEK per worker in 1968 constant producer prices. The standard deviations of mean age and mean years of education are fairly low and get even lower in the larger plants. While there is a drift upward in both mean age and mean education over the period, most of this is due to selective firing of the young and the less educated in the recession Sweden experienced in the beginning of the 1990s.

Age effects on productivity without controlling for fixed, plant-level effects

In Table 2 we present the results from estimating age effects on productivity when no plant-level fixed effects are used. Four specifications are presented: only age shares (1), age shares and education (2), age shares and education estimated for small and larger plants separately (3, 4). The break-off point between large and small plants has arbitrarily been set at an average of 50 employees during the existence of an establishment.

TABLE 2 Age share model without plant-level fixed effects, with dependent variable log value added per worker, Sweden, mining and manufacturing industry, 1985–96

Dep.var: log VA/empl.	(1)	(2)	(3)	(4)
Log share ≤29	0.020	0.006	0.005	0.095
	(5.66)**	(1.77)	(1.30)	(9.26)**
Log share 30–49	0.128	0.080	0.060	0.229
	(20.38)**	(12.91)**	(9.28)**	(10.11)**
Log share ≥50	−0.043	−0.023	−0.016	0.016
	(13.78)**	(7.51)**	(5.08)**	(1.53)
Mean education		0.146	0.133	0.179
		(61.05)**	(49.15)**	(34.30)**
Constant	4.255	2.628	2.728	2.640
	(393.37)**	(91.61)**	(84.86)**	(37.95)**
Plant size restriction			<50	50 or more
Observations	95,443	95,443	66,819	28,624
R-squared	0.01	0.05	0.04	0.05

Absolute value of t statistics in parentheses.
* significant at 5%; ** significant at 1%

The estimates give strong support to the hypothesis that plant-level productivity is positively influenced by a high share of prime-age adults in the workforce, whereas a high share of young adults has a less beneficial effect. Note also that the effect of old workers is negative. The results here, thus, fit with what we should expect from studies of age effects on individual productivity. The result is also in line with the findings of other studies of this issue (Haltiwanger et al. 1999; Haltiwanger, Lane, and Spletzer 2007; Crépon et al. 2002; Ilmakunnas and Maliranta 2002; Hellerstein and Neumark 2004; Ilmakunnas and Maliranta 2005).

Introducing controls for education does not change this conclusion. The age effects become less pronounced but the basic pattern is still very strong. The pattern is also present among both small and large plants, although it is much stronger in the sample of large plants. This is what one should expect given that small plants will be more constrained in achieving an optimal mix of workers.

Because the shares sum to one, care has to be taken in interpreting the coefficients in the table because the age share variables cannot vary independently of each other. Thus, an increase in the share below age 30 must be accompanied by a decrease in the other age group shares, and the effect on productivity depends on how this decrease is distributed over the age groups. For example, according to column (1), an increase in the young workforce share has a positive elasticity of 0.02, but if the corresponding decrease takes place in the prime-age group the net effect is predicted to be negative nevertheless, while if it takes place in the 50+ group the positive effect would be reinforced. Therefore understanding how shares shift over age groups is essential for the interpretation. A swelling of the prime-age group at the expense of the young will have positive effects while an increase of the old-age group at the expense of the young in this case will have negative effects.

Since the estimated coefficients are elasticities and a one percent change in the share of young workers automatically corresponds to a percentage change in the other age shares that differs depending on their initial size, the outcome is not straightforward. Assume for instance that the distribution is 30 percent young, 45 percent middle age, and 25 percent old, then the estimates in column (1) imply that a 10 percent decrease in the young to 27 percent combined with a corresponding increase of the old to 28 percent will decrease productivity by around 0.3 percent. However, if the prime-age group increases by 3 percentage points, this is only two-thirds of a 10 percent increase for that share and hence productivity will increase in this case by $(0.128*(10*(0.30/0.45))) - (0.02*10)$ percent, that is, around 0.65 percent. In general the effect of a change thus depends on the initial values. In practice, however, we will have a distribution of age shares counteracting extreme effects.

Table 3 presents an alternative estimation of the age effects with a much simpler interpretation. Here the log of mean age of the workforce at the plant is the age variable instead of age shares for young, prime-age, and older workers. If the Horndal hypothesis is valid, we should expect mean age to have a clear positive effect on labor productivity. However, these estimates give the opposite results. Increasing workforce age is associated with lower productivity. To get an impression of the magnitude, consider that mean age is around 40 and a one-year increase therefore corresponds to an increase of 2.5

TABLE 3 Mean age model without plant-level fixed effects, with dependent variable log value added per worker, Sweden, mining and manufacturing industry, 1985–96

Dep.var: log VA/empl.	(1)	(2)	(3)	(4)
Log mean age	–0.302	–0.075	–0.074	–0.317
	(19.60)**	(4.80)**	(4.28)**	(8.82)**
Mean education		0.151	0.135	0.187
		(62.51)**	(48.70)**	(37.76)**
Constant	5.295	2.807	2.946	3.383
	(93.41)**	(41.07)**	(37.95)**	(23.12)**
Plant size restriction			< 50	50 or more
Observations	95,443	95,443	66,819	28,624
R-squared	0.00	0.04	0.04	0.05

Absolute value of t statistics in parentheses.
* significant at 5%; ** significant at 1%

percent, which according to the estimate in column (4) results in a decrease in productivity by a little less than 0.8 percent. The conclusion is that when labor productivity across plants and over time is compared without taking into account the possible effect of plant-level quasi-fixed factors, workforce aging stands out as a potential threat to productivity. Judging from these estimates, managers would be well advised to consider how to dismiss older employees and instead hire prime-age adults with higher levels of productivity.

Age effects on productivity with control for fixed, plant-level effects

Table 4 presents the results from estimating the same specification as in Table 2, with the difference that plant-specific effects have been controlled for. This has been done by subtracting the mean value over time of plant-level value added per worker, age shares, and education levels from the variables before they are put into the regression. The regressions, thus, are performed on deviations from the plant-level, time-series mean.

The rationale for this procedure is that plant-level productivity may be substantially influenced by the basic design of the plant at the time it was established. Examples of factors that can be costly to change in an established plant are location in relation to transport infrastructure, the size of the premises and buildings, systems for internal transport, the physical set-up of the production flow, and the dimension of tubes, vessels, and so on. To the extent that buildings have been designed to accommodate a specific type of

TABLE 4 Age share model with plant-level fixed effects, with dependent variable log value added per worker, Sweden, mining and manufacturing industry, 1985–96

Dep.var: log VA/empl.	(1)	(2)	(3)	(4)
Log share ≤29	−0.022	−0.021	−0.009	−0.023
	(7.94)**	(7.54)**	(2.90)**	(2.86)**
Log share 30–49	0.039	0.032	0.023	0.138
	(7.21)**	(5.98)**	(4.19)**	(6.72)**
Log share ≥50	0.011	0.012	0.004	0.081
	(4.40)**	(4.69)**	(1.49)	(7.70)**
Mean education		0.098	0.070	0.201
		(29.36)**	(19.23)**	(24.66)**
Plant size restriction			< 50	50 or more
Fixed plant effect	Yes	Yes	Yes	Yes
Observations	95,443	95,443	66,819	28,624
R-squared	0.00	0.01	0.01	0.03

Absolute value of t statistics in parentheses.
* significant at 5%; ** significant at 1%

machinery, it may also be difficult and costly to make major changes in the type of machinery used in the plant. Taken together, the quasi-fixed factors imply that the production characteristics of plants may largely reflect the technological level and relative prices of production factors at the time they were designed and built. If, in addition, the age structure of the labor force is influenced by how long a plant has been in operation, then the estimated parameter for different age variables may not capture the productivity effect on labor force aging but may instead serve as an indirect measure of the technological age of the industrial plant.

By removing the plant-level mean of the variables, we control for this risk. What we get then is a within-plant estimate of the aging effects that should not be influenced by partial correlations between quasi-fixed factors and labor-force age structure.

As shown in Table 4, removing plant-level means from the variables changes the estimated age effects. In the base regression the strong positive effect of prime-age workers is reduced, whereas the effect of older workers goes from negative to positive. Furthermore, the positive effect of young workers becomes negative. The implied hump shape of productivity over age thus tilts such that an older workforce becomes comparatively more productive than implied by the estimates in the previous section. Comparing the estimates obtained for large and small plants, it is clear again that the age effects are much more pronounced for large plants than for small plants. In both cases, however, the age profile gives some support for the Horndal hypothesis: large shares of young adults in the workforce have a negative effect on productivity; prime-age adults have positive effects on productivity and so have old workers, albeit to a lesser extent. Thus, an aging of the workforce can improve productivity depending on the composition of aging.

A positive relation between aging and productivity is also demonstrated in Table 5 where productivity is related to the mean age of the workforce. Here the same specifications as in Table 3 are used, with the difference that plant-level means have been subtracted from the variables. The removal of plant-level fixed effects has a strong influence on the estimated age effects in this case. In Table 3 age effects were negative. The within-plant estimation of age effects, however, indicates substantial positive effects of aging on productivity. The largest estimates are found among large plants. This, then, is the same pattern that was observed in the Horndal steelworks: increasing workforce age accompanied by increases in productivity.

So far, then, testing the Horndal hypothesis vis-à-vis the individual-effect hypothesis has led to apparently contradictory results. Tables 2 and 3 show conclusively that plants with a workforce dominated by older workers are less productive than plants with a dominance of prime-age workers. When the relation between aging and productivity is estimated within

TABLE 5 Mean age model with plant-level fixed effects, with dependent variable log value added per worker, Sweden, mining and manufacturing industry, 1985–96

Dep.var: log VA/empl.	(1)	(2)	(3)	(4)
Log mean age	0.249	0.262	0.136	0.633
	(13.76)**	(14.58)**	(6.93)**	(14.53)**
Mean education		0.101	0.072	0.202
		(30.28)**	(19.82)**	(24.88)**
Plant size restriction			< 50	50 or more
Fixed plant effect	Yes	Yes	Yes	Yes
Observations	95,443	95,443	66,819	28,624
R-squared	0.00	0.01	0.01	0.03

Absolute value of t statistics in parentheses.
* significant at 5%; ** significant at 1%

plants, however, the Horndal pattern starts to emerge. A result in the same direction is obtained by Haltiwanger et al. (1999) when they analyze the effect of workforce age not on the level of but on changes in productivity.

The conclusion, as we see it, is that the lower productivity of plants with many older workers is not due to declining productivity of individual workers. Instead it should, as we show below, be explained by the fact that high concentrations of older workers are found in older plants where the production technology is not entirely up-to-date. Even if efficiency increases as the workforce ages, the productivity of an older plant can still be lower than that of a newly built, modern plant. Or, to rephrase the conclusion: if we observe a plant with a very old workforce, we would probably be correct to assume that this plant has relatively low labor productivity. It would be erroneous to infer from this, however, that rejuvenating the workforce could increase productivity. Instead, our empirical evidence indicates that dismissing older workers and replacing them with young adults could in fact lower productivity. From Table 4 it is apparent that a replacement with prime-age adults on the other hand would be advantageous. However, the average mobility is much less for prime-age than for young adult workers, so the former mechanism tends to dominate.

The Horndal story provides some evidence also on this point. During the 1930s managers had become preoccupied with the high mean age of the workforce at the Horndal steelworks. During a crisis in 1937 they decided to get rid of the oldest workers, some of them above age 70 years. Contrary to their expectation, however, the ensuing decline in the mean age of workers did not contribute to higher productivity. Instead the overall positive trend in productivity was broken and it did not recover until after about eight years when the mean age of the workers started to increase again.

Instrumental variable regressions of the aging effect

In the previous section we used fixed plant effects to control for a possible influence of plant age on both workforce age and productivity. This approach controls for any systematic differences across plants that affect productivity and remain constant over time. But it cannot capture the possible effect of an externally generated productivity shock. Such a shock can generate correlated changes in labor-force age structure and labor productivity that are not related to the effects of workforce aging per se. The argument here is that changes in the age structure of the workforce can be endogenous and, therefore, that OLS estimates of the aging effect can be biased. Even worse, the control for fixed effects can introduce such a correlation if there are persistent but not constant differences in reactions across plants. This well-known problem in panel estimation is often handled by using instrumental variable (IV) regressions.

To make this point concrete, suppose a negative productivity shock hits a plant, and assume that this leads to departures of older workers preferentially, not because they are less productive but because they have other options like early retirement. That would introduce a spurious positive correlation between productivity and the share of older workers. In the Swedish context this may have occurred to some extent, although labor market regulations would tend to create the opposite bias by making it more difficult and costlier to fire the old than the young.

Controlling for fixed effects, which is tantamount to subtracting the averages of variables within plants, may introduce endogeneity bias, even if there is no such correlation between explanatory variables and the contemporary random shocks. This well-known dynamic bias problem arises because random shocks in the current period may be correlated with the average age structure even if there is no such correlation with the current age structure. This is because the average includes future values and thereby any future influence from the shocks, so even if the composition of the workforce in a given year is independent of the productivity shocks encountered this year, its adaptation the next year will be part of the average, which thus may exhibit a correlation that creates endogeneity bias.

Another possible critique is that the model we have estimated above suffers from omitted variables, for example, by ignoring the influence of demand factors. One way around this problem is to use fixed time effects or regime dummies that can account for the changes over time in variables that are not in the model.

In this section, therefore, we present results in which the effect of labor force aging is estimated using instruments for both age structure and education as well as estimation results for models using fixed time effects. A regime dummy (regime=1 if year ≥ 1991, otherwise zero) was also tested as a more parsimonious way to account for the recession.

IV regression depends on the availability of good instruments for the endogenous variables. For the education variable and the mean age variable we were able to find such instruments. This is not the case for the age share model. We have found instruments that are valid in the sense that they are not correlated with the residuals in the second-stage regression. However, these instruments have been weak with respect to their ability to generate good predictions of the endogenous age share variables.[2] Below, therefore, we only present the results for the mean age model.

Moreover, we have not tried to establish whether the relation between log productivity and log mean age could be curved instead of linear. While that is likely to be the case, an instrumentation of the squared variable is precarious. In any case, the actual variation in mean age of the plant workforce in our sample is not sufficient to admit extrapolation to the extremes of age variation. Although it is common practice in the literature to estimate age-productivity profiles in this way, it cannot be considered a rigorous estimation practice. Since it is not our purpose here to compare productivity and earnings profiles, there is no need to make precise the nonlinearity that is likely to be present. Over the ranges encountered in empirical data, the linear approximation seems sufficient to conclude that workforce aging per se can hardly be considered a major future problem.

The results of the instrumental variable regressions are presented in Table 6. These results show that controlling for possible endogeneity bias further strengthens the contention that workforce aging at the plant level is associated with increasing productivity. The IV-based estimates of the aging effect are about six to eight times higher than the fixed-effect estimates. According to these estimates, a one-year increase in the mean age of the workforce from 40 to 41 years, that is a 2.5 percent increase, would imply a 4–5 percent increase in productivity. The IV estimates, thus, suggest that the Horndal effect is very much alive and that ordinary OLS estimates are seriously biased downward as they appear in Table 5 and even more in Table 3.

A similar result is obtained by Aubert and Crépon (2003). Looking only at the OLS estimates in the pooled data they find, as we did, a negative correlation between age and productivity. However, when they use instrumental variables to control for the endogeneity of workforce age structure and fixed establishment effects, this negative correlation turns positive.

Moreover, the two-stage least squares estimates in Table 6 are only marginally affected when we include a regime dummy in order to control for unexplained time effects. Inserting a full set of year dummies (not reported) does not change this conclusion. Thus, the identification problem that usually arises from the correlation between age effects and time effects (and to some extent education) is also ameliorated in the IV estimates.

TABLE 6 Instrumental variable regressions, with dependent variable log value added per employee: Shea partial R^2 measures relevance of multivariate instrument model, Sweden, mining and manufacturing industry, 1985–96

Dep.var: log VA/empl.	(1)	(2)	(3)	(4)
Log mean age	1.784	1.662	1.703	2.084
	(12.29)**	(10.79)**	(14.45)**	(12.32)**
Shea partial R^2	0.0256	0.0231		
Partial R^2	0.0673	0.0824		
Education	0.235	0.217	0.156	0.250
	(37.10)**	(28.55)**	(10.59)**	(14.24)**
Shea partial R^2	0.3342	0.2441		
Partial R^2	0.8774	0.8707		
Regime		0.078		−0.070
(=1 if year ≥ 1991)		(8.95)**		(6.49)**
Constant	−4.917	−4.323	−3.755	−6.138
	(8.31)**	(6.79)**	(10.43)**	(8.87)**
Sargan statistic	1.898	2.008		
Sargan p-value	(0.387)	(0.366)		
Fixed plant effect			Yes	Yes
Observations	54,006	54,006	54,006	54,006
Number of plant ID			9,794	9,794
Instruments:				
Lag −2 log share ≤29			x	x
Lag −3 log share ≤29			x	x
Lag −1 log share 30–49	x	x	x	x
Lag −3 log share 30–49				
Lag −3 log share ≥50			x	x
Lag −1 education	x	x	x	x
Lag −2 education	x	x	x	x
Lag −3 education	x	x	x	x

Absolute value of z statistics in parentheses. x = Instrument used in the regression reported in column. Full results available from authors on request (see endnote 1).
* significant at 5%; ** significant at 1%

Start-ups and closures

The sample used in the estimations above contains plants that have been in existence during the entire 1985–96 period as well as plants that have opened up or closed down during that time. This allows for a check of the assumption that productivity levels and labor-force age structure are correlated with technological age.

If it is the case that new plants are more up to date and more likely to employ young workers, then we should expect that plants with high value added per worker and high shares of young workers are more likely to be start-ups than plants with low value added per worker and low shares of young workers. Similarly, plants with low mean age of workers should be likely to be start-ups.

These predictions are tested in Table 7. Here a plant is defined as a start-up during the first year it is present in our sample (if this year is not 1985). The test has been performed with a binomial logit model. As can be seen from the results, plants with high value added per worker, high shares of young workers, and, to some extent, plants with high shares of prime-age workers are more likely to be start-ups. Plants with high shares of older workers and a high mean age of the workforce, on the other hand, are less likely to be start-ups.

This dataset, thus, strongly supports the idea that new plants embody a technology that generates higher value added per worker and, also, that new plants tend to have a younger workforce.

In Table 8 the focus is shifted to the closure plants. Here, a plant is defined as a closure plant during the last year it is present in our dataset (if this year is not 1996). If firm behavior is rational, a plant should not be closed down if it would be possible to restore profitability by an adjustment in the labor force or by changes in the production process. However, if a plant has become technologically out-of-date a closure is often the most viable alternative. This assumption is corroborated by the estimates presented in Table 8. These estimates show that plants with high levels of value added per worker are unlikely closure candidates. Similarly, plants with a high share of young

TABLE 7 Effect on log odds of being a start-up from age and productivity variables, productivity expressed as log value added per worker: Binomial logit models, Sweden, mining and manufacturing industry, 1985–96

Start-up=1	(1)	(2)	(3)	(4)	(5)
Log VA/empl	0.071 (3.41)**				
Mean age		–0.072 (27.41)**			
Share ≤29			1.558 (20.73)**		
Share 30–49				0.596 (6.62)**	
Share ≥50					–2.848 (29.17)**
Constant	–2.811 (31.80)**	0.269 (2.68)**	–3.000 (108.59)**	–2.791 (63.22)**	–1.885 (81.70)**
Observations	95,443	95,443	95,443	95,443	95,443

Absolute value of z statistics in parentheses.
* significant at 5%; ** significant at 1%

TABLE 8 Effect on log odds of being a closure plant from age and productivity variables, productivity expressed as log value added per worker: Binomial logit models, Sweden, mining and manufacturing industry, 1985–96

Closure=1	(1)	(2)	(3)	(4)	(5)
Log VA/empl	–0.466				
	(24.35)**				
Mean age		0.031			
		(13.00)**			
Share ≤29			–0.679		
			(8.77)**		
Share 30–49				0.042	
				(0.48)	
Share ≥50					0.745
					(9.20)**
Constant	–0.515	–3.692	–2.239	–2.454	–2.621
	(6.57)**	(37.59)**	(90.13)**	(58.53)**	(109.44)**
Observations	95,443	95,443	95,443	95,443	95,443

Absolute value of z statistics in parentheses.
* significant at 5%; ** significant at 1%

adult workers, indicating a more modern plant, are less likely to be closed down. Increasing mean age of the workforce and increasing shares of older workers, on the other hand, strongly increase the closure probability. Thus, if plant closure is an indication of technological obsolescence, then an aged workforce can indeed be seen as a characteristic of plants approaching the end of their life cycle.

Both start-ups and closure plants, thus, have distinctive age profiles. Moreover, both types of plants demonstrate rapid changes in their age structure in the year following start-up or preceding closedown (see Table 9). This implies that the presence of start-ups and closure plants contributes to a variation in age structure that goes beyond the time trends in age structure change that are due to a shifting aggregate age structure of Sweden's working-age population.

The picture emerging here is that plant life cycles interact with the aging of workers in a way that tends to bias estimates of older worker productivity downward. It is not far-fetched to conjecture that this tendency may be reinforced by the selectivity in the closure process. Most closures are probably foreseen and those employees with the best labor market prospects leave at an early stage, introducing a negative selection within the age group. For start-ups, on the other hand, there is uncertainty about the productivity of newly employed people, who are predominantly young, and the matching process will give a positive selection bias for productivity.

TABLE 9 Change in age structure in plants after start-up and prior to closure, Sweden, mining and manufacturing industry, 1985–96

	Share ≤29	Share 30–49	Share ≥50	Obs	Mean age
Start year	0.354	0.468	0.178	1,732	37.4
Start (+1)	0.342	0.470	0.188	1,732	37.8
Start (+2)	0.331	0.474	0.195	1,732	38.1
Start (+3)	0.319	0.475	0.205	1,732	38.5
Start (+4)	0.306	0.477	0.217	1,732	38.9
Last (−4)	0.301	0.447	0.252	3,200	39.7
Last (−3)	0.295	0.446	0.260	3,200	40.0
Last (−2)	0.289	0.447	0.264	3,200	40.3
Last (−1)	0.274	0.449	0.277	3,200	40.8
Last year	0.256	0.454	0.290	3,200	41.4

Discussion

According to the estimates presented in this chapter, there is little need to worry about the productivity consequences of workforce aging. Although individual performance in many areas peaks in young or in prime ages, an accumulation of high shares of older adults in manufacturing plants does not seem to have negative effect on plant-level productivity. To be more precise, there is no negative effect, on average, from aging within the ranges that we empirically observe. On the contrary, when plant-level effects are controlled for, high shares of older adults are associated with higher productivity than high shares of young adults. While it is possible that this result holds only for changes in the neighborhood of mean ages around 40, this is well within the relevant range that foreseeable workforce aging in the developed world will lead to.

A positive effect on productivity of workforce aging runs counter to many popular conceptions. Macro-level evidence, however, indicates that a shift from a working-age population dominated by young adults to domination by older workers is indeed positive for economic growth. An early study showing this is Romer (1987). McMillan and Baesel (1990) for the United States and Malmberg (1993) for Sweden also give evidence for positive old-workforce effects. Lindh and Malmberg (1999) give evidence for such effects in an OECD panel. Andersson (2001) presents evidence from Scandinavian time series. Feyrer (2002) and Gómez and Hernández de Cos (2003) are recent working papers demonstrating the positive effects of an older workforce. A positive relation between workforce aging and increases in per capita income is also evidenced by the relation between economic development and the long-term transformation of the age structure that is associated with the demographic transition (Malmberg and Sommestad 2000). Most of today's highest-ranked economies have secured this rank during the decades when population growth was concentrated on the middle-age population. Examples include Germany, Sweden, and the United States during the early period following World War II; Japan in the 1960s, 1970s, and 1980s; and Korea, Singapore, and Chile in the 1980s and 1990s. In this study we have shown that this macro-pattern may have an underpinning also on the micro-level within the manufacturing industry.

A positive relation between workforce aging and productivity growth also has an implication for the relation between mortality and economic growth. If it was the case that weaker individual-level performance during the later years of working life would exert a downward pressure on firm-level productivity, then high mortality among workers above age 50 years would not necessarily be negative for economic growth. High mortality would have a negative effect on the profitability of educational investment and possibly saving, but part of this could be compensated by a weeding out of older, less-efficient workers. However, in empirical studies increasing longevity has consistent positive effects on per capita income, and this indicates that labor-force aging can lead to higher productivity unless taken to extremes not generally encountered in the aggregate economy. In fact, as shown in Malmberg and Lindh (2004), a model that takes into account both age structure shifts and changes in longevity can account for much of the global variation in income growth since 1960.

The labor productivity and change in total productivity in a plant might, among other factors, depend on the composition of workers and not only on some simple measure of age. If, for example, the prime-age workers are deemed the most productive and the learning-by-doing argument holds, then there might exist some optimal mix of employees. For instance, a certain share of prime-age workers might have to be combined with certain shares of both young and old workers for a plant to achieve its maximum productivity.

A certain share of older workers might influence and enhance the ability to learn among both young and prime-age workers. This would symbolize a kind of learning-by-seeing or learning-by-interacting relationship between workers of different age groups. But it is apparently not only age that matters—industry or even establishment experience may play a large role in the complicated pattern of labor productivity.

Young workers might also play an important part by introducing new knowledge into the workforce. By our estimates it looks as if this group might not have a highly positive impact on total labor productivity. Experience might be needed to understand how this new knowledge is supposed to raise productivity. It might also be that prime-age and older workers are stuck in their old work habits and unwilling to change.

According to our estimates age composition seems to have a greater influence in larger plants: this might be due to increased interaction and more change of ideas when more people are involved in production. On the other hand, and perhaps even more realistically, it might also be due to larger plants having a greater possibility to achieve an optimal mix of employees, a possibility that might not exist for smaller plants because of restrictions on hiring and firing.

If corroborated by additional studies, the findings presented here have potentially important policy implications, with special significance for many countries in the European Union. In Europe since the 1970s, a common measure against unemployment has been early retirement for older workers. The results presented here indicate that early retirement may well be detrimental for productivity in established plants if the retirees are replaced by young adults.

If workforce aging is good for productivity growth, policies should instead be geared toward finding means to stimulate continued labor-force participation among older workers. Such policies should help employers to design work practices that take advantage of the services of such workers. Of equal importance is to amend regulations, pension plans, and employment contracts that stimulate early retirement. In addition, more focus should be given to factors that can improve the health of people who are approaching older age. Such measures, of course, would be of value not only for their potential to stimulate productivity. Increased labor force participation by people above age 55 years is also almost a necessity if the fiscal viability of current welfare arrangements is to be preserved when increased longevity greatly increases the population share of persons above age 65.

If workforce aging leads to productivity growth, then how should the practice of mandatory retirement in some firms be explained? One possible answer is mortality risks. For much of the period since World War II, mortality rates among men aged 50 and older were at a relatively high level. Moreover, mortality risks increase rapidly above 60 years of age. If employees were to be allowed to work indefinitely this would imply that the firm would face a very high risk that some time in the future they would, often without warning, permanently lose an employee. By introducing mandatory retirement this uncertainty can, at least partly, be transformed into a deterministic process that may be easier for management to handle, in particular if it is financed from public pay-as-you-go systems. Retirement can occur at a specific, predetermined date not because of a sudden change in productivity but because an undisturbed process of production can, by itself, be essential to the individual plant's performance.

For further research it should be emphasized that our results here also point out several difficulties in estimating the productivity effects of aging. The age composition and educational composition of the workforce are determined in conjunction with technical change and changing demand conditions as well as in the interplay with local factor supplies, in particular local labor markets. We find clear evidence of endogeneity bias and our attempts to solve this by instrumental variables may not be the final word on this issue. The interaction that we find between plant life cycles and the composition of the workforce raises issues about the identification of productivity effects from aging that fixed-effects estimates can only begin to disentangle.

Notes

The establishment of the dataset used in this study has been funded by the Swedish Council for Working Life Research. We further thank Fredrik Andersson, Hans Schwartz, Björn Andersson, and Christian Svendsen for their efforts in cleaning and organizing the database.

1 More detail is provided in a technical appendix available on request from the authors «bo.malmberg@humangeo.su.se».

2 In the technical appendix referred to in endnote 1, we make this assertion precise. Although the age-share results are not robust, the basic hump shape and its tilt toward older age groups as we introduce fixed plant effects are still apparent.

References

Andersson, B. 2001. "Scandinavian evidence on growth and age structure," *Regional Studies* 35(5): 377–390.
Arrow, K. J. 1962. "The economic implications of learning by doing," *The Review of Economic Studies* 29(3): 155–173.
Aubert, P. and B. Crépon. 2003. "La productivité des salariés âgés: une tentative d'estimation," *Economie et Statistique* (368): 95–119.
Crépon, B. et al. 2002. "Wages, productivity, and worker characteristics: A French perspective," Serie des Documents de Travail du CREST, Institut National de la Statistique et des Etudes Economiques.
Feyrer, J. 2002. "Demographics and productivity," Dartmouth College Working Paper No. 02-10.
Genberg, M. 1992. *The Horndal Effect: Productivity Growth Without Capital Investment at Horndalsverken between 1927 and 1952*. Uppsala: Uppsala University.
Gómez, R. and P. Hernández de Cos. 2003. "Demographic maturity and economic performance: The effect of demographic transitions on per capita GDP growth," Banco de España, Working Paper No. 0318.
Haltiwanger, J. C. et al. 1999. "Productivity differences across employers: The roles of employer size, age, and human capital," *American Economic Review* 89(2): 94–98.
Haltiwanger, J., J. Lane. and J. Spletzer. 2007 "Wages, productivity, and the dynamic interaction of businesses and workers," *Labour Economics* 14: 575–602.
Hellerstein, J. K. and D. Neumark. 2004. "Production function and wage equation estimation with heterogeneous labor: Evidence from a new matched employer–employee data set," NBER Working Paper Series, Cambridge, MA.
Ilmakunnas, P. and M. Maliranta. 2002. "Labour characteristics and wage–productivity gaps," *New Zealand Economic Papers* 36(1): 73–74.
———. 2005. "Technology, labour characteristics and wage-productivity gaps," *Oxford Bulletin of Economics and Statistics* 67: 623–645.
Lindh, T. and B. Malmberg. 1998. "Age structure and inflation—A Wicksellian interpretation of OECD data," *Journal of Economic Behavior & Organization* 36: 17–35.

———. 1999. "Age structure effects and growth in the OECD, 1950–1990," *Journal of Population Economics* 12: 431–449.

———. 2007a. "Demographically based global income forecasts up to the year 2050," *International Journal of Forecasting* 23: 553–567.

———. 2007b. "Effects of age structure on investment, saving and trade," in R. Clark, N. Ogawa, and A. Mason (eds.), *Population Aging, Intergenerational Transfers and the Macroeconomy*. Edward Elgar Publishing.

Lundberg, E. 1961. *"Produktivitet och räntabilitet: studier i kapitalets betydelse inom svenskt näringsliv,"* Stockholm, Studieförb. Näringsliv o. samhälle: Norstedt (distr.).

Malmberg, B. 1993. "Age structure effects on economic growth: Swedish evidence," *Arbetsrapporter / Kulturgeografiska institutionen, Uppsala universitet*, 41. Uppsala, Institutionen: 20 bl.

Malmberg, B. and T. Lindh. 2004. "Demographically based global income forecasts up to the year 2050," Institute for Futures Studies Working Paper 2004: 7.

Malmberg, B. and L. Sommestad. 2000. "The hidden pulse of history: Population and economic change in Sweden, 1820–2000," *Scandinavian Journal of History* 25(1-2): 130–146.

McMillan, H. M. and J. B. Baesel. 1990. "The macroeconomic impact of the baby boom generation," *Journal of Macroeconomics* 12(2): 167–195.

Romer, P. M. 1987. "Crazy explanations for the productivity slowdown," *NBER Macroeconomics Annual* 2: 163–202.

Older Workers and National Productivity in Japan

ROBERT L. CLARK
NAOHIRO OGAWA
SANG-HYOP LEE
RIKIYA MATSUKURA

Historically, economic development in most countries has been accompanied by declines in total fertility rates, increases in life expectancy, and an aging of the population. Together these changes affect national economic growth, savings rates, and worker productivity. These demographic trends place increased financial pressure on national retirement systems. In most developed countries, labor force participation rates of older persons have declined, exacerbating these economic challenges. Work and retirement decisions are influenced by a series of social, family, and economic variables. A significant factor influencing the age of retirement is the presence of health limitations. Physical problems in accomplishing certain tasks affect the value of older persons in the labor market and increase their preferences for leisure so that individuals with such limitations are more likely to retire.

Health limitations tend to reduce employment opportunities and lower compensation offers. In response to lower earnings potential, older persons with health limitations are likely to reduce hours of work and retire at earlier ages. Poor health also changes the individual's own assessment of the value of his or her time away from work. This reevaluation often occurs because the worker's job becomes more stressful and demanding given reduced physical or mental capacity. The importance of health status for the age of retirement in the United States and Western Europe has been well documented. Less is known about the relationship between health and retirement in the rapidly aging countries of Asia.

Japan provides a case study of the role of health in retirement decisions. Japan has the most rapidly aging population in the world and currently has the highest proportion of people aged 65 years and older. In 1980, only 9.1

percent of the population was aged 65 and older. By 2004, this percentage had increased to 19.5, and current projections indicate that in 2025, 31.0 percent of the Japanese population will be aged 65 and older (Ogawa 2003).

Despite rapid economic development, a mature social security system, and the widespread imposition of mandatory retirement, the proportion of Japanese who remain in the labor force at older ages is relatively high. Rapid population aging and declines in the working-age population have significant implications for the rate of national economic growth and the ability to finance the country's social security system.[1] The ability to support an aging population may well depend on maintaining high labor force participation rates among the elderly. In this chapter, we examine the retirement decisions of a cohort of older Japanese who were aged 65 and older in 1999. Combining our findings from this longitudinal survey with other national surveys, we investigate the potential effect of institutional changes in employment and retirement policies to keep older workers in the labor force as a means of sustaining a relatively higher population in the labor force in the coming decades.

Work and retirement

Labor force participation rates among men 65 and older in the developed countries of Europe tend to be below 10 percent, while the proportion of men 65 and older who remain in the labor force in the United States is about 18 percent. In comparison, the labor force participation rate for men 65 and older in Japan is over 30 percent. Older women in Japan are also more likely to continue working than older women in Europe and the United States. Figure 1 shows participation rates for men and women aged 65 and older in Japan from 1960 until 2003. Participation rates declined from 1960 to 1980. In the 1980s, the proportion of older persons in the labor force remained relatively stable; however, during the "lost decade" of the Japanese economy,[2] the proportion of older persons in the labor force again fell.

Why are older Japanese more likely to remain in the labor force and postpone retirement than elderly persons in other developed countries? Will these high employment rates continue in the future? Can continued high levels of labor force participation among the elderly serve as a check to declines in the number of persons of traditional working ages? To examine these questions, we provide a brief overview of employment and retirement policies in Japan. The human resource policies of large companies continue to be centered on low rates of turnover, seniority-based pay, and long job tenure (Hashimoto and Raisian 1985; and Clark and Ogawa 1992a). However, these corporate giants also have mandatory retirement policies that require workers to leave the company at a relatively young age, typically age 60 (Seike 2008 forthcoming).

Virtually all Japanese companies employing 30 workers or more have some type of retirement program. These company plans can be traditional

FIGURE 1 Labor force participation rates for persons aged 65 and older by sex: Japan, 1960–2003

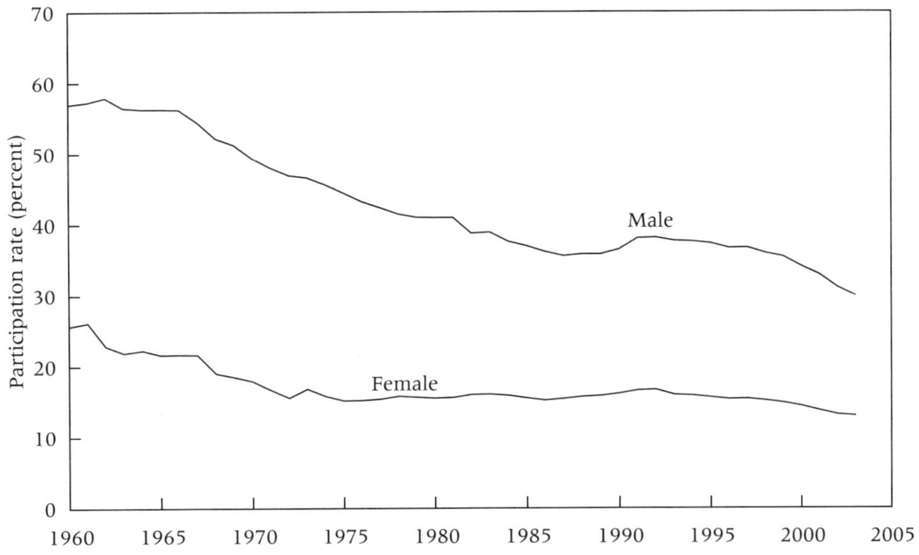

SOURCE: Statistics Bureau, Ministry of Public Management, Home Affairs, Posts and Telecommunications, *Annual Report on the Labour Force Survey*, 2003.

lump sum severance pay plans or pension plans (Clark 1990; Clark and Mitchell 2002). In addition, all paid employees are covered by a national security program that provides a monthly benefit for the worker and his spouse that represents approximately 60 percent of average monthly career earnings. The widespread use of mandatory retirement at age 60 coupled with employer pensions and a relatively generous social security system typically would not result in high rates of labor force participation among the elderly.

The industrial structure of the Japanese economy may provide some insight into the older ages at retirement. While many smaller companies also have mandatory retirement policies, retirees from large companies often find second careers with smaller companies (Clark and Ogawa 1992b, 1997). In addition, the Japanese economy retains a relatively large agricultural sector as well as family-owned enterprises that provide work opportunities for older persons. Thus, the transition from corporate careers to full-time retirement often includes a shift to a new job with a smaller company or a move into self-employment. The higher incidence of agricultural employment and entrepreneurship also allows older workers in these sectors of the economy to remain on the job until older ages.

The desire to work because of the status it provides and the income it yields may differ across regions and cultures of the world. Stronger work preferences among the Japanese elderly than among those in Europe or North

America could be one explanation for the higher work rates among older Japanese men and women. Every five years, the Japanese government conducts an employment survey. Older persons are asked their reason for leaving their last job. Table 1 presents the results of the Employment Status Survey from 1977 to 2002. Among people 65 and older in 1977, about two-thirds indicated that they left their job because of illness or old age. The proportion of respondents indicating that health issues were the primary cause of their retirement has declined sharply in the past two decades, especially among older men. In contrast, there has been a significant increase in the proportion of older Japanese indicating that they left the labor force because they had reached the retirement age.

The increasing number of persons citing company policies as the reason for retiring reflects the continued improvement in the health status of older

TABLE 1 Reasons for leaving one's job among those aged 65 and older, Japan 1977–2002

Reason for leaving	1977	1982	1987	1992	1997	2002
Men						
Personnel curtailment, or company liquidation, or bankruptcy	9.0	9.6	6.9	4.1	4.8	10.4
Job was temporary or not secure	0.7	0.6	0.0	1.2	0.8	1.8
Low pay	0.7	1.1	0.6	0.6	0.8	0.5
Unsatisfactory working conditions	1.4	1.1	0.6	1.7	0.9	3.0
Did not like job	—	0.7	0.6	0.6	5.2	0.3
Job transfer, or company relocation, or family member found or changed job	0.7	0.6	0.0	0.6	0.4	0.1
Reached retirement age	18.6	23.6	30.2	26.2	43.7	38.9
Illness or old age	60.7	53.4	52.8	54.1	38.1	33.1
To care for elderly or sick family member	—	—	—	1.7	1.1	1.3
Other	8.3	9.0	8.2	9.3	8.5	10.1
Women						
Personnel curtailment, or company liquidation, or bankruptcy	3.6	5.7	2.1	3.8	5.8	11.9
Job was temporary or not secure	1.8	1.1	1.0	1.0	0.8	1.5
Low pay	1.8	1.1	2.1	1.0	1.2	0.7
Unsatisfactory working conditions	0.0	2.3	1.0	1.0	0.9	2.6
Did not like job	—	0.0	0.0	0.0	2.9	0.2
Job transfer, or company relocation, or family member found or changed job	1.8	1.1	1.0	1.0	0.8	0.4
Reached retirement age	7.1	10.3	14.6	12.5	22.0	19.1
Illness or old age	69.6	66.7	61.5	61.5	51.8	43.8
To care for elderly or sick family member	—	—	—	5.8	4.9	5.5
Other	14.3	10.3	12.5	10.6	11.1	13.4

SOURCE: Management and Coordination Agency, Employment Status Survey, several years.

persons, their rising life expectancy, and the effect of these improvements on the desire for delayed retirement. As more people reach the traditional retirement age in good health, more want to remain on the job. Company practices and retirement policies have changed more slowly, and most companies continue to impose mandatory retirement at age 60. With life expectancy and good health improving rapidly but institutions adjusting only slowly, the constraint of mandatory retirement has become more binding on the employment of older Japanese.

The Longitudinal Study of Aging

The statistical analysis of retirement decisions employs data from the Nihon University Japan Longitudinal Study of Aging. The Japan Study is designed to be comparable in many respects to the US Longitudinal Study of Aging (Ogawa, Retherford, and Saito 2008 forthcoming). The first round of the Japan Study was conducted in November 1999,[3] and the initial sample size in the first wave of the survey was 6,700. Proxy respondents were allowed to answer questions in cases where the original respondent was not competent to do so or not available at the time of the interview. Interviews were conducted with 4,997 persons aged 65 and older. Persons aged 75 and older were over-sampled by a factor of two. When analyzing the data, weights are used so that the observations in the sample are representative of the Japanese population aged 65 and older. Despite efforts to include institutionalized persons in the Japan Study, such persons remain underrepresented. The second wave of the survey was conducted in November 2001. The sample size for the second wave was 4,621 including 631 new respondents added to the sample.

We examine the initial employment status of persons aged 65–84 in 1999 and estimate the change in employment between 1999 and 2001. Despite the widespread imposition of mandatory retirement, Japanese men and women tend to remain in the labor force until advanced ages. The age-specific employment rates for men and women are shown in Table 2. The data show that in 1999 about half of the men aged 65–69 were still employed. In addition, 40 percent of those aged 70–74 remained on the job as did 29 percent of men aged 75–79. Even among men aged 80–84, one out of six was still working. For women, the age-specific employment rates are lower but still very high in comparison to other developed countries. Among women aged 65–69, almost 33 percent were working in 1999, and 18.5 percent of women aged 70–74 and 12.4 percent of those aged 75–79 were still working.

These high work rates among older Japanese raise questions concerning the determinants of work and retirement decisions of elderly Japanese. This analysis seeks to provide evidence on the key factors governing the retirement choices of older persons. The transition to retirement was examined in two steps. First, we used a logit model to estimate whether individuals were work-

TABLE 2 Employment rates by sex and age, Japan, 1999 and 2001

Ages	1999	2001
Men		
65–69	47.7	50.8
70–74	39.8	31.3
75–79	29.2	26.0
80–84	14.9	15.2
Women		
65–69	31.8	28.1
70–74	18.5	18.3
75–79	12.4	9.3
80–84	8.0	5.8

SOURCE: Nihon University Japan Longitudinal Study of Aging.

ing at the time of the survey. Second, we estimated the change in employment status between 1999 and 2001. Both models were estimated separately by sex. Employment status was estimated as a function of the respondent's health status as measured by the Nagi score, whether the respondent was living in an urban or rural area, age of the respondent, level of education, and whether the person's longest job was in the agricultural sector or whether the person was self-employed. The Nagi score of health status is a widely used measure of the physical abilities of older persons (Nagi 1965, 1979). In the Japan Study, information was gathered with respect to nine categories that indicate levels of physical limitations.[4]

The transition from work to retirement between 1999 and 2001 is shown in Figure 2. Among men, 64 percent of those working in 1999 remained on the job in 2001, while just over half of the women who were working were still employed two years later. Once older Japanese leave the labor force, there is relatively little reentry: fewer than 10 percent of men and women not working in 1999 reported that they were employed in 2001.

FIGURE 2 Labor force transition of survey respondents aged 65–84, Japan, 1999–2001

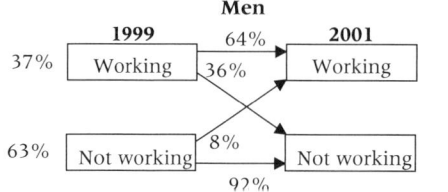
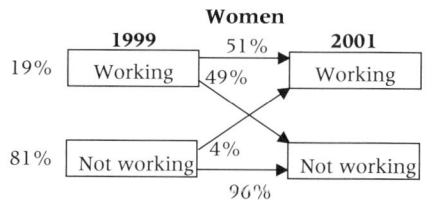

SOURCE: Nihon University Japan Longitudinal Study of Aging.

Health status was measured by the Nagi score, which indicates whether the respondent had difficulty in performing at least one of the nine specific tasks. Figure 3 shows the proportion of individuals who reported having difficulty with each of these activities in both survey years. In 1999, about 30 percent of the sample had difficulty lifting objects weighing 10 kilograms and standing for two hours, while 25 percent of the respondents had difficulty bending over, sitting for two hours, and climbing ten steps. In 1999, 46 percent had some difficulty with at least one of the tasks in the Nagi score while 54 percent reported no difficulties.

Changes in health status affect the ability of workers to remain in the labor force. By 2001, 25 percent of respondents who had no difficulties in 1999 reported that they now had difficulty with at least one of the tasks (see Figure 4). Table 3 illustrates the deterioration and improvement in health as measured by the number of changes in the Nagi score. Among men, 58 percent had no change in the index between the surveys. In 2001, 16 percent of the male respondents improved their Nagi score on one or two activities, and 8 percent had a reduction in the number of problems by three or more activities. During the same period, 14 percent had an increase in the Nagi score by one or two activities and almost 5 percent reported an increase of three or more problem areas. Female respondents were more likely to show improvement in their Nagi score.

FIGURE 3 Percent of survey respondents (ages 65–84) having difficulty performing physical ("Nagi") activities, Japan, 1999 and 2001

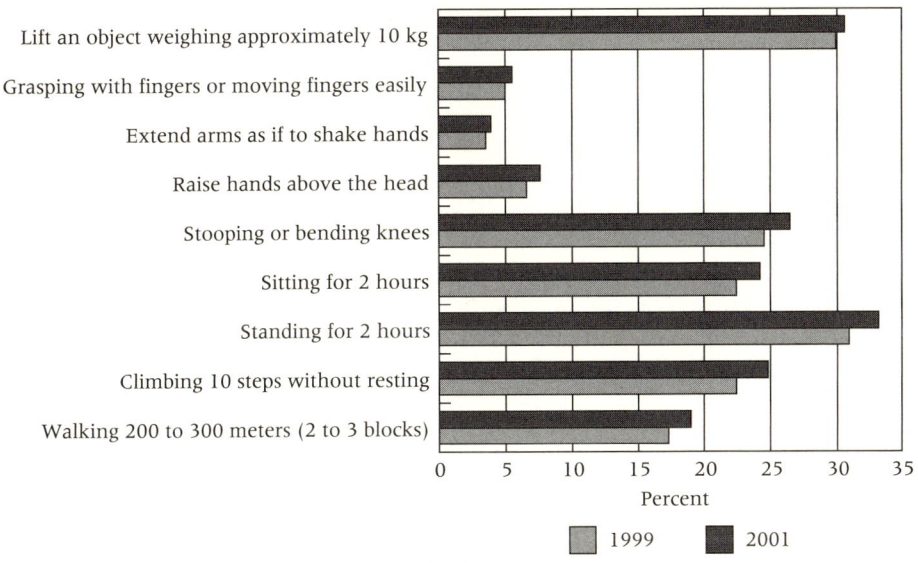

SOURCE: Nihon University Japan Longitudinal Study of Aging.

FIGURE 4 Percent of survey respondents aged 65–84 having difficulty performing physical ("Nagi") activities, Japan, 1999 to 2001

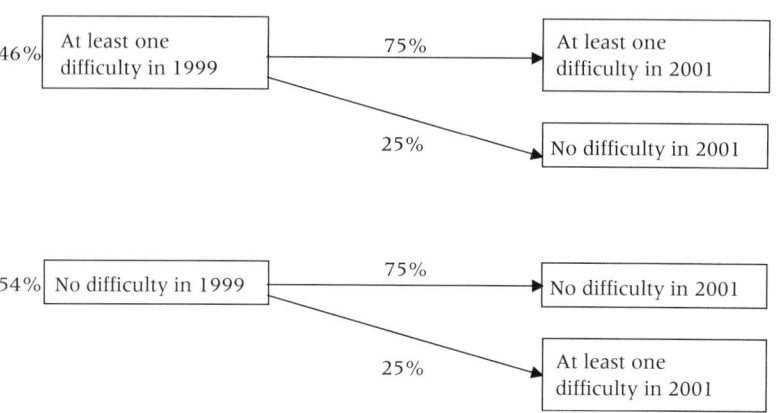

SOURCE: Nihon University Japan Longitudinal Study of Aging.

TABLE 3 Change in physical limitation ("Nagi") score between 1999 and 2001, Japan

Change in number of difficulties	Men (percent)	Women (percent)
–3 or more items	7.8	12.1
–2	6.1	7.4
–1	9.8	13.0
No change	58.1	42.7
+1	9.4	12.1
+2	4.3	6.6
+3 or more items	4.5	6.2

Source: Nihon University Japan Longitudinal Study of Aging.

Work status in 1999

The probability of being in the labor force in 1999 was estimated separately by sex, and the results are reported in Appendix Table 1. Being employed was estimated as a function of age, education, health, family characteristics, home ownership, and living arrangements. The predicted probabilities of working for individuals hold all other variables constant at their mean values. The dependent variable is "whether the respondent was still working," with 1 indicating that the person was working at the time of the survey and 0 indicating that the individual was not in the labor force. Unfortunately, the Japan Study does not contain data on current or past wage rates or the level of nonlabor income. However, several of the explanatory variables were included as proxies for value of time in the market. These included age, education, and health. The results are consistent with predictions of economic theory.

Employment declined with age for both men and women. The predicted employment rate for men aged 65–69 was 49.3 percent. The employment rate fell to 42.0 percent for men aged 70–74 and further to 35.1 percent for men aged 75–79. The predicted employment rate for women aged 65–69 was 30.9 percent. The employment rate declined to 23.1 percent for women aged 70–74 and to 18.8 percent for those aged 75–79.

For men, more education, which should correspond to higher market wage rates, was associated with a higher probability of being employed. Persons with a high school degree were 4.5 percentage points more likely to be employed than those without a degree, while individuals with a junior college or university degree were 3.9 percentage points more likely to be employed than those with a high school degree. Women whose highest level of education was high school were more likely to be working than women with higher or lower educational attainment.

Persons working in agriculture or who were self-employed were more likely to be in a setting that enables them to remain employed in their career job and to gradually reduce their hours of work. Our estimates indicated that men whose longest occupation was either agricultural employment or self-employment were 27.8 percentage points more likely to be employed than other men. Women whose longest job was in agriculture or self-employment were over twice as likely to be working as other women (31.9 percent versus 12.2 percent). Consistent with this finding, women who lived in rural areas were more likely to be working than women in urban areas.

Health limitations as measured by the Nagi score significantly reduced the likelihood that men were working. Men reporting some health limitations were 13.7 percentage points less likely to be employed. Married men whose spouse was healthy were 9.7 percentage points more likely to be employed than men whose spouse reported having health problems. Women with some problems on the Nagi score were 12.4 percentage points less likely to be working than women who reported no problems. In addition, women whose spouse was healthy were more likely to be working than women whose husband had health problems and more likely to be working than single women.

These results indicate that Japanese men and women are influenced by the same economic, health, and family variables that determine the work and retirement decisions of older persons in other countries. However, the results also illustrate that older Japanese are much more likely to remain employed than the elderly in other developed countries.

Longitudinal analysis of retirement

This section examines the change in work status between 1999 and 2001 for respondents in the Nihon University Japan Longitudinal Study of Aging. Limiting the sample to individuals who were working in 1999, we estimated whether they were still employed in 2001. Remaining employed is estimated as a function of change in health status, change in marital status, age in 1999, education in 1999, residence in 1999, childhood residence, home ownership, presence of preschool children in the household, co-residence with adult children, and sector of employment for the longest job. These results are reported separately for men and women in Appendix Table 2.

Among respondents who were working in 1999, health played a dominant role in determining whether they remained employed in 2001. Preexisting health conditions in 1999 and the deterioration of health both influenced individuals to retire. First, men with some health problems in 1999 were 7.1 percentage points less likely to be working in 2001 than those with no health problems. Women with health problems in 1999 were even less likely to still be employed in 2001. Second, changes in health status were also important. Compared to men with no change in their Nagi score, men who had an additional three problems were 23.0 percentage points less likely to remain employed, while women who had developed three new health limitations were 27.9 percentage points less likely to be working in 2001.

Men with a college degree were approximately 16.8 percentage points more likely to be still working in 2001 than those with less education. Because only a few women had a university degree, women with college degrees were combined with those with high school degrees in the retirement equation for women. For both men and women, there was no significant difference in the probability of working for those with a high school degree compared to those with only junior high school. As would be expected, younger men and women were more likely to delay retirement than were older persons. The only other significant determinant of continued employment among men was whether their longest job had been in agriculture or self-employment. Men in either of these categories were 9.3 percentage points more likely to remain employed between 1999 and 2001. This finding suggests that there may be important differences in the employment opportunities for persons depending on whether they reside in urban or rural areas. This possibility is explored in the following section.

Urban/rural differences in retirement patterns

In Japan the proportion of the total population living in rural areas declined from 63 percent in 1950 to 21 percent in 2000. The proportion of elderly persons aged 65 and over residing in rural areas diminished from 71 to 27 percent during the same period. The labor force participation rate for elderly Japanese men is considerably higher in rural than in urban areas. For instance, in 1999, 41 percent of rural men aged 65 and over were in the labor force compared to 32 percent of urban men of the same age.

To examine these regional differences in retirement rates, we estimated probabilities of remaining employed for both rural and urban elderly men aged 65–84 using the same sample as the previous analysis.[5] Appendix Table 3 presents the results of logit estimates of the determinants of continued employment for men by urban/rural residence. The dependent variable is whether the respondent was still working in 2001 given that he was working in 1999.

A key factor determining the continued employment of men in rural areas was the change in the Nagi score from 1999 to 2001. In contrast, changes in health status had no effect on the continued employment of urban men. This result is consistent with the view that most rural elderly workers are less likely to be subject to institutional factors such as mandatory age of retirement than their urban counterparts. Therefore, rural elderly workers are able to continue working until their health deteriorates. In contrast, most urban elderly workers are likely to be affected by mandatory retirement age before their health deteriorates. Preexisting health conditions in 1999 made it less likely that urban men would be working in 2001. Having a university degree significantly increases the probability of continued employment for urban elderly men but not for rural men. Many of the well-educated urban elderly workers are self-employed or hold top managerial posts, so that members of this particular subgroup of the labor force do not have such institutional constraints as a mandatory retirement age.

Implications for national productivity

Older persons in Japan have much higher employment rates than the elderly in other developed countries. The analysis presented above indicates that retirement is very sensitive to health status and changes in health status. As health has improved and life expectancy increased, employment constraints and national economic conditions have become more important in influencing the age of retirement. In another study that we are conducting in conjunction with the Japanese Statistics Bureau, we have been examining five waves of the Employment Status Survey, from 1982 to 2002. Our analysis shows two important changes in the employment patterns of older persons. First, in the adverse economic environment of the 1990s, the participation rates of persons aged 60 and over have declined. Second, as mandatory retirement ages have been increased from 55 to 60 and the age of eligibility for social security benefits has been raised, the employment rates of persons aged 55–59 have come to look more like those of persons aged 50–54 and less like the employment patterns of persons aged 60–64.

These findings lead us to consider the implications of the continued evolution of national retirement policies. To set the stage, remember that the population is rapidly aging and the absolute size of the Japanese labor force is beginning to decline. Current projections from the NUPRI (Nihon University Population Research Institute) macro model, which assumes broadly unchanged labor force participation rates by age and occupation, indicate that the labor force will decline from 67.0 million persons in 2005 to 59.1 million in 2025. Such a decline will affect the growth rate of GDP and the ability to pay future retirement benefits.

With the prospect of a declining labor force, the Japanese government may consider additional steps to facilitate the continued employment of older persons. In fact some steps are already underway. Let us assume that the legal age of mandatory retirement is raised from 60 to 65 and that companies comply with this change and that the age of eligibility for retirement benefits continues to rise to 65 as it is currently scheduled to do. Finally, let us assume that economic growth returns to the level assumed by the NUPRI model's base assumptions.

Based on our findings from the 1982–2002 Employment Status Surveys, we make the following assumptions that may be regarded as upper bounds of the effect of these changes on the Japanese labor force. First, we assume that the employment rates of persons aged 60 to 64 approach those of persons 55–59. This would be consistent with the historical experience that the rates for persons aged 55–59 approached those of persons aged 50–54 as the age of mandatory retirement was increased from 55 to 60. Second, we assume that the employment rates of persons 65 and over increase to the rates observed in the 1980s before the end of the bubble economy, or 10 percentage points higher than current rates.

The effect of these changes is shown in Table 4. These changes in the employment rates of older persons would produce a significant increase in potential GDP and potential GDP per capita. The base projection of the NUPRI model is that potential GDP in 2025 will be 619.1 trillion yen and that potential GDP per capita will be 5.1 million yen. The changes in the total labor force implied by the assumptions stated above produce a potential GDP in 2025 of 692.3 trillion yen and a potential GDP per capita in 2025 of 5.7 million yen. These levels are 12 percent higher than those implied by the base NUPRI model.

Given the existing high employment rates of men younger than age 60 and the projected decline in the traditional working-age population, there are two potential sources of increases in the labor force: a higher employment rate among older persons and a higher employment rate among younger women.

TABLE 4 Economic projections from the NUPRI macro model, Japan, 2005–2025

	NUPRI model base case		Simulation with more older workers	Percent change
	2005	2025	2025	
Potential GDP (trillion yen)	561.2	619.1	692.3	11.8
Potential GDP per capita (million yen)	4.4	5.1	5.7	12.3
Labor force (thousands)	66,958	59,172	70,921	19.9

Our analysis of the NUPRI macro model explores the implications of changes in national retirement policies for the potential labor force. If health status continues to improve and life expectancy at age 60 continues to increase, we would expect that more Japanese over the age of 60 will wish to remain in the labor force; however, changes in industrial relations policies are needed to accommodate this wish.

Conclusion

Our analysis uses a unique longitudinal survey to provide new evidence on the determinants of retirement for older Japanese men and women. The results help explain the relatively high labor force participation rates of older persons in Japan. The probability of men aged 65–84 working in 1999 was 35.6 percent; it was 20.4 percent for women of the same age. Key determinants of the probability of males working were education, health, and sector of employment for the longest job. Men with a college degree were 8.4 percentage points more likely to be working in old age than those with only a junior high degree. Men with no difficulties on the Nagi scale had a 13.7 percentage point higher probability of working than those with at least one health limitation, while those who spent their careers working in agriculture or in self-employment were 27.8 percentage points more likely to be working in old age. Similar effects on health and sector of employment were observed for women.

The main determinant of the probability of remaining on the job between 1999 and 2001 was changes in health status as measured by the increase in the number of Nagi limitations. Further analysis showed that among men this factor primarily affected persons in rural areas; however, for women, declining health had a major effect on the employment rates of those in urban as well as rural areas. Thus, the primary finding of this analysis is that health status influences the probability of older persons remaining in the labor force.

Evidence suggests that elimination of employment restrictions that currently confront older workers and already-legislated changes in social security benefits will raise the employment rates of older persons. Increases in the proportion of persons aged 60 and older provide the opportunity for Japan to partially offset the projected declines in its labor force. The effect of potential increases in employment of older persons could result in an increase in GDP of 12.3 percent by 2025.

APPENDIX TABLE 1 Estimated probabilities of working (percent) by sex, Japan, 1999

	Men	Women
Predicted	35.6	20.4
Actual	35.6	20.4
Age		
65–69	49.3**	30.9**
70–74	42.0**	23.1**
75–79	35.1**	18.8**
80–84+	20.5	13.0
Education		
Jr. high +	33.3	18.7
Sr. high	37.8*	24.1**
University or jr. college	41.7**	15.8
Nagi score		
Some difficulty	26.1**	14.2**
No difficulty +	39.8	26.6
Marital status and spouse's health		
Married, spouse healthy	37.7	24.1**
Married, spouse not healthy	28.0*	17.6
Not married +	35.5	18.8
Current residence		
Urban	34.0	17.9**
Rural	37.6	23.1
Childhood residence		
Urban	33.4	23.0
Rural	36.9	19.0
Longest job		
Self-employment or agriculture	54.3**	31.9**
Other +	26.5	12.2
Living with child		
Yes	37.4	20.0
No	33.9	20.8
Living with pre-schooler		
Yes	38.8	21.5
No +	35.3	20.3
Home ownership		
Owns a home	35.7	20.1
Owns a condominium	26.4	17.7
Does not own a home +	36.4	24.0
Log likelihood	−842.2	−671.8
Sample size	1,499	1,551

+ = reference group; *significant at the 10 percent level; **significant at the 5 percent level

APPENDIX TABLE 2 Estimated probabilities of working (percent) in 2001 conditional on working in 1999 by sex, Japan

	Men	Women
Predicted	63.3	52.7
Actual	63.3	52.7
Age		
65–69	74.1**	61.5**
70–74	61.2	60.9**
75–79	57.6	42.4
80–84 +	57.4	37.2
Education		
Jr. high +	60.3	49.7
Sr. high	62.6	56.4
University or jr. college	79.4**	77.4
Nagi score		
Some difficulty	57.6*	43.1**
No difficulty +	64.7	56.9
Change in Nagi score from 1999		
–3	32.8*	23.1**
–2	42.8*	32.1**
–1	53.5*	42.4**
0	63.8*	53.4**
1	73.1*	64.0**
2	80.8*	73.5**
3	86.8*	81.3**
Marital status and spouse's health		
Married, spouse healthy	66.2	51.2
Married, spouse not healthy	70.5*	49.1
Not married +	34.8	55.4
Marital status change		
Married in 1999 and 2001	60.7	54.2
Other +	77.1	50.8
Current residence		
Urban	61.4	51.5
Rural	65.1	53.7
Childhood residence		
Urban	61.5	56.0
Rural	64.2	50.8
Longest job		
Self-employment or agriculture	67.9**	54.5
Other +	58.6	49.3
Living with child		
Yes	65.7	49.9
No	60.7	56.6
Living with pre-schooler		
Yes	63.6	42.1
No+	63.2	53.5
Home ownership		
Owns a home	61.9*	52.0
Owns a condominium	80.3	65.9
Does not own a home +	75.0	58.1
Log likelihood	–324.244	–194.264
Sample size	525	310

+ = reference group; *significant at the 10 percent level; **significant at the 5 percent level

APPENDIX TABLE 3 Estimated probabilities of working (percent) in 2001 conditional on working in 1999, by urban/rural residence, Japan

	Urban	Rural
Predicted	61.6	63.2
Actual	61.6	63.2
Age		
65–69	73.8**	74.4*
70–74	61.1	61.4
75–79	53.2	60.2
80–84+	50.9	55.6
Education		
Jr. high +	57.9	62.7
Sr. high	58.3	63.6
Univ or jr. college	77.3**	71.1
Nagi score		
Some difficulty	64.0*	63.8
No difficulty +	53.8	60.4
Change in Nagi score from 1999		
−3	61.7	38.6**
−2	61.6	47.5**
−1	61.6	56.6**
0	61.6	65.3**
1	61.5	73.1**
2	61.5	79.7**
3	61.5	85.1**
Marital status and spouse's health		
Married, spouse healthy	64.4	70.3
Married, spouse not healthy	62.7	77.6
Not married +	41.0	4.9
Marital status change		
Married in 1999 and 2001	58.3	58.2
Other +	78.1	91.7
Longest job		
Self-employment or agriculture	66.6	68.3**
Other +	57.8	55.8
Living with child		
Yes	67.3*	63.6
No	56.6	62.7
Living with pre-schooler		
Yes	46.7	73.8
No+	62.4	62.2
Home ownership		
Owns a home	59.8	63.3
Does not own a home +	70.7	59.2
Log likelihood	−176.287	−150.021
Sample size	286	259

+ = reference group; *significant at the 10 percent level; **significant at the 5 percent level

Notes

Research for this chapter was funded by two grants from the National Institutes of Health, NIA R01-AG025488 and AG025247. This work was also supported by a grant obtained by the Nihon University Population Research Institute from the Academic Frontier Project for Private Universities: matching fund subsidy from MEXT (Ministry of Education, Culture, Sports, Science and Technology), 2006–2010.

1 Amendments to the social security system covering employees have made future benefits a function of the rate of growth of total earnings by covered workers. Thus, augmenting the labor force with additional older workers will increase revenues owing to the larger labor force, reduce expenditures owing to delayed retirement, and keep the income replacement ratio from declining as fast as currently projected.

2 Japan's lost decade refers to the 1990s when the bubble economy collapsed, economic growth stalled, unemployment rose, and the value of most assets sharply declined. In addition to the dramatic change in the economy, "The people were shocked and confused as a wave of anxiety and pessimism rapidly pervaded Japanese society" (Yoshikawa 2001: 1). This represented a severe reversal of fortune and attitudes of the population from the view presented only a few years earlier in Vogel 1979.

3 Data from the first survey conducted in 1999 are available from the Nihon University Population Research Institute: ogawa@eco.nihon-u.ac.jp.

4 The nine categories of the Nagi score include activities such as lifting objects, raising hands above the head, sitting, standing, walking, and climbing stairs. The complete list of items is shown in Figure 3 along with the proportion of respondents reporting difficulties with each activity.

5 The sample of women who were working in 1999 in urban and rural areas was deemed too small for useful analysis.

References

Clark, Robert. 1990. *Japanese Retirement Systems*. Homewood, IL: Dow Jones-Irwin.
Clark Robert and Olivia Mitchell. 2002. "Strengthening employment-based pensions in Japan," *Benefits Quarterly* (2nd quarter): 22–43.
Clark, Robert and Naohiro Ogawa. 1992a. "Employment tenure and earnings profiles in Japan and the United States: Comments," *American Economic Review* 82(1): 336–345.
———. 1992b. "The effects of mandatory retirement on earnings profiles in Japan," *Industrial and Labor Relations Review* 45(2): 258–266.
———. 1997. "Transition from career jobs to retirement in Japan," *Industrial Relations* 36(2): 255–270.
Hashimoto, Masanori and John Raisian. 1985. "Employment tenure and earnings profiles in Japan and the United States," *American Economic Review* 75: 721–735.
Management and Coordination Agency. Various years. *Employment Status Survey*. Tokyo.
Nagi, Saad Z. 1965. "Some conceptual issues in disability and rehabilitation," in M. B. Sussman (ed.), *Sociology and Rehabilitation*. Washington, DC: American Sociological Association, pp. 100–113.
———. 1979. "The concept and measurement of disability," in E. D. Berkowitz (ed.), *Disability Policies and Government Programs*. New York: Praeger, pp. 1–15.
Nihon University Japan Longitudinal Study of Aging. Nihon University Population Research Institute, Tokyo.
Ogawa, Naohiro. 2003. "Population aging and its impact on the socioeconomic system in Japan," *Aging in Japan 2003*. Tokyo: Japan Aging Research Center, pp. 123–150.

Ogawa, Naohiro, Robert D. Retherford, and Yasuhiko Saito. 2008 (forthcoming). "Care of the elderly and women's labour force participation in Japan," in Naohiro Ogawa and Shripad Tuljapurkar (eds.), *Riding the Age Waves: Responses to Aging in Advanced Industrial States*. Kluwer.

Seike, Atsushi. 2008 (forthcoming). "An economic analysis of age discrimination: The impact of mandatory retirement and age limitation in hiring on the utilization of human resources in an aging society," in Naohiro Ogawa and Shripad Tuljapurkar (eds.), *Riding the Age Waves: Responses to Aging in Advanced Industrial States*. Kluwer.

Statistics Bureau, Ministry of Public Management, Home Affairs, Posts and Telecommunications. 2003. *Annual Report of the Labour Force Survey*.

Vogel, Ezra. 1979. *Japan as Number One: Lessons for America*. Cambridge, MA: Harvard University Press.

Yoshikawa, Hiroshi. 2001. *Japan's Lost Decade*. Tokyo: International House of Japan.

Growth Effects of Age-Related Productivity Differentials in an Aging Society: A Simulation Study for Austria

HELMUT HOFER
THOMAS URL

Demographic projections throughout Europe show similar patterns of rapidly aging societies. Although long-run population projections depend crucially on their assumptions about migration, the outcomes are reliable enough to bring about a steady flow of studies and policy recommendations. All major international organizations devote resources to long-term analysis and concentrate on the impact of population aging on public finances (Leibfritz et al. 1996; Koch and Thimann 1997; World Bank 1994; Holzmann and Stiglitz 2001; Economic Policy Committee 2001, 2002; European Commission 2001, 2002).

Another strand of literature emphasizes the consequences of demographic change for long-run economic growth. Andersson (2001), for example, estimates the effect of population aging on the average growth rate and concludes that within Scandinavian countries, changes in the relative size of age groups contribute significantly to the growth rate of output. Andersson's approach, however, does not allow decomposition into direct effects resulting from productivity differentials and indirect effects from changing capital accumulation. Bloom and Williamson (1998) add demographic variables to Barro-type cross-country growth regressions and plug dependency ratios—that is, the ratio of the non-working-age population to the working-age population—into the equation to assess the role of demographic change in the Asian growth experience between 1965 and 1990. Bloom and Williamson suggest that a baby boom generation would create a wavelike pattern of real GDP per capita over time. As the baby boomers increase the head count immediately after birth, they reduce per capita income. At the same time they draw on available resources for caring and education and consequently reduce savings. When baby boomers enter the working-age population, their additional labor supply contributes to higher output, and life cycle consumption smoothing generates more savings. When the baby bust period follows, output tends to fall below the baseline scenario, because the labor force shrinks and the elderly run down their assets. Cutler et al. (1990) achieve a similar result using a Ramsey-type growth model. They show that the baby bust phase requires lower capital accumulation to equip new workers and to house new families, while permitting more consumption for a given capital–output ratio.

Both approaches recognize the potential effects of demographic change on long-run growth performance, but the transmission channel of demographic change is limited to its direct effect on the size of labor supply and its indirect effect on capital accumulation. In this chapter we extend the analysis by introducing age-specific productivity profiles into a calibrated neoclassical growth model for the Austrian economy, that is, we supplement the direct and indirect effects of demographic change by transforming labor input into efficiency units. This extension is comparable to the approach in Bryant and McKibbin (2004) where the aggregate wage bill depends on age-specific earnings profiles. Bryant and McKibbin show that baby boom shocks reduce output during the baby bust phase by some 20 percentage points as compared to a scenario without hump-shaped age-earning profiles. Miles (1999) also uses age-related productivity profiles in an overlapping generations model, but he concentrates on the consequences of the resulting hump-shaped earnings path of private households for their savings behavior.

Baumgartner et al. (2005) calibrate a long-run neoclassical growth model for the Austrian economy (A-LMM), which is based on the population projections made by Statistics Austria and is used to forecast the effect of population aging on the development of potential output, employment, public finances, and other macroeconomic variables. The social security system also plays a central role in the model. Aging results mainly in a shift of the relative size of age cohorts with differential participation rates. Because of the shrinking size of the working-age population and age-specific activity rates for each cohort, the labor force declines over time. Here we go a step further and introduce age-specific productivity differentials into this model. We take the population projection with a declining working-age population as given and analyze what happens if, on top of the changing head count of individual cohorts, age-related productivity profiles affect the aggregated labor supply expressed in efficiency units.

There are two main arguments why productivity should vary with age. First, on-the-job training and experience add to human capital; second, physical and cognitive abilities diminish with increasing age. The upward slope of the age-productivity profile over the early years of the working career results from the accumulation of human capital acquired by education and training on the job. Becker (1975) provides a comprehensive analysis of the incentives to human capital accumulation. His optimality constraint for investing in human capital equates the present value of investment costs with the present value of additional income from this investment. Assuming constant investment costs, the accumulated gains from investment automatically decrease as workers grow older and as the number of years over which gains can be appropriated shrinks. Consequently, the incentive to invest in human capital decreases with age, which motivates at least concavity of the age-productivity profile.

Physical and cognitive abilities, competency of inductive reasoning, and retentiveness start to decline from a peak around the age of 50. At the same time people need more time to receive signals, aggravating the loss in productivity due to age (Verhaegen and Salthouse 1997; Skirbekk 2002, 2003a). Interestingly, interactive skills do not depreciate with age; but as structural change accelerates, demand for experience-based skills abates. This is a universal phenomenon across countries, population subgroups, sexes, and people with high or low ability level. Training programs can soften or even halt the decline but are not yet widespread across industrialized countries. Summarizing Skirbekk's (2003a) overview, the empirical evidence suggests a hump-shaped relation between age and productivity with a peak around age 50 and with different estimates of the reduction in productivity for younger and older workers. The size of the reduction depends on the measurement method. Supervisory ratings do not usually support a clear link between age and productivity, whereas employer–employee matched data series show more pronounced differentials.

The long-run simulation model A-LMM is a highly aggregated macroeconomic model with an aggregate production function. Capital and labor measured in full-time equivalents are combined to produce aggregate output. We relate aggregate labor in full-time equivalents to age-specific labor productivities following the approach developed by Fürnkranz-Prskawetz and Fent (2004). We apply three aggregation functions (linear, Cobb–Douglas, CES) with deviating assumptions on the substitutability of age groups in order to compute an average productivity index that aggregates cohort-specific productivity differentials. The advantage of integrating age-specific productivity into a long-run simulation model is a complete feedback between the aging labor force and the production possibility frontier.

In the next section we present the relevant subset of equations determining the transformation of the labor input into efficiency units. (The Appendix describes the model in detail.) In the third section we present estimates for productivity differentials and various aggregation functions for the computation of labor efficiency units. After presenting the simulation results in the fourth section, we summarize and draw some conclusions.

The simulation model

A-LMM has been designed to analyze the macroeconomic impact of long-term trends on the Austrian economy, to develop long-term scenarios, and to perform simulation studies. The current version of the model has a time horizon of 2075 and is documented in Baumgartner et al. (2005). The model

FIGURE 1 A-LMM structure

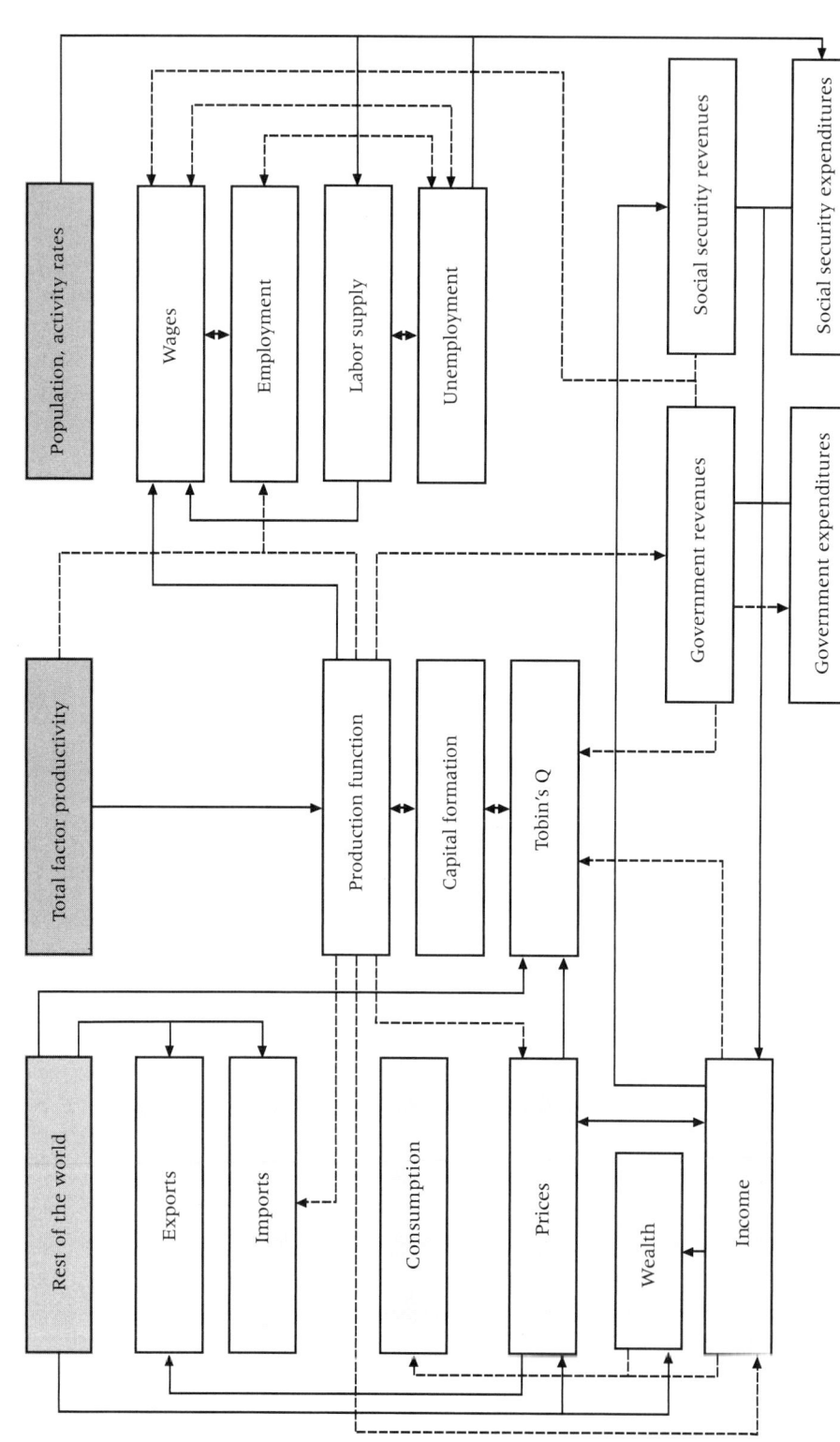

NOTE: Shading indicates exogenous developments.

is firmly based on neoclassical growth theory with exogenous Harrod-neutral technological progress. In combination with a Cobb–Douglas production function, this implies constant factor income shares over the simulation horizon and is consistent with stylized facts about growing market economies. The model attains a steady-state growth path determined by exogenous rates of change of the working-age population and technical progress.

The model is populated by two kinds of agent—private firms and private households—whose actions result from forward-looking optimizing behavior. Private agents' behavioral equations are derived from dynamic optimization principles and are based on perfect foresight. As the third major actor, we consider the national government. We assume a constant legal and institutional framework for the whole projection period. The government is constrained by the balanced-budget requirement according to the European Union's Stability and Growth Pact. The structure of A-LMM is shown in Figure 1.

The long-run growth path of the model is determined by supply side factors. Thus, the modeling of firm behavior becomes decisive for the properties of our model (see, for example, Allen and Hall 1997). Firms are assumed to produce goods and services using capital and labor as inputs. Factor demand is derived under the assumption of profit maximization subject to resource constraints and the production technology. Capital accumulation is based on a modified neoclassical investment function with forward-looking properties. In particular, the rate of investment depends on the ratio of the market value of additional investment goods to their replacement costs. This ratio (Tobin's Q) is influenced by expected future profits net of business taxes. Domestic saving creates no limit for investment activities since Austria is modeled as a small open economy with perfect and open capital markets. Labor demand is derived from the first-order condition of the firms' profit maximization problem.

Private households' behavior is derived from intertemporal utility maximization according to an intertemporal budget constraint. Within this set-up, decisions about consumption and savings (financial wealth accumulation) are formed in a forward-looking manner. Consumption depends on the present value of expected future disposable income from wages and transfers (human wealth) and from financial wealth including overseas claims, but also on current disposable income since liquidity constraints are binding for some households.

Households offer their labor services to firms and receive income in return. A special characteristic of A-LMM is the highly disaggregated labor supply. The labor force equals the product of the cohort-specific population and labor market participation rates. In the model we use highly disaggregated (by sex and by six age groups) participation rates. This gives us the opportunity to account for the different behavior of males and females (where part-time work is a major difference) and young and elderly employees (where early retirement comes into consideration).

Another special characteristic of A-LMM is a disaggregated model of the social security system as part of the public sector. We explicitly model the expenditure and revenue side for pension, health and accident, and unemployment insurance. We also model expenditures on long-term care. Demographic developments are important explanatory variables in the social security model. Individual branches of the public sector may run permanent deficits; however, for the public sector as a whole, a short-run balanced-budget condition is forced to hold.

A-LMM as a long-run model is supply side driven. The demand side adjusts in each period to secure equilibrium in the goods market. The adjustment mechanism runs via disequilibria in the trade balance. The labor market equilibrium is characterized by a time-varying natural rate of unemployment. We do not model prices and financial markets explicitly; rather we view Austria as a small open economy. Consequently, the real interest and inflation rates coincide with their foreign counterparts. Real output growth in the rest of the world is set above the Austrian trend level to allow for the convergence of per capita income in the rest of the world toward Austria's level. As a consequence, the real interest rate in Austria is above the real rate of output growth, and hence dynamic efficiency conditions apply. Furthermore, we assume that the European Central Bank continues to follow an inflation target of just under 2 percent. To achieve equilibrium in the capital market and to close the model, we require that domestic excess savings correspond to the transfer balance in the current account. This closure rule allows for a significant build up of the net foreign assets position as the baby boom generation approaches retirement and for a reduction of foreign assets during their retirement phase. In the long-run steady state, the model converges to a zero net foreign asset position because private households regard net foreign assets as part of their expected financial wealth and consequently adjust their consumption.

Because of the long projection horizon and a comparatively short record of available economic data for Austria, the parameterization of the model draws extensively on economic theory.[1] This shifts the focus toward theoretical foundations, economic plausibility, and long-run stability conditions and away from statistical inference. As a consequence, many model parameters are either calibrated or estimated under theory-based constraints.[2] For a short description of the production function and the labor market in the simulation model, we refer readers to the Appendix.

Implementing age-related productivity

The implementation of age-related productivity into the model mimics the approach we use to account for part-time work, maternity leave, and absence due to military service; see equation (A.7) in the Appendix. The number of dependent employees, LE_t, is the starting point for this transformation. Our source of employment data is the Federation of Austrian Social Security Institutions, which counts people on maternity leave and in military service, $LENA_t$, as dependent employees. Therefore, we use the ratio of employment measured in full-time equivalents, LD_t, to the number of dependent employees excluding people on maternity leave or in military service, QLD_t, and an index of the weekly average working time, QWT_t, for the transformation of the head count into labor measured in full-time equivalents.

We account for changes in labor productivity by introducing another correction factor. The labor productivity index, IAP_t, reflects the changing composition of the labor force and the shift in average labor productivity associated with the aging process. Thus LE_t is given by

$$LE_t = \frac{LD_t}{QLD_t \, QWT_t \, IAP_t} + LENA_t, \quad (1)$$

where IAP_t is normalized, such that its value in 2002 is equal to one. This normalization guarantees that the values in the starting year fully reflect the data from labor market statistics and the national accounts.

There are several ways to compute the labor productivity index, each associated with a different assumption on the substitutability of labor across age cohorts. Baumgartner et al. (2005) use six age cohorts because participation rates do not vary much within each of these age brackets.

We project the participation rates separately for six male (PRM_{1t} to PRM_{6t}) and six female (PRF_{1t} to PRF_{6t}) age cohorts. The following age groups are used: 15 to 24 years, 25 to 49 years, 50 to 54 years, 55 to 59 years, 60 to 64 years, 65 years and older. $POPM_{1t}$ to $POPM_{6t}$ and $POPF_{1t}$ to $POPF_{6t}$ denote the corresponding population groups. Total labor supply, LF_t, is given by

$$LF_t = \sum_{i=1}^{6} \left(PRM_{it} POPM_{it} + PRF_{it} POPF_{it} \right). \quad (2)$$

In order to consider economic repercussions of changes in the social security law and the tax code on future labor supply, we model future activity rates as a combination of trend activity rates, PRT_t, which are exogenous in A-LMM, and a second component that is dependent on the development of wages and unemployment:

$$PRM_{it} = PRTM_{it} + ELS \cdot WA_t; \quad (3)$$

$$PRF_{it} = PRTF_{it} + ELS \cdot WA_t. \quad (4)$$

ELS denotes the uniform participation elasticity with respect to WA_t, where WA_t is given by

$$WA_t = \log\left(\frac{w_t (1-u_t)}{w_{2002}(1+g_{wa})^t (1-u_{wa})} \right). \quad (5)$$

The variable WA_t is a proxy for the development of the ratio of the actual wage to the reservation wage. It measures the (log) percentage difference between the actual wage at time t, w_t, weighted by the employment probability $(1-u_t)$, and an alternative wage.[3] The path of the alternative wage (see the denominator in 5) is based on a constant employment probability $(1-u_{wa})$ and on wages growing at a constant rate g_{wa}. In our simulations we set g_{wa} to 1.8 percent and u_{wa} to 5.4 percent.

Since no actual estimate for the Austrian participation elasticity is available, we use an estimate for Germany with respect to gross wages and set $ELS = 0.066$ (Steiner 2000). This estimate implies that a 10 percent increase in the (weighted) wage differential leads to a 0.66 percentage point increase in the participation rate. For detailed motivation of the activity rate scenarios see Baumgartner et al. (2005).

The aggregation of age-specific productivity

The base version of the model assumes homogeneous labor and thus ignores possible age-related productivity differentials between cohorts. Skirbekk (2002, 2003a, 2003b) provides an overview of sources for age-related productivity differentials and estimates of their magnitude. Productivity reductions at older ages are small for tasks with a need for experience and communication skills, whereas older workers show a declining ability for tasks requiring problem solving, learning, and speed. Skirbekk (2003b) presents an estimate of age-related productivity differentials. We have to adjust our age-cohort structure in equation (2) to model age-specific productivities and calculate labor supply by sex for the following six age groups: 15–19, 20–24, 25–34, 35–44, 45–49, and 50 years and older. This grouping is more disaggregated as compared to the activity rates, PRM_{it} and PRF_{it}, used in equation (2) because we need to map the hump-shaped pattern of age-related productivity differentials more adequately. We denote the activity rates in this slightly different age classification as $PRAM_{1t}$ to $PRAM_{6t}$ (males) and $PRAF_{1t}$ to $PRAF_{6t}$ (females), and the corresponding population groups as $POPAM_{1t}$ to $POPAM_{6t}$ and $POPAF_{1t}$ to $POPAF_{6t}$.

The first column of Table 1 replicates Skirbekk's estimates, standardized such that the productivity of 25–34-year-olds equals one. The productivity of the youngest age group is 8 percent smaller than that of the reference group. A similar picture emerges for the oldest age group, 50 years and older. This group shows a productivity deficit of 6 percent. Since other studies like Hansen (1993) provide evidence for productivity deficits of some 25 percent, we multiply Skirbekk's values by a factor of three and use those values for a sensitivity analysis. The version with a higher productivity differential also corresponds to the shape implied by the linear-quadratic function used by Miles (1999). For the implementation of the model we standardize the pro-

TABLE 1 Productivity differentials, weighting factors, and per capita wage distribution across age groups

Age group	Productivity differentials relative to age group 25–34		Weighting factors AP_i		Distribution of per capita wages
	Small	Large	Small	Large	
Up to 19	0.92	0.76	0.16	0.14	0.03
20 to 24	0.93	0.80	0.16	0.15	0.10
25 to 34	1.00	1.00	0.17	0.19	0.16
35 to 44	1.01	1.03	0.18	0.19	0.21
45 to 49	0.97	0.92	0.17	0.17	0.22
50 to 65	0.94	0.81	0.16	0.15	0.27
			1.00	1.00	1.00

NOTE: Productivity differentials are defined with respect to age group 25 to 34. Weighting factors and income distribution represent shares adding up to 1.
SOURCE: Productivity differentials from Skirbekk (2003b), distribution of per capita wages across cohorts from Statistics Austria, "Wage and Income Tax Statistics 2001," based on the wage per employee.

ductivity differentials such that they sum to one. This guarantees homogeneity of degree one in the aggregation function, that is, a proportional increase of labor supply in all age groups will result in an equivalent proportional increase in efficiency labor units. The age-specific productivity weights are given in columns 3 and 4 of Table 1.

For comparison we also tabulate the distribution of per capita wages across age groups in Table 1. There is a remarkable difference between the distribution of per capita wages across age brackets and the distribution of productivity levels. Very likely this is the result of different degrees of part-time work and lower wages for apprentices. The deviation of age-specific wages from the age-specific marginal product, that is, seniority wages, may also form part of the explanation.

In the base version of the simulation model we do not distinguish between different age-related productivity levels. The equation relating the headcount of labor input to full-time equivalents assumes that the age-related productivity index IAP_t equals one for all periods. We now follow Fürnkranz-Prskawetz and Fent (2004) and use three possible ways to construct this index. First we allow for perfect substitutability between different age groups by using a linear specification of the aggregation function:

$$IAP_t = \frac{\left(\sum_{i=1}^{6} AP_i \left(PRAM_{it} POPAM_{it} + PRAF_{it} POPAF_{it}\right)\right)}{LF_t} \bigg/ IAP_{2002}, \quad (6)$$

where AP_i is the weight of the ith age group from Table 1 and IAP_{2002} is the value of the productivity index for the last sample year 2002. In order to isolate the effect of the shift in population structure from the change in population size, we divide the weighted sum of labor force components by the unweighted sum used in the base scenario. Division by the initial value of the age-related productivity index guarantees that we replicate the data for the starting year 2002 exactly. The productivity weights AP_i can also be interpreted as the elasticities of the efficiency of labor with respect to a ceteris paribus change in the size of one age group. An alternative specification that restricts the substitutability of age groups is a Cobb–Douglas function:

$$IAP_t = \frac{\prod_{i=1}^{6}\left(PRAM_{it}POPAM_{it} + PRAF_{it}POPAF_{it}\right)^{AP_i}}{LF_t} \Big/ IAP_{2002} . \qquad (7)$$

The elasticity of substitution between different age groups for this aggregation function is restricted to one. A further alternative is to allow for elasticities of substitution that differ between age cohorts. For this purpose we use a nested constant elasticity of substitution (CES) function with three different age groups, where we assume perfect substitutability of labor within each age group but imperfect substitutability between these three age groups. We distinguish between middle-aged workers (25 through 49), old workers (50 and older), and young workers (up to 24). Middle-aged workers can be most easy substituted for by someone from the old age group with slightly lower relative productivity (see Table 1). The substitutability of older workers by younger ones is smaller. This sequence of nesting is also suggested by the magnitude of the productivity differentials in Table 1. The two nested CES-aggregation functions are:

$$IAP_t = \frac{\left((1-AP_a)P_1^{-\rho_1} + AP_a\left(\sum_{i=3}^{5} AP_i\left(PRAM_{it}POPAM_{it} + PRAF_{it}POPAF_{it}\right)\right)^{-\rho_1}\right)^{-\frac{1}{\rho_1}}}{LF_t} \Big/ IAP_{2002} \qquad (8)$$

$$P_1 = \left[(1-AP_b)\left(\sum_{i=1}^{2} AP_i\left(PRAM_{it}POPAM_{it} + PRAF_{it}POPAF_{it}\right)\right)^{-\rho_2} + \left(AP_b\right)\left(PRAM_{6t}POPAM_{6t} + PRAF_{6t}POPAF_{6t}\right)^{-\rho_2}\right]^{\frac{1}{\rho_2}}, \qquad (9)$$

where ρ_1, and ρ_2 are the parameters of substitution at each level of nesting, P_1 represents the nested labor aggregate of older and younger workers, and AP_a and AP_b are the corresponding productivity weights of the respective age groups. The parameters AP_i correspond to the values in the linear case in equation (6) given in Table 1 but normalized such that their respective sums equal one. We assume that the substitution parameters fulfill the condition $\rho_1 < \rho_2$. This implies that the elasticity of substitution between workers of different age groups declines from middle-aged people to elderly workers and again from the elderly to the younger age group (Layard and Walters 1978). Kratena (2004) calibrates a static CGE model for Austria in which he draws a distinction between skilled and unskilled labor. His Allan elasticity of substitution between skilled and unskilled labor in manufacturing is 1.88, implying a parameter of substitution, ρ, of 1.53. For the rest of the economy Kratena assumes a substitution parameter of 2.06. A weighted average for the total economy would be 1.96. We use the two extreme values for our simulation and set $\rho_1=1.53$ and $\rho_2=2.06$. For all aggregation functions (6) through (9) of age groups into efficiency labor units, we use high and low productivity differentials (cf. Table 1).

Simulation results

Demographers expect a pronounced change in the future age structure of the Austrian population. The effect of the decline in the work force on the Austrian economy has been detailed in Baumgartner et al. (2005). The base scenario uses the main variant of the population forecast for Austria (Hanika et al. 2004). In this variant the working-age population (15–64) increases until 2012, reaching a peak value of 5.61 million. Thereafter, the working-age population diminishes rapidly until 2030 and continues to shrink at a lower rate until 2050. Despite the decline in the size of the working-age population starting in 2012, the labor force continues to grow until 2015 and then shows a weak downward trend until 2070. This pattern is due to the increase in the overall labor force participation rate throughout the simulation period by 8 percentage points. With only modest capital deepening and lower employment due to the decelerating size of the working-age population, the model predicts an average annual growth rate of real GDP of 1.6 percent. We use this base scenario as the reference point and present our simulation results as deviations from this baseline.

Given the hump-shaped profile of individual productivity over the life time, we expect an additional effect on output growth resulting from the aging labor force. Figure 2 shows how aging results in a slightly shrinking share of juveniles. The size of the youngest age group—up to 19 years, those with the lowest productivity—declines between 2002 and 2075 by 1.3 percentage points. The age group 20–24 declines by 1.8 percentage points. On the other hand, the share of 50–65-year-olds increases by 12.8 percentage points and shows by far the strongest consequence of aging. The size of the age group 45–49 is unaffected by the structural shift, whereas the sizes of the most productive age groups shrink—by 6.3 percentage points (35–44 years) and 3.5 percentage points (25–34 years). Overall, about a quarter of the decrease in average productivity related to the growing size of older age groups is compensated by a reduction in the size of younger age groups. Demographic

FIGURE 2 Distribution of labor supply by age group over time

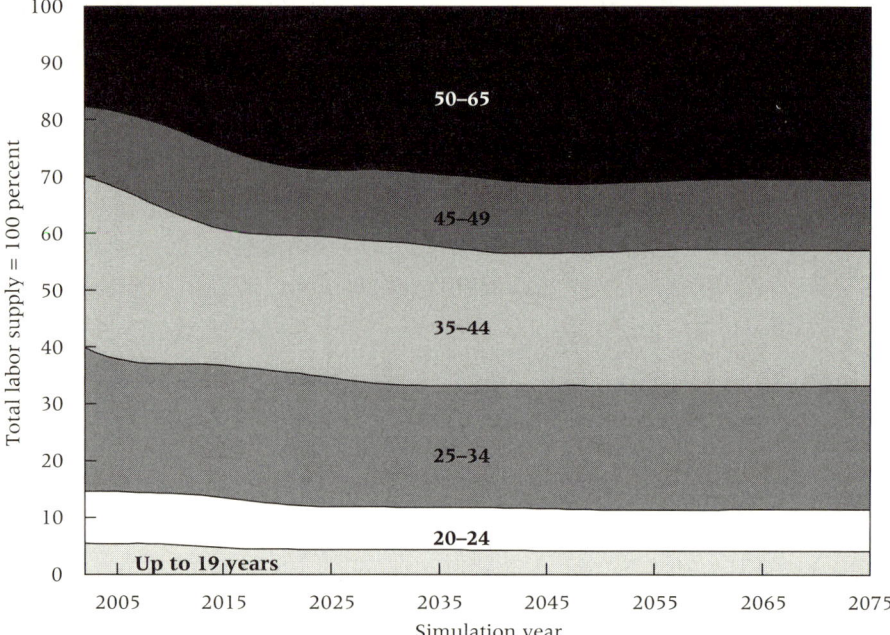

change will occur mainly in the period up to 2030 and flatten out thereafter. After 2050 the demographic structure remains stable.

Correspondingly, the age-related productivity index declines in the long run. The size of the productivity differential depends on the choice of the aggregation function, that is, the size of the elasticity of substitution and whether the productivity differential is assumed to be small or large (Figure 3). Under the assumption of perfect substitution and small productivity differentials, we find negligible effects of aging on average productivity. Even for large differentials we identify a decline in average productivity of only 2.3 percentage points. Relaxing the assumption of full substitutability and allowing for unit elasticity causes a long-run drop in the productivity index by some 6 percentage points, regardless of the assumption on the size of the productivity differential. The nested CES-aggregation shows almost the same picture, although both substitution elasticities are lower than in the case of the unit elasticity. The response to the transitory expansion of high-productivity groups is very strong under CES-aggregation and peaks around 2015. The similarity between Cobb–Douglas and CES aggregation is also due to the small number of age cohorts in the nested CES-function (young, middle, old). Allowing for six age groups in a CES-function but using uniform elasticities of substitution between age groups exposes a considerable weakening of productivity by 13 and 18 percentage points for $\rho = 1$ and $\rho = 2$ respectively (not

FIGURE 3 Index of age-related productivity for linear, Cobb–Douglas, and nested CES-aggregation

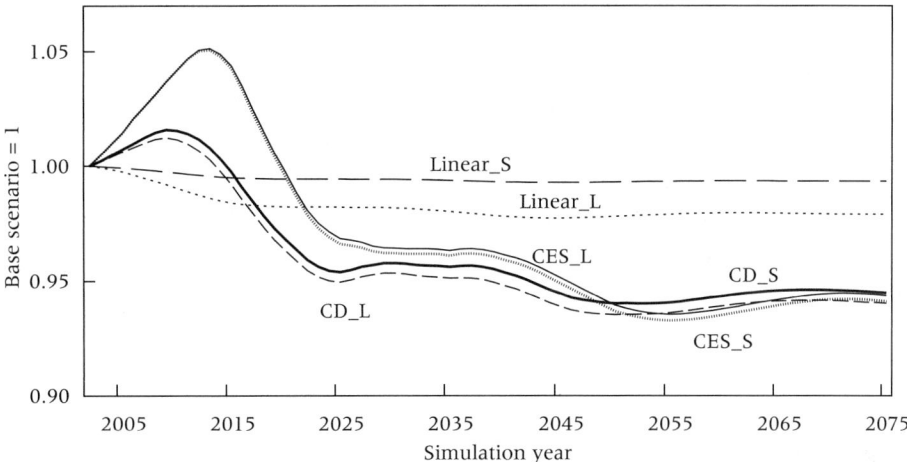

NOTE: Linear represents linear aggregation, CD represents Cobb–Douglas aggregation, nested CES represents a nested constant elasticity of substitution aggregation, suffix L indicates large productivity differential, and suffix S indicates small productivity differential.

shown in Figure 3). The trough in the productivity index occurs between 2045 and 2055, when the share of the oldest age group reaches a maximum.

Figure 4 presents results for real GDP under various scenarios for the IAP_t as a relative deviation from the base scenario. A number greater than one indicates that the simulated solution gives a higher output, whereas a

FIGURE 4 Simulation results for real GDP, 1995 = 100

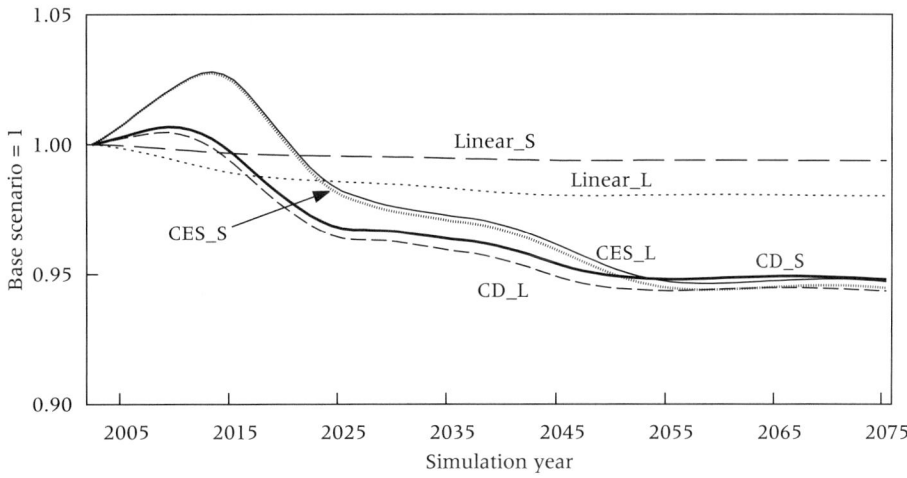

NOTE: For labels, see note to Figure 3.

number below one shows a lower output as compared to the base scenario. The overall impression is that the response of output matches the productivity index in shape, but the size is somewhat smaller. The stability properties of the model guarantee that perturbations from the changing working-age population eventually disappear, and the model solution will return to a steady-state growth path. Consequently, the deviation from the base scenario becomes constant. Nevertheless, the growth rate of real output drops from around 2 percent per year in the first 15 simulation years to a meager 1.4 percent per year at the end of the simulation period. More important, the wavelike pattern of the productivity index translates directly into a similar cycle for output growth rates, and this has a direct consequence for the level of output at the end of the simulation horizon. The strong increase in efficient labor during the first 15 simulation years creates a higher base from which the declining productivity index exerts its negative force. The development of the wage per employee is almost identical to real output. This wavelike pattern supports the suggestion by Bloom and Williamson (1998) that an increase in per-worker wages occurs when baby boomers enter the age brackets with high productivity, and a decline sets in after their movement into lower-productivity age brackets and into retirement.

So, first, why does age-related productivity have only a comparatively small effect, and second, why do swings in productivity not translate fully into ups and downs in output and per-worker wages? The main answer to this question is that the simulation model uses first-order optimality conditions for factor demand, which respond to the development of the marginal productivity of labor and capital. Figure 5 shows how the marginal productivity of labor evolves over time. Essentially, the productivity-related increase in labor efficiency at the beginning of the simulation period is mirrored by a temporary decline in the marginal productivity of labor, which in the long run is reversed into a small (oscillating) gain. The marginal productivity of capital, on the other hand, has a pattern more or less in line with the development of the productivity index. This is reasonable, since ceteris paribus capital becomes more productive when labor input in efficiency units rises. Figures 6 and 7 show the response of the investment–output ratio and the capital–labor ratio to aging. The investment–output ratio increases first and then drops by about 0.1 units, with the trough occurring between 2015 and 2020. In the long run, the investment–output ratio converges back to the steady state. Starting from a capital–labor ratio of 2.4, only small adjustments are to be expected. Accumulated over time, the reduction in investment lowers the capital–labor ratio of the economy by roughly 2 percent (linear case) and 6 percent (all other cases). The adjustment in the capital–labor ratio mirrors in a dampened way the projected response of output to aging (cf. Figure 4).

An equally important reason for the similarity between the development of productivity, output, and per-worker wages is that our experiment

FIGURE 5 Simulation results for marginal product of labor

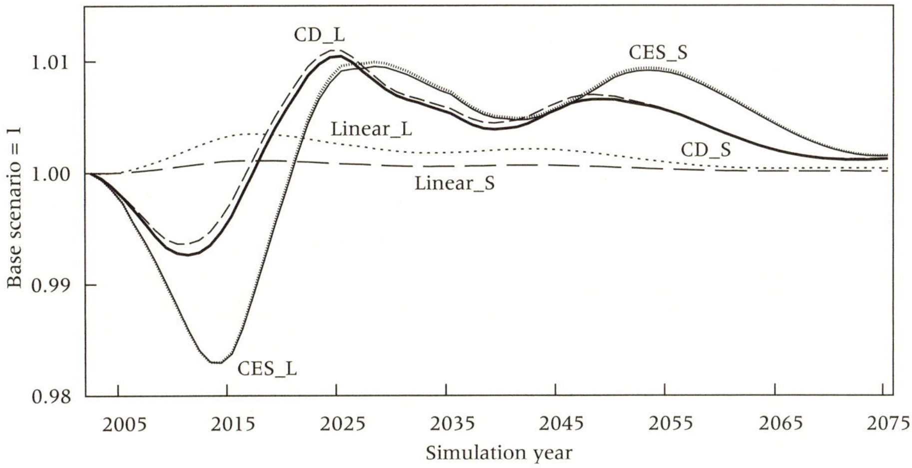

[Figure: Line graph showing simulation results from 2005 to 2075, with base scenario = 1 on y-axis ranging from 0.98 to 1.01. Curves labeled CD_L, CES_S, Linear_L, Linear_S, CD_S, and CES_L are shown. CES_L dips to about 0.985 around 2015, while CD_L peaks around 2025 near 1.01.]

NOTE: For labels, see note to Figure 3.

did not affect the exogenous rate of technical progress, *TFP* (cf. equation A.1). There is no feedback mechanism in the model that links aging to the rate of productivity growth. With the exogenous value of 0.85 for total factor productivity growth, the rate of technical progress is the obvious driving force in the model. Reductions in labor efficiency units have only a temporary effect on output growth.

Relaxing this assumption mitigates the already small negative effect from age-specific productivity differentials. Cutler et al. (1990) suggest a possible negative relationship between the growth of the labor force and the rate of technical progress: if labor becomes scarce, innovation will be focused on labor-saving technical progress and aging will feed positively back on the overall rate of technical progress. In a cross-section of industrialized countries Cutler et al. demonstrate a significant negative relationship between total factor productivity growth and labor force growth with a coefficient between –0.26 and –0.97, depending on the specification of the model. Accordingly, a decline in the long-run growth rate of the labor force by one percentage point would improve the annual rate of total factor productivity growth by roughly 0.3 to 1.0 percentage points per year.

In our base scenario the average growth rate of the labor force over the simulation period from 2003 through 2075 is 0.7 percentage points below its value during the three decades before 2003. The estimates by Cutler et al. (1990) thus imply an upsurge in total factor productivity growth in the range between 0.2 and 0.7 percentage points. This is a remarkable magnitude, given the expected lower receptivity of an aging society to new technologies. To get an idea of the necessary amount of additional total factor productivity growth

FIGURE 6 Simulation results for investment-to-GDP ratio

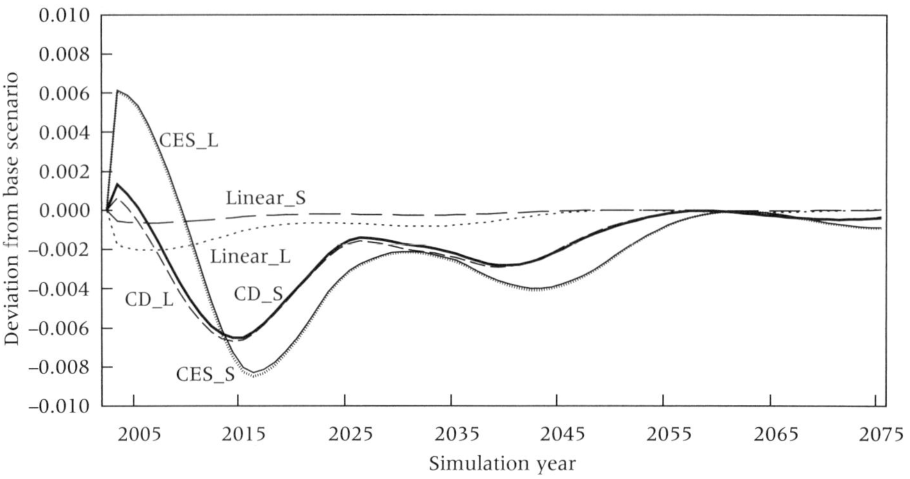

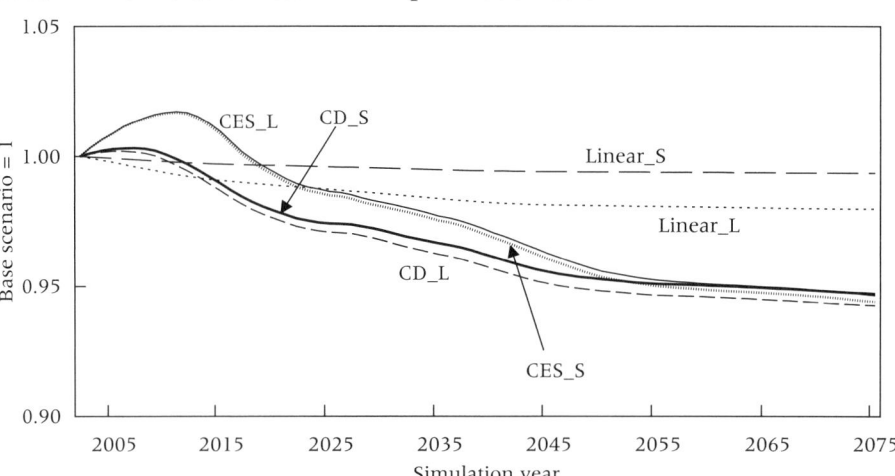

NOTE: For labels, see note to Figure 3.

that is needed to fully compensate for the reduced age-related productivity, we introduce into A-LMM an endogenous feedback mechanism from changes in the labor force to total factor productivity growth. We calibrate the adjustment parameter of total factor productivity to labor force growth such that the level of output per worker in 2075 corresponds to the base scenario with homogeneous labor. The rate of total factor productivity has to increase from 1.67 percent per year to 1.674 (linear aggregation with small productivity

FIGURE 7 Simulation results for capital–labor ratio

NOTE: For labels, see note to Figure 3.

differentials) or 1.722 (Cobb–Douglas aggregation with large productivity differentials) to eliminate the effect of age-related productivity differentials on the level of output per worker in 2075.

Summary and conclusions

We integrate age-specific productivity differentials into a long-run calibrated neoclassical growth model for the Austrian economy that fully integrates the actual population forecast. The model is based on an aggregate production function of the Cobb–Douglas type with exogenous technological progress. The labor market in this model is highly disaggregated, with six age groups for males and females in the working ages, and incorporates age-specific participation rates. The literature on age-specific productivity differentials emphasizes that on-the-job training builds up human capital and that, around age 50, physical and cognitive abilities, competency of inductive reasoning, and retentiveness start to decline. This results in a hump-shaped profile of age-specific productivity.

We use two age-productivity profiles reflecting either small or large differentials in productivity relative to the age group 25–34 years. This assumption results in a more or less hump-shaped pattern for age-specific productivity. Then we compute an average productivity index using three aggregation functions with different degrees of substitutability between age groups: linear, Cobb–Douglas, and a nested constant elasticity of substitution (CES). The productivity index allows us to rescale labor in the simulation model from full-time equivalents into efficiency units.

The advantage of a model-based approach for gauging the effect of age-related productivity differentials on other macroeconomic key variables is that the feedback between labor supply and capital accumulation is fully reflected in the model results. We compare simulations using alternative patterns for the age-related productivity differential and various aggregation functions to a base scenario with homogeneous labor supply. This approach requires assumptions about the future development of variables such as the extent of part-time employment, weekly working hours, activity rates, and the like, which themselves might be related to productivity development. Although these variables are critical to the model outcome, the base scenario and the simulated alternatives respond similarly to alterations, and our conclusions are thus not affected by those assumptions.

If we restrict the aggregation function to the linear case, the simulation results show only a small variation in output and other key macroeconomic variables. If one assumes perfect substitutability of labor, the consequences of aging for long-run growth potential are negligible. Introducing imperfect substitutability by using Cobb–Douglas or nested CES aggregation functions creates relatively small long-run effects on average productivity, real output, and per-worker wages in the magnitude of –6 percent as compared to the base scenario with homogeneous labor.

An important reason for the small effect of age-related productivity differentials is that the development of the size and structure of the working-age population is not unidirectional over the whole simulation horizon. In the first 15 years of the simulation, demographers expect an increase in the age bracket with the highest productivity, that is, 35–44 years. Starting in approximately 2015, the age group 50–65 years will gain in size, mainly at the expense of high-productivity middle-aged cohorts. Age-related productivity and less than perfect substitutability imply comparatively high growth over the early years of the simulation. Lower growth rates start to set in around 2015 but the higher base reached in 2015, as compared to the base scenario, generates only small differences at the end of the simulation period.

The marginal productivity conditions for factor demand act as stabilizing forces in the model. The marginal products of labor and capital react in opposite directions. The declining amount of labor input (measured in efficiency units) associated with aging is accompanied by a lower capital stock such that the marginal product of capital converges to the same long-run value as in a model with homogeneous labor productivity.

The predicted increase in life expectancy and the aging of the population will also change the savings behavior of forward-looking individual households. While the increase in life expectancy extends the prospective individual retirement period, the aging process will shift the population structure toward more elderly households with shorter remaining life spans. Our simulation model is designed for small open economies; therefore the resulting adjustment in savings behavior will affect only the net foreign asset position, and we do not present results. For large economies, however, part of the change in savings will have an effect on domestic capital accumulation.

Finally, we show that the negative growth effect from age-specific productivity profiles can be easily compensated, if one is willing to believe that the declining dynamism in an aging society is compensated by a slightly larger increase in ingenuity and innovation caused by the advancing scarcity of labor. The rate of total factor productivity growth has to be increased from 1.67 percent per year to 1.674 to eliminate the negative output effect of age-related productivity differentials. This fully compensating increase is far below estimates for the feedback between productivity growth and changes in the labor force from a cross-section of countries, and it remains clearly within the confidence interval for estimates of the rate of total factor productivity growth. All in all, we conclude that age-specific productivity profiles appear likely to have small consequences on future economic performance.

Appendix: The production function and the labor market in the Austrian Long-run Macromodel (A-LMM)

Output is produced with a Cobb–Douglas production function by combining labor and physical capital under constant returns to scale. After taking the natural logarithm, the Cobb–Douglas production function is given by:

$$\log(Y_t) = CONY + (1 - ALPHA)TFP \cdot t + ALPHA \log(K_t) + (1 - ALPHA)\log(LD_t), \qquad (A.1)$$

where Y_t denotes gross domestic product at constant 1995 prices at time t. $CONY$ is a shift parameter in the production function, TFP is the constant growth rate of labor-enhancing technical progress, LD_t is the number of full-time equivalent employees,[4] and K_t is the stock of capital. The parameter $ALPHA = 0.491$ is the output elasticity of capital. The value of $(1-ALPHA)$ corresponds to the share of labor income in nominal GDP in 2002. The labor income share in Austria is lower than in most other developed countries. This can be explained by Austria's practice of including incomes of the self-employed in the gross operating surplus, that is, profits, and this makes our specification closer in spirit to the augmented neoclassical growth model along the lines of Mankiw, Romer, and Weil (1992). By augmenting the production function with human capital, these authors obtain an estimate of the labor coefficient of 0.39. In the baseline, we assume a constant annual growth rate for labor productivity of $TFP=1.67$ percent. The corresponding annual growth rate for total factor productivity is $TFP(1-ALPHA)=0.85$ percent.

The labor market block of the model consists of four parts: labor supply, labor demand, wage setting, and unemployment. First, aggregate labor supply is projected through 2075. Total labor supply is determined by the projected head count of the working-age population, by the population shares of disaggregated sex–age cohorts, and by their respective activity rates. Labor demand is derived from the first-order conditions of the firm's cost minimization problem. Real wages are assumed to be determined in a bargaining framework and depend on the level of (marginal) labor productivity, the unemployment rate, and a vector of so-called wage push factors (the tax burden on wages and the income replacement rate from unemployment benefits).

The development of the Austrian labor force depends on future activity rates and the population scenario. In our model population development is exogenous. We use only the main variant of the most recent population projections for 2000–2075 by Statistics Austria[5] (Statistics Austria 2003; Hanika et al. 2004). Total labor supply, LF_t, comprises the dependent employed, LE_t, the self-employed, LSS_t, and the unemployed, LU_t. We take our labor market data for LE_t from the Federation of Austrian Social Security Institutions,[6] for LU_t from the Public Employment Service, and for LSS_t from the Austrian Institute for Economic Research.[7] Using data from these sources provides consistent long-run time series for the calculation of labor force participation rates. For administrative reasons LE_t includes persons on maternity leave and in military service, denoted as $LENA_t$.[8] Dependent labor supply (employees and unemployed), LS_t, and the unemployed are calculated as:

$$LS_t = QLS_t LF_t \tag{A.2}$$

$$LU_t = LS_t - LE_t, \tag{A.3}$$

where QLS_t denotes the share of self-employed in the total labor supply. In the projections we set $QLS_t = 0.9$, the value for the year 2002. Therefore, LSS_t amounts to 10 percent of LF_t over the whole simulation horizon.

We use the number of dependent employed in full-time equivalents, LD_t, as labor input in the production function (cf. equation A.1). The data source for employment in full-time equivalents is Statistics Austria. Employment (in persons) is converted into employment in full-time equivalents through the factor QLD_t. For the past, QLD_t is calculated as $LD_t/(LE_t - LENA_t)$. QLD_t is kept constant over the whole forecasting period at 0.98, the value for 2002.

Consistent with the production technology, optimal labor demand, LD_t^*, can be derived from the first-order conditions of the cost minimization problem as follows:

$$\log(LD_t^*) = \log(1 - ALPHA) - \log(W_t) + \log(Y_t). \tag{A.4}$$

Labor demand rises with output, Y_t, and is negatively related to real wages, W_t. Because firms require time to adjust to their optimal workforce (Hamermesh 1993), we assume the following partial adjustment process for employment; the partial adjustment parameter ALD denotes the speed of adjustment:

$$\left(\frac{LD_t}{LD_{t-1}}\right) = \left(\frac{LD_t^*}{LD_{t-1}}\right)^{ALD}, \tag{A.5}$$

with $0 < ALD < 1$. Actual labor demand is then given by

$$\log(LD_t) = ALD\left(\log(1 - ALPHA) - \log(W_t) + \log(Y_t)\right) + (1 - ALD)\log(LD_{t-1}). \tag{A.6}$$

We fix the speed of adjustment parameter ALD at 0.5.

For the transformation of employees, LE_t, into full-time equivalents, LD_t, we need information about the number of hours spent at work. For this purpose we use an index, QWT_t, which is calculated as the share of females in the total labor force times females' average working hours plus the share of males in the labor force times the average working hours of males. The average working time for females is 32.8 hours per week and that for males is 38.7 hours per week. These values are taken from the Microcensus 2002. QWT_t is standardized to 1.0 in 2002. In our scenarios we assume constant working hours for both males and females, but the increasing share of females in the labor force implies that total average working time will decline over the simulation horizon. The relationship between LE_t and LD_t is:

$$LE_t = \frac{LD_t}{QLD_t QWT_t} + LENA_t. \tag{A.7}$$

Real wages per full-time equivalent, W_t, are determined in a bargaining framework. We postulate the following wage equation:

$$\log(W_t) = CONW_t + \alpha_1 MPL_t - \alpha_2 U_t + \alpha_3 TWED_t + \alpha_4 GRR_t, \qquad (A.8)$$

where the real wage depends in the long run on the level of the marginal product of labor, MPL_t, the unemployment rate, U_t, and several wage push factors, such as the tax wedge on labor taxes, $TWED_t$, and the gross replacement rate, GRR_t, that is, the relation of unemployment benefits to gross wages. $CONW_t$ is an exogenous variable used to calibrate the rate of structural unemployment. Based on theoretical considerations we set the coefficient for MPL_t equal to 1.0. We estimate α_2, the coefficient of the dampening influence of unemployment on wages, to be around 2. For α_3 and α_4 we set values of 0.4 and 0.3, respectively.

Under the condition that real wages have to be equal to equilibrium real wages in the long run, the unique equilibrium rate of unemployment, U_t^* is

$$U_t^* = \frac{CONW_t + \alpha_3 TWED_t + \alpha_4 GRR_t}{\alpha_2}. \qquad (A.9)$$

Notes

We thank Ryan Edwards, Walter Fisher, Rudolf Winter-Ebmer, and participants at the Symposium on Population Aging and Economic Productivity in Vienna, the Austrian Economic Association Meeting in Innsbruck, and the 4th Austrian labor market workshop in Vienna for their helpful comments. We are also grateful to Ursula Glauninger for valuable research assistance.

1 For consistency A-LMM relies on the system of national accounts. On the basis of the current European System of National Accounts framework (ESA 1995), official data are available from 1976, in part only from 1995, onward. The projection exceeds the estimation period by a factor of three.

2 "[S]o called 'calibrated' models [...] are best described as numerical models without a complete and consistent econometric formulation [...]" Dawkins et al. (2001, p. 3655). Parameters are usually calibrated so as to reproduce the benchmark data as equilibrium. A typical source for calibrated parameters is empirical studies that are not directly related to the model at hand, for example, cross-section analysis or estimates for other countries, or simple rules of thumb that guarantee model stability. For a broader introduction and discussion of the variety of approaches subsumed under the term "calibrated models" see Hansen and Heckman (1996), Watson (1993), and Dawkins et al. (2001).

3 We use lagged WA_t instead of current WA_t to avoid convergence problems for the solution algorithm of the model.

4 Following the convention of the National Accounts, the compensation of the self-employed is included in the gross operating surplus and therefore is not part of the compensation of employees. We therefore exclude labor input by the self-employed from the production function.

5 We received extended population projections from Statistics Austria through the year 2150. Given the forward-looking behavior of households and firms, this mitigates endpoint problems for our simulation period from 2003 through 2075.

6 Hauptverband der österreichischen Sozialversicherungsträger.

7 For a description of the respective data series see Biffl (1988).

8 In the projection of $LENA_t$ we assume a constant relationship, $QLENA_t$, between $LENA_t$ and the population aged 0 to 4 years, $POPC_t$, which serves as proxy for maternity leave.

References

Allen, C. and S. Hall. (eds.). 1997. *Macroeconomic Modelling in a Changing World, Towards a Common Approach*, Series in Financial Economics and Quantitative Analysis, John Wiley & Son.

Andersson, B. 2001. "Scandinavian evidence on growth and age structure," *Regional Studies* 35: 377–390.

Barro, R. J. and X. Sala-i-Martin. 1995. *Economic Growth*. London: McGraw Hill.

Baumgartner, J., H. Hofer, S. Kaniovski, and A. Schuh. 2005. "A long-run macroeconomic model of the Austrian economy (A-LMM): Model documentation and simulations," in Oesterreichische Nationalbank, *Macroeconomic Models and Forecasts for Austria, Workshop Proceedings of OeNB Workshops* No. 5. Vienna: Oesterreichische Nationalbank, pp.170–271.

Becker, G. S. 1975. *Human Capital*. Chicago: University of Chicago Press.

Biffl, G. 1998. "Arbeitsmarkt 2000," *Forschungsberichte aus Sozial- und Arbeitsmarktpolitik* Nr. 21, Vienna: Bundesministerium für Arbeit und Soziales.

Bloom, D. E. and J. G. Williamson. 1998. "Demographic transitions and economic miracles in emerging Asia," *World Bank Economic Review* 12: 419–455.

Bryant, R. C. and W. J. McKibbin. 2004. "Incorporating demographic change in multi-country macroeconomic models: Some preliminary results," in P. Onofri (ed.) *The Economics of Aging Population: Macroeconomic Issues*. Edward Elgar, Cheltenham, pp. 349–408.

Cutler, D. M., J. M. Poterba, L. M. Sheiner, and L. H. Summers. 1990/1."An aging society: opportunity or challenge," Brookings Papers on Economic Activity, pp. 1–74.

Dawkins, C., T. N. Srinivasan, and J. Whalley. 2001. "Calibration," Chapter 58, in J. J. Heckman and E. Leamer (eds.)., *Handbook of Econometrics*, Vol. 5, Elsevier Science B.V., pp. 3653–3703.

Economic Policy Committee. 2001. "Budgetary challenges posed by aging populations: The impact on public spending on pensions, health and long-term care for the elderly and possible indicators of the long-term sustainability of public finances," EPC/ECFIN/655/01-EN final, Brussels, 24 October «http://europa.eu.int/comm/economy_finance/epc/documents/aging_en.pdf».

———. 2002. "Reform challenges facing public pension systems: The impact of certain parametric reforms on pension expenditure," EPC/ECFIN/237/02 final, Brussels, 5 July «http://europa.eu.int/comm/economy_finance/epc/documents/para2002_en.pdf».

European Commission. 2001. "Public finances in EMU 2001," *European Economy* (3), Directorate-General for Economic and Financial Affairs, Brussels.

———. 2002. "Public finances in EMU 2002," *European Economy* (3), Directorate-General for Economic and Financial Affairs, Brussels.

Fürnkranz-Prskawetz, A. and T. Fent. 2004. "Workforce aging and economic productivity: The role of supply and demand of labor: An application to Austria," Oesterreichische Nationalbank, *Current Issues of Economic Growth, Proceedings of OeNB Workshops* (2).

Hamermesh, D. S. 1993. *Labor Demand*. Princeton.

Hanika, A., G. Lebhart, and S. Marik. 2004. "Zukünftige Bevölkerungsentwicklung Österreichs bis 2050 (2075)," *Statistische Nachrichten* (1): 18-33.

Hansen, G. D. 1993. "The cyclical and secular behaviour of the labour input: Comparing efficiency units and hours worked," *Journal of Applied Econometrics* 8(1): 71–80.

Hansen, L. P. and J. J. Heckman. 1996. "The empirical foundations of calibration," *Journal of Economic Perspectives* 10(1): 87-104.

Holzmann, R. and J. E. Stiglitz (eds.). 2001. *New Ideas about Old Age Security*. Washington DC: World Bank Publications.

Koch, M. and C. Thimann. 1997. "From generosity to sustainability: The Austrian pension system and options for its reform," IMF Working Paper No. 10, Washington DC.

Kratena, K. 2004. "Intra-industry trade and input demand," Austrian Institute for Economic Research Working Paper No. 238/2004, Vienna.

Layard, P. R. G. and A. A. Walters. 1978. *Microeconomic Theory.* New York: McGraw Hill.
Leibfritz, W., D. Roseveare, D. Fore, and E. Wurzel. 1996. "Aging populations, pension systems and government budgets, how do they affect saving?" in OECD (ed.), *Future Global Capital Shortages: Real Threat or Pure Fiction?*, Paris, pp. 47–102.
Mankiw, N. G., D. Romer, and D. N. Weil. 1992. "A contribution to the empirics of economic growth," *Quarterly Journal of Economics* 106: 407–437.
Miles, D. 1999. "Modelling the impact of demographic change upon the economy," *Economic Journal* 109: 1–36.
Skirbekk, V. 2002. *Variations in Productivity over the Life Span: A Review and Some Implications.* Laxenburg: International Institute for Applied Systems Analysis, Interim Report IR-02-061.
———. 2003a. "Age and individual productivity: A literature survey," Max Planck Institute for Demographic Research Working Paper (WP 2003-028), Rostock.
———. 2003b. "Age and individual productivity potential: New evidence based on ability levels and industry-wide task demand," International Institute for Applied Systems Analysis, Laxenburg, mimeo.
Statistics Austria. 2003. *Demographisches Jahrbuch 2001/2002*, ST.AT, Vienna.
Steiner, V. 2000. "Können durch einkommensbezogene Transfers am Arbeitsmarkt die Arbeitsanreize gestärkt werden?," *Mitteilungen aus der Arbeitsmarkt- und Berufsforschung* 33: 385–396.
Verhaegen, P. and T. A. Salthouse. 1997. "Meta-analysis of age differences in job performance," *Journal of Applied Psychology* 71: 33–38.
Watson, M. W. 1993. "Measures of fit for calibrated models," *Journal of Political Economy* 101(6): 1011–1041.
World Bank, 1994. "Averting the old age crisis," Oxford: Oxford University Press.

Workforce Aging and Labor Productivity: The Role of Supply and Demand for Labor in the G7 Countries

ALEXIA PRSKAWETZ
THOMAS FENT
ROSS GUEST

It is well accepted that future economic output in most industrialized countries must be achieved by a smaller and older labor force. A key question is how this development might affect labor productivity as measured by output per worker.[1] In the view of many economists, an aging population has negative consequences for growth in output per capita for two reasons. First, the support ratio changes because a decreasing ratio of the working-age population to the total population increases the ratio of consumers to producers. This contributes negatively to growth in output per capita. Second, behavioral effects, that is, negative effects of an aging population, may reduce labor productivity as measured by output per worker. It is the latter effect that we investigate in this chapter.

We shall study the sensitivity of projected labor productivity with respect to assumptions concerning three key characteristics of the labor market: the projected labor force participation rates,[2] the age–productivity profile of workers, and the degree of substitutability between labor of different ages. The first two characteristics determine the labor supply and the third characteristic determines the labor demand curve.[3] The assumption that workers of different ages are not perfectly substitutable and exhibit different levels of productivity implies that there is an optimal age mix of the workforce (in terms of output maximization) and that demographic change can move the actual age mix either closer to or further from the optimal mix and therefore affect labor productivity. The magnitude of this age-distribution effect depends on the degree to which workers of different ages are substitutable. As shown by Guest (2005) for Australia and by Prskawetz and Fent (2007) for

Austria, the age-distribution effect could easily be as important for economic growth as policies that aim to increase the labor force participation rates of older workers and women.

The assumption of imperfect substitutability of workers at different ages is one of the main arguments why cohort size may be negatively associated with labor market outcomes such as wages and unemployment (cf. Bloom et al. 1987; Korenman and Neumark 2000; Welch 1979). However, as noted in Gottschalk (2001), the literature on effects of cohort size and composition on labor market outcomes cannot be applied straightforwardly to the labor market implications of population aging that will be observed in the coming years. One reason is the increase in the demand for educated workers associated with technological progress. The second reason, more closely related to our study, is that labor market outcomes in the future will depend on the substitutability of older workers with young and prime age workers as contrasted with the substitutability of young with prime age workers during the time when the baby boom generation entered the labor force.

We present qualitative results and rough orders of magnitude rather than propose detailed projections of the future development of labor productivity. Following the work of Blanchet (1992) and Lam (1989), we choose a pure labor economy as our theoretical framework to study the impact of labor force aging on economic output. For our numerical simulations we use age-specific demographic data provided by the UN's *World Population Prospects: The 2004 Revision* (medium variant projections) and age-specific labor market data provided by OECD labor market statistics.

A restrictive assumption in Blanchet (1992) is that production technology allows for perfect substitution between workers of different ages. Although this assumption was relaxed in Blanchet (2002) and a CES (constant elasticity of substitution) production function was applied instead, the study is restrictive since it only considers the effect of workforce aging in a stable population. However, as is well known from the economic growth literature relating differences in economic growth rates to changes in demographic structures (e.g., Higgins and Williamson 1997), an analysis that restricts itself to steady states of population distribution may at best be insufficient and at worst misleading in times of severe demographic change. Since many industrialized countries will experience pronounced fluctuations in the working-age population in the coming decades (caused by the baby boom generation, which is expected to start retiring around 2020), a focus on transitional dynamics is essential.

By focusing on a pure labor economy and ignoring physical capital, we disregard one of the most important channels through which the negative impact of labor force shrinkage on economic growth may be attenuated. As we know from neoclassical growth theory, population decline increases the steady-state capital–labor ratio since fewer people have to be equipped with capital.[4] Moreover, as argued in Mason and Lee (2004), the accumulation of capital and wealth constitutes the source of the second demographic dividend. These effects are captured in general equilibrium models, which commonly constitute the theoretical framework to study the economic consequences of population aging. However, most of those models are restrictive with respect to production technology, which in most cases aggregates labor of all ages into one production factor. Since our aim is to introduce imperfect substitutability across age groups in the labor market and consider its implications for labor productivity during times of rapid labor force shrinkage and aging, we regard our decision to concentrate on a pure labor economy as "an important departure for more complete models" (in the words of Lam 1989, p. 192, who made a similar assumption).

In the next section we review the methodology applied in projecting future impacts of demographic change on labor productivity. We outline our theoretical framework in the third section. In the fourth section we present the demographic and labor supply forecasts in the G7 countries from 2005 to 2050 and outline two scenarios for the size and structure of the future labor supply. We apply alternative assumptions about the substitutability, productivity, and labor force participation of workers of different ages to arrive at scenarios of future labor productivity in the fifth section. We conclude with a discussion of the main results and an outlook for further research.

Projecting the future impact of demographic change on labor productivity

To project the future impact of an aging labor force on macroeconomic variables, computable general equilibrium models (CGE models) are applied. In a recent study on labor market effects of population aging, Börsch-Supan (2002) shows that about half of the decline (of 15 percent) in per capita output that results from the decrease in the labor force through 2035 can be compensated by induced higher capital intensity. However, he states, "... any possible age-structure related reduction in aggregate productivity ... would reduce the effect of higher capital intensity" (p. 42). He then concludes that an increase of productivity growth from 1.39 to 1.65 percent would be necessary to maintain the per capita level of GDP as of 2000. Hence, strong productivity growth, which in turn depends on increased capital intensity and human capital, is necessary to maintain the consumption level if labor force participation starts to decline.

A different approach—more closely related to demographic accounting than to sophisticated economic modeling—to forecasting the effect of labor force aging on labor productivity is taken in Blanchet (1992 and 2002). Interacting fixed and exogenously chosen age–productivity profiles with alternative projected demographic structures and age-specific labor force participation, Blanchet (1992) shows that the effect of labor force aging on labor productivity is moderate. To explain these results, he refers to stable population theory, which provides simple rules of thumb to assess the conditions under which the average value of an age-dependent variable may be sensitive to changes in the population growth rate. He shows that a change in the population growth rate of 1 percentage point cannot have an aggregate impact of more than 20–25 percent on any age-dependent phenomenon (see Appendix A, where we review Blanchet's argument).

Not only is aggregate economic productivity determined by the change in individual-based productivity, which works through a change in the age composition of the workforce, but, as we know from the theory of factor demand, the impact of labor force aging and labor force shrinkage on labor productivity depends on the substitutability of different factors of production—in particular, the substitution of capital for labor and the substitutability between workers of different ages and levels of education. Empirical studies indicate that the human capital of young workers and that of old workers are imperfect substitutes in production: young and old workers have comparative advantages in complementary tasks (cf. Kremer and Thomson 1998). As documented in Hamermesh (1993, chapter 3), the result of a relative decline in the supply of labor in a world consisting of homogeneous capital and labor would be declining returns to capital and an increase in wage rates. The results are much less clear, however, if one introduces restrictive substitution patterns between workers disaggregated by age (Hamermesh 1993, Table 3.9).

Although Blanchet (2002) has taken up the role of imperfect substitutability of workers of different ages and its impact on labor productivity when population growth changes, his analysis focused only on a stable population. To study the effect of imperfect substitutability between workers of different ages in times of population aging, it is necessary to focus on transitional dynamics. We therefore extend Blanchet's analysis to investigate the time path of labor productivity in a pure labor economy where workers of different ages are not perfect substitutes. Hence, we concentrate on dynamic features of population aging. In addition to studying the sensitivity of projected labor productivity with respect to the labor demand function, we investigate how future labor productivity will change depending on such labor supply factors as the individual age–productivity profile and labor force participation rates.

Theoretical framework

Imperfect substitution of workers by age

Macroeconomic models of population aging have typically assumed that once workers of different ages are adjusted for their productivity differences, they become identical inputs in economic terms. That is, they are perfectly substitutable, hence an aggregate employment index can simply be calculated as the sum of the (productivity-adjusted) employment levels of workers of different ages. The seminal example of this approach in the context of population aging is Cutler et al. (1990). The shortcoming of this assumption is that it ignores synergies between workers of different ages. Yet evidence from the management literature indicates that older and younger workers exhibit different attributes (for a short summary of this literature, see Guest and Shacklock 2005). For example, employers report that younger workers tend to have greater physical strength and endurance, vision, hearing, cognitive processing, intellectual capital, and adaptability. Older workers are perceived as having better people management skills, judgment that depends on experience, reliability/dependability, loyalty, and attendance. These differences suggest synergies and therefore imperfect substitution between younger and older workers.

Imperfect substitutability implies that the age mix of a given workforce affects output and leads to the notion of an optimal age mix that maximizes output. Demographic change can move the actual age mix either closer to or further from the optimal mix, thereby affecting aggregate output and, by implication, aggregate labor productivity. If the actual age distribution moves closer to the optimal distribution, a labor productivity dividend accrues to the economy. Conversely, if the actual distribution moves further from the optimal mix, a deadweight loss occurs.

The magnitude of the dividend or deadweight loss depends on two factors. One is the degree to which younger and older workers can be substituted in producing a given output. The other is the relative productivity of younger and older workers. These factors are expressed in a formula for the optimal age mix in Lam (1989), which is given in Appendix B. Intuitively, the greater the relative productivity of workers of a given age, the greater their optimal share of the workforce. This circumstance arises from the desire to equate the marginal product of workers of different ages. The degree to which the optimal workforce share adjusts to the relative productivity of workers increases with the elasticity of substitution between workers. To illustrate this relationship, suppose that there are only two types of workers—young and old. Suppose further that young workers become more productive relative to older workers. Firms will want to employ a greater share of younger workers to equate marginal products of workers. If the elasticity of substitution is low, young and old workers are highly complementary, and therefore only a small increase in the share of younger workers is required to equate marginal products. If the elasticity is high, a large increase in the share of younger workers is required. A duality exists between the elasticities of substitution and complementarity, as both reflect the underlying technology of production (this duality is discussed in Sato and Koizumi 1973). In our empirical model we use the elasticity of substitution.

Among the empirical studies of elasticities of substitution and complementarity of labor by age, Card and Lemieux (2001) estimate constant elasticities of substitution between different age groups for the United States, United Kingdom, and Canada in the range of 4 to 6. Estimates from the earlier literature, surveyed in Stapleton and Young (1988), range from 2 for highly educated workers to elasticities greater than 10 for workers with low education.

Functional forms of the production function

In the simulations presented in the following sections we analyze the sensitivity of projected labor productivity with respect to alternative assumptions about future labor supply and the substitutability and productivity of the labor force at different ages. We assume that the output of a particular economy depends solely on the input of labor and that individuals aged 15–74 years participate in the labor force according to the age-specific labor force participation rates given by the OECD labor market statistics.

We apply four production functions. The first is the *additive production function*, which assumes perfect substitutability between labor at different ages. In this modeling framework the output at time *t* is given by

$$Y(t) = \sum_{x=15}^{70} \alpha_x \, {}_5L_x(t), \text{ with } \sum_{x=15}^{70} \alpha_x = 1, \tag{1}$$

where α_x indicates the productivity of the labor force in the five-year age interval $[x,x+5)$, and ${}_5L_x$ indicates the labor force in this age interval, that is, the population within the age interval, ${}_5N_x(t)$, multiplied by the age-specific labor force participation rate $lfpr_x(t)$, where we distinguish between female and male labor force participation rates. The functional form (1) implies that once workers of different ages are adjusted for their productivity differences, they become identical inputs in economic terms. This is clearly unrealistic because it does not account for any degree of complementarity between workers of different ages. Examples of complementary age-dependent skills include the physical strength of young male workers, which complements the skills of older workers in managing people, including mentoring younger workers, and making decisions. Such complementarities are assumed away in the additive production function (1). Yet this is the typical functional form that has been adopted to define the labor index in macroeconomic models of demographic change.

Second, we consider the *Cobb–Douglas production function*,

$$Y(t) = \prod_{x=15}^{70} {}_5L_x(t)^{\alpha_x}, \text{ with } \sum_{x=15}^{70} \alpha_x = 1, \tag{2}$$

where the elasticity of substitution between any two input factors is constant and equals one. Alternatively, we assume a *constant elasticity of substitution production function* (CES) of the form

$$Y(t) = \left(\sum_{x=15}^{70} \alpha_x \,_5 L_x(t)^\rho \right)^{\frac{1}{\rho}}, \qquad (3)$$

with $\sigma = 1/(1-\rho)$ denoting the elasticity of substitution between the labor force of different ages and $\rho \in (-\infty, 1]$. The additive and Cobb–Douglas production functions are included in this general formulation as special cases if $\rho=1$ and $\rho \to 0$, respectively. As indicated in Blanchet (2002) the assumption of the CES production technology is restrictive as well. When workers from one age group are substituted by members of any other age group, the actual age difference does not matter. In reality one might assume that a person aged 25 years can easily be substituted by a person aged 26 but not easily by a person aged 64.

To take this into account we propose as the third alternative another kind of CES production function,

$$Y(t) = \left[\alpha_{15} \left(\frac{3 \,_5 L_{15}(t) + \,_5 L_{20}(t)}{4} \right)^\rho + \sum_{x=20}^{65} \alpha_x \left(\frac{\,_5 L_{x-5}(t) + 2 \,_5 L_x(t) + \,_5 L_{x+5}(t)}{4} \right)^\rho \right.$$
$$\left. + \alpha_{70} \left(\frac{\,_5 L_{65}(t) + 3 \,_5 L_{70}(t)}{4} \right)^\rho \right]^{\frac{1}{\rho}}, \qquad (4)$$

which we call *fuzzy CES*. This function takes into consideration that members of two neighboring age groups are better substitutes than those in age groups that are further apart. Instead of having just one age group within each addend of the production function—as in formula (3)—we use a weighted average of three neighboring age groups. This assumes that the direct elasticity of substitution of workers of different ages is higher when they belong to consecutive age groups. Therefore, each member of the labor force contributes not only to the age group he or she actually belongs to, but also—with a lower weight—to neighboring age groups. While the previous production functions (1), (2), and (3) implicitly assume that an individual moves from age group x to $x + 5$ at a certain moment, the fuzzy CES takes into account that aging is a continuous process. This idea can be generalized by combining $2n+1$ age groups instead of three (with n being an arbitrary number), which leads to expressions such as

$$\alpha_x \left(\sum_{j=x-n}^{x+n} \beta_{x,j} x_j \right)^\rho,$$

with $\sum_{j=x-n}^{x+n} \beta_{x,j} = 1$ and $\beta_{x,x-n} < \beta_{x,x-n+5} < \ldots < \beta_{x,x-5} < \beta_{x,x}$ and $\beta_{x,x} > \beta_{x,x+5} > \ldots > \beta_{x,x+n-5} > \beta_{x,x+n}$. Assigning $\beta_{x,j} = 0$ for all $j < x - 5$ or $j > x + 5$, $\beta_{x,x-5} = \beta_{x,x+5} = 1/4$, and $\beta_{x,x} = 1/2$, we obtain the production function given in (4).

The fuzzy CES implies that the elasticity of substitution between workers of different age groups depends (negatively) on the distance between age groups.[5] This is an appealing notion. Another appealing notion is that workers of some ages are inherently more flexible than workers of other ages; such workers are more substitutable with workers of any given age than are other workers. For example, it is reasonable to suppose that middle-aged workers are more flexible than either young or older workers, because middle-aged workers have some characteristics of both young workers and older workers. For example, they have moderate physical abilities, though not as great as young workers, and they have some of the attributes that come with age and maturity, such as skills in managing people. The fuzzy CES production function allows us to take this property into consideration by assigning appropriate parameters $\beta_{x,j}$ to each particular age group.

Another way of capturing this idea is to assign to each age group a parameter that captures their degree of flexibility. This can be achieved through a *CRESH function* (Hanoch 1971) of labor inputs distinguished by age that constitutes our fourth alternative for the production function:

$$\sum_{i=1}^{k} \alpha_i \left[\frac{L_i}{f(Y)} \right]^{\rho_i} = 1, \qquad (5)$$

where α_i is the productivity weight of labor of age i; k is the number of age groups; L_i is the number of workers of age i; Y is the index of composite labor inputs; and ρ_i is a parameter that determines the flexibility, or versatility, of L_i, meaning the degree to which L_i can substitute for any other input, L_j. We assume here that all labor inputs are substitutes to some degree, which restricts ρ_i such that $\rho_i \in (-\infty, 1]$. Note that if $\rho = 1$ ($\rho_i = \rho$), the additive (CES) production function results. As ρ approaches zero and $-\infty$, the Cobb-Douglas and the Leontief[6] production function result.

The elasticity of substitution, σ_{ij}, between L_i and L_j is given by Hanoch (1971, p. 699).

$$\sigma_{ij} = \frac{a_i a_j}{\sum_{m=1}^{k} s_m a_m}, \qquad (6)$$

where $a_i = 1/(1-\rho_i)$ and s_m is the factor share of L_i. The larger the value of a_i, the more easily L_i is substitutable for any other labor input. This implies that two labor inputs with high values of a_i will be good substitutes, and two inputs with low values of a_i will be poor substitutes. Restrictions exist on the range of values of σ_{ij} that yield a unique solution for the CRESH function (Hanoch 1971). The binding restriction in the present application is that for all i, either $0 < \rho_i < 1$ ($a_i > 1$) or $\rho_i < 0$ ($0 < a_i < 1$).

In applying the CRESH function we assume that middle-aged workers are more flexible than either young workers or old workers. The degree of flexibility is a hump-shaped function of age, rising to middle age then falling to old age. Appendix C gives the matrix of values of σ_{ij} that are used in the simulations. These values were chosen arbitrarily, subject to the restrictions on the parameters mentioned above, and such that the resulting values for the elasticity of substitution are in the range that is commonly used in applications of CES functions.

Demographic and labor supply forecasts for the G7 countries

Figure 1a plots the development of the total population in the G7 countries from 2005 to 2050. The populations of Canada and the United States are continuously increasing during the period of observation, whereas the populations of all other G7 countries have already started to decrease or will start to do so in the first half of the twenty-first century. As outlined in McDonald and Kippen (2001, p. 2), population can be maintained in the United States and Canada because of high/moderate fertility and moderate/high net immigration. The United Kingdom and France are characterized by moderate levels of fertility and low levels of net immigration, while the situation is more extreme for Germany, Japan, and Italy where fertility and net migration are rather low.

The projected demographic change will have an impact on the size and structure of the labor force through (1) a compositional effect that works via the age structure and (2) a direct or behavioral effect that operates via a change in age-specific labor force participation rates. As Johnson (2002) notes, "[D]emography is not the only, or even the most important, factor influencing the relative size and structure of the labor force.... Furthermore, behavioral factors which determine age- and sex-specific participation rates are more important than the population age structure in determining economy-wide employment shares" (pp. 113–114). Changes in age-specific rates may be caused by individual factors, as well as by institutional and macroeconomic variations, which include shifts in the demand for and supply of labor (e.g., economic swings and institutional incentives for delayed labor market entry due to prolonged education and early retirement exits). These micro- and macro-level determinants may in turn be related to demographic changes as proposed by Easterlin (1978) and more recently by Shimer (2001).

Figures 2a and b show the age-specific labor force participation rates of the G7 countries in 2004. For males the variance of labor force participation rates among the G7 countries is especially pronounced at older ages. The highest labor force participation rates for older males can be observed in Japan followed by the United States, Canada, and the United Kingdom. For France, Germany, and Italy the labor force participation rates at older ages are much smaller. (Among male workers aged 60–64 in these three countries only 19, 35, and 30 percent are in the labor force. The corresponding numbers for Japan, the United States, Canada, and the United Kingdom are 70, 57, 53, and 56 percent.) For females the variance of the labor force participation rates across the G7 countries is most pronounced in the middle ages, with Italy and Japan hav-

FIGURE 1 Total population and labor/population ratio, G7 countries

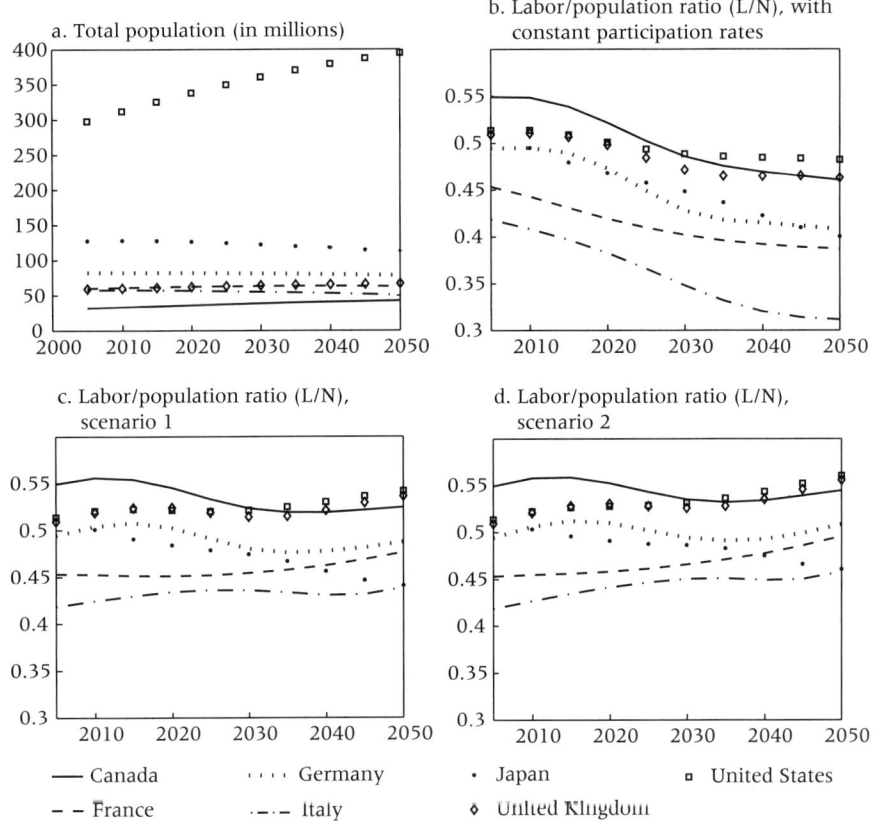

NOTE: See text for scenario 1 and 2 assumptions.
SOURCE: *World Population Prospects: The 2004 Revision*, medium variant.

ing the lowest rates; female labor force participation rates at ages 25–59 range between 60 and 70 percent and reach values as low as 30 percent for females in Italy aged 55–59. At older ages females exhibit patterns similar to those of males: the highest labor force participation rates can be observed for females in Japan, the United States, Canada, and the United Kingdom, where 40, 45, 35, and 30 percent of females are still in the labor force at ages 60–64.

If we combine the age-specific population data with the labor force participation rates and assume that the labor force participation rate is kept constant from 2005 to 2050, we obtain the support ratios depicted in Figure 1b. These computations clearly neglect the changes in labor force participation rates that will take place from 2005 onward. Therefore, these graphs are illustrations of the age-compositional effect rather than a projection of the actual support ratios. The simulations highlight the strong demographic pressures that interact with disincentives for labor force participation in the

FIGURE 2 Labor force participation rates by age and sex, 2004

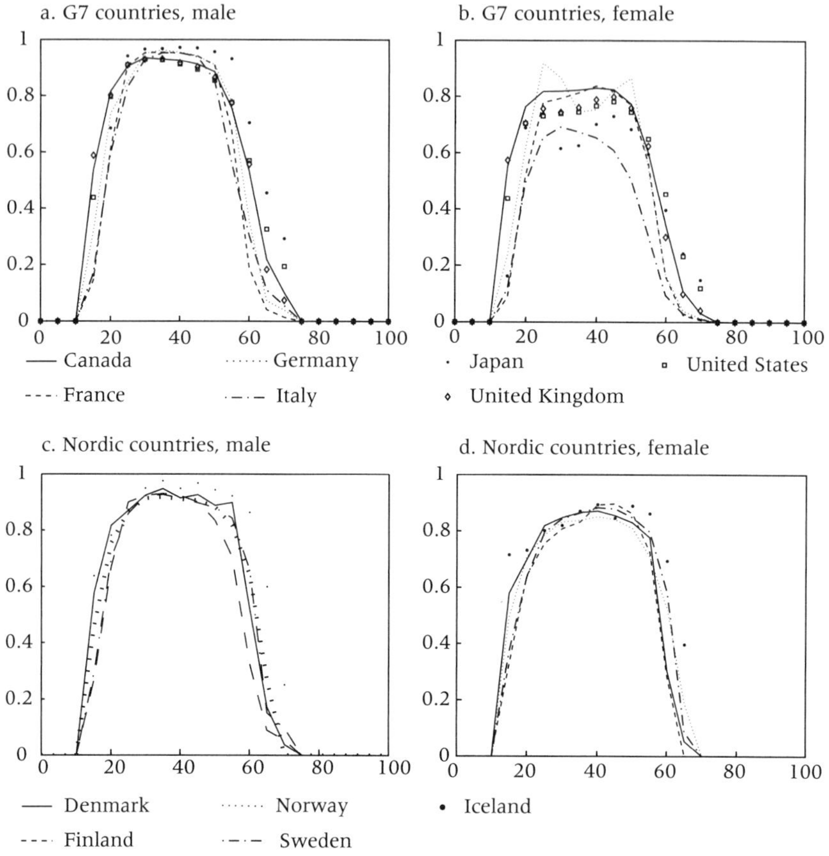

a. G7 countries, male

b. G7 countries, female

——— Canada   ········ Germany   · Japan   ▫ United States
---- France   ·-·- Italy   ◇ United Kingdom

c. Nordic countries, male

d. Nordic countries, female

——— Denmark   ········ Norway   · Iceland
---- Finland   ·-·- Sweden

SOURCE: OECD labor market statistics.

countries considered. Only for the United States, the United Kingdom, and Canada is the support ratio currently above 50 percent. For United Kingdom and the United States a fall of the support ratio by approximately 5 percent is projected, while Canada will experience one of the most pronounced declines in its support ratio (by approximately 10 percent). For all other countries the support ratio has already fallen below 50 percent in 2005 and is projected to decline further during the next five decades. Italy's support ratio will fall as low as 30 percent by 2050, while the ratio will stabilize around 40 percent for Japan, Germany, and France.

A decrease in the working-age population is expected in many developed countries. Since immigration and fertility cannot compensate this trend, the need to integrate women and the elderly into the workforce arises (see Mc-Donald and Kippen 2001 for an extensive discussion on labor supply prospects in developed countries). Comparing the labor force of the G7 countries with those in the Nordic countries illustrated in Figures 2c and d indicates that the potential labor force in the G7 countries is not yet exploited completely. A gradual increase of the labor force participation rates to those levels already achieved in the Nordic countries in 2004 would at least mitigate the negative impact of shrinking populations and higher age compositions. Since labor force participation rates in Iceland are extremely high, we will discuss two labor force scenarios. In scenario 1 we take the maximum of the age- and sex-specific labor force participation rates in the G7 plus the Nordic countries (not including Iceland) as an upper bound, and in scenario 2 we include Iceland as well. Starting from the country-specific labor force participation rates as observed in 2004, we assume that this upper bound is reached gradually by 2050.

Thus, in the first scenario there is no possibility to increase the labor force participation rates of males in Japan in the future, while in the second scenario this possibility exists. The impact of these two labor force scenarios on the support ratio from 2005 to 2050 is depicted in the two lower panels of Figure 1 (c and d). For all countries except Japan, an increase in labor force participation rates to levels currently observed for Nordic countries will stabilize or even increase the support ratio. Obviously, the largest potential to raise overall employment exists in countries with lower employment rates and/or larger working-age populations.

Simulation results

In the following we compute the dynamics of output per worker, Y/L, for the G7 countries and compare different scenarios. Since labor is the only production factor in our model, labor productivity is entirely determined by output per worker. To project labor productivity we multiply the age-dependent productivity schedule α_x by the distribution of the workforce by age and divide by the total size of the labor force. First we investigate the sensitivity of those projections assuming equal productivity schedules across ages, but varying the elasticity of substitution across age groups. We base this first set of simulations on the constant labor force participation scenario as of 2004. Next, we allow for alternative shapes of the age–productivity schedules and labor force participation rates to study the sensitivity with respect to labor supply as opposed to the labor demand function.

Equal productivity across age, constant labor force participation

The graphs in Figure 3 illustrate output per worker Y/L in the G7 countries assuming that the age-specific labor force participation rates remain at the level of 2004 and productivity is the same for all age groups from 15–19 to 70–74. We compare only relative levels of output per worker because alternative production functions applied to these trajectories lead to different levels of output per

FIGURE 3 Output per worker (*Y*/*L*), with constant 2004 labor force participation rates and constant productivity by age, under alternative production functions, G7 countries, 1950–2050 (index: *Y*/*L* in 2005 = 100)

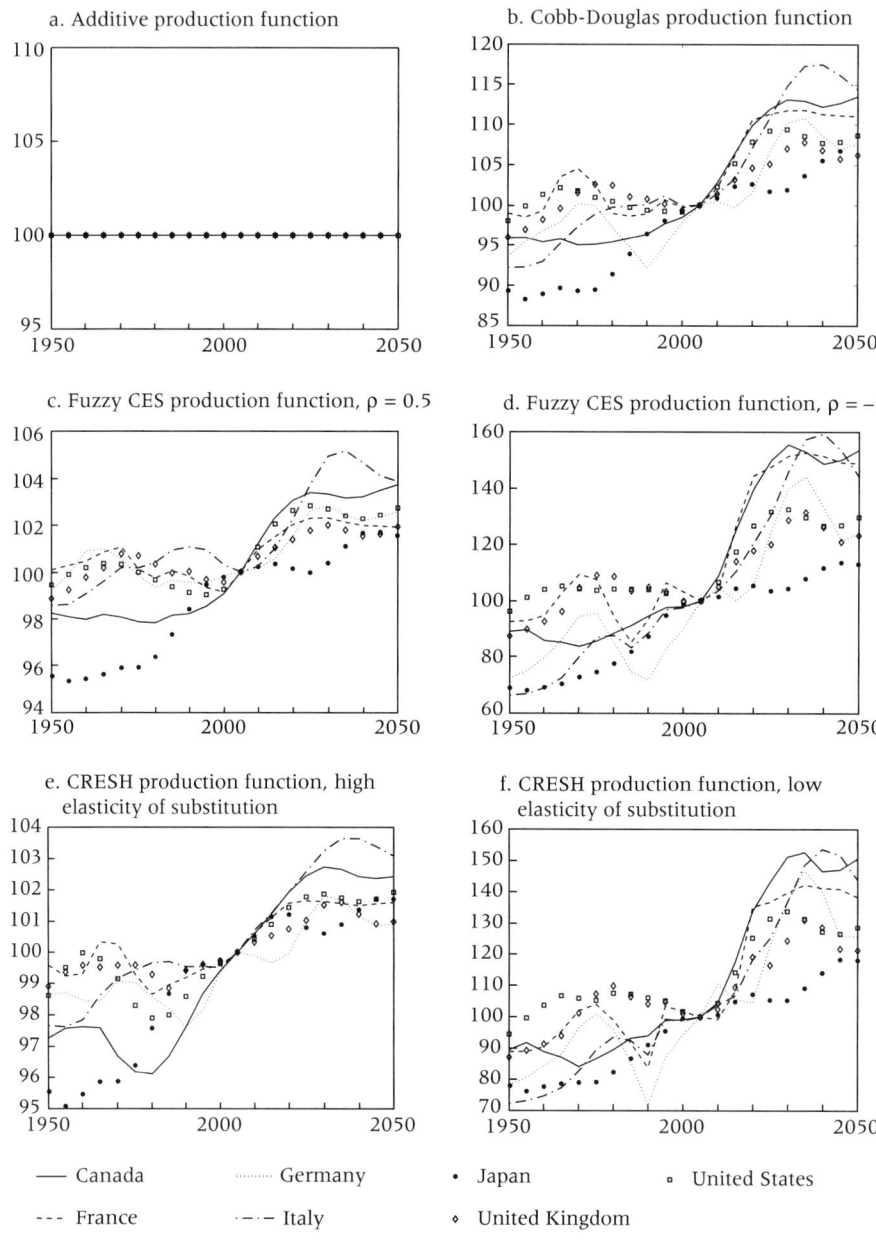

SOURCE: Authors' calculations.

capita, which do not allow for meaningful comparisons. Relative output means that we scale the whole trajectory such that the output in 2005 is 100.

Figure 3a depicts the results obtained from an additive production function where the index of labor is independent of the age distribution of the labor force as reflected in the horizontal line. Figure 3b is the same with a Cobb–Douglas production function. Figures 3c and d illustrate the outcome applying the fuzzy CES production function with parameters $\rho = 0.5$ and -1 while Figures 3e and f depict the outcome applying the CRESH production function with high and low elasticity of substitution.

If we relax the assumption of perfect substitutability between workers of different ages, the change in the size and composition of the workforce will no longer be neutral for forecasts of output per worker. The lower the elasticity of substitution between workers of different ages (i.e., the lower the value of ρ), the more pronounced we expect the fluctuations of output per worker to be. The results are qualitatively similar for the fuzzy CES and CRESH production functions.

All the scenarios presented in Figure 3 are based on the assumptions of constant labor force participation rates and equal productivity for all age groups. Therefore, the derived trajectories of future output per worker reflect the impact of changes in the age composition of the workforce. The results are intuitive since output maximization for a CES-type production function with equal productivity for all ages is achieved if the age distribution is uniform (see Appendix B, where we review the argument advanced by Lam 1989, Section 3.) The magnitude of the age-distribution effect across the G7 countries depends on the differences between the optimal age distribution and the projected actual distribution.

For all G7 countries during the next several decades the actual age distribution of the workforce can be expected to shift closer to the optimal age distribution since the deviation from the optimal uniform age distribution is currently high (due to the post–World War II baby boom). As a result, output per worker, Y/L, will increase under the assumptions of our modeling framework. Taking this average output per worker as a proxy for labor productivity, the future shifts in age composition may generate a dividend in terms of aggregate labor productivity. Our simulations indicate that the size of the effect depends on the elasticity of substitution and differs across G7 countries. While Japan will experience the lowest dividend, Canada, Italy, and France are expected to experience the greatest dividends.

Age-specific productivity, constant labor force participation

We modify our model by assuming that workers of different ages have different productivity levels. Figure 4 illustrates two age–productivity profiles.

FIGURE 4 Model age-productivity profiles

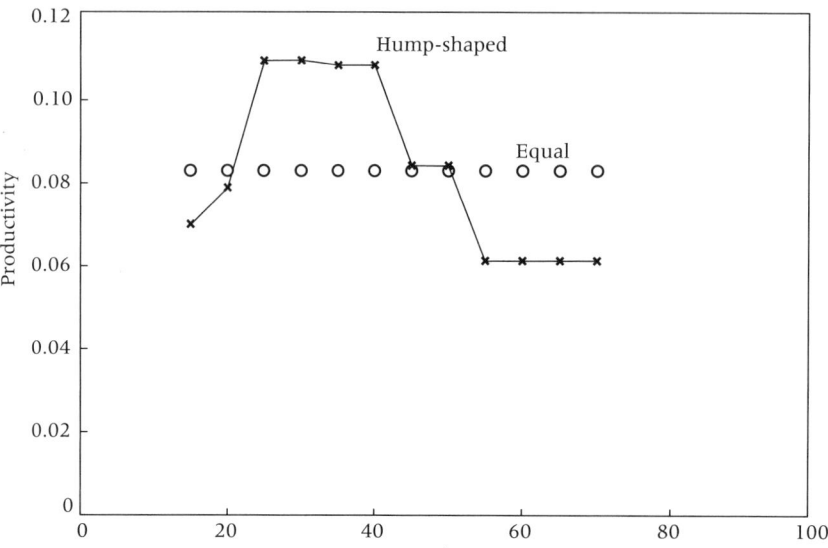

SOURCE: Based on estimates by Skirbekk (2005).

The "equal" profile is the one that we applied to compute the results shown in Figure 3. The "hump-shaped" profile assumes that workers are most productive in the middle of their working life. We applied estimates by Skirbekk (2005) assuming that individual productivity within a ten-year age group is the same for both five-year age groups within that range and that individual productivity does not decrease between ages 65 and 75. The graphs in Figure 4 depict the relative productivity indices α_x in equation 1 and are normalized to meet the restriction

$$\sum_{x=15}^{70} \alpha_x = 1 \quad .$$

Applying such a heterogeneous age–productivity profile has an impact on the optimal age structure with respect to aggregate labor productivity. The optimal age composition is no longer a uniform distribution, but a distribution with a greater weight on those age groups with higher average productivity. The extent of this non-homogeneity depends on the elasticity of substitution. Perfect substitutability (additive production function) requires a workforce with all workers in the age group with the highest average productivity. Lowering the elasticity of substitution mitigates the inequality of the optimal age distribution. If we apply this profile to the same labor force participation rates and production functions as before, we obtain the results depicted in Figure 5.

When productivity is allowed to vary by age, the projected changes in the size and composition of the labor force have an effect on output per worker even under an additive production function that assumes perfect substitut-

FIGURE 5 Output per worker (Y/L), with constant 2004 labor force participation rates and hump-shaped age-productivity profiles, under alternative production functions, G7 countries, 1950–2050 (index: Y/L in 2005 = 100)

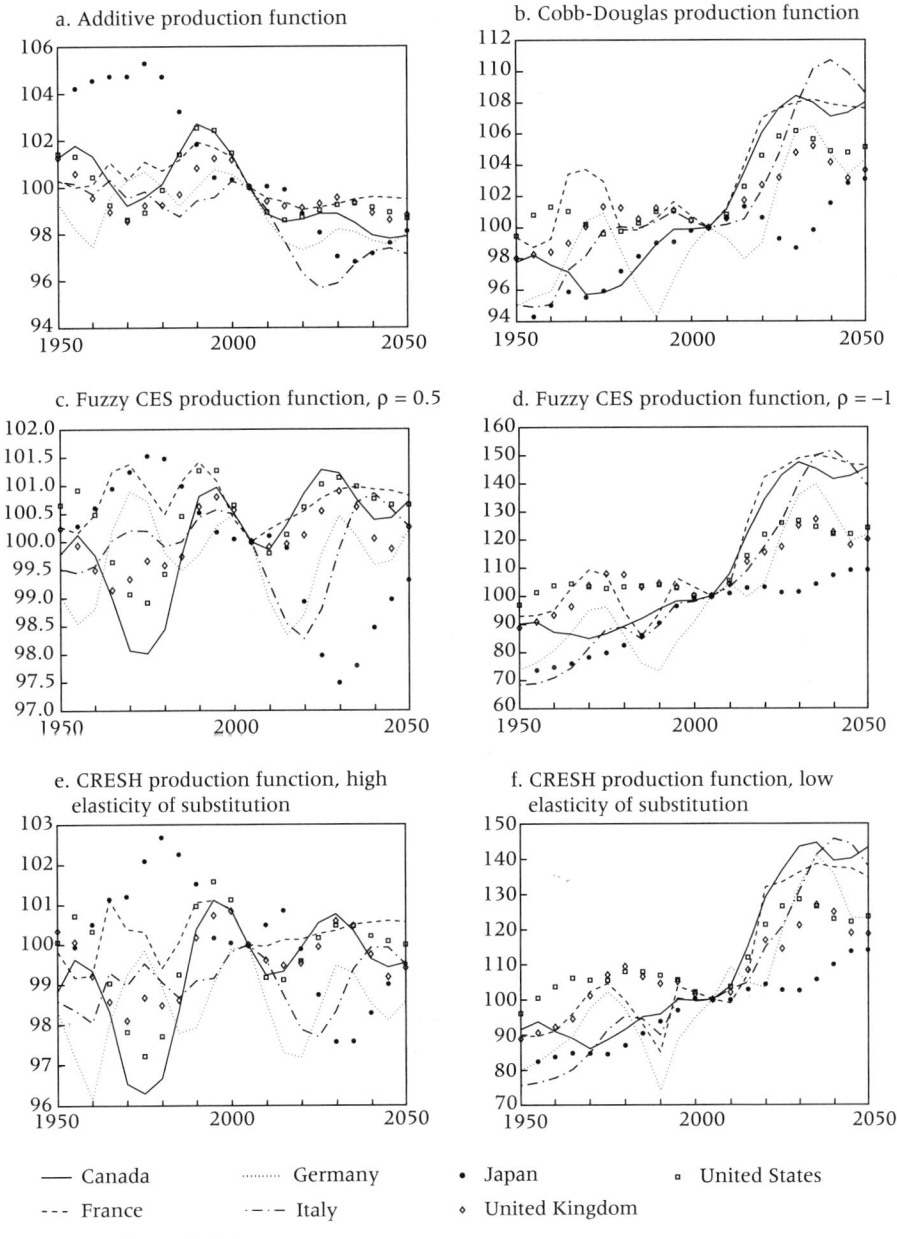

SOURCE: Authors' calculations.

ability of workers of different ages. Combined with an aging labor force, the assumption of decreasing productivity with age will lead to slightly lower output per worker compared to a scenario with age-independent productivity. However, the effect of age-specific productivity is modest compared to the effect related to the choice of the production function. As in the previous section our simulations indicate that Japan will experience the lowest dividend from workforce aging while Canada, Italy, and France will experience the greatest dividends.[7]

Age-specific productivity, increasing labor force participation

In the next step, rather than keeping the labor force participation rates constant at the 2004 values we apply labor force participation scenarios 1 and 2 discussed on p. 309. To facilitate comparison of the different scenarios, we group the results by country. Output per worker (Y/L) over 2005–50 under alternative participation scenarios and age–productivity profiles are shown in Figures 6, 7, and 8 for France, Japan, and the United States, respectively.[8] The three lefthand panels in each figure assume that workers of different ages have the same productivity, while those on the right are based on the hump-shaped age–productivity profile. The graphs in the top row are generated by keeping the labor force participation rates constant at the level of 2004—these are the results shown in the previous graphs (Figures 3 and 5) but now sorted by country. The graphs in the second row illustrate labor force scenario 1 (excluding Iceland for computing the upper bound), and the graphs in the bottom row describe scenario 2 (including Iceland).

We can draw the following conclusions from the set of simulations: (1) The effect of age-specific productivity—at least given the age-specific schedule we assume—is rather modest compared to the effects that are related to the choice of the production function and the labor force projections. Compared to simulation results that assume an equal productivity schedule by age (lefthand panels), we find that labor productivity is slightly lower if we apply the hump-shaped pattern of productivity by age (righthand panels). A hump-shaped pattern of age productivity will more likely depress labor productivity in countries where our labor force scenarios imply a pronounced increase in the number of older workers (compared to the base level as observed in 2004). For instance, this is the case for France as can be seen by comparing the corresponding lefthand and righthand panels in Figure 6. (2) The lower the substitutability of workers at different ages, the greater the increase in the workforce dividend. A production function assuming a lower level of substitutability among different age groups is more sensitive to deviations from the optimal age distribution. The lower the substitutability of workers of different

FIGURE 6 France: Output per worker (*Y/L*), 2005–50, under alternative age-productivity profiles, labor force participation scenarios, and production functions (index: *Y/L* in 2005 = 100)

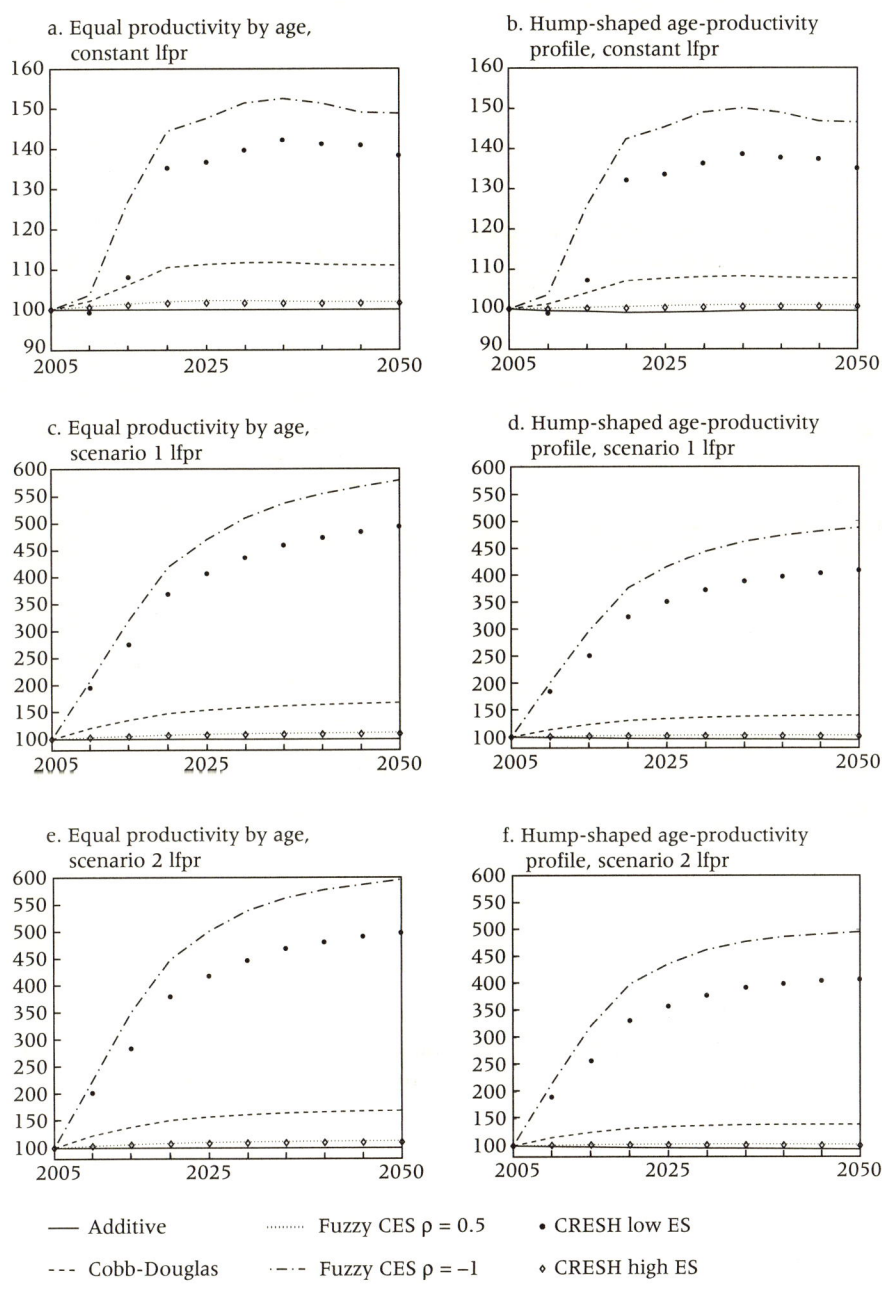

SOURCE: Authors' calculations.

FIGURE 7 Japan: Output per worker (*Y/L*), 2005–50, under alternative age-productivity profiles, labor force participation scenarios, and production functions (index: *Y/L* in 2005 = 100)

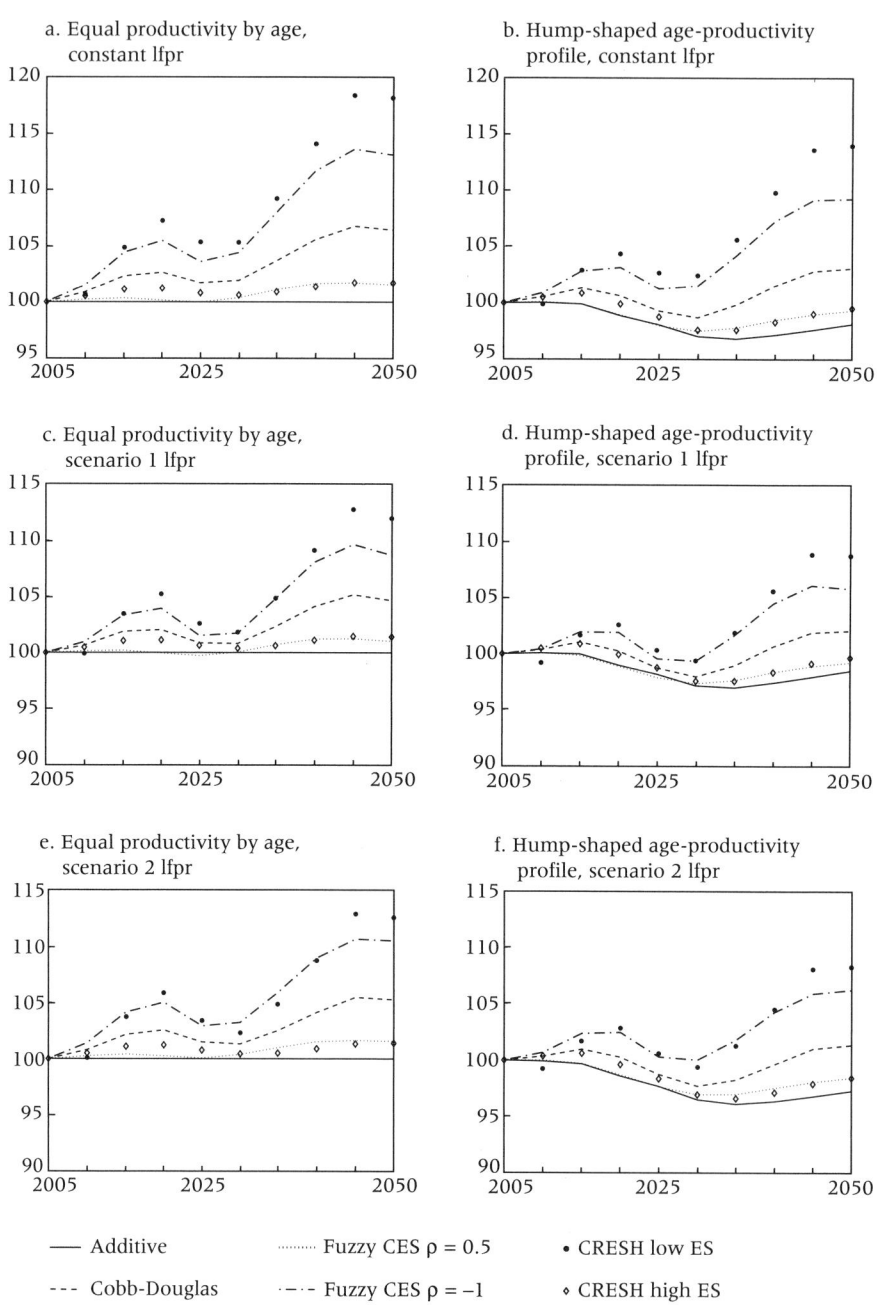

SOURCE: Authors' calculations.

FIGURE 8 United States: Output per worker (*Y/L*), 2005–50, under alternative age-productivity profiles, labor force participation scenarios, and production functions (index: *Y/L* in 2005 = 100)

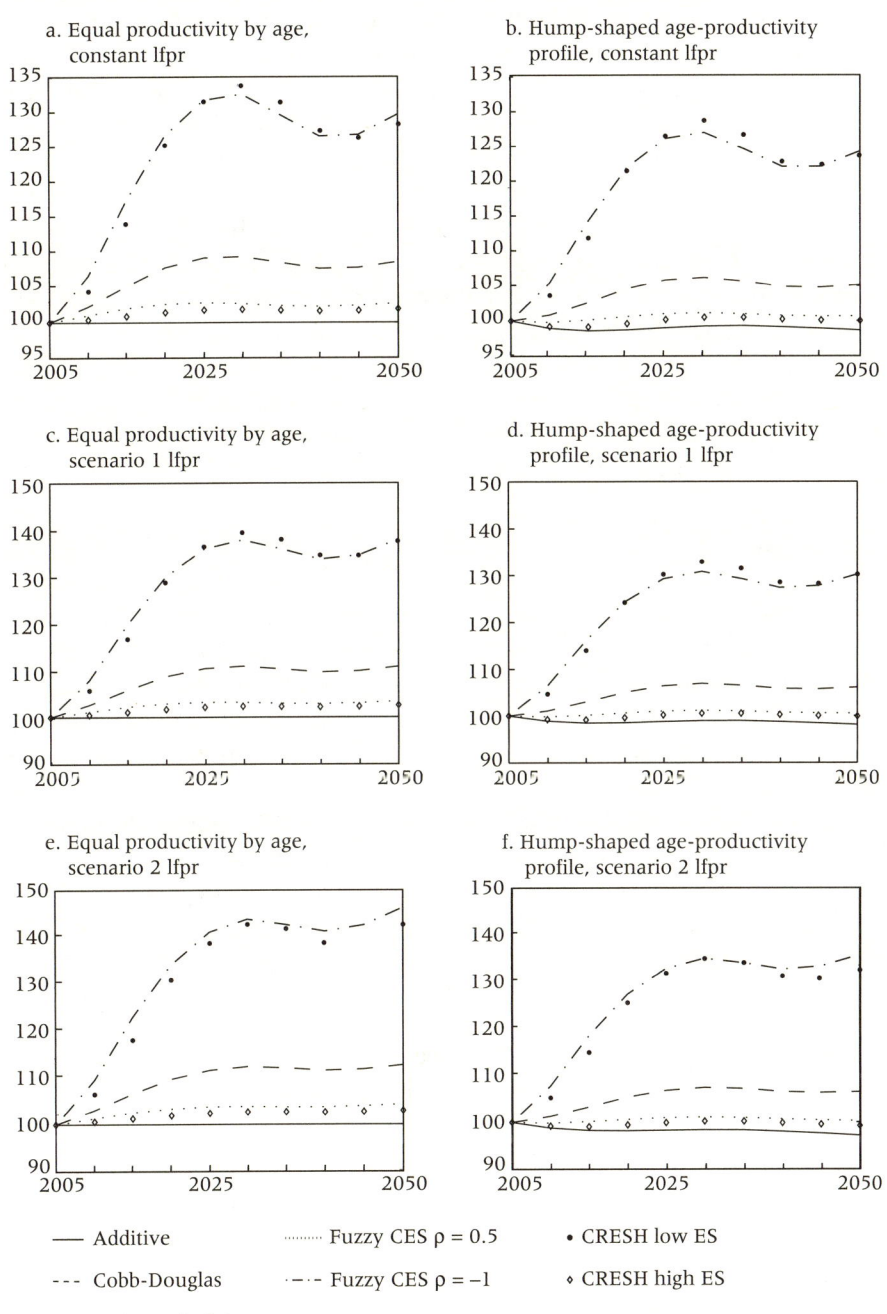

SOURCE: Authors' calculations.

ages, the greater the difference between the fuzzy CES and CRESH function. (3) A comparison across rows indicates that the dividend of workforce aging is more pronounced if we also add the assumption of increasing labor force participation rates.[9] However, the extent of this further increase in the dividend differs across countries. It is most pronounced in France (Figure 6) and least pronounced in Japan (Figure 7) and the United States (Figure 8). Since we compare output per worker relative to the year 2005, a pronounced increase can result from a high level of labor productivity in the future but also from a low level in the past. The outstanding increase in the case of France results from a low level of departure in 2005 and a high gain in the future. For Japan, the increase in labor force participation rates even leads to a decline in projected relative output per worker during the next three decades as opposed to the scenario where we keep labor force participation rates constant. For Italy the projected increase in labor force participation rates does not yield an increase in labor productivity similar to the one indicated for France. As argued also in McDonald and Kippen (2001, p. 19) for Italy: "In the longer term, however, labor supply can only be maintained through increases in fertility."

Discussion

The shrinkage and aging of the workforce are expected to depress labor productivity in the future. Policies aimed at increasing labor force participation rates (mainly among females and the elderly) and policies that promote human capital at all ages are high on the agenda. So far, only the labor supply side has been emphasized in the literature. However, as we argue in this chapter, projected labor productivity (measured by output per worker) will depend as well on labor demand (measured by the degree of substitutability of workers at different ages). The fact that workers of different ages are not perfect substitutes in production has been studied by economists as well as demographers. In particular, the entry of the baby boom cohort into the labor market has initiated a vast literature on the complementarity of workers at different ages and by sex. Although it is difficult, if not impossible, to project the labor demand structure over a time horizon of five decades, our simulations indicate that in a pure labor economy, the assumption of imperfect substitution of workers at different ages implies a dividend from workforce aging during the next decades. Workforce aging implies that the actual age distribution of the workforce can be expected to shift closer to the optimal age distribution, generating a dividend in terms of labor productivity. Simulations suggest that the dividend is likely to be nontrivial and it is negatively related to the elasticity of substitution of workers at different ages.

Within our framework of a pure labor economy, changes in age-specific productivity schedules have only a small impact on projected labor productivity. Increases in labor force participation rates over the next five decades to levels currently observed in Nordic countries have a pronounced impact. The efficacy of increasing labor force participation rates is contingent upon the scope of increase and the assumption that workers induced not to retire are good substitutes for younger workers (cf. McDonald and Kippen 2001). A key question is how firms will be able to adjust to shifts in the composition of the workforce that will result given the demographic projections and our alternative scenarios of labor force participation rates.

While our chapter ignores equilibrium analysis and only indicates partial effects of population aging, we have shown that issues surrounding labor demand are central to how population aging will affect labor productivity. Scenarios on the future quantity and quality of labor supply, as implicitly represented by our scenarios on labor force participation rates and age–productivity schedules, will interact with the labor demand pattern. The question of the degree of substitution of workers at different ages has been addressed before, but we need new empirical studies (most promising at the firm level) and new theoretical models that allow us to understand possible implications of population aging for the structure of labor demand. Furthermore, we need to extend our framework to include physical and human capital, factors that, themselves, will change in an aging society and will be complementary to or substitutable for workers of different ages.

Appendix A: The effect of labor force aging on labor productivity in a stable population

The average value of an age-specific variable $x(a)$ over ages a_1 to a_2 in a stable population that grows at rate n and has a survivorship function $s(a)$ can be written as:

$$\bar{x} = \frac{\int_{a_1}^{a_2} x(a)s(a)e^{-na}da}{\int_{a_1}^{a_2} s(a)e^{-na}da}. \qquad (7)$$

The logarithmic derivative of $\bar{x}$ is then equal to

$$d\log\bar{x} = \frac{d\bar{x}}{\bar{x}} = (-A_x + A)dn, \qquad (8)$$

where A is the mean age of the population and A_x is the mean age associated with the characteristic $x(a)$.

If one limits labor force participation to ages $[\alpha,\beta]$, it follows that $A-A_x$ is bound in absolute values by $(\beta-\alpha)/2$, i.e., about 20 to 25 years or half the length of a typical workforce age range. Hence, a change of the population growth rate by 1 percentage point cannot have an aggregate impact of more than 20–25 percent.

Appendix B: Output maximization with CES technology

Lam (1989, Section 3) considers a CES production function $Y = [\alpha L_1^\rho + (1-\alpha) L_2^\rho]^{1/\rho}$, which can be rewritten as $Y = L[\alpha \pi^\rho + (1-\alpha)(1-\pi)^\rho]^{1/\rho}$ with π denoting the proportion of the labor force in the young age group. It can be shown that for given values of ρ and α there exists a unique value of the share of the labor force in the young age group π that maximizes the value of total output, that is, the unique value which equates the marginal products of the two ages of workers. More specifically, output per period attains a maximum when

$$\frac{\pi}{1-\pi} = \left[\frac{\alpha}{1-\alpha}\right]^\sigma, \qquad (9)$$

with $\sigma = 1/(1-\rho)$ denoting the elasticity of substitution between the young and old labor force age groups. From (9) it follows that if the two types of workers have equal productivity ($\alpha = 0.5$), output will be maximized when $\pi = 0.5$, that is, when the age distribution of the labor force is uniform. If $\alpha \neq 0.5$, however, the elasticity of substitution will determine the division of labor that maximizes output. For instance, if $\alpha < 0.5$ the optimal value of π will be less than 0.5 since a greater proportion of older workers will be required to equate the marginal products of the two age groups. As the degree of substitutability increases, a higher ratio of older workers to younger workers is required to equilibrate their marginal products, and the output maximizing value of π will decrease.

The above considerations can be applied to the labor demand function as given in (3). Denoting by π_x and π_y the share of the labor force in age group x and y, the output maximization condition is:

$$\frac{\pi_x}{\pi_y} = \left[\frac{\alpha_x}{\alpha_y}\right]^\sigma. \qquad (10)$$

For an age-independent productivity schedule $\alpha_x = \alpha_y$ we obtain $\pi_x = \pi_y$ for any pair of ages x and y. In other words, a uniform age distribution within the labor force ensures maximum output per worker.

In case of age-dependent productivity—for instance, decreasing or hump-shaped—the optimal age distribution of the workforce will differ from the uniform age distribution. Formula (10) indicates that an optimal age structure requires a higher share of those age groups with higher productivity and a lower share of those with lower productivity.

Appendix C: Parameters chosen in applying the CRESH production function

HIGH elasticity of substitution

α_i	ρ_i	s_i		15–19	20–24	25–29	30–34	35–39	40–44	45–49	50–54	55–59	60–64	65–69	70–74
2	0.500	0.051	15–19	1.65											
2.2	0.545	0.084	20–24	1.80	1.98										
2.4	0.583	0.128	25–29	1.95	2.15	2.35									
2.6	0.615	0.132	30–34	2.10	2.32	2.53	2.74								
2.8	0.643	0.139	35–39	2.26	2.48	2.71	2.93	3.16							
3	0.667	0.161	40–44	2.26	2.48	2.71	2.93	3.16	3.38						
3	0.667	0.119	45–49	2.10	2.32	2.53	2.74	2.95	3.16	3.16					
2.8	0.643	0.100	50–54	1.95	2.15	2.35	2.54	2.74	2.93	2.93	2.74				
2.6	0.615	0.052	55–59	1.80	1.98	2.17	2.35	2.53	2.71	2.71	2.53	2.35			
2.4	0.583	0.025	60–64	1.65	1.82	1.93	2.15	2.32	2.48	2.48	2.32	2.15	1.98		
2.2	0.545	0.007	65–69	1.65	1.82	1.93	2.15	2.32	2.48	2.48	2.32	2.15	1.98	1.65	
2	0.500	0.003	70–74	1.50	1.65	1.83	1.95	2.10	2.26	2.26	2.10	1.95	1.80	1.65	

$\sum \alpha_i s_i = 2.66$

LOW elasticity of substitution

α_i	ρ_i	s_i		15–19	20–24	25–29	30–34	35–39	40–44	45–49	50–54	55–59	60–64	65–69	70–74
0.6	−0.667	0.051	15–19	0.50											
0.66	−0.515	0.084	20–24	0.54	0.60										
0.72	−0.389	0.128	25–29	0.59	0.65	0.70									
0.78	−0.282	0.132	30–34	0.63	0.69	0.75	0.82								
0.84	−0.190	0.139	35–39	0.68	0.74	0.81	0.88	0.95							
0.9	−0.111	0.161	40–44	0.68	0.74	0.81	0.88	0.95	1.01						
0.9	−0.111	0.119	45–49	0.63	0.69	0.76	0.82	0.88	0.95	0.95					
0.84	−0.190	0.100	50–54	0.59	0.65	0.70	0.76	0.82	0.88	0.88	0.82				
0.78	−0.282	0.052	55–59	0.54	0.60	0.65	0.70	0.76	0.81	0.81	0.76	0.70			
0.72	−0.389	0.025	60–64	0.50	0.55	0.60	0.65	0.69	0.74	0.69	0.65	0.60	0.54		
0.66	−0.515	0.007	65–69	0.45	0.50	0.54	0.59	0.63	0.68	0.68	0.63	0.59	0.54	0.50	
0.6	−0.667	0.003	70–74												

$\sum \alpha_i s_i = 0.88$

Notes

1 The recent development accounting literature (Hall and Jones 1999) has stressed that only workers can contribute to production, and therefore understanding differences in output per worker is more important than understanding differences in output per capita. Note that output per capita can be decomposed into output per worker times the worker-to-population ratio.

2 The labor force participation rate is a measure of the proportion of a country's working-age population that engages actively in the labor market, either by working or looking for work; the rate provides an indication of the relative size of the supply of labor available to engage in the production of goods and services. International Labor Organization, «http://www.ilo.org/public/english/employment/strat/kilm/indicators.htm».

3 Recall that the production function determines the degree of substitutability of workers at different ages, and the labor demand curve can be derived from the production function. Hence, the degree of substitutability of workers at different ages determines labor demand.

4 As shown in Cutler et al. (1990, p. 18), this "Solow effect" offsets the long-run dependency effect on US per capita consumption in the short run. On the other hand, one can argue that significant proportions of excess savings may be invested abroad and not in the domestic capital stock, so that the positive effects of higher capital intensity are of a smaller order of magnitude.

5 In a separate note that can be requested from the authors (afp@econ.tuwien.ac.at), we show that the direct elasticity of substitution of the CES production function constitutes a lower bound for the direct elasticity of substitution between any two inputs of the fuzzy CES production function.

6 The general form of the Leontief production function is $q = \min(x_1, x_2, ..., x_n)$ where q denotes output and x_i, $i = 1,...,n$ are quantities of input. The assumption is that factors are used in fixed proportion.

7 For the additive production function and assuming age-varying productivity, the optimal age structure, i.e., the age distribution that optimizes output, is achieved if all workers belong to the age group with the highest productivity. However, the concentration of the population distribution toward these ages declines over the next few decades.

8 Results for the other G7 countries are available from the authors (afp@econ.tuwien.ac.at).

9 For our computations we decompose output per capita Y/N as $Y/N = Y/L * L/N$. Obviously increasing labor force participation rates leads to an increase of L/N. However, our simulations reveal that the first multiplier Y/L also increases. Therefore, an increase of labor force participation rates has a twofold positive impact on output per capita.

References

Blanchet, D. 1992. "Does an ageing labour force call for large adjustments in training or wage policies?,' in P. Johnson and K. F. Zimmermann (eds.), *Labor Markets in an Ageing Europe*. CEPR, Cambridge University Press.

Blanchet, D. 2002. "Le vieillissement de la population active: ampleur et incidence," *Economie et Statistique* 355–356: 123–138.

Bloom, D., R. B. Freeman, and S. D. Korenman. 1987. "The labour market consequences of generational crowding," *European Journal of Population* 3: 131–176.

Börsch-Supan, A. 2002. "Labor market effects of population aging," Discussion Paper 11-2002, Mannheim Research Institute of the Economics of Aging.

Card, D. and T. Lemieux. 2001. "Can falling supply explain the rising return to college for younger men? A cohort-based analysis," *The Quarterly Journal of Economics* 116(2): 705–746.

Cutler, D. M., J. M. Poterba, L. M. Sheiner, and L. H. Summers. 1990. "An aging society: Opportunity or challenge?," *Brookings Papers on Economic Activity* 1990(1): 1–56.

Easterlin, R. 1978. "What will 1984 be like? Socioeconomic implications of recent twists in the age structure," *Demography* 15(4): 116–147.

Gottschalk, P. 2001. "What can we learn from the cohort size literature about the future demand for the greying baby boomers?," paper prepared for a Roundtable on the Demand for Older Workers Sponsored by the Retirement Research Consortium, The Brookings Institution, 23 March.

Guest, R. 2005. "A dividend from workforce ageing in Australia," Griffith University, Australia, mimeo.

Guest, R. and K. Shacklock. 2005. "The impending shift to an older mix of workers: Perspectives from the management and economics literatures," *International Journal of Organisational Behaviour* 10(3): 713–728.

Hall, R. and C. I. Jones. 1999. "Why do some countries produce so much more output per worker than others?," *The Quarterly Journal of Economics* 114: 83–116.

Hamermesh, D. S. 1993. *Labor Demand*. Princeton: Princeton University Press.

Hanoch, G. 1971. "CRESH production functions," *Econometrica* 39(5): 695–712.

Higgins, M. and J. G. Williamson. 1997. "Age structure dynamics in Asia and dependence on foreign capital," *Population and Development Review* 23: 261–293.

Johnson, P. 2002. "The impact of ageing: The supply of labour and human capital," in H. Siebert (ed.), *Economic Policy for Aging Societies*. Berlin: Springer, pp. 111–130.

Korenman, S. and D. Neumark. 2000. "Cohort crowding and youth labor market: a cross-sectional analysis," in Blanchflower, D. G. and R. B. Freeman (eds.), *Youth Employment and Joblessness in Advanced Countries*. NBER Comparative Labor Market Series. Chicago: University of Chicago Press.

Kremer, M. and J. Thomson. 1998. "Why isn't convergence instantaneous? Young workers, old workers, and gradual adjustment," *Journal of Economic Growth* 3: 5–28.

Lam, D. 1989. "Population growth, age structure, and age-specific productivity: Does a uniform age distribution minimize lifetime wages?," *Journal of Population Economics* 2: 189–210.

Mason, A. and R. Lee. 2004. "Reform and support systems for the elderly in developing countries: Capturing the second demographic dividend," International Seminar on the Demographic Window and Healthy Aging: Socioeconomic Challenges and Opportunities, China Centre for Economic Research, Peking University, Beijing.

McDonald, P. and R. Kippen. 2001. "Labor supply prospects in 16 developed countries, 2000–2050," *Population and Development Review* 27: 1–32.

Prskawetz, A. and T. Fent. 2007. "Workforce ageing and the substitution of labour: The role of supply and demand for labour in Austria," *Metroeconomica* 58(1): 95–126.

Sato, R. and T. Koizumi. 1973. "On the elasticities of substitution and complementarity," *Oxford Economic Papers* 25.

Shimer, R. 2001. "The impact of young workers on the aggregate labor market," *The Quarterly Journal of Economics* 116: 969–1007.

Skirbekk, Vegard. 2005. *Age and Individual Productivity-Potential: New Evidence Based on Ability Levels and Industry-Wide Task Demand*. International Institute for Applied Systems Analysis.

Stapleton, D. and D. Young. 1988. "Education attainment and cohort size," *Journal of Labor Economics* 6(3): 330–361.

United Nations. 2004. *World Population Prospects: The 2004 Revision*. New York: United Nations.

Welch, F. 1979. "Effects of cohort size on earnings: The baby boom babies' financial bust," *Journal of Political Economy* 85: 65–97.

AUTHORS

DAVID E. BLOOM is Professor of Economics and Demography, Harvard School of Public Health.

AXEL H. BÖRSCH-SUPAN is Director, Mannheim Research Institute for the Economics of Aging, Department of Economics, University of Mannheim, Germany.

RAOUF BOUCEKKINE is Professor, Department of Economics and CORE, Université catholique de Louvain, and University of Glasgow.

DAVID CANNING is Professor of Economics and International Health, Harvard School of Public Health.

ROBERT L. CLARK is Professor, North Carolina State University, Raleigh.

DAVID DE LA CROIX is Professor, Department of Economics and CORE, Université catholique de Louvain.

RYAN D. EDWARDS is Assistant Professor of Economics, Queens College, City University of New York.

THOMAS FENT is Research Scientist, Vienna Institute of Demography, Austrian Academy of Sciences, Vienna.

JAMES FEYRER is Assistant Professor of Economics, Dartmouth College, New Hampshire.

ANNE GOUJON is Researcher, Vienna Institute of Demography, Austrian Academy of Sciences, and part-time Research Scholar, World Population Program, International Institute for Applied Systems Analysis, Laxenburg, Austria.

ROSS GUEST is Professor, Department of Accounting, Finance and Economics, Griffith University, Australia.

MAX HALVARSSON is Research Assistant, Institute for Futures Studies, Stockholm.

HELMUT HOFER is Economist, Institute for Advanced Studies, Vienna.

RONALD LEE is Professor of Demography and Jordan Family Professor of Economics, University of California, Berkeley.

SANG-HYOP LEE is Associate Professor, Department of Economics, University of Hawaii at Manoa.

THOMAS LINDH is Professor of Economics, Växjö University, Sweden.

WOLFGANG LUTZ is Leader, World Population Program, International Institute for Applied Systems Analysis, Laxenburg, Austria, and Director, Vienna Institute of Demography, Austrian Academy of Sciences, Vienna.

BO MALMBERG is Professor, Department of Geography, Stockholm University.

ANDREW MASON is Professor, Department of Economics, University of Hawaii at Manoa, and Senior Fellow, Population and Health Studies, East-West Center, Honolulu.

RIKIYA MATSUKURA is Staff Researcher, Nihon University Population Research Institute, Tokyo.

NAOHIRO OGAWA is Professor, Nihon University, Tokyo.

DOMINIQUE PEETERS is Professor, Department of Geography and CORE, Université catholique de Louvain.

ALEXIA PRSKAWETZ is Professor, Institute for Mathematical Methods in Economics (Research Unit Economics), Vienna University of Technology, and Deputy Director, Vienna Institute of Demography, Austrian Academy of Sciences, Vienna.

VEGARD SKIRBEKK is Research Scholar, World Population Program, International Institute for Applied Systems Analysis, Laxenburg, Austria.

THOMAS URL is Economist, Austrian Institute of Economic Research, Vienna.

ANNABABETTE WILS is Research Director, Education Policy and Data Center, Academy for Educational Development, Washington, DC.